DEVIANT BURIAL
in the Archaeological Record

STUDIES IN FUNERARY ARCHAEOLOGY

Vol. 1 *Social Archaeology of Funerary Remains*
Edited by Rebecca Gowland and Christopher Knüsel

Vol. 2 *Deviant Burial in the Archaeological Record*
Edited by Eileen M. Murphy

Vol. 3 *The Archaeology of the Dead*
Henry Duday

Vol. 4 *Burial in Later Anglo-Saxon England c. 650–1100 AD*
Jo Buckberry and Annia Cherryson

Vol. 5 *Living Through the Dead: Burial and Commemoration in the Classical World*
Edited by Maureen Carroll and Jane Rempel

Vol. 6 *Living with the Dead: Ancestor Worship and Mortuary Ritual in Ancient Egypt*
Nicola Harrington

Studies in Funerary Archaeology: Volume 2

DEVIANT BURIAL IN THE ARCHAEOLOGICAL RECORD

edited by

Eileen M. Murphy

Oxbow Books
Oxford & Philadelphia

Published in the United Kingdom in 2008. Reprinted in 2015 by
OXBOW BOOKS
10 Hythe Bridge Street, Oxford OX1 2EW

and in the United States by
OXBOW BOOKS
908 Darby Road, Havertown, PA 19083

Paperback Edition: ISBN 978-1-84217-338-1
Digital Edition: ISBN 978-1-78297-535-9

A CIP record for this book is available from the British Library

For a complete list of Oxbow titles, please contact:

UNITED KINGDOM
Oxbow Books
Telephone (01865) 241249, Fax (01865) 794449
Email: oxbow@oxbowbooks.com
www.oxbowbooks.com

UNITED STATES OF AMERICA
Oxbow Books
Telephone (800) 791-9354, Fax (610) 853-9146
Email: queries@casemateacademic.com
www.casemateacademic.com/oxbow

Oxbow Books is part of the Casemate Group

Printed and bound in Great Britain by
Marston Book Services Ltd, Oxfordshire

Front cover: Drawing by Libby Mulqueeny, Queen's University Belfast, of a decapitated male from Driffield Terrace, York (© York Archaeological Trust)

Back cover: Reconstruction drawing by David A. Walsh of the so-called 'live burial' at Sewerby, East Yorkshire (Hirst 1985, frontispiece). Reproduced by permission of English Heritage.

This volume is dedicated to my children –
Abigail, Jude and Saul Murphy-Donnelly

Contents

Contributors

EDELTRAUD ASPÖCK
Department of Archaeology, University of Reading, Whiteknights, PO Box 217, Reading RG6 6AH, England.
Email: e.aspoeck@reading.ac.uk, edeltraud.aspoeck@gmail.com

JO BUCKBERRY
Biological Anthropology Research Centre, Archaeological Sciences, University of Bradford, Bradford BD7 1DP, England.
Email: J.Buckberry@bradford.ac.uk

PHILIPPE CHARLIER
Laboratory of Paleopathology, Department of Legal Medicine and Forensic Pathology, Raymond Poincaré University Hospital, 92380 Garches, France; HALMA-IPEL, UMR 8164 CNRS, Lille 3 University, Vilelneuve d'Ascq, France.
Email: ph_charlier@yahoo.fr

ANNIA KRISTINA CHERRYSON
School of Archaeology and Ancient History, University of Leicester, University Road, Leicester LE1 7H, England.
Email: akc6@leicester.ac.uk

COLM J. DONNELLY
Centre for Archaeological Fieldwork, School of Geography, Archaeology and Palaeoecology, Queen's University Belfast, Belfast BT7 1NN, Northern Ireland.
Email: c.j.donnelly@qub.ac.uk

MARK GORDON
86 Kenilworth Park, Harold's Cross, Dublin 6W, Republic of Ireland.
Email: markgordon@ireland.com

JAMES HOLLOWAY
Department of Archaeology, Cambridge University, Downing St., Cambridge CB2 3DZ, England.
Email: jeh30@cam.ac.uk

Stephany Leach
Department of Archaeology, School of Human and Environmental Sciences, University of Reading, Whiteknights, PO Box 217, Reading RG6 6AH, England.
Email: stephleach@hotmail.co.uk

Eileen M. Murphy
School of Geography, Archaeology and Palaeoecology, Queen's University Belfast, Belfast BT7 1NN, Northern Ireland.
Email: eileen.murphy@qub.ac.uk

Valeriu Sîrbu
Museum of Brăila, 3 Traian Square, 810153 – Brăila, Romania.
Email: valeriu_sirbu@yahoo.co.uk

Alison Taylor
40 Hertford Street, Cambridge CB4 3AG, England.
Email: alison.taylor@archaeologists.net

Anastasia Tsaliki
Marias Hatzikiriakou 117, Kallipolis – Piraiki 185 39, Piraeus, Greece.
Email: anastasia@connectfree.co.uk

Estella Weiss-Krejci
Im Hoffeld 59/4, 8046 Graz, Austria.
Email: estellawk@hotmail.com

Acknowledgements

This volume arose as a result of a session of the same name held at the 11th annual conference of the European Association of Archaeologists which took place in Cork, Ireland, in September 2005. I am very grateful to the conference's organisers and members of the Scientific Committee for enabling the session to take place and for providing an international forum which allowed the presentation of a wide range of fascinating papers on the subject of deviant burial. The volume would of course not have been possible without the efforts of all the contributors and I am extremely grateful to each of them for the efficient production of their papers and for their prompt responses to my various editorial queries.

I am also very grateful to Libby Mulqueeny of the School of Geography, Archaeology and Palaeoecology, Queen's University Belfast, for her help with much of the illustrative material contained within the volume and for producing the front cover illustration. Thanks are also due to Richard Hall of the York Archaeological Trust for permitting a drawing of the decapitated male excavated from Driffield Terrace, York, to be used on the front cover of the volume.

Individual acknowledgements are included as appropriate in the papers which follow.

Introduction

Eileen M. Murphy

It has long been recognised by archaeologists and anthropologists that certain individuals in a variety of cultures from diverse time periods and geographical locations have been accorded different treatment in burial relative to other members of their society (e.g. Saxe 1970; Binford 1972; O'Shea 1984; Shay 1985). These individuals can include criminals, women who died during childbirth, unbaptised infants, people with disabilities, and supposed revenants, to name but a few. Such burials can be identifiable in the archaeological record from an examination of the location and external characteristics of the grave site. Furthermore, the position of the body in addition to its association with unusual grave goods can be a further feature of non-normative burials. The motivation behind these differential burial practices is also diverse and can be associated with a highly complex array of different social and religious beliefs.

A range of high quality academic texts have been produced in recent years that cover the funerary practices and beliefs of past societies (e.g. McHugh 1999; Parker Pearson 1999; Taylor 2002). These generally make reference to the evidence for non-normative burials but the current volume focuses specifically on the evidence for minority and atypical burial in the archaeological record. As such, it is envisaged that the collection of papers contained within this book will go some way towards enabling a clearer understanding to be gained concerning the nature of the people accorded such funerary rites within the broader social and religious beliefs of the societies from which they each originated. The volume comprises some 12 papers that focus on non-normative burial practices from the Neolithic through to the Post-Medieval period and includes case studies from a diverse array of countries including Austria, England, France, Germany, Greece, Ireland, Italy, Romania, Scotland and Sweden. Both the broad time-span and the wide geographic nature of the contributions is a testament to the fact that certain individuals have been accorded a differential form of burial to the majority of their peers in most human societies at some stage in their history.

The issue of terminology when referring to non-normative burial is discussed in depth in the contribution by Edeltraud Aspöck (Chapter 2). Although the current volume is entitled 'Deviant Burial in the Archaeological Record' it is appreciated that the use of the word 'deviant' might be perceived to have overtly negative connotations, thereby suggesting that the individuals accorded unusual burial practices had in some way been deliberately rejected by their societies for some wrongdoing. As the papers by Estella Weiss-Krejci (Chapter 10), and Colm Donnelly and Eileen Murphy (Chapter 11) demonstrate, however, this is by no means always the case. Individuals can be accorded deviant or non-normative burial practices for a variety of reasons, and in some cases the reasons lie well beyond their control, such as death before baptism, during childbirth or as a result of an infectious disease. A further problem with the use of the term 'deviant' is highlighted particularly well in the contributions of Annia Cherryson (Chapter 7) and James Holloway (Chapter 8). The former chapter looks at burial variation in Late Saxon Wessex, while the latter discusses the phenomenon of charcoal burial in a variety of European countries. Both Cherryson and Holloway are of the opinion that minority burial practices are not strictly 'deviant' but rather just a less commonly used form of burial which should be considered as part of the repertoire of normal burial practices.

The volume begins with two papers which primarily focus on theoretical aspects of the study of atypical archaeological burials. The remainder of the volume is ordered chronologically and comprises case study papers. In the first paper Anastasia Tsaliki introduces the concept of an 'Archaeology of Fear' and discusses a range of practices apparent in the global archaeological funerary record which appear to be indicative of necrophobia or a fear of the dead. She stresses the need for archaeologists and anthropologists to adopt a multidisciplinary approach, which draws on information derived from social, biological and burial evidence, to enable a clearer understanding of atypical burials in the past. The final section of her paper presents five case studies derived from Cyprus, Greece and Italy where individuals appear to have been accorded atypical burial practices as a consequence of necrophobia.

In Chapter 2 Edeltraud Aspöck compares European German-language and Anglophone research on 'deviant burials' which leads to her to challenge the usefulness of the concept of 'deviant burial'. She states that the term *Sonderbestattung* is the German-language equivalent to 'deviant burial' although, interestingly, this is a completely neutral term lacking the negative connotations of the English word 'deviant'. She charts the development of research on *Sonderbestattung* from the 1920s onwards before turning her attention to the Anglophone research. She believes the research in the two archaeological traditions displayed parallels until the 1970s when they then diverged. In recent years the post-processual approach, with its emphasis on 'individualism, agency and marginal groups in society' (Aspöck, this volume), has dominated Anglophone research, whereas the European German-language research has tended to focus mainly on classificatory issues which have arisen from the archaeological evidence itself. Aspöck concludes by discussing the problems associated with both approaches and suggests the way forward is not to view atypical burials in isolation but rather as an integral part of the normal mortuary practices of a society.

Stephany Leach's contribution (Chapter 3) focuses on a re-evaluation of human skeletal remains recovered from five cave and rock shelter sites in the Yorkshire Dales in England. A recent programme of radiocarbon dating has revealed the remains to be of Early Neolithic date, and not Late Neolithic or Early Bronze Age as previously thought. Furthermore, it had previously been believed that the remains had derived from articulated burials but Leach's research has revealed evidence for the differential treatment and representation of the human remains. The paper includes a review of the evidence that exists for the Earlier Neolithic treatment of the dead in Britain and discusses the complex funerary rites employed by these communities, before the final deposition of often extensively manipulated human body parts within long barrows, chambered tombs and the ditches of causewayed enclosures. She questions the motivations that may have lain behind the various rites before attempting to interpret the reasons why the skeletons recovered from the cave and rock shelter sites may have been disarticulated. The osteological analysis indicated that the remains included those of young children as well as adults whose bones displayed signs of injury and disease. In her discussion Leach postulates that the remains recovered from the cave and rock shelter sites could simply have been deposited there as a result of random occurrences, the season of death or other practical matters. She also suggests, however, they might have been deliberately placed within the subterranean sites as a result of deeper community beliefs and that they represent specifically selected members of the community. In the conclusion she stresses that her study is based on a relatively small quantity of skeletal remains but she suggests that a clearer understanding of the diverse array of Early Neolithic mortuary rituals in Britain might be gained by undertaking similar detailed osteological analysis on other contemporary collections of human remains.

In Chapter 4 Philippe Charlier presents the evidence for two Mediterranean examples of atypical burial and demonstrates how a multidisciplinary approach can be used in the interpretation of such burials. The first case involves the burial of a girl with Trisomy 21, or Down's Syndrome, in Late Bronze Age Rome. He provides a detailed account of the palaeopathological characteristics of the skeleton and makes reference to the unusual nature of her burial context within an uninhabited marshy area. The presence of a perimortem blunt force trauma on the individual's skull in addition to the unusual nature of her burial, leads Charlier to suggest that she had been ritually sacrificed. In the second case study he discusses the burial of two female skeletons of late second century BC or early first century BC date recovered from the cistern of the House of Fourni on Delos Island, Greece. One of the individuals appeared to have been decapitated and both were associated with a series of iron nails. Charlier suggests that the nails represent the remains of hobbles which had been employed to restrict physical movement. Drawing on contemporary historical accounts he then proceeds to suggest reasons why the women were apparently tortured and killed. He concludes by advocating that a multidisciplinary approach is essential when attempting to interpret the evidence from atypical burials.

The paper by Valeriu Sîrbu (Chapter 5) discusses the various manners employed for the burial of children during the fourth century BC to the first century AD in the Carpato-Danubian region, the territory of the Geto-Dacians or northern Thracians. During this period the remains of young children appear to have been accorded a variety of funerary rites and their burials comprise whole skeletons, partial skeletons, skulls or isolated cranial or post-cranial bones. The children's remains included in his study were recovered from a variety of site types, including settlements, isolated pits and apparently cultic sites referred to by archaeologists as 'fields of pits'. It is particularly interesting that the majority of the child burials date from the first century BC to the first century AD, a time when ordinary Geto-Dacian burials are extremely rare. The paper deals in depth with the enclosure of Grădina Casteluliu in Hunedoara where the burials of some 39 children were discovered. The features of these burials lead Sîrbu to conclude that they were the result of either human sacrifice or ritual inhumation.

In Chapter 6 Alison Taylor provides a comprehensive review of deviant burial practices in Roman Britain, drawing on evidence derived from an impressive array of archaeological cases and contemporary documentary accounts. She ends her introduction by citing examples to demonstrate the often ambiguous nature of such burial evidence and the difficulties involved with its interpretation. She then proceeds to run through possible explanations that may account for deviant burial, including human sacrifice, infanticide, execution, mutilation after death, witchcraft, and the fear of ghosts. This section is followed by an in depth discussion of the various types of physical evidence that Roman deviant burial might take, including decapitation, prone burial and unusually secure burial. The paper concludes by again referring to the potential ambiguity of the archaeological evidence for deviant burial across the Roman World. Taylor suggests that the creation of a database of all Roman burials and a greater understanding of Continental European burial evidence is necessary to enable British archaeologists to gain a clearer understanding of atypical burials. Furthermore, she believes they need to remain open-minded when attempting to interpret such burials.

Annia Cherryson's paper (Chapter 7) uses variation in the burial evidence from Late Saxon Wessex to address the issue of when should a burial be considered to be deviant rather than simply representing unusual, but acceptable, mortuary behaviour. The paper begins with an overview of what are regarded as normal burial practices for the period – primarily churchyard burial in addition to the growing body of evidence for the persistence of burial in field cemeteries. The following section provides a review of Late Saxon execution cemeteries in the region, burials which are readily classed as deviant. Cherryson then proceeds to discuss contemporary isolated burials and barrow burials. These have traditionally been classified as deviant but she queries this categorisation in light of the increasing evidence for the persistence of burial outside churchyards during the period. While some of the isolated burials appear to display characteristics that might be considered as deviant, others – although atypical – do not display features that might warrant such a classification. She suggests that one category of isolated burial in particular – those discovered in settlements and displaying nothing unusual apart from their location – should in fact be considered as a part of the normal range of Late Saxon funerary practices. She concludes by stating that each isolated burial needs to be examined individually within the wider context of contemporary burial practices.

The phenomenon of charcoal burials – in which the body is laid on, or beneath, a layer of wood charcoal – forms the subject of James Holloway's work (Chapter 8). Such burials have been found in tenth to twelfth-century contexts in England, Ireland, Scotland and Scandinavia, while a similar rite is also known from Merovingian France. This minority burial rite is poorly understood and a variety of explanations have been proposed to account for it, including hygiene and as a symbolic comfort for the deceased. Holloway's paper provides a review of the different forms of charcoal burial in addition to their distribution and chronology. He looks in depth at the phenomenon in five cemeteries from five different areas before reviewing the various interpretations that have been proposed to account for such burials. He concludes by stressing that charcoal burial should be considered as a variant rite within the boundaries of normal Medieval Christian burial practices. He suggests that Medieval burial practice as a whole should not be considered in terms of normal and deviant burials, but rather 'as a vocabulary of symbolic elements from which a range of rites are produced and reproduced'.

In Chapter 9 Jo Buckberry's research focuses on the archaeological and osteological evidence derived from excavations undertaken during the 1960s at Walkington Wold, East Yorkshire, in England. Originally the burials were interpreted as representing a massacre that took place during the Late Roman period. This interpretation was later questioned by Andrew Reynolds (1997) who proposed that it was actually an Anglo-Saxon execution cemetery. Buckberry's research has confirmed this latter interpretation through a programme of radiocarbon dating and a detailed re-examination of the human skeletal remains. The new radiocarbon dates confirmed that the burials were of Mid to Late Saxon date. The osteological findings derived from each individual are provided in full in the text, and this demonstrates that all of the individuals were adult males, many of whom displayed evidence for perimortem decapitation and physiological stress. The location of the cemetery (around a Bronze Age barrow, close to the local Hundredal boundary), and the variation in the orientation and position of the bodies all assist in the verification of the site as an execution cemetery but, interestingly, this example is the most northerly in England.

The paper of Estella Weiss-Krejci (Chapter 10) examines how deviant behaviour during life, unusual circumstances of death, and death at a young age affected the mortuary treatment accorded to historically documented individuals from the Habsburg and Babenberg Dynasties of Medieval and Post-Medieval Europe. The study focussed on some 257 individuals whose lives or deaths were considered to be atypical, and the paper provides an introduction as to what proper burial should have constituted for these high status individuals; how their corpses should have been treated, where they should have been buried and who they should have been buried with. The author then proceeds to describe in detail individuals who were considered likely candidates for differential burial practices. The results indicated that 'social deviants' in addition to those who had died during warfare or had been the victims of disease or murder, as well as young children were provided with differential mortuary treatment. A particularly interesting finding is the fact that deviant treatment of the corpse could also happen to individuals who had made very positive contributions to society during their lifetimes. In these cases the unusual funerary treatment was a sign of high and special status. Bearing this finding in mind, Weiss-Krejci suggests that in the absence of historical documents it can be difficult for archaeologists to understand why an individual may have been treated differentially in death and she advises that the interpretation of any atypical burial be undertaken in a cautious manner.

In Chapter 11 Colm Donnelly and Eileen Murphy undertake a detailed review of the dating evidence for *cillíní* – a class of Irish burial grounds reserved for the remains of individuals considered unsuitable for interment within consecrated ground. These poignant sites are most frequently associated with unbaptised babies and are found the length and breadth of Ireland. The paper focuses on the general lack of clarity concerning the origin of the monuments that exists within the Irish archaeological community. A review of the dating evidence obtained from 16 excavated sites, however, suggests that the *cillín* is a monument of the Post-Medieval period, and it is suggested that their proliferation in this period is associated with the Irish Counter-Reformation. The Council of Trent had reaffirmed Catholic doctrine and Canon Law and the new Continental seminaries produced priests and friars who returned to Ireland to administer the reformed Catholicism to the people. The importance of correctly administering the sacraments, including baptism, was emphasised and the authors suggest that this was the necessary catalyst for the creation of the *cillín*.

The final chapter of the volume is Mark Gordon's study of an eighteenth-century Irish mausoleum built outside the confines of the graveyard of Mainham Church, Co. Kildare. The work demonstrates how a consideration of funerary sculpture and architecture from an archaeological perspective can help elucidate further information concerning the motivational factors that may have lain behind the construction of a funerary monument. Planned by Stephen Fitzwilliam Browne as a mausoleum for his family and himself, it appears that the monument was constructed outside the graveyard following a dispute with the Anglican minister, John Daniel. This information is related to us in a plaque placed above the door of the mausoleum. Gordon, however, suggests that this may not be the entire story and proposes that Browne may have used the dispute as a means of deflecting attention away from the fact that he had constructed a large, elaborate monument to himself and his family – something that may have been frowned upon by his peers. As such, the dispute at Mainham may have actually provided Browne with an opportunity – a conclusion only apparent when the researcher looks beyond the obvious external plaque and interprets the more subtle clues held within the mausoleum's architecture and sculpture.

It is hoped that the current volume of papers will make some contribution towards our understanding of the complexities involved when dealing with non-normative burials in the archaeological record. The papers make reference to a wide variety of burial practices which can in some cases clearly be regarded as 'deviant' although, for others, the negative association of this terminology would appear inappropriate. In these latter cases the use of more neutral terms, such as 'differential', 'atypical', or 'non-normative', is more suitable. In some situations the burials appear to be displaying 'minority' rites which are simply part of the normal range of funerary practices utilised by a particular society. Whatever the terminology, an underlying theme within the volume is an emphasis on the need to study atypical burials within the context of the normal burial rites of a particular society, rather than in isolation. It is clearly apparent that unusual forms of burial can be difficult to interpret and invariably a multidisciplinary approach is required.

References

Binford, L. R. 1972. Mortuary practices: their study and their potential, pp. 208–43 in Binford, L. R., *An Archaeological Perspective*. London: Seminar Press.

McHugh, F. D. 1999. *Theoretical and Quantitative Approaches to the Study of Mortuary Practice* (BAR International Series 785). Oxford: Archaeopress.

O'Shea, J. M. 1984. *Mortuary Variability: An Archaeological Investigation* (Studies in archaeology series). Orlando: Academic Press.

Parker Pearson, M. 1999. *The Archaeology of Death and Burial.* Stroud: Sutton Publishing.

Reynolds, A. 1997. The definition and ideology of Anglo-Saxon execution sites and cemeteries, pp. 33–41 in De Boe, G. and Verhaege, F. (eds), *Death and Burial in Medieval Europe.* Zellick: I. A. P. Rapporten.

Saxe, A. A. 1970. *Social Dimensions of Mortuary Practices.* Unpublished Ph.D. thesis, University of Michigan. Ann Arbor, Michigan: University Microfilms Inc.

Shay, T. 1985. Differentiated treatment of deviancy at death as revealed in anthropological and archaeological material. *Journal of Anthropological Archaeology* 4, 221–41.

Taylor, T. 2002. *The Buried Soul – How Humans Invented Death.* London: Fourth Estate.

1. Unusual Burials and Necrophobia: An Insight into the Burial Archaeology of Fear

Anastasia Tsaliki

Abstract

'Unusual' or 'deviant' burials are considered to be cases where the individual has been buried in a different way relative to the norm for the period and/or the population under examination. Deformity and disease received scholarly attention in antiquity but, at the same time, they have also been the focus of social prejudice and superstition. Anthropological and ethnographical investigation has revealed that socially deviant and diseased individuals may receive different mortuary treatment relative to unaffected members of a society. In some cases, unusual disposal is accompanied by evidence for practices, which indicate fear of the dead (necrophobia). These practices usually include methods for the restriction of the dead in the grave by weighing down the body with large rocks, decapitation or the use of nails, wedges and rivets. For example, vampirism can be seen as a notion based on necrophobia, since legend indicates the vampire is a reanimated dead body. Anthropology and folklore have studied superstitional social fear for long but the 'Archaeology of Fear', based on the study and interpretation of evidence from the funerary archaeological record, is a relatively new concept. Although deviant individuals were not always treated differently in life or death, and were not necessarily regarded as outcasts or misfits, it is important for anthropologists and archaeologists to combine social, biological and burial data, as this approach may enable us to improve our understanding of atypical burials in the past.

Introduction

In an effort to understand ancient humans, archaeology obtains a plethora of evidence from cemeteries and the burials within. By exploring the manner of death and the treatment of the dead it may be possible to gain a clearer picture of the living – of their society, practices and spirituality. Archaeological investigation has revealed the phenomenon of unusual burials: these are cases where an individual has been buried in a different way than what is considered the norm for the period and/or the population under examination. Unusual burials can also be termed 'atypical', 'anomalous', 'extraordinary', 'non-normative', 'abnormal' or 'deviant'.

Methodology

The theoretical premise of the research presented hereinafter is that the type of burial together with the analysis of associated human skeletal remains may reveal significant information about the nature of the life, status, and manner of death of an individual. For instance, evidence of trauma, disease, and/or deformity in the skeleton may offer an insight into an individual's deviant treatment. An extensive literature review has been conducted for the purposes of establishing the necessary theoretical basis concerning death and its related subjects and to identify the usual burial customs and beliefs for the groups and periods under study. This was necessary to enable the detection and selection of the case studies included in the paper, and to enable these findings to be placed within their broader funerary context.

Unusual burials are often difficult to locate in the archaeological record as this depends on the experience of the excavators and recorders in addition to the background knowledge and aims of those responsible for interpreting the finds. Furthermore, it is difficult to associate every atypical burial with specific causes of crime or marginality. Both the bones and the burial context play an important role towards the achievement of this aim. As special treatment in the burial record can take many different forms within different cultures, a list of unusual human burial traits has been provided in Table 1.1. The list is not considered to be exhaustive, but rather as a reference guide to help with the adequate recording and categorisation of unusual cases.

In some cases unusual disposal is accompanied by evidence of practices, which appear to indicate fear of the dead (necrophobia). Necrophobia can be defined as a morbid fear of death and the dead. It is a term used also within medicine, which implies that the phobia may cause extreme and morbid reactions, such as intense anxiety, obsessions, or even a panic attack associated with acute distress, mental confusion and fear of impending death

Basic criteria applied to distinguish unusual burials:

- Primary and secondary burials in unusual places and/or positions when compared to the ordinary burial customs of the cultural group or of the time period (e.g. skeletal remains in wells, pits or kilns, skeletons laid in a prone position).
- Mass burials (inhumations and cremations), especially those without evidence or historical documentation for a crisis (e.g. epidemic, war, civil unrest) or those unique in the given burial ground.
- Inhumations or cremations, in cemeteries or isolated, associated with indicators of unusual ritual activity (e.g. cut marks, unusual artefacts of possible symbolic or ritual use).
- Cremations found in an inhumation site and vice-versa.
- Skeletons with evidence that may be indicative of crime, torture or special mortuary ritual (e.g. victims of infanticide, senicide, human sacrifice, cannibalism).

Table 1.1. Basic criteria applied to enable the identification of unusual burials.

(Youngson 1992). It is a Greek word deriving from 'necros' (*νεκρός*), which means 'dead', and 'phobos' (*φόβος*), which means 'fear', and in Latin it is known as 'terror mortis'.

Necrophobic practices usually include methods of restriction of the dead within the grave (Table 1.2). The fear of the dead seems to have had a substantial influence on burial customs from at least as far back as the Neolithic period, and it would appear to have had a worldwide impact (Tsaliki 2001).

Pathology and Deviancy

It has been hypothesised that pathological conditions which cause deformities, pathologies that can affect an individual's mental state and behaviour, diseases with social stigma, or a violent death, may be linked to the nature of an individual's burial. Social marginalisation during life and/or death can occur for a wide variety of reasons, including disease (e.g. smallpox, leprosy, tuberculosis and other epidemic infections), congenital and mental conditions, an immoral life, murder, the nature of one's birth, family status, witchcraft, a curse, excommunication, heresy, death prior to baptism, violent death, death by suicide, and improper burial rites (Ucko 1969; Shay 1985; Sledzik and Bellantoni 1994). In his *Natural History* of AD 77, Pliny made a clear connection between a cross-eyed person and evil eye traditions. In Britain, information derived from folk superstition would tend to suggest that personal disability or deformity was often regarded as unlucky in the past (Roud 2004, 81).

Shay (1985) drew attention to pertinent information within the field of sociology and formed three hypotheses regarding deviancy, which were all tested and confirmed by burial data derived from ethnographic cases, but could not always be confirmed in archaeological material due to the often insufficient nature of the evidence. She proposed that:

- The criteria of deviancy vary in different societies.
- Deviant burials may not reflect the status of the deceased during his/her life, but the social identity they acquired by certain actions or circumstances of death.
- In simple societies volitional and non-volitional forms of deviancy are not distinguished, so they are treated equally at death.

– Skeletons with evidence of tied body parts.
– Skeletons in prone position.
– Bodies buried unusually deep in the ground.
– Burials being covered by rocks or other weights.
– Bodies found cremated in an inhumation site.
– Skeletons with evidence of decapitation.
– Burials with evidence of rivets/stakes.

Table 1.2. Possible indicators of necrophobia apparent in burials.

Although deviant individuals were not always treated differently in life or death, and were not necessarily seen as outcasts or misfits, it is important for anthropologists and archaeologists to combine information derived from social, biological and burial data, as this approach may improve our understanding of atypical burials in the past.

The 'Special Dead'

Ucko (1969) successfully demonstrated the variability of body treatment and the dynamic nature of human societies as early as in the 1960s using ethnographic parallels, which he believed could widen the horizons of archaeological interpretation. For instance, fear of the dead has been noted in Kenya and amongst other African people. These groups treated a wide variety of individuals within their society – leprosy sufferers, young children, those killed by lightning, those who died in childbirth, those who had a violent death in battle, those who drowned, those who died from smallpox or dropsy, witches, twins, priests, chiefs, murderers, suicide victims and the very old – differently at burial. The very young (infants who did not yet have their first teeth) and the very old could be considered to be closer to the land of spirits (Ucko 1969, 271).

In other cultures, such as among the Romans, neonates and infants were buried at night in a closed family ceremony, because the very young had a marginal status and no public identity, so their burial could not be a social event of the community (Norman 2002). Roman writers referred to the death of young children as 'mors acerba' (unripe death) or 'mors immatura' (untimely death) (Norman 2002). Similarly, special dead in the ancient Greek World were the 'aoroi' (*άωροι*, the untimely dead), such as infants, young adults, and the unmarried. They were feared because witches saw them as suitable couriers of 'katadesmoi' (*κατάδεσμοι,* curse-tablets) (Garland 1985; Kurtz and Boardman 1994). Special dead also included heroes and the war dead, who were highly respected, as well as the murdered and their killers. The latter constituted feared and 'unquiet' dead (*βιαιοθάνατοι*). The murdered were angry against their killers and those who did not avenge their violent death. The killers, on the other hand, were afraid of being haunted by their victims and were condemned to shamefully wander after death, as Aeschylus wrote about Klytaimnestra (Garland 1985). Plato in his *Laws* recommended that murderers should be executed and their bodies cast out of the victim's country without any burial rites performed. He stated that those found guilty of the murder of a family member or infanticide should be executed and dumped naked at a crossroads outside the city. He also suggested that a stone should be thrown by all the archons on the corpse's head in the name of the state, using overkill as an expiatory act for the crime, and that the body should then be left outside the city without burial. Xenophon in *Hellenica* wrote that in Athens traitors and tomb robbers would be thrown to the 'varathron' (*βάραθρον*, gulch or pit) situated in, or near, the demos of Melite (Stalley 1983; Garland 1985; Mikalson 2005). In Sparta the bodies of condemned criminals were thought to have been thrown into Keadas (also spelled as 'Kaiadas' or 'Kaeadas'), although there is no conclusive archaeological evidence to support this assertion (Pitsios *et al.* 2003).

Another category, suicide victims, were condemned by Christianity as early as the fifth century AD. It is difficult to determine the ancient Greek attitude towards such individuals, however, as Homer and the tragic poets saw suicide as appropriate under certain circumstances, although Pythagoreanism and Platonism condemned it as a kind of hubris (Garland 1985, 97). Aristotle indicates that suicide was seen as socially irresponsible and illegal in Athens (Garland 1985, 98; Brody 1989; Marks 2003). Suicide was viewed as an untimely and violent death; Aischines and Plato indicate the spirits of these dead were feared and that the interpreters of sacred law ('exegetai'/ *εξηγηταί*) needed to be consulted on purification rituals and the burial of a suicide victim (Garland 1985, 96–8; Brody 1989; Marks 2003).

'Diobletoi' (*διοβλητοί*), those struck by lightning, were regarded with reverence by ancient Greeks, as they were thought to have been killed by Zeus himself. Plutarch reported that their bodies were believed to be incorruptible and sometimes they were left where they had been struck without burial. 'Deuteropotmoi' (*δευτερόποτμοι* or *υστερόποτμοι*), those who were thought to have died abroad but subsequently returned home alive, were considered impure and had to go through cleansing rites. Finally, the most fearful and dangerous category of dead were the 'ataphoi' (*άταφοι*) – those who remained unburied. In epic poetry and tragedy it was stated they could not enter Hades and that they haunted the living (Garland 1985; Barber 1988; Johnston 1999; Lawson 2003).

The attribution of proper burial rites was a matter of dignity and responsibility for the living, as witnessed by Homer's *Iliad* and *Odyssey*, and the tragedy *Antigone* by Sophocles. If the body was not found, it was necessary to create a cenotaph burial, sometimes with a stone as a substitute for the body (Kurtz and Boardman 1994).

Harmful Entities: Ghosts, Demons and the Undead

Many peoples believe the soul of the deceased does not reach its final destination immediately after death but remains for a time marginally between worlds. During this liminal period the soul is believed to be vulnerable to attack by evil spirits. The fear of revenants is based on this theory (Barber 1988; Summers 1996). The corpse is thus seen as polluting, and cathartic measures are applied both before and after the funeral (Kurtz and Boardman 1994; Johnston 1999; Lawson 2003). Even in non-Western cultures, as in ancient and contemporary Japan, the spirits of the dead are considered to be potentially dangerous and may wander for many weeks. If appropriate rituals are not performed the soul cannot move on to the land of the dead to meet the ancestors. These wandering spirits suffer from bitterness and malice and can curse their descendants. Those who died a violent or untimely death ('bad death') are also believed to be filled with hate and spite and it is anticipated they will return to hurt the living. It is thus necessary to be purified by a series of rites before and after the funeral (Mullins 2004). Ghost stories are abundant in Japan.

In the ancient Greek and Roman Worlds, there was a plethora of harmful entities such as the 'lamiae' or 'larvae', the 'empussae' or 'lemures', the 'striges', the 'mormo', and the 'ephialtae' or 'hyphialtae', equivalent to 'incubi' and 'succubi', who were thought to attack people in their sleep. There were also special festivals for the honour and appeasement of the dead, such as the *Anthesteria* in Athens and the Roman *Lemuria*, *Laralia* and *Saturnalia*, which were very closely connected to the idea that malignant spirits or ghosts existed who wanted to feed upon the vitality of the living (Summers 1996).

Ancient Greek and Roman beliefs concerning ghosts, witches and revenants have been preserved mainly in the writings of the following Classical authors (Summers 1996; Felton 1999; McIlveen 2001; Keightley 2003; Raucci 2005):

- Photius, in a summary of Antonius Diogenes', *The Wonders Beyond Thule* (c. second century AD), included the story of Paapis, an evil Egyptian priest, who had ensorcelled the siblings Dercyllis and Mantinias to make them live during the day and be corpses at night.
- Philostratus, a famous sophist of the late second century AD. He narrated the *Life of Apollonius of Tyana*, a wise man. It included an account of a Corinthian revenant in the story of Menippus, also known as *Bride of Corinth* (4.25). A vampiric or ghoulish creature in the form of a woman haunted men, devoured their flesh and drank their blood.
- Phlegon of Tralles, the Greek writer and freedman of the Emperor Hadrian (second century AD). In his *Mirabilia* (*Book of Marvels*) he presented the story of a young girl named Philinnion, who got out of her grave and seduced young Machates. A diviner ordered her body to be burned to ashes in a remote spot outside the city walls. After that the whole city was ritually cleansed with holy lustrations. In another story, Polycrites died suddenly but then returned from his grave to kill and eat his newborn hermaphrodite child, who was considered to be an ill-omen by the priests and the augurs. *Mirabilia* also includes other stories concerning the resurrection of corpses.
- Lucan (AD 39–65), in his poem *Pharsalia* (Book VI) talked about the Thessalian witch Erichtho, who slept in her grave and had the ability to raise the dead.
- Apuleius (second century AD) in his book *Metamorphoses*, also known as the *Golden Ass* (*Asinus Aureus*), narrated stories of witches who drank blood, hurt the living, and mutilated and stole members from corpses in graveyards.
- Propertius, a Latin poet of the first century BC, in his *Elegies* (4.7 and 4.11) referred to two women, Cynthia and Cornelia, who returned from the dead as spectres to proclaim their final wishes.
- Ovid (43 BC–AD 17), in his Latin poem, *Fastes/Fasti* (*Festivals*) (6.125–6.180), presented the 'striges' as blood-drinking birds.
- Pliny the Younger (first to second century AD), in one of his letters (7.27), narrated the story of Athenodorus and a house in Athens that was for sale at a bargain price because it was supposed to be haunted by a murdered man; the body was subsequently found and a proper burial put the ghost to rest.
- Finally, stories of haunting and haunted houses are also found in the writings of Plautus' *Mostellaria* and Lucian's *Philopseudes*.

It is probably the case that people sometimes practiced unusual burials with apotropaic and preventive purposes in order to deal with the fear of the rising dead and revengeful ghosts. According to Kyle (2001), pagan Romans were scared of the bodies of executed Christians, even more so because they were aware that Christians believed in resurrection. As a response to this fear they burned the corpses of Christians to assure that they would not resurrect and seek revenge.

Despite a widespread general belief to the contrary, stories of the undead also existed in Medieval Britain. In William of Newburgh's *Chronicles*, Chapters xxii–xxiv narrate relative events, which allegedly occurred in AD 1196, during the reign of King Richard I. One story in the county of Buckinghamshire describes how a dead man wandered out of his grave, attacked his wife, harassed his brothers and beset animals. The living sought help from the church and the Bishop of Lincoln wrote a chartula of Episcopal absolution and sent it to the local archdeacon with orders to open the grave and lay the chartula upon the breast of the corpse. When the tomb was opened, the body was found to have been incorrupt but after the archdeacon acted as instructed, it was reported that the dead man never wandered from his grave again (Summers 1996, 78–82). In fact, the British vampire of this story shares a lot in common with traditions concerning the Greek vampire, which have been found to be slightly different to those of Slavonic vampires. In Greece, the term for a vampire is used to delineate a corpse reanimated by a demon who does not necessarily drink blood but seeks to harm the living by attacking them, killing their animals and disturbing the household (Mouzakis 1989; Tsaliki 2001).

After the twelfth century AD, however, the tradition of vampires seems to have died out in Britain, while the fear of witchcraft increased (Bunson 1993). It is interesting to note though that the classic study of witchcraft – *Malleus Maleficarum* – written in AD 1486 by two Dominican friars, Fathers Kramer and Sprenger, also mentions remedies against the vampiric demons 'incubi' and 'succubi' (Kramer and Sprenger 1996).

It is known that until AD 1823 those who committed suicide in Britain were denied burial in consecrated ground and were interred by the public roadway or at a crossroads, in some cases with a wooden stake having been driven through their bodies. Written evidence for this practice exists, for instance, from Derbyshire dating to AD 1573. This custom is believed to have been applied as a deterrent to others, but since a suicide victim's body was considered to be cursed by the church and deprived of a religious burial, the fear of the dead cannot be excluded. An Act of Parliament of AD 1823, banned the driving of a stake through the body and, after this time, suicide victims were interred in a proper burial ground, but between nine and twelve at night and without religious rites. These limitations were removed in AD 1882 (Roud 2004, 61–3).

As noted above, Greece has a long tradition of revenants and bloodsucking creatures dating back to ancient times. In Byzantium, Slavic influence in conjunction with the precepts of the Greek Orthodox Church formed the legend of the Greek vampire species 'vrykolakas' (*βρυκόλακας*). Related superstitions have been recorded in Byzantine and Post-Byzantine Christian texts, orthodox canon laws, novels, folk songs and manuscripts, which were written both by Greeks and Western travellers in Greece (Mouzakis 1989). Priests attempted to explain the phenomenon and also carried out destruction of the revenants. Major aetiologies for the creation of vampires were considered to have been excommunication and the incorruptibility of the corpse; so special prayers were applied to enable priests to revoke an excommunication (Summers 1996). Related texts have been found in the codices of the monasteries of Mount Athos and Meteora. Many of them originate from the peak period of the 'vampire craze' in Greece – the seventeenth to nineteenth centuries AD. Protective amulets in the shape of crosses and pentagrams were worn by the living, placed on the corpse, or hung around the house. In addition, salt, garlic, vinegar, sulphur, onion, and quicklime were used as apotropaic substances, probably because of their strong smell and/or caustic action (Mouzakis 1989; Davias 1995).

Case Studies

Researchers in anthropology and folklore have long studied superstitional social fear, but the interest in the 'Archaeology of Fear', based on the study and interpretation of evidence from the funerary archaeological record, is relatively recent. Five examples of deviant burials – one from Cyprus, three from Greece, and one from Italy – will now be presented and briefly discussed. The aim of this section of the text is to demonstrate the wide chronological and geographic span of the phenomenon.

1. Khirokitia in Cyprus (Neolithic period: 4500–3900/3800 BC)

Burials at Khirokitia have been found within the settlement and in most cases they were placed under the house floor. The bodies were buried in pit graves in a flexed position. Heavy millstones, which were placed on the head or the body, may attest to necrophobic beliefs and practices (Niklasson 1991). Similar practices have been reported from other Neolithic and Chalcolithic Cypriot sites as well, such as Lemba and Kissonerga-Mosfilia. In addition, the first excavator of the Khirokitia site, Porphyrios Dikaios, identified two unusually flexed and prone individuals – Tholos XVII and especially one at Tholos XVII, Burial II (Figure 1.1). He interpreted the individuals as having been human sacrifices and considered the individual from Tholos XVII, Burial II, to have been associated with foundation rituals (Tsaliki 2000).

2. Capo Colonna, Trani, Italy (c. ninth–eighth century BC)

Two cist graves excavated by Dr. Ada Riccardi in a possible sacred area and dated to Protogeometric times, on the basis of associated pottery, are considered to be unusual since a large sandstone had been placed over each of the interred individuals. The area was considered to be sacred because a building, which may have been a temple, and a circular pit of unknown function were located near the graves (A. Riccardi 2002, pers. comm.). Grave 1 was found to have included the remains of two young adult males and an adolescent, while Grave 2 contained the remains of a young adult male. All three of the individuals recovered from Grave 1 displayed palaeopathological lesions in addition to perimortem or postmortem tooth ablation of the right central maxillary incisor. Lesions apparent in the spine of one of the adult males from Grave 1 were considered to suggest that he may have suffered from spondylitis of traumatic origin (Saponetti *et al.* 2007). In addition, it was

Figure 1.1. Khirokitia, Cyprus. Tholos XVII, Burial II. Note the unusual flexed and prone body position, where the arms seem to have been tied behind the back. The skull is intentionally artificially deformed, a common trait for this population (after Dikaios 1953).

thought that he may have sustained facial trauma which had resulted in the loss of four frontal teeth (Saponetti and Scattarella 2003). A very tall young adult male recovered from the disproportionally small Grave 2 had been placed in a prone and tightly flexed position and his remains were considered to display signs of severe cranial trauma (Saponetti and Scattarella 2003). It has been speculated that all four of the individuals were sacrificial victims, with the large rocks having been deposited on the bodies out of fear, to prevent them rising from their graves and seeking revenge on those responsible for their deaths (S. S. Saponetti 2002, pers. comm.; Saponetti *et al.* 2007).

3. Kalyvia in Attica, Greece (mid eighth–fifth century BC)

A. Tsaravopoulos and K. Papathanasiou excavated a multi-period cemetery at Kalyvia, where cremation was the predominant burial rite and individuals were associated with a wide variety of grave goods (Papatsarouha 2001). A few unusual inhumations, however, have also been discovered at the site dating from a variety of periods. These inhumations occur in simple pits and are not constrained to a specific area of the cemetery (A. Tsaravopoulos 2003–05, pers. comm.). A number of the inhumation burials have been found to contain simple grave goods, mainly in the form of small crude jars. Unfortunately, the preservation of the inhumations is generally extremely poor, with only a couple of exceptions, and the human remains have not yet been fully studied. In at least two cases, a large rock had been deliberately positioned at the centre of the body. In another case the skeleton was positioned within the pit in a contorted supine position, with the forearms bent parallel to the arms and the legs slightly flexed. This latter individual appears to have had a major fracture of the tibia, which was malaligned and possibly infected (Figure 1.2). The presence of these unusual inhumation burials within a cremation site in addition to the relatively simple nature of their grave goods may suggest that these burials were deviant.

4. Merenda in Attica, Greece (c. fourth century AD)

The second Ephorate of Prehistoric and Classical Antiquities (B'EPKA), under the direction of Dr. O. Kakavogianni, conducted large scale rescue excavations at the site of Merenda in Attica. A collection of disarticulated human remains were discovered in a limekiln during 2002. According to the excavators (O. Kakavogianni and V. Vlachodimitropoulou 2003, pers. comm.), the limekiln was in disuse when the burial took place. The deep pit of the kiln appeared to have been deliberately sealed with large rocks, which were located predominantly over the human remains.

Figure 1.2. Kalyvia, Attica. An unusual pit inhumation in a cemetery where cremation predominates. Despite the poor preservation it is obvious that the body is in a supine position with the forearms bent parallel to the arms and the legs slightly flexed. Note the fracture of the right tibia (courtesy of A. Tsaravopoulos).

The author has studied the skeletal remains and they were found to comprise one 'main' individual, a probable female 25–35 year old adult, along with the incomplete remains of a probable adult male. The body position of the 'main' individual was abnormal and she appears to have been deliberately cut in half before the body had fully decomposed and while the skeleton was still articulated. It is not possible to ascertain, however, if this had occurred during the ante-, peri- or postmortem periods. The head, torso and upper limbs along with part of the right ilium were found deposited prone in anatomical articulation, while the lower part of the body, consisting of the rest of the pelvic bones and the femora, tibiae, fibulae and bones of the feet rested next to, and parallel to, the upper part in a flexed articulated position. Hence the pelvis was lying approximately parallel to the head and the flexed legs were parallel to the torso (Figure 1.3). The very specific positions of the two body halves *in situ* cannot be explained by processes associated with taphonomy, decay or animal scavenging, but only by the intentional placement of the body in this manner. In the former situations the lower vertebrae would have been the location where the body would have been likely to naturally sub-divide. As such, the nature of the division of the body could only have been achieved by having cut it in half when flesh was still present on the corpse.

While cleaning the area of the 'main' individual's lower torso, between the arms, a segment of a third pelvic bone was found in articulation with the head and neck of an additional left femur. These body parts probably belonged to an adult male. The excavators are adamant that no other skeletal remains were found in the kiln. This raises the question of what happened to the rest of the second body.

Dismemberment and mutilation are perceived by different cultures and in various periods as strong punishments and a further humiliation of a wrong-doer (Riley Scott 1995; Spyropoulos 1998; Taylor 2003). The modest burial of these skeletal remains was performed in a pagan way, with a small plain trefoil Roman jar having been placed near the body in addition to a coin from the reign of Constantine (AD 307–337). The latter object may well have been the boat-fare to Charon (Davies 1999, 149). In an effort to interpret this unusual case, one probable scenario could be religious persecution against pagans. However, in this case one would expect a larger scale of events and more victims present. Alternatively, the study of the position of women in Greco-Roman and Byzantine societies, in addition to Roman law and the Roman perception of ritualised punitive executions, could suggest adultery (Carey 1995; Smythe 1997). Another, even more serious crime, was the relationship between a free woman and a slave. In the fourth century AD, Constantine enacted a number of laws against marriages between partners of different social status. If such unions were then discovered the offenders were to be executed (Evans-Grubbs 1993; Tsaliki forthcoming a).

5. Taxiarhis Myrintzou, Lesbos island, Greece (c. eighteenth–nineteenth centuries AD)

During 1999 the fourteenth Ephorate of Byzantine Antiquities (14th EBA), under the direction of A. C. Loupou, conducted salvage excavation of a few Post-Byzantine graves situated to the north of the church of Taxiarhis Myrintzou at the site of Ano Halikas

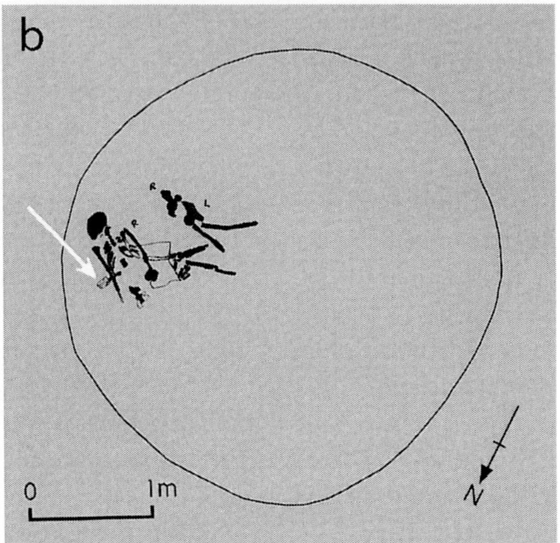

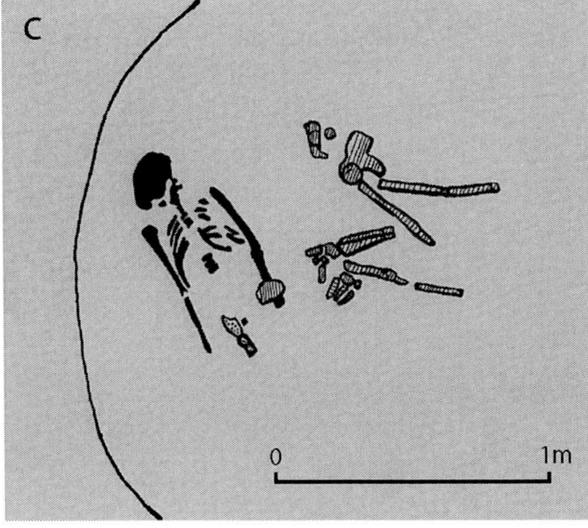

Figure 1.3. Merenda, Attica. Unusual burial in a kiln. (a) Photograph of the remains in situ. *Note the small jar near the left arm (courtesy of B' Ephorate of Prehistoric and Classical Antiquities). (b) Drawing of the kiln and the skeletal remains* in situ. *Note the small jar near the left arm (adapted from the drawings of A. Petrou, courtesy of B' Ephorate of Prehistoric and Classical Antiquities). (c) Detail drawing of the human remains in which differential shading has been used to highlight the different but associated bone assemblages. The upper body part of the 'main' individual is shaded in black, its lower body parts are striated, while the skeletal elements belonging to a second individual are stipled (A. Tsaliki).*

(M. Fountouli 2001, pers. comm.). The author undertook the osteological and palaeopathological analysis of the burials and radiographic examination was done by F. Takis. A male of 60+ years of age had been buried in a cist grave (Grave II). According to the excavators (A. C. Loupou and M. Fountouli 2001, pers. comm.), three bent spikes, each approximately 16 cm long with square sections and large heads, were found in association with the bones of the individual (Figure 1.4). The grave was considered to have been too narrow for a coffin and there was no evidence that one had been used. As such, the location of the long wedges within the grave was very unusual and they cannot be explained as coffin fittings.

The remains of the individual displayed a wide range of pathologies and deformities, some of which may explain his atypical postmortem treatment (Tsaliki forthcoming b):

- Frontal sinusitis with a large cloaca formation to the right of the nasion, which had resulted in asymmetry of the supraorbital ridges (Figure 1.5).
- Nasal, maxillary and mandibular deformities. A possible aetiology could be facial paralysis due to neurological problems of the facial and trigeminal nerves (C. Rodrígu-

Figure 1.4. An example of a spike similar to those found in association with the human skeleton at Taxiarhis Myrintzou, Lesbos, Greece. NB: The three spikes associated with the Taxiarhis Myrintzou individual were all bent, although their tips were straight (A. Tsaliki, courtesy of the wardens of the Castle of Mytilene).

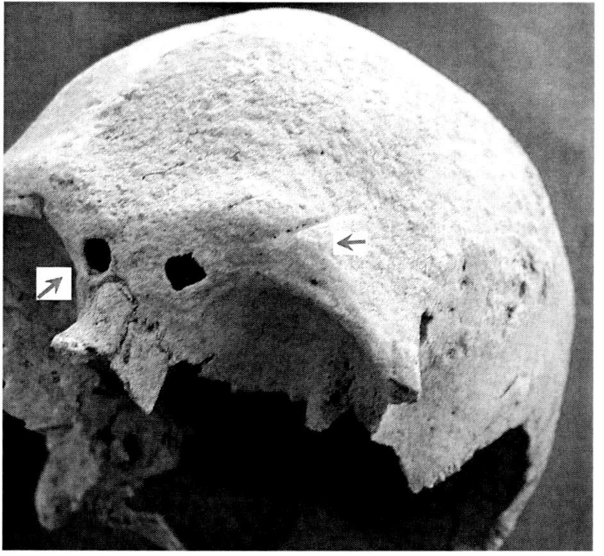

Figure 1.5. Cranium of the individual from Grave II at Taxiarhis Myrintzou, Lesbos, Greece. Note the frontal sinusitis with a large cloaca on the right (the hole on the left is probably due to taphonomy), the nasal deformity and the healed linear fracture over the left orbit (A. Tsaliki).

ez-Martín 2004–05, pers. comm.). The deformity of the mandible may alternatively have been due to biomechanical adaptation of the maxilla during occlusion and mastication. Radiographs did not reveal any evidence of fractures or other pathology.
– A healed linear fracture, approximately 16 mm long, over the left eye orbit which appeared to have arisen as a consequence of sharp-force trauma.

The man appears to have managed to live a long life despite his deformities. The nature of the frontal injury, however, may suggest that he had engaged in interpersonal violence and it is possible that he had been socially stigmatised because of his facial deformities. The spikes in his grave may be related to rituals that were known to have been undertaken in order to prevent a corpse from becoming a vampire. Physical disability is known to be a factor that can predispose an individual to become a vampire and means of prevention include among others – proper burial, pounding nails into various body parts, and putting stakes and nails in the coffin to prevent the bloating of the corpse, which in the popular mind was a sign of vampiric transformation (Bunson 1993; Tsaliki 2001).

Conclusions

To summarise, folklore and literary sources have long provided information on necrophobia, deviancy and marginality in human societies, as has been shown above through the writings of Classical and Medieval authors and the brief analysis of the vampire legend. Archaeology on the other hand is largely based on excavation and evidence, as demonstrated from the case studies discussed above. This paper aspires to show the potential benefits that could be gained from a collaborative framework between anthropology, palaeopathology, sociology, literature, archaeology, and related disciplines for the optimum recovery, recording and interpretation of the remains of past societies.

Beyond the facts provided by osteological examination, the process of interpretation in archaeology and anthropology, especially of unusual burial contexts, can sometimes be perceived as 'risky', with the formulation of hypotheses that may appear farfetched. However, when undertaken with reference to scientific methods and by following an objective approach, interpretation is vital in order to provide an understanding of skeletal remains and to enable insights to be gained concerning the material and cognitive aspects of past cultures.

Acknowledgements

This paper is based on my doctoral research thesis entitled – *An Investigation of Extraordinary Human Body Disposals with Special Reference to Necrophobia*. I would like to thank Dr E. Murphy for the invitation to participate in her initiatives relating to deviant burials, Dr C. Gerrard, and all the Ephorates and excavators who allowed me to study the burials derived from their excavations; they are mentioned individually in the text. Last but not least, I would like to express my gratitude to the institutions that funded my research, especially the (former) Bioanthropology Foundation, UK, and the P. Bakalas Bros. Foundation, Greece.

References

Barber, P. 1988. *Vampires, Burial, and Death: Folklore and Reality*. New Haven: Yale University Press.

Brody, B. A. (ed.) 1989. *Suicide and Euthanasia: Historical and Contemporary Themes*. Dordrecht: Kluwer Academic Publishers.

Bunson, M. 1993. *Vampire, The Encyclopaedia*. London: Thames and Hudson.

Carey, C. 1995. Rape and adultery in Athenian Law. *The Classical Quarterly, New Series* 45, 407–17.

Davias, O. (ed.) 1995. *Μόνταγκ Σάμμερς – Ο Έλλην Βρυκόλαξ*. Athens: Delfini. (Montague Summers – The Greek Vampire).

Davies, J. 1999. *Death, Burial and Rebirth in the Religions of Antiquity*. London: Routledge.

Dikaios, P. 1953. *Khirokitia: Final Report on the Excavation of a Neolithic Settlement in Cyprus on Behalf of the Department of Antiquities, 1936–1946*. Oxford: Oxford University Press.

Evans-Grubbs, J. 1993. Marriage more shameful than adultery: slave-mistress relationships, mixed marriages, and Late Roman Law. *Phoenix* 47, 125–54.

Felton, D. 1999. *Haunted Greece and Rome: Ghost Stories from Classical Antiquity*. Austin: University of Texas Press.

Garland, R. 1985. *The Greek Way of Death*. London: Duckworth.

Johnston, S. I. 1999. *Restless Dead: Encounters Between the Living and the Dead in Ancient Greece*. London: University of California Press.

Keightley, T. 2003. *Ovid's Fasti – Notes and an Introduction*. The Project Gutenberg EBook, Release Date: August, 2005 [EBook #8738], http://www.gutenberg.org/dirs/etext05/8fsti10.txt, accessed 16/2/2006.

Kramer, H. and Sprenger J. (with translation, an introduction, bibliography and notes by M. Summers) 1996. *Malleus Maleficarum. The Classic Study of Witchcraft* (reprint of 1928 edition). London: Brachen Books.

Kurtz, D and Boardman, J. 1994. *Έθιμα Ταφής στον Αρχαίο Ελληνικό Κόσμο* (translated from 1971 British edition by O. Vizyinou and Th. Xenos). Athens: Kardamitsas. (Greek Burial Customs).

Kyle, D. G. 2001. *Spectacles of Death in Ancient Rome*. London: Routledge.

Lawson, J. C. 2003. *Modern Greek Folklore and Ancient Greek Religion: A Study in Survivals* (reprint of 1910 edition). Whitefish: Kessinger Publishing.

Marks, A. H. 2003. Historical suicide, pp. 309–18 in Bryant, C. D. (ed.), *Handbook of Death and Dying*. London: Sage Publications.

McIlveen, R. 2001. *Greeks and Romans Knew How to Spin a Ghostly Tale*. http://homepages.indiana.edu/102601/text/ghost.html, accessed 16/2/2006.

Mikalson, J. D. 2005. *Ancient Greek Religion*. Oxford: Blackwell Publishing.

Mouzakis, S. A. 1989. *Οι Βρυκόλακες στους Βυζαντινούς και Μεταβυζαντινούς Νομοκανόνες* και στις Παραδόσεις του Ελληνικού Λαού. Athens: Bibliopoleio ton Bibliofilon. (The Vampires in Byzantine and Post-Byzantine Canons and in the Greek Traditions).

Mullins, M. R. 2004. Japanese Christians and the world of the dead. *Mortality* 9, 61–75.

Niklasson, K. 1991. *Early Prehistoric Burials in Cyprus* (Studies in Mediterranean Archaeology 96). Jonsered: Paul Åströms Förlag.

Norman, N. 2002. Death and burial of Roman children: the case of the Yasmina cemetery at Carthage – Part I, setting the stage. *Mortality* 7, 302–22.

Papatsarouha, E. 2001. Καλύβια Αττικής. Ανασκαφές σε ένα από τα κέντρα των αριστοκρατών-γαιοκτημόνων της αρχαίας Αθήνας. *Corpus* 31, 20–7. (Kalyvia in Attica. Excavations in one of the centres of the nobles-landowners of ancient Athens).

Pitsios, Th., Mihelogonas, I., Zafiri, V. and Mihelogona, A. 2003. Ritual death in the ancient Keadas. *International Congress of Anthropology: Homo sapiens Past, Present and Future, Paleoanthropology and Modern Human Populations of Eastern Mediterranean. Athens. November 21–23, 2003. Abstracts*, 59.

Raucci, S. 2005. Return of the living dead: elegiac and epic female spectral images. *The 136th Annual Meeting of the American Philological Association, Boston, MA, January 6–9, 2005.* http://www.apaclassics.org/AnnualMeeting/05mtg/abstracts/RAUCCI.html, accessed 16/2/2006.

Riley Scott, G. 1995. *A History of Torture.* London: Senate.

Roud, S. 2004. *A Pocket Guide to the Superstitions of the British Isles.* London: Penguin Books.

Saponetti, S. S. and Scattarella, V. 2003. Probabili pratiche necrofobiche in tombe della prima età del ferro (IX–VII sec. AC) a Capo Colonna (Trani, Bari). *XV Congresso degli Antropologi Italiani, Chieti 28–30 Settembre 2003. Abstracts*, 171. (Probable Necrophobic Practices in Tombs of the Early Iron Age – IX–VII centuries BC).

Saponetti S. S., Scattarella F., De Lucia A. and Scattarella V. 2007. Paleobiology, palaeopathology and necrophobic practices in Early Iron Age burials (IX–VII century BC) in Capo Colonna, Trani, Apulia, Southern Italy – the State of health of a small sample from Iron Age. *Collegium Antropologicum* 31, 339–44.

Shay, T. 1985. Differentiated treatment of deviancy at death as revealed in anthropological and archaeological material. *Journal of Anthropological Archaeology* 4, 221–41.

Sledzik, P. and Bellantoni, N. 1994. Brief communication: bioarchaeological and biocultural evidence for the New England vampire folk belief. *American Journal of Physical Anthropology* 94, 269–74.

Smythe, D. C. 1997. Women as outsiders, pp. 149–67 in James, E. (ed.), *Women, Men and Eunuchs. Gender in Byzantium.* London: Routledge.

Spyropoulos, H. S. 1998. *Τα Ερωτικά και τα Αιμοσταγή του Ηροδότου*. Athens: Patakis Publications. (On Herodotus' Love and Slaughterous stories).

Stalley, R. F. 1983. *An Introduction to Plato's Laws.* Indianapolis: Hackett Publishing Company.

Summers, M. 1996. *The Vampire in Europe* (reprint of 1929 edition). London: Brachen Books.

Taylor, A. 2003. Burial with the Romans. *British Archaeology* 69, 14–19.

Tsaliki, A. 2000. *Environmental Remains and Burials from Neolithic and Chalcolithic Cyprus* (in Greek with English abstract). Ancient Cyprus Web Project. http://www.ancientcyprus.ac.uk/papers/Tsaliki1/page1.html, accessed 25/7/2003.

Tsaliki, A. 2001. Vampires beyond legend: a bioarchaeological approach, pp. 295–300 in La Verghetta, M. and Capasso, L. (eds), *Proceedings of the XIII European Meeting of the Paleopathology Association, Chieti, Italy, 18–23 Sept. 2000.* Teramo: Edigrafital S.p.A.

Tsaliki, A. forthcoming a. *Burial in a Kiln: Deviancy and Crime Punishment in Ancient Attica.* Athens: ASCSA publications.

Tsaliki, A. forthcoming b. Les Figures des légendes: conceptions, exemples et pathographie in the *Proceedings of the 2e Colloque International de Pathographie*, Loches 6–8 April 2007.

Ucko, P. J. 1969. Ethnography and archaeological interpretation of funerary remains. *World Archaeology* 1, 262–80.

Youngson, R. M. 1992. *Collins Dictionary of Medicine.* Glasgow: Harper Collins Publishers.

2. What Actually is a 'Deviant Burial'? Comparing German-Language and Anglophone Research on 'Deviant Burials'

Edeltraud Aspöck

Abstract

'Deviant burials' are generally associated with bizarre practices like decapitations and strange body positions. Archaeologically 'deviant burials' are those that are different from the normative burial ritual of the respective period, region or cemetery. This paper will examine the research history of 'deviant burials' in the Anglophone and the German-language archaeological traditions. In both traditions the interpretation of 'deviant burials' started with the denial of the intentionality of these burials and then slowly moved to the insight in the 1960s and 1970s that 'deviant burials' are part of normal burial practices. By comparing the two research traditions we will see how the interpretation of 'deviant burials' has changed over time, in the context of two different archaeologies, finally arriving at two completely different approaches. This challenges the usefulness of the concept of 'deviant burials' as such.

Introduction

'Deviant burials' are first of all associated with bizarre practices like decapitations and strange body positions, bearing testimony to particularly unusual mortuary practices of the past, such as the 'live burial' at Sewerby, East Yorkshire (Figure 2.1). More objectively, the minimal definition of 'deviant burials' that most archaeologists would agree to is that they are burials different from the normative burial ritual of the respective period, region and/or cemetery. These differences may occur in body position or treatment, location or construction of the grave or types of grave goods.

The characteristics of German archaeology and the differences in archaeological practice between Germany and the Anglophone area have been outlined by Härke (1991; 1995; 2000). In the 'culture-historical' epoch of archaeology similarities between the two areas prevailed and the concept of an 'archaeological culture' can be traced back to the ideas of the German archaeologist Kossina (Härke 1991, 188). During the Nazi regime archaeol-

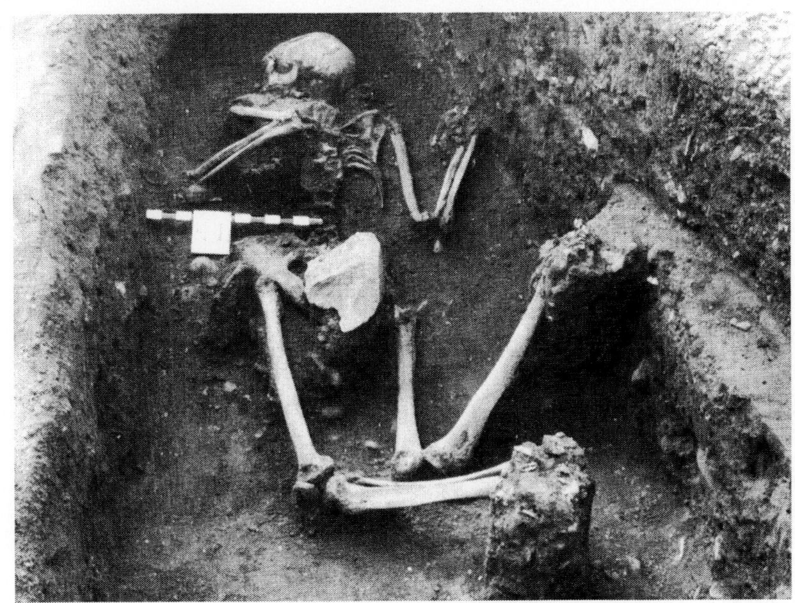

Figure 2.1. A so-called 'live burial' at the Anglo-Saxon cemetery at Sewerby, East Yorkshire. The top image shows the grave during the excavation (Hirst 1985, plate 2b), while a reconstruction of the burial drawn by David A. Walsh is depicted at the bottom (Hirst 1985, frontispiece). Reproduced by permission of English Heritage.

ogy in Germany was utilised for political purposes, leading to a subsequent fear of over-interpretation and the desire to remove all ideology from archaeology after the Second World War (Härke 1991; 1995). Consequently, since 1945 German archaeology has been characterised by being mainly descriptive, with meticulous excavations and artefact studies connected with an almost complete absence of theoretical debate. This of course stands in sharp contrast to developments within the English-speaking world of archaeology. One exception to this has been in German burial archaeology of the Early Historic period, which in the 1970s had a lively debate on the social interpretation of burials, showing many parallels to the contemporary Anglo-American debate. Unfortunately there was no communication between the two traditions at this time (Härke 1991, 195–7; 2000).

This paper compares European German-language studies of 'deviant burials' with how 'deviant burials' have been studied in Anglophone archaeology. The review of German-language research is based on studies from Austria, Germany, Hungary, Poland, Slovakia and Switzerland, but the bulk of the studies come from Germany.

German-language Research on 'Deviant Burial' Rites

The term *Sonderbestattung* is the German-language equivalent to the English term 'deviant burial'. *Bestattung* being the German word for *burial*, the prefix *sonder-* means something *special* or *exceptional*. Most importantly, in contrast to the English term 'deviant burial', *Sonderbestattung* is a neutral term, and has neither a positive nor a negative connotation. 'Deviant burials' and *Sonderbestattung* are used to describe the same phenomenon.

Early Discussions

One of the main concerns of early studies of the '*Bestattung in Bauchlage und verwandte Bräuche*' ('face-down burials and related customs', Wilke 1933) was to prove that they were intentional practices. This was probably first stated in a 1931 paper, emphasising that unusual burials form a specific group of burials, and were not the result of accidents, soil pressure or carelessness (Wilke 1931). Early papers from the 1920s and 1930s were followed by a research gap until the 1960s, when the study of unusual burials together with the same approaches and interests of the earlier studies was taken up again. First there was an interest in the temporal and spatial distribution of unusual burials, and secondly in the beliefs surrounding them. Examples of unusual burials from all over the world and across all periods were listed (Wilke 1933; Kyll 1964), which led to the notion of a 'continuity' of these burial rituals from the Palaeolithic period until the middle of the twentieth century AD (Wilke 1933; Kyll 1964). Based on this assumption of 'continuity', Kyll (1964, 175) suggested that unusual burials were manifestations of latent archaic beliefs, forming very powerful rituals which 'emerged' at certain occasions when the living felt endangered. Furthermore it was suggested that these rituals might have been practiced secretly, because they were different from the prevailing belief systems of the leading social groups (Salin 1952, 216; Kyll 1964, 175). Interpretations were based on social anthropological research. The practice of turning the corpse face-down was viewed in connection with the animistic belief that the soul leaves the body through the mouth, either as an attempt to prevent the soul from leaving the body, or from returning to it (Wilke 1933, 460; Kyll 1964, 178). Another explanation was that turning the body on the face for burial was meant to protect the living from the 'evil eye' (Wilke 1933, 457; Kovrig 1963, 86–102).

The Concept of Sonderbestattungen

The term *Sonderbestattungen* was created in the field of palaeodemography. The physical anthropologist Schwidetzky (1965), asked why human remains from cemeteries are not always a representative sample of a living population. In an analysis of ethnographic reports she found evidence for different treatment at death that would influence population statistics: different places or manners of burial for certain age, sex and social groups would lead to a statistically significant absence of certain groups in demographic statistics. Children were the population group most frequently reported as being subject to special burial rites (Schwidetzky 1965, 233). The large amount of evidence for special disposal within societies, and the fact that it was seldom reported that everybody received the same funerary treatment, left her sceptical about the validity of population statistics based on prehistoric cemeteries (Schwidetzky 1965, 243–4).

Subsequently, the term *Sonderbestattung* was adopted in archaeology, but with a different meaning, that of exceptional burials (Pauli 1975). *Sonderbestattung* therefore means something completely different in the two disciplines: in palaeodemography it is used as an explanation for statistically missing, or in other words invisible burials, while in archaeology it is used to classify special – visible – burials (Wahl 1994).

For a long time, possibly the most influential research on *Sonderbestattungen* has been Pauli's (1975) study *Keltischer Volksglaube* ('Celtic folk belief'). Pauli analysed amulet finds and unusual burial rites in central European cemeteries from 600 to 200 BC. He found an increased presence of amulets, frequently accompanied with unusual body positions and body treatment in graves from the end of the sixth to the fourth centuries BC. This period, at the end of the Hallstatt and the beginning of the La Tène period, was a time of profound changes in religious, cultural and political spheres manifesting itself in a peak of imported goods from the Mediterranean, resettling of hilltop settlements and radically new artistic expressions (Pauli 1975, 207–13). Pauli suggested that the increased use of amulets has to be understood in this context, as along with these changes came an uncertainty about future developments and a stronger individual urge for protection (Pauli 1975, 199). He developed his general hypothesis that times of profound changes caused an increase in amulets in graves as well as an increase in unusual burial rituals (Pauli 1975, 185–90). Like the custom of *Sonderbestattungen*, the belief in the power and effectiveness of amulets was thought to be part of a folk belief rather than official religion (Pauli 1975, 212).

Both Pauli and Schwidetzky based their research on ethnographic, historic and folklore accounts. Pauli categorised two main groups who received different treatment at death. The first were those who died a *mors immatura* (children, in some occasions also unmarried women) and the second group were what he called the 'dangerous dead', comprising individuals who were already different during their lifetime (like shamans, witches, medicine men), or whose circumstances of death were different. At the same time it became standard practice to write one chapter on *Sonderbestattungen* as part of each cemetery analysis. Within individual cemeteries, different types of abnormal burials were identified and interpreted, resulting in a wide range of explanations including magical associations, surviving elements of previous populations (Kovrig 1963), burial rites as a final punishment (Fettich 1965), 'deviant burials' as a kind of sacrifice or substitute for human sacrifice (Pauli and Glowatzki 1979; Tempelmann-Macynska 1989) and burials of social outcasts, low status individuals or disabled people (Pauli and Glowatzki 1979; Neugebauer 1992; Lauermann 2003). These interpretations were sometimes supported by historical or folklore evidence, but also many of them were *ad hoc* arguments without any theoretical foundations. A tendency towards morbid interpretations can often be seen as well as a projection of a 'dark side of the past' into these burial rituals (e.g. Pauli and Glowatzki 1979, 147–50). Nevertheless, from the 1970s onwards, *Sonderbestattungen* have had an established place in German-language burial archaeology. Furthermore, the link between these unusual burials and the unique treatment of certain dead as reported in ethnographies and folklore sources has also been established.

The Fear of the Dead

A fixed theme in German-language archaeology of 'deviant burial' rites has been the 'fear of the dead'. From the earliest studies (e.g. Wilke 1931) onwards authors referred to the fear of certain dead, often not specified, but commonly the fear of *Wiedergänger* (dead people returning) to lie behind the special treatment of some dead. Burial practices, but also post-burial manipulations of the grave and body, were frequently interpreted as practical measures to prevent the dead from returning. They include: face down body position; tightly bound bodies; feet tightly bound (trammelled by chains); amputated limbs; dislocated or missing skulls; and stone covers (e.g. Ament 1992, 4).

The idea of the un-restful dead has been obviously influenced by folklore and a lot of arguments are explicitly based on them. Unsurprisingly, in eastern European Slavic countries, where vampire stories originated and are still part of folklore tales, this tradition is even stronger. The vampire is supposed to be more dangerous than the *Wiedergänger* because not only is it returning to the living in the night, but it is also said to drain their blood (Grenz 1967, 255). Many 'deviant burials' from the Early Medieval period to the twentieth century have been interpreted as the remains of supposed vampires and as anti-vampire practices in the Slavonic areas of Germany, Poland, Czechia and Slovakia (Grenz 1967; Warnke 1982; Hanuliak 1995; 1999). Hanuliak has found a climax of anti-vampire practices in ninth to twelfth century AD Slovakia. He has linked this increase with social changes, connected with the crisis at the end of the pre-Christian, 'heathen' period (Hanuliak 1995, 133–5). This dominance of fear in the interpretations of *Sonderbestattungen* has rightly received criticism, mainly because it cannot be applied to such a variety of phenomena, ranging from decapitations to unusual grave goods (Torbrügge 1979, 51–2; Meyer-Orlac 1997, 5–8). Also there is a lack of specification of what is feared – the corpse, death in general, assumed actions of the dead – something which has been criticised (Meyer-Orlac 1997, 5–8), but in most cases it is quite clear that what was meant was the fear of the dead returning.

In Search of a Definition of Sonderbestattung

In a diagram Meyer-Orlac (1997, 10) described how the life and circumstances of death of every dead person are 'evaluated', leading to the burial ritual appropriate for that particular individual (Figure 2.2). The outer circle stands for the evaluation of life, and the inner circle for the evaluation of death. The idea is that various lives and deaths were assigned an extremely positive or extremely negative evaluation, which consequently was expressed in a 'deviant burial' rite. The section of these extreme evaluations has been called *sacer*, expressing an often ambivalent meaning, something that is accursed and divine at the same time (Meyer-Orlac 1997, 2).

Meyer-Orlac's paper is part of a volume that has come out of a 1990 conference in Switzerland on *Sonderbestattungen* in Bronze Age Eastern Central Europe (Rittershofer 1997).

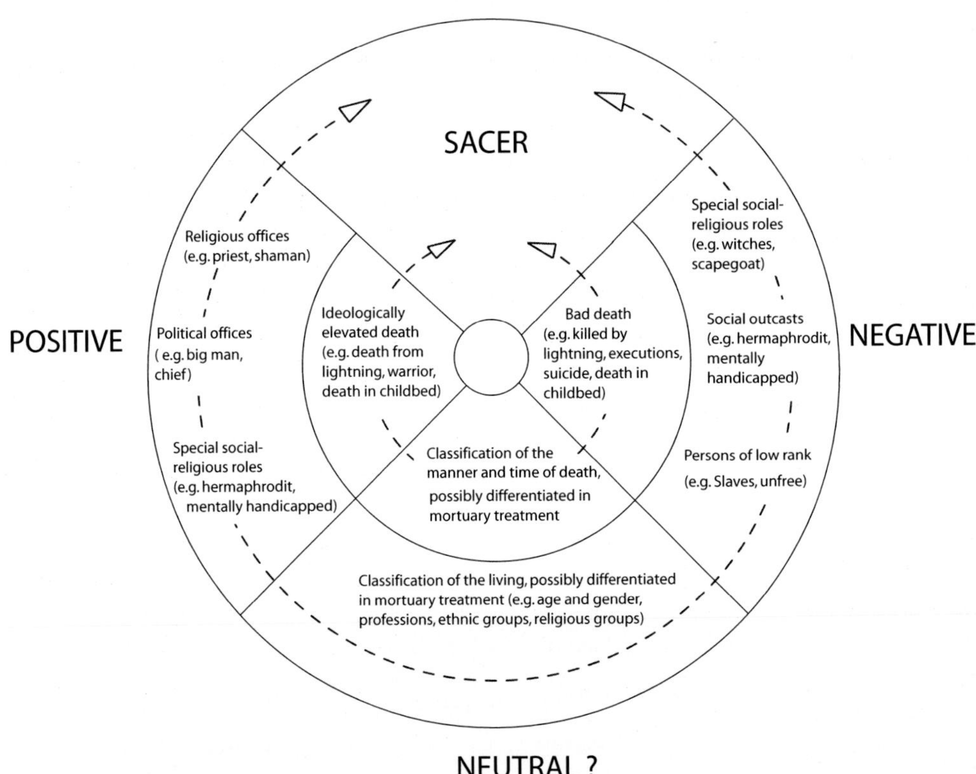

Figure 2.2. Diagram describing how the life and circumstances of death might be evaluated at a burial situation (drawn after Meyer-Orlac 1997, 10). Meyer-Orlac has suggested that extremely positive or negative evaluations might lead to a 'deviant burial'. These extreme evaluations have in common that they are ambivalent, expressed by allocating them the same area in the diagram, which is called sacer *(Meyer-Orlac 1997, 2). Reproduction and translation permitted by Verlag Marie Leidorf GmbH.*

A wide range of different kinds of topics were addressed at this conference, ranging from settlement burials to pendants made of human skulls, all of which are listed in Table 2.1a. This shows how 'broad' the classification *Sonderbestattung* has become and how there has been a move away from the previously rather limited use of the word as a category of burial different from the normal burial rite within a certain period or cemetery. This is also reflected in other current publications, where the *translatio* (exhumation, transport and storage) of corpses and skeletons of martyrs, multiple burials and buried pots which contain placenta have been labelled *Sonderbestattung* (Table 2.1b).

Understandably, other papers are concerned with the actual definition and meaning of *Sonderbestattung*. First of all, the use of the same term for different (but ultimately linked) phenomena in archaeology and physical anthropology has been criticised (Wahl 1994). Another question has been whether there should be any statistical limitation placed on the term, or in other words, where does the category *Sonderbestattung* end and a 'subgroup' of burials begin (Wahl 1994, 104; Meyer-Orlac 1997, 1)? Other papers at the Swiss Bronze Age *Sonderbestattungen* conference have been concerned with establishing criteria to classify human remains recovered from settlements (Furmanék and Jakab 1997; Gedl and Szybowicz 1997; Schultz 1997). It has also been questioned whether post-depositional manipulated burials belong to the 'deviant burial' category and, if so, whether they should be called 'apparent deviant burials' (Schultz 1997, 11–13). Similarly, it has been debated if evidence of supposedly human sacrifice or executions belong to 'deviant burials' (Meyer-Orlac 1997, 1). The big concern with finding criteria for classification and the establishment of typologies has to be understood in the context of German-language archaeology as outlined in the beginning of the paper. It reflects the fundamental importance traditionally given to typology not only in German-language archaeology, but also within other archaeologies on the continent (Härke 1991).

An important criticism of the current study of *Sonderbestattungen* is that the category is simply used too often (Wahl 1994). Peter-Röcher (1997) has pointed out that archaeologists have been ready to call a minority of burial evidence of a period the 'normal' burial rite, only because it is concordant with our Western perception of what a normal burial rite looks like. At the same time, burials have been called *Sonderbestattungen* which are actually normal in the respective archaeological period but are conspicuous and exotic to our modern Western taste.

Anglophone Research on 'Deviant Burials'

Culture-historical Search for Normative Burial Rites

In Anglophone culture-historical debate, as with its German-language counterpart, initially there was a lot of doubt whether unusual burials result from deliberate burial practices. Explanations of Anglo-Saxon face-down burials or burials with strange body positions include the famous statements that the undertaker might have been drunk (Rolleston 1869, 477), or that he was too lazy to 'excavate a grave of sufficient length' (Leeds and Harden

(a) 1990 conference in Switzerland on 'Special burials in the Bronze Age of Eastern Central Europe' (Rittershofer 1997):	
Settlement burials	Lauermann 1997
Graves containing special finds	Coblenz 1997
Burials of children and of metallurgists	Coblenz 1997
A type of barrow	Breddin 1997
Graves without burials (cenotaph)	Plesl 1997
Post-depositional manipulated graves	Bönisch 1997; Meyer-Orlac 1997; Schultz 1997
Cremations lacking cremated bone	Eibner 1997
Un-cremated bones in cremation cemeteries	Plesl 1997
Sacrifice	Gedl and Szybowicz 1997
Cannibalism	Gedl and Szybowicz 1997; Grimm 1997
Pendants made of human skull	Coblenz 1997

(b) Other more recent studies:	
Burials covered with animal skulls	Peschek 1996
Exhumation, transfer and storage of the corpses or skeletons of martyrs	Glaser 1997
Double and multiple burials, succeeding burials	Lauermann 2003
Buried pots containing placenta	Frieser 2003

Table 2.1. List of evidence which has been classified Sonderbestattung *in current German-language publications.*

1936, 30). Another idea was that the ends of the grave were not vertical and when the corpse decayed, the skull, together with two vertebrae rolled backwards (Leeds and Harden 1936, 30). But also more recently, the intentionality of face-down burials and 'live-burials' has been questioned and it has been argued that this kind of evidence resulted from soil movements, connected with the decomposition of wooden structures at some time after deposition (Reynolds 1988). This is not the place to provide a detailed argument against that position, but to mention one counter-argument, the orderly body-position of some prone burials can hardly have resulted from the decomposing corpse turning in the grave due to wood decomposition and gas formation. Therefore while many will agree that post-depositional processes have to be more often taken into account (e.g. Nilssen Stutz 2003,

131–59), and that some cases are indeed ambiguous (e.g. the Sewerby live-burial in Figure 2.1; Hirst 1985, 38–43; 1993, 42–3) in the bulk of cases, body position or manipulation were deliberate and part of the burial ritual.

To return to the research history and culture-historical search for archaeological cultures, which were assumed to be the remains of a 'people' or race (Childe 1929, v–vi), it was Childe's belief that unusual burials were those of immigrants or, in other cases, that they were 'foreign rituals' which might have been introduced by chiefs from somewhere else (e.g. Childe 1947, 4, 7, 69, 125, 298). The same approach was taken by Faull (1977), who interpreted the Early Anglo-Saxon 'deviant burials' as those of Romano-British people.

The Deviant Social Persona

In contrast to culture-historical archaeology's search for norms, variability and differences in burial rituals became the focus of the ensuing processual branch of burial archaeology. Probably as a result of the frequent use of quantitative methods, the use of the term 'deviant' to refer to an unusual burial became common in this period, and it seems to have been first used in the work of Saxe (1970).

According to the 'processual' model, at times of death the survivors have a 'duty relationship' to the deceased and what gets symbolised in mortuary ritual is the so-called 'social persona', a composite of social identities, consisting of age, sex and the various social roles or membership affiliations of the deceased (Binford 1972, 225–6). The concept of a 'deviant social persona' was developed by Saxe (1970, 10–12). He basically argued that certain circumstances of life and death can alter the obligations of the burying community towards the dead person (their 'duty relationship'), who consequently loses the right to a normal funerary treatment and gets treated according to what is suitable for this category of 'deviant' dead. This means that the burial rite for this individual will not refer to the age, sex or status of the deceased, but would normally show less appreciation for that dead individual ('a shallow social persona'). Those circumstances that are considered 'deviant' and that alter what happens after death differ from society to society (Shay 1985, 222). This understanding of 'deviant burials' was quite a big step towards viewing them as an integral part of the normal mortuary behaviour of a community.

Saxe has suggested that in less complex societies it will not be distinguished whether a deviance is volitional or non-volitional, all will be perceived and treated the same. In more complex societies, along with the development of law and medicine, the notion of what constitutes a deviant life or death will become more differentiated and criminal acts (volitional), for example, will be treated differently from illness (non-volitional), with illness possibly being treated in the same way as a normal life or death (Saxe 1970, 11–12). This was expressed in Saxe's Hypothesis Seven: 'The simpler a sociocultural system, the less divergence will be evident in the treatment of different kinds of deviant social personae and conversely' (Saxe 1970, 118).

While Binford and Saxe have only used ethnographic evidence, the later studies of O'Shea (1984) and Shay (1985) have combined the ethnographic material with archaeological data. In his case study on three Native American groups from the mid-seventeenth to the mid-eighteenth century AD O'Shea (1984) analysed the differences in the burial record and compared them with what was known about the groups from historical sources. Some forms of 'deviant burial' rites found in the cemeteries did not have any ethnographic precedents (O'Shea 1984, 250) and vice versa, disposal in a location other than the corporate cemetery of course did not show up archaeologically (O'Shea 1984, 254). O'Shea has doubted whether it is possible to recover all kinds of 'deviant burial' rites employed by a society, or to determine their precise meaning or significance with solely archaeological analysis (O'Shea 1984, 254). Shay's analysis of ethnographic and historical data, as well as sociological studies, has confirmed Saxe's model and showed that 'deviancy' can be valued high or low (Shay 1985, 223–5, 231; tables 1 and 2). Her application of the model to examples of 'deviant burials' has shown that the 'processual' model provides a logical explanation. For example, an exceptional Bronze Age burial of an adult male in Jericho who has been trepanned during life, did not show the usual treatment given to adult males (Shay 1985, 231). He did not receive secondary burial, a feature regarded as showing group affiliation by Shay, and the grave assemblage was poor in quantity and quality. Consequently, the burial did not reflect the social identities maintained by the deceased during his life, but treatment appropriate to the deviancy related to the particular circumstances of his death (Shay 1985, 231).

The Saxe approach has also been applied to human remains of the British Iron Age. For most of the British Iron Age the majority of people were disposed of in a way that did not leave direct archaeological traces and burials have rarely been found in the archaeological record. Wait's (1985, 120) interpretation was simply to equate most of the human remains of the British Iron Age with 'deviant burials', rites performed for 'a series of unclean and outcast statuses'. Other research on Iron Age human remains has shown patterns in depositional practices (e.g. Walker 1984; Fitzpatrick 1992). This suggests that the relationship between normal and 'deviant burial' rites in the British Iron Age is more complex, and that the concept of 'deviant burials' cannot be applied at all or at least in not as straightforward a manner as in other periods.

The Context and Meaning of 'Deviant Burials'

After the above studies, which can be summarised as 'processual', there was not much attention given to the theoretical study of 'deviant burials'. At the same time, as in German-language archaeology, 'deviant burials' have been studied in analyses of individual cemeteries and have been interpreted very similarly to those that occur in analyses of Continental cemeteries.

Current studies have embraced 'deviant burials' again and look at them from current perspectives in Anglophone theory. One is the specific meaning of places of deposition in a natural landscape or within areas of human activity. Reynolds (2002, 188) has interpreted the Early Anglo-Saxon 'deviant burials' within cemeteries differently from the ones of the later Anglo-Saxon period, which were placed on boundaries. In particular, research on out-of cemetery human remains has focussed on the place of deposition as a means of interpretation (Isserlin 1997, 92; Cleary 2000, 138). Taylor (2002, 144–69) has argued that the 'liminal' character of bogs was an important aspect for the rituals performed on the so-called bog bodies. Based on ritual theory, Taylor as well as Williams have developed detailed scenarios for the deaths of the individuals who became bog bodies (Taylor 2002; Williams 2003). In Britain, disability and social inclusion/exclusion have gained attention as an academic topic in particular since the Disability Discrimination Act of 1995 (Roberts 2000, 47). In an interdisciplinary volume on 'Madness, Disability and Social Exclusion' the question of how to find the disadvantaged and socially excluded in the archaeological and skeletal record has been addressed (Hubert 2000). Whether disabled people have been buried normally or differently may tell how they were perceived during their lifetime and provide information about the 'attitude' shown towards disabled people in past societies (Murphy 2000, 74–5; Papadopoulos 2000; Roberts 2000, 56).

In the above studies, all belonging to what is conventionally summarised as 'post-processual' approaches, the study of 'deviant burials' is given a more prominent position than it was in the previous 'processual' studies. 'Deviant burials' incorporate many of the aspects of 'post-processualism', such as individualism, agency and marginal groups in society. This is in contrast with the focus of processual studies on society as a system, in which 'deviant burials' were one part of burial practices, but otherwise unimportant. In the context of 'post-processual' archaeology 'deviant burials' are not only a by-product of mortuary practices of any society but also of major interest.

Comparing Anglophone and German-language Research on 'Deviant Burials'

The research on 'deviant burials' and *Sonderbestattungen* respectively in the two archaeological traditions shows parallels until the 1970s, but from then on they developed in different directions. Early in both traditions, 'culture-historical' approaches shared the notion that unusual burials originate in something completely different from the normal burials. This may be either due to a different belief or religion, or a different ethnicity or race. In the 1960s and 1970s the concept of 'deviant burials' developed. It was recognised that firstly, the postmortem treatment of a dead person, which is very different from what would normally be expected, is part of the mortuary rites in most societies. And secondly, what leads to this difference are special circumstances of the life or death of an individual.

This concept of 'deviant burials' developed simultaneously in the Anglophone and the German-language tradition. Although there was no communication between the two traditions the studies of 'deviant burials' share the same characteristics. Firstly, there were quantitative analyses of ethnographic accounts, leading to the conclusion that an unusual life or an unusual death can be the reason for a different mortuary treatment of some dead individuals. Secondly, hypotheses have been created which integrate the study of 'deviant burials' into the study of socicty (Saxe 1970; Pauli 1975; see above). This situation corresponds well with the overall picture, as German and Anglophone burial archaeology of that time generally show many similarities, and both were occupied with the social analysis of mortuary evidence (Härke 2000). But one important difference between the German and the Anglophone studies of 'normal burials' was that German research was only based on historical sources, while the Anglophone studies derived their hypotheses from ethnographic cases (Härke 2000, 377). This does not apply to the study of 'deviant burials'. The interpretation of 'deviant burials' was also in German-language archaeology based on ethnographic analogies. This is interesting, as the research on *Sonderbestattungen* therefore forms an exception within German-language burial archaeology and in a way mirrors the abnormality of its research subject.

This tendency to study 'deviant burials' under different assumptions than normal burials, or to project ideas about macabre behaviour or rites of the past into them, is not restricted to German-language archaeology. One famous British example was 'Crime and punishment in an Anglo-Saxon cemetery' (Hawkes and Wells 1975). Based on an over-interpretation of the skeletal evidence of a female prone burial, and some random information from textual sources, the story of a gang-rape which was followed by pregnancy and then collective punishment was reconstructed. Unfortunately, this paper is one of the very few that can frequently be found quoted in Continental papers as well.

Interpretations of 'deviant burials' in cemetery analyses are quite similar in Anglophone and German-language traditions. The main difference is that the 'fear of the dead' is part of literally every interpretation of 'deviant burials' on the Continent. This has been criticised and interpreted as a phenomenon of *zeitgeist* in Continental archaeology and anthropology since the eighteenth century, connected with the recognition that we still are not able to control death (Meyer-Orlac 1997, 8–9). However, there is a striking contrast between the roles the dead play in both archaeologies. While the British archaeologists venerate their ancestors (Whitley 2002), Continental, German-language archaeologists fear their dead. Archaeological interpretation, like all other research, does not happen on its own and is embedded into contemporary society (Shanks and Tilley 1987). In this sense, the interpretations of Continental archaeologists might reflect a general uneasiness towards recent dead after a history of wars on the Continent during the twentieth century, and in particular due to the Second World War.

Another line of research pursued in both traditions has been the investigation of the skeletal remains of 'deviant burials' (Pauli 1978; Pauli and Glowatzki 1979; Harman *et al.* 1981; Schleifring 1999). The idea has been that skeletal analysis might provide motives for differentiated treatment at death. However, in the majority of cases, there were no pathologies, signs of disease or other skeletal marks telling of conspicuous physical characteristics of the dead, which would have made them different during their lifetimes (Pauli 1978; Pauli and Glowatzki 1979; Harman *et al.* 1981; Schleifring 1999).

While similarities between the Continental German-language studies and the Anglophone research on 'deviant burials' prevailed until the 1970s, since then the development has diversified. In recent years, 'post-processual' emphasis on individuals and on people on the margins of society as well as ritual itself led to an increasing interest in 'deviant burials', which have been studied from all these perspectives. At the same time, Continental German-language archaeology has remained close to the archaeological evidence itself, which has led to the discussion of mainly classificatory issues. However, sometimes Anglophone ideas and approaches have been adopted by younger Continental researchers or students, e.g. a German Master's thesis has looked at female 'deviant burials' from the perspective of female individuality (Hoffmann 1999). This also reflects a more general trend (Härke 2000, 16–17).

A final point concerns terminology. As I noted earlier, the German-language term *Sonderbestattung* refers to the exclusivity of these burials and is otherwise neutral. The English word 'deviant' has a negative and sexual connotation and might imply that first, the buried person was a social 'deviant' or that the burial ritual itself was perverse. The use of this term is problematic as a lot of interpretations actually follow that line. The use of the term 'deviant' began in 'processual' archaeology, when statistical methods were employed, which explains that the original meaning was in a neutral statistical sense – describing 'something that deviates from normal' (The Oxford English Dictionary 1989, 565–6). It has been pointed out to me that in North American and Canadian archaeology the term 'deviant' is avoided in favour of classifications such as 'unusual burials' or 'non-normative' burials and also in French these burials are called *extraordinaire* (extraordinary) or *atypique* (atypical) (A. Tsaliki 2006, pers. comm.). It is worth considering and applying alternative terms more widely in British archaeology as well.

Conclusions

Recent research on 'deviant burials' in the Anglophone debate and in Continental German-language studies has gone in two completely different directions. German-language studies have been concerned with trying to gain a closer definition of what actually makes a burial 'deviant'. But recent papers have shown the problems when trying to achieve a more precise definition than 'that *Sonderbestattungen* are burials different from the normative burials'. At the same time, Anglophone archaeology is not really interested in the classification of burials as being deviant or not. Current studies tend to analyse certain categories of 'deviant burials' in terms which are of current interest in Anglophone archaeology. This raises the question of the usefulness of the archaeological concept of 'deviant burials'.

Analyses of ethnographic evidence in both research traditions have shown that due to special lives or deaths some individuals do not receive a normal funeral but are treated differently after death. This different treatment may be apparent in the archaeological record. Ethnographic sources therefore support the existence of a group of burials, which are different from the normal burials and which are the remains of individuals who were excluded from a normal funerary treatment for differing reasons. What has to be emphasised is that what we call 'deviant burial' rites are at the same time an integral part of the normal mortuary practices of most communities. Being part of the funerary rituals of a particular society means that 'deviant burials' can only be studied in this context. Therefore, the archaeological definition of what a 'deviant burial' is, as well as their interpretation is only possible in the immediate context of any burial, which is either within a cemetery, region and period of time. To conclude, what needs to be studied together with what is 'deviant' is what is 'normal'. Norm and exception – normal and 'deviant burials' – are ultimately linked together. The definition and meaning of 'deviant burials' can only be assessed in the context of the normal burial rituals, as well as other historical and archaeological evidence.

Acknowledgements

This paper is part of my Ph.D. research titled '*Deviant burials* as signifiers for periods of change from the Iron Age to the Anglo-Saxon period in Southern Britain' at the University of Reading. I want to thank my supervisors Heinrich Härke and Bob Chapman, as well as Richard Bradley and Linda Hulin for reading and commenting on drafts of this paper, and Eoin Lenihan for checking the English (all University of Reading). Gerhard Trnka (University of Vienna) kindly helped me with the search for previous research on *Sonderbestattungen*.

References

Ament, H. 1992. *Das Alamannische Gräberfeld von Eschborn (Main-Taunus-Kreis)* (Materialien zur Vor- und Frühgeschichte von Hessen 14). Wiesbaden: Selbstverlag des Landesamtes für Denkmalpflege Hessen. (The Alamannic Cemetery of Eschborn, Main-Taunus-Kreis, Germany).

Binford, L. R. 1972. Mortuary practices: their study and their potential, pp. 208–43 in Binford, L. R., *An Archaeological Perspective*. New York and London: Seminar Press.

Childe, V. G. 1929. *The Danube in Prehistory*. Oxford: Clarendon Press.

Childe, V. G. 1947. *The Dawn of European Civilization*. London: Kegan Paul.

Clarke, G. 1979. *Pre-Roman and Roman Winchester 2: The Roman Cemetery at Lankhills*. Oxford: Clarendon Press.

Cleary, S. E. 2000. Putting the dead in their place: burial location in Roman Britain, pp. 127–42 in Pearce, J., Millett, M. and Struck, M. (eds), *Burial, Society and Context in the Roman World*. Exeter: Oxbow Books.

Faull, M. L. 1977. British survival in Anglo-Saxon Northumbria, pp. 1–55 in Laing, L. (ed.), *Studies in Celtic Survival* (BAR British Series 37). Oxford: British Archaeological Reports.

Fettich, N. 1965. *Das Awarenzeitliche Gräberfeld von Pilismarót-Basaharc* (Studia Archaeologica 3). Budapest: Verlag der Ungarischen Akademie der Wissenschaften. (The Avar-period Cemetery of Pilismarót-Basaharc, Hungary).

Fitzpatrick, A. P. 1992. *Archaeological Excavations on the Route of the A27 Westhampnett Bypass, West Sussex, 1992, 2: The Cemeteries* (Wessex Archaeology Report 12). Salisbury: Trust for Wessex Archaeology.

Furmánek, V. and Jakab, J. 1997. Menschliche Skelettreste aus bronzezeitlichen Siedlungen in der Slowakei, pp. 14–23 in Rittershofer, K. F. (ed.), *Sonderbestattungen in der Bronzezeit im Östlichen Mitteleuropa* (Internationale Archäologie 37). Espelkamp: Verlag Marie Leidorf GmbH. (Human remains in Bronze Age settlements in Slovakia).

Gedl, M. and Szybowicz, B. 1997. Bestattungen in bronzezeitlichen Siedlungen Polens, pp. 24–41 in

Rittershofer, K. F. (ed.), *Sonderbestattungen in der Bronzezeit im Östlichen Mitteleuropa* (Internationale Archäologie 37). Espelkamp: Verlag Marie Leidorf GmbH. (Burials in Bronze Age settlements in Poland).

Grenz, R. 1967. Archäologische Vampirbefunde aus dem westslawischen Siedlungsgebiet. *Zeitschrift für Ostforschung* 16, 255–65. (Archaeological evidence of vampires in the west-Slavic area).

Hanuliak, M. 1995. Ungewöhnliche Bestattungen in Siedlungsgruben des 9. bis 12. Jh. *Ethnographisch-Archäologische Zeitschrift* 36, 125–36. (Unusual burials in settlement pits of the ninth to twelfth century AD in Slovakia).

Hanuliak, M. 1999. Vampirismus auf Gräberfeldern von der Wende des Früh- zum Hochmittelalter. *Ethnographisch-Archäologische Zeitschrift* 40, 577–85. (Vampirism in cemeteries at the turn of the Early to the High Medieval period in Slovakia).

Härke, H. 1991. All quiet on the Western Front? paradigms, methods and approaches in West German archaeology, pp. 187–222 in Hodder, H. (ed.), *Archaeological Theory in Europe*. London: Routledge.

Härke, H. 1995. 'The hun is a methodical chap': reflections on the German tradition of pre- and proto-history, pp. 46–60 in Ucko, J. (ed.), *Theory in Archaeology. A World Perspective* (Theoretical Archaeology Group series). London: Routledge.

Härke, H. 2000. Social analysis of mortuary evidence in German protohistoric archaeology. *Journal of Anthropological Archaeology* 19, 369–84.

Harman, M., Molleson, T. I. and Price, J. L. 1981. Burials, bodies and beheadings in Romano-British and Anglo-Saxon cemeteries. *Bulletin of the British Museum of Natural History (Geol.)* 35, 145–88.

Hawkes S. and Wells, C. 1975. Crime and punishment in an Anglo-Saxon cemetery? *Antiquity* 49, 118–23.

Hirst, S. M. 1985. *An Anglo-Saxon Inhumation Cemetery at Sewerby, East Yorkshire* (Archaeological publications, York University, 4). York: University Archaeological Publications.

Hirst, S. M. 1993. Death and the archaeologist, pp. 41–3 in Carver, M. (ed.), *In Search of Cult*. Woodbridge: The Boydell Press.

Hoffmann, H. 1999. *Furcht oder Ehrfurcht? Besondere Frauen – Weibliche Sonderbestattungen*. Unpublished Masters Dissertation, Hamburg University. URL: http://www.archaeologisch.de/totefrauen1.html (08.03.2006). (Fear or reverence? Special women – female 'deviant burials').

Hubert, J. (ed.) 2000. *Madness, Disability and Social Exclusion: The Archaeology and Anthropology of 'Difference'* (World Archaeology 40). London: Routledge.

Isserlin, R. M. J. 1997. Thinking the unthinkable: human sacrifice in Roman Britain?, pp. 91–9 in Meadows, K., Lemke, C. and Heron, J. (eds), *The Theoretical Roman Archaeology Conference Proceedings 6, 1996*. Oxford: Oxbow Books.

Kovrig, I. 1963. *Das awarenzeitliche Gräberfeld von Alattyán* (Archaeologia Hungarica, ser. nov. 50). Budapest: Verlag der Ungarischen Akademie der Wissenschaften. (The Avar-period cemetery of Alattyán, Hungary).

Kyll, N. 1964. Die Bestattung der Toten mit dem Gesicht nach unten. *Trierer Zeitschrift* 27, 168–83. (Burial of the dead with the face downwards).

Lauermann, E. 1997. Sonderbestattungen im Bereich einer frühbronzezeitlichen Siedlung in Unterhautzental, NÖ, pp. 42–6 in Rittershofer, K. F. (ed.), *Sonderbestattungen in der Bronzezeit im Östlichen Mitteleuropa* (Internationale Archäologie 37). Espelkamp: Verlag Marie Leidorf GmbH. ('Deviant burials' in the area of an Early Bronze Age settlement in Unterhautzental, Lower Austria).

Lauermann, E. 2003. *Studien zur Aunjetitz-Kultur im nördlichen Niederösterreich 2* (Universitätsforschungen zur prähistorischen Archäologie 99). Bonn: Dr. Rudolf Habelt GmbH. (Studies of the Aunjetitz Culture in northern Lower Austria 2).

Leeds, E. T. and Harden, D. B. 1936. *The Anglo-Saxon Cemetery at Abingdon, Berkshire*. Oxford: Ashmolean Museum.

Macdonald, J. L. 1979. Religion, pp. 404–33 in Clarke, G. (ed.), *Pre-Roman and Roman Winchester 2: The Roman Cemetery at Lankhills*. Oxford: Clarendon Press.

Meyer-Orlac, R. 1997. Zur Problematik der 'Sonderbestattungen' in der Archäologie, pp. 1–10 in Rittershofer, K. F. (ed.), *Sonderbestattungen in der Bronzezeit im Östlichen Mitteleuropa* (Internationale Archäologie 37). Espelkamp: Verlag Marie Leidorf GmbH. (On the problem of 'deviant burials' in archaeology).

Murphy, E. M. 2000. Developmental defects and disability: the evidence from the Iron Age semi-nomadic peoples of Aymyrlyg, South Siberia, pp. 60–80 in Hubert, J. (ed.), *Madness, Disability and Social Exclusion: The Archaeology and Anthropology of 'Difference'* (World Archaeology 40). London: Routledge.

Neugebauer, J. W. 1992. Früh- und mittelbronzezeitliche Sonderbestattungen in Ostösterreich, pp. 433–44 in Lippert, A. and Spindler, K. (eds), *Festschrift zum 50jährigen Bestehen des Institutes für Ur- und Frühgeschichte der Leopold-Franzens-Universität Innsbruck* (Universitätsforschungen zur prähistorischen Archäologie 8). Bonn: Dr. Rudolf Habelt GmbH. (Early and Middle Bronze Age deviant burials in Eastern Austria).

Nilsson Stutz, L. 2003. *Embodied Rituals and Ritualized Bodies: Tracing Ritual Practices in Late Mesolithic Burials* (Acta Archaeologica Lundensia 8, 46). Lund: Wallin and Dahlholm Boktryckeri AB.

O'Shea, J. M. 1984. *Mortuary Variability: An Archaeological Investigation* (Studies in archaeology series). Orlando: Academic Press.

Papadopoulos, J. K. 2000. Skeletons in wells: towards an archaeology of social exclusion in the ancient Greek world, pp. 96–118 in Hubert, J. (ed.), *Madness, Disability and Social Exclusion: The Archaeology and Anthropology of 'Difference'* (World Archaeology 40). London: Routledge.

Pauli, L. 1975. *Keltischer Volksglaube: Amulette und Sonderbestattungen am Dürrnberg bei Hallein und im Eisenzeitlichen Mitteleuropa* (Münchner Beiträge zur Vor- und Frühgeschichte 28). München: Beck. (Celtic folk belief: Amulets and deviant burials from the Dürrnberg near Hallein and in Iron Age Central Europe).

Pauli, L. 1978. Ungewöhnliche Grabfunde aus Frühgeschichtlicher Zeit: archäologische Analyse und anthropologischer Befund. *Homo* 29, 44–52. (Unusual burial evidence from the protohistoric period: archaeological analysis and skeletal evidence).

Pauli, L. and Glowatzki, G. 1979. Frühgeschichtlicher Volksglaube und seine Opfer. *Germania* 57, 143–52. (Protohistoric folk belief and its victims).

Peter-Röcher, H. 1997. Menschliche Skelettreste in Siedlungen und Höhlen: kritische Anmerkungen zu herkömmlichen Deutungen. *Ethnographisch-Archäologische Zeitschrift* 38, 315–24. (Human remains in settlements and caves: a criticism of traditional interpretations).

Reynolds, A. 2002. Burials, boundaries and charters in Anglo-Saxon England: a reassessment, pp. 171–94, in Lucy, S. and Reynolds, A. (eds), *Burial in Early Medieval England and Wales*. Leeds: Meaney Publishing.

Reynolds, N. 1988. The rape of the Anglo-Saxon women. *Antiquity* 62, 715–18.

Rittershofer, K. F. (ed.) 1997. *Sonderbestattungen in der Bronzezeit im Östlichen Mitteleuropa* (Internationale

Archäologie 37). Espelkamp: Verlag Marie Leidorf GmbH ('Deviant burials' in the Bronze Age in Eastern Central Europe).

Roberts, A. R. 2000. Did they take sugar? The use of skeletal evidence in the study of disability in past populations, pp. 46–59 in Hubert, J. (ed.), *Madness, Disability and Social Exclusion: The Archaeology and Anthropology of 'Difference'* (World Archaeology 40). London: Routledge.

Rolleston, G. 1869. Researches and excavations carried on in an ancient cemetery at Frilford near Abingdon, Berks, in the years 1867–68. *Archaeologia* 42, 417–85.

Ross, A. 1967. *Pagan Celtic Britain: Studies in Iconography and Tradition.* London: Routledge and Kegan Paul.

Salin, E. 1952. *La Civilisation Mérovingienne, D' après les Sépultures, les Textes et le Laboratoire* 2. Paris: A. et J. Picard.

Saxe, A. A. 1970. *Social Dimensions of Mortuary Practices.* Unpublished Ph.D. thesis, University of Michigan. Ann Arbor, Michigan: University Microfilms Inc.

Schleifring, J. 1999. Menschliche Skelette in Bauchlage vom kaiserzeitlichen Gräberfeld Groß-Gerau „Auf Esch", pp. 625–35 in Herrmann, F. R. (ed.), *Festschrift für Günter Smolla* 2 (Materialien zur Vor- und Frühgeschichte von Hessen 8). Wiesbaden: Selbstverlag des Landesamtes für Denkmalpflege Hessen. (Human skeletons in a prone position from the Roman period cemetery of Groß-Gerau „Auf Esch", Germany).

Schultz, M. 1997. Sonderbestattungen in der Bronzezeit aus der Sicht der Anthropologie, pp. 11–12 in Rittershofer, K. F. (ed.), *Sonderbestattungen in der Bronzezeit im Östlichen Mitteleuropa* (Internationale Archäologie 37). Espelkamp: Verlag Marie Leidorf GmbH. (The anthropology of deviant burials from the Bronze Age).

Schwidetzky, I. 1965. Sonderbestattungen und ihre paläodemographische Bedeutung. *Homo* 16, 230–47. (Deviant burials and their palaeodemographic significance).

Shanks, M. and Tilley, C. 1987. *Social Theory and Archaeology.* Cambridge: Polity in association with Blackwell.

Shay, T. 1985. Differentiated treatment of deviancy at death as revealed in anthropological and archaeological material. *Journal of Anthropological Archaeology* 4, 221–41.

Taylor, T. 2002. *The Buried Soul: How Humans Invented Death.* London: Fourth Estate.

Tempelmann-Maczynska, M. 1989. Totenfurcht und Totenglauben bei den Germanen im 4. bis 7. jahrhundert n. Chr. aufgrund der sog. Sonderbestattungen und des Grabraubs. *Zeitschrift der Savigny-Stiftung für Rechtsgeschichte, Germanistische Abteilung* 106, 274–83. (Fears and beliefs about the dead among Germanic people from the fourth to the seventh century AD on the basis of the so-called deviant burials and grave robbery).

Torbrügge, W. 1979. *Die Hallstattzeit in der Oberpfalz* (Materialhefte zur Bayerischen Vorgeschichte A 39). Kallmünz/Opf.: Verlag Michael Lassleben. (The Hallstatt period in Oberpfalz, Germany).

Veit, U. 1996. *Studien zum Problem der Siedlungbestattung im Europäischen Neolithikum* (Tübinger Schriften zur Ur- und Frühgeschichtlichen Archäologie 1). Münster: Waxmann Verlag GmbH. (Studies of settlement burial in the European Neolithic).

Wahl, J. 1994. Zur Ansprache und Definition von Sonderbestattungen, pp. 85–106 in Kokabi, M. and Wahl, J. (eds), *Beiträge zur Archäozoologie und Prähistorischen Anthropologie* (Forschungen und Berichte zur Vor- und Frühgeschichte in Baden Württemberg 53). Stuttgart: Konrad Theiss Verlag. (On the terminology and definition of deviant burials).

Wait, G. A. 1985. *Ritual and Religion in Iron Age Britain* (BAR British Series 149). Oxford: British Archaeological Reports.

Walker, L. 1984. The deposition of human remains, pp. 442–63 in Cunliffe, B., *Danebury: An Iron Age Hillfort in Hampshire* 2 (Council for British Archaeology research report 52). London: Council for British Archaeology.

Warnke, D. 1982. Eine "Vampir-Bestattung" aus dem frühgeschichtlichen Hügelgräberfeld in den "Schwarzen Bergen" bei Ralswiek auf Rügen. *Ausgrabungen und Funde* 27, 3. (A 'vampire-burial' from the protohistoric cairn in the 'Black Mountains' near Ralswiek on Rügen, Germany).

Whitely, J. 2002. Too many ancestors. *Antiquity* 76, 117–26.

Wilke, G. 1931. Die Bestattung in Bauchlage. *Mannus* 23, 202–6. (Prone burial).

Wilke, G. 1933. Die Bestattung in Bauchlage und verwandte Bräuche, pp. 449–60 in *Homenagem a Martins Sarmento.* Guimaraes: Sociedade Martins Sarmento, subsidiada pelo Ministério da Instruçao publica e pela Junta de educaçao nacional. (Prone burial and related customs).

Williams, M. 2003. Tales from the dead: remembering the bog bodies in the Iron Age of North-Western Europe, pp. 89–112 in Williams, H. (ed.), *Archaeologies of Remembrance: Death and Memory in Past Societies.* New York: Kluwer/Plenum.

Zeiten, M. K. 1997. Amulets and amulet use in Viking Age Denmark. *Acta Archaeologica* 68, 1–74.

3. Odd One Out? Earlier Neolithic Deposition of Human Remains in Caves and Rock Shelters in the Yorkshire Dales

Stephany Leach

Abstract

Reanalysis of human skeletal material from natural subterranean sites in the Yorkshire Dales has highlighted diverse treatment and a range of activities with regard to the deposition of human remains. Possible motivation for this variation in treatment is discussed in relation to Earlier Neolithic mortuary practices. Prior to this reanalysis, the human remains excavated from these sites were all generally considered to be Late Neolithic or Early Bronze Age in date and derived from articulated burials. However, a recent radiocarbon dating programme has identified a group of five Earlier Neolithic cave and rock shelter sites; these dates represent the earliest known deposition of human remains in this upland region relating to Neolithic mortuary activity.

The observed differential treatment of the remains is considered in relation to a number of variables including demographic factors, manner of death, health and evidence for disfigurement and disability in the skeletal record, in order to identify possible motivation for this behaviour and dealings with their dead. The noted range of mortuary treatment represents actions within the normal spectrum of corpse 'management' during the Earlier Neolithic, but can the bones of these individuals provide an indication of the process of selection for specific treatment? In this upland region, caves and rock shelters could have played a significant role as foci for community activities and meeting places. The deposition of human remains at these locations might be viewed, therefore, as a highly significant part of community life and ritual negotiations. Variation noted in the treatment of the human corpse might simply relate to random occurrences and practical issues, alternatively, it could relate to deeper community concerns and deliberate, meaningful manipulation of the remains of specific individuals. By looking at the bones of the Earlier Neolithic people we might gain further understanding of their mortuary rituals and, by implication, the beliefs and concerns of the living.

Introduction

Reanalysis by the author of human skeletal material from more than 20 subterranean sites in the Yorkshire Dales and North York Moors has highlighted diverse treatment and a range of activities with regard to the deposition of human remains. This diversity of behaviour denotes the complexity and significance of use of these subterranean sites and their relationship with other features in the landscape. Only minimal direct anthropological or taphonomic analysis has been carried out on these human remains, excavated from cave and rock shelter sites during the nineteenth and twentieth centuries. Neglect of the archaeological record derived from the sites has resulted in a lack of recognition of the key and unique role caves played in landscape development and interaction in general and as mortuary centres in particular. This paper discusses possible motivation for variation in the treatment of human remains from five cave and rock shelter sites in North Yorkshire.

Prior to this reanalysis, the human remains excavated from these sites were all generally considered to be Late Neolithic or Early Bronze Age in date and derived from articulated burials (Keith 1936; Raistrick 1936; Simpson 1950; Jackson 1962; King 1970; 1974; Gilks 1976; 1988; 1989; 1995; Pierpoint 1984; White 1997; Manby *et al.* 2003). No direct radiocarbon dating of human bone had been carried out on the material; the belief that the remains related to burials of the Late Neolithic or Early Bronze Age was based on an assumed association with artefacts recovered from many of the sites. Assemblages excavated from the Yorkshire cave sites include flint tools, and Peterborough, Grooved Ware and Beaker pottery. Prehistoric pottery sherds were absent from some cave sites, however, and a number contained Iron Age and Romano-British artefacts. Nevertheless, the belief that the remains represented articulated burials associated with the earlier prehistoric pottery became entrenched in the archaeological thought and literature pertaining to this upland region (Keith 1936; Raistrick 1936; Simpson 1950; Jackson 1962; King 1970; 1974; Gilks 1976; 1988; 1989; 1995; Pierpoint 1984; White 1997; Manby *et al.* 2003). Gilks (1976, 98) has stated that 95% of burials excavated from cave sites in North Yorkshire derived from this time period: 'An analysis of the finds from all sites has shown that about 80% are, without question, of Late Neolithic date, 15% are EBA and 5% cannot be accurately dated, but might well be Late Neolithic'. Initial research for the author's project was based on the assumption that these individuals represented the strata of society that were excluded from the constructed burial monuments. The main focus of the analysis was to try to determine the reason for their exclusion from the more formal burial contexts and deposition in these liminal locations.

A recent radiocarbon dating programme has, however, provided evidence that extended the duration of cave use from the Earlier Neolithic to the Romano-British period; so far only four cave sites have generated dates from human bone that relate to the suggested period of use for burial purposes. The direct dating of human bone has provided a chronological framework for the events witnessed in these subterranean death assemblages. As a result of this research, a group of Earlier Neolithic cave and rock shelter sites were identified (Figure 3.1, Table 3.1). These dates represent the earliest known deposition of human remains in this upland region relating to Neolithic mortuary activity.

Within this contemporary group of sites, differential treatment and representation of human remains was noted. Although these sites had all previously been described as repositories for burials, the osteological profiles for two of the five sites suggested either head or secondary cranial deposition rather than articulated burials. The observed differential treatment of the remains is considered with regard to a number of factors – age and sex of the individuals, manner of death, health and evidence for disfigurement and disability in the skeletal record – to identify possible motivation for this range of behaviour and dealings with their dead. The observed range of mortuary treatment in the osteological profiles from these five sites represents actions within the normal range of corpse 'management' during the Earlier Neolithic. Can the bones of these individuals, however, provide an indication of the process of selection for specific treatment?

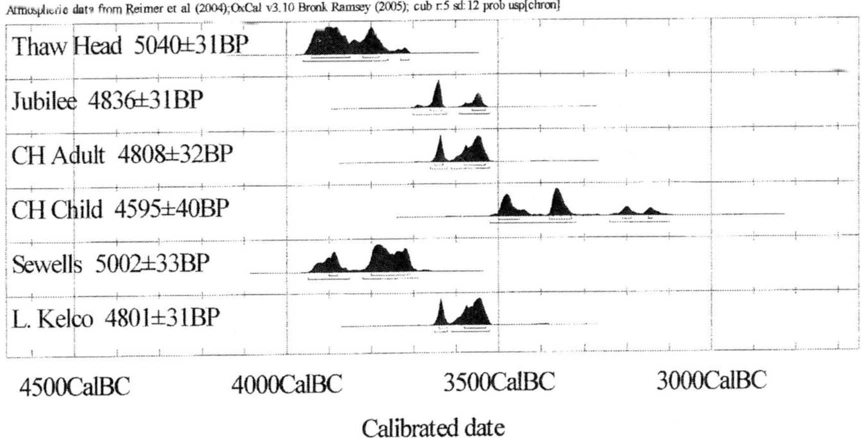

Figure 3.1. Calibrated radiocarbon dates of human bone samples – the first four dates relate to whole corpse deposition, while the last two relate to cranial depositions (OxCal Program v3.10, copyright Bronk Ramsey (1995; 2001; 2005)).

Site	Specimen Submitted	Lab No.	Date BP	±	Date cal. BC	Mode of deposition
Thaw Head	Young adult ♀	OxA-14264	5040	31	3960–3710	Whole corpse
Sewell's	Mid adult ♂	OxA-13537	5002	33	3950–3690	cranium and mandible
Jubilee	Mid adult ♂	OxA-14262	4836	31	3700–3520	Whole corpse
Cave Ha 3	Mature adult ♂	OxA-13539	4808	32	3660–3520	Whole corpse
L. Kelco	Adult ♀	OxA-13538	4801	31	3650–3520	cranium
Cave Ha 3	Child c. 2 yrs	OxA-14266	4595	40	3520–3100	Whole corpse

Table 3.1. Earlier Neolithic sites in chronological order compared with the mode of deposition of human remains (CH = Cave Ha 3).

The Sites

The five identified Earlier Neolithic sites are all located within a 12 mile radius, close to Settle and Ingleton in the Yorkshire Dales. They are situated in caves and rock shelters that occur within outcrops of rock or cliffs, known as scars, dividing a series of valleys in the region. Three sites are located in Giggleswick Scar, near Settle, one within (Cave Ha 3 Rock Shelter) and two on the periphery (Sewell's Cave and Lesser Kelco Cave) of the Cave Ha Rock Shelter Complex. The fourth site, Thaw Head Cave, the earliest and most westerly of the group, is located approximately one mile north of Ingleton and the fifth site, Jubilee Cave, is located in a scar north of Settle (Figure 3.2).

Cave Ha Rock Shelter Complex

The Cave Ha Rock Shelter Complex consists of a group of rock shelter and cave sites. Cave Ha 1 is an impressive natural rock formation shaped like a half dome into the cliff face, similar to an amphitheatre, with unusual multicoloured rock formations. The geomorphology of the site and its location within the scar generate some interesting acoustic qualities. The human remains were excavated from Cave Ha 3, a medium sized rock shelter with a

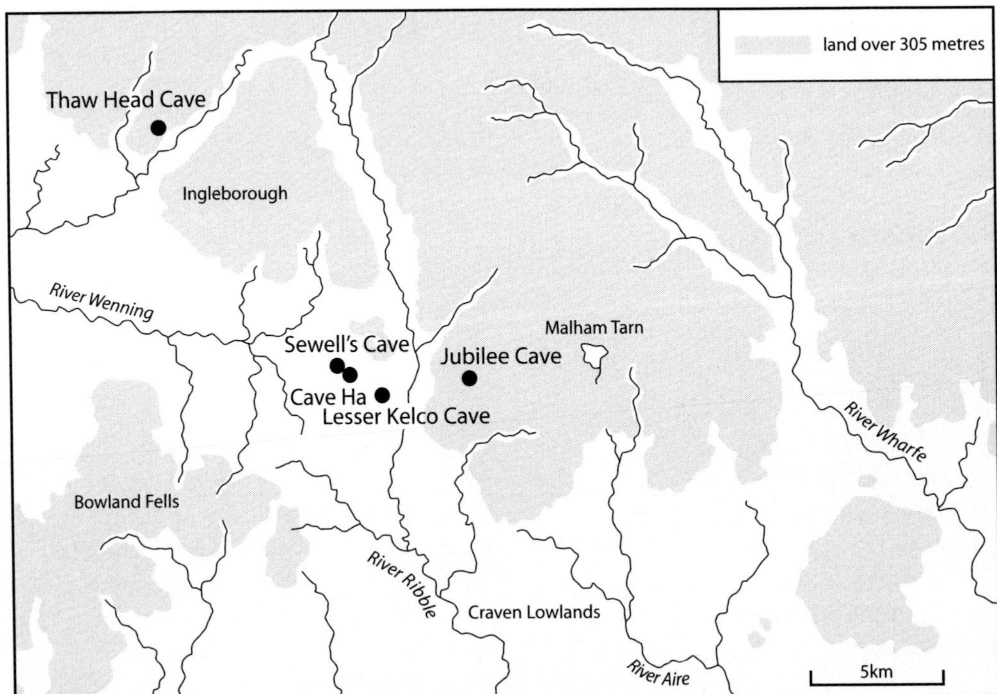

Figure 3.2. Location of cave sites containing Earlier Neolithic human skeletal remains (copyright Lord Cave Archive 2006).

long, gentle curve into the cliff face. There are natural cavities or alcoves at the back of the shelter and it was from these that the majority of the remains were excavated. Again the morphology is unusual since the shelter contains relic Holocene tufa as well as active formations of this substance. Many of the skeletal remains were found to have been coated with tufa (Figure 3.3).

Excavations at the complex took place during the nineteenth and twentieth centuries (Hughes 1874; Tobin 1955). The excavation of Cave Ha 1 recovered very little in the way of artefacts – a few flint flakes and a flat stone bead, and the bones of a mixture of wild and domestic animal species – but no human remains (Hughes 1874). Excavation of Cave Ha 3 produced the remains of four individuals, one adult male and three infants, including both cranial and postcranial bones. In addition, the remains of a large hearth and many heavily processed animal bones, mostly of large domestic cattle, were also recovered. Two flint scrapers were found close to the human remains. Tobin (1955) noted that one of the most unusual features of the site was the large amount of tufa that was present throughout the entire excavation, the consistency of which ranged from solid rock to a soft mealy substance. Excavation at the Cave Ha Complex remains incomplete.

Figure 3.3. Cave Ha 3, tufa surrounding articulated adult foot bones (S. Leach).

Sewell's Cave

Sewell's Cave is located on the western periphery of the Cave Ha Complex, approximately 200 m west of Cave Ha 1. The appearance of the cave is more representative of a rock shelter; the entrance is at the base of a cliff and, before excavation enlarged the area, access to the site would have involved some degree of difficulty. The shelter is approximately 11 m long, 2 m high and extends back 4 m into the cliff face (Brook *et al.* 1976). Work at the site was directed by Raistrick during the 1930s and resulted in complete excavation of the cave and the area immediately in front of the entrance (Raistrick 1936). Upper levels of the site were found to have contained an assemblage of Romano-British artefacts, while lower levels produced three fragments of worked flint, including one Earlier Neolithic leaf-shaped flint arrowhead, two sherds of Peterborough Ware and fragments of Beaker pottery (Raistrick 1936). The human skeletal remains were recovered from the lower level and entirely comprised cranial material. A minimum number of four individuals were identified – two adults, including one male, a young child and an older infant.

Lesser Kelco Cave

Lesser Kelco Cave lies on the eastern periphery of the Cave Ha Complex, approximately 1.5 miles from Cave Ha 1. The morphology of this site is different to the other sites; before excavation access was quite restricted and progress through to the back of the cave involved a long low crawl for approximately 8 m to the end of this single chambered cave (Simpson 1950). Two phases of excavation took place within the cave in the period between 1928 and 1936, and resulted in the complete excavation of the site (Simpson 1950; Jackson 1962). Romano-British artefacts were recovered from the cave, in addition to sherds of Peterborough Ware, a flint tool and a polished stone axe (Simpson 1950; Jackson 1962). The human skeletal material excavated from Lesser Kelco consisted of cranial material, calvaria and fragments of maxillae; these were located towards the back of the cave, two against the western wall of the chamber. During the initial analysis a minimum number of five individuals was determined on the basis of the crania present (Cameron 1950, 258). Only three crania remain in the private collection, however, and the location of the other crania is unknown. The extant assemblage consists entirely of adult remains – one female and two males are represented.

Thaw Head Cave

Thaw Head Cave is the site that contains the oldest human skeletal material from caves in this region. It is a small cave situated in the southwestern face of Twisleton Scar, north of Ingleton. A steep scree slope leads to a small entrance, approximately 0.5 m in width and height, and the cave itself only comprises one chamber, which measures 4 m by 2 m, and has a gently sloping roof (Gilks 1995, 1). Although the cave was not an obvious feature in the landscape, it is located in an area of outstanding natural features. The scar is bordered on each side by two rivers, Twiss and Doe, and these flow into the lower part of the valley above Ingleton in a series of waterfalls (Figure 3.4).

Figure 3.4. Thornton Force Waterfall situated below Thaw Head Cave (S. Leach).

The cave was discovered quite recently – in 1986 – and was fully excavated (Gilks 1995). During the excavation in excess of 1250 pottery sherds were recovered; these represented five vessels from the Late Neolithic to Late Bronze Age, including Grooved Ware, Beakers, and an Early Bronze Age cordoned barrel urn which was perhaps associated with part of a cremated human mandible. A flint scraper, flint plano-convex knife and a bronze pin were also recovered from the cave sediment in addition to animal bones that included both wild and domestic species (Gilks 1995, 5). The inhumed human remains – the disturbed remains of a young woman and infant represented by both cranial and postcranial bones – were found at the back of the cave. A tufa deposit was found to have covered a number of the bones.

Jubilee Cave

The final site, Jubilee Cave, is the most easterly of the five being situated in quite a remote location in the north end of Kingscar, above Settle. Various excavations have been conducted within the chambers of this cave complex, but little work has been published regarding the archaeology of the site (Lord 2004). Human remains from the main burial were located under a rock shelf, with a scatter of disarticulated bone fragments having been found along the corridor of the fissure. The nature of their association with the main individual, however, remains unclear. Artefacts recovered during excavation of the site included Mesolithic microliths, Peterborough Ware, Romano-British artefacts and animal bones of domesticated species. The human remains comprised the fairly complete skeleton of a robust adult male, along with a small assemblage of disarticulated human bone. All of the remains were submitted to Sir Arthur Keith for anthropological examination.

Previous Interpretation of the Human Remains

During the initial reanalysis of the collections, before the chronology of the sites was established through radiocarbon dating, the osteological profiles of the remains from both Sewell's Cave and Lesser Kelco Cave seemed at odds with the established view that the remains represented articulated burials. These seemed to be the 'odd ones out'. In the case of both caves those who excavated or initially examined the remains, although acknowledging the complete absence of postcranial material, never once considered the possibility that the sites represented locations exclusively for the purposes of cranial deposition (Keith 1936, 203; Raistrick 1936, 193; Simpson 1950, 261; Jackson 1962, 264). This situation may perhaps have been due to their conviction that the remains were of Late Neolithic date and that the prehistoric pottery present at the sites represented associated grave goods.

Simpson (1938) suggested the activities of burrowing animals together with the flow of water through Lesser Kelco Cave had removed all trace of postcranial human remains even though postcranial animal bones were present in the assemblage. Jackson (n.d.) suggested that human agency was responsible for the removal of the postcranial portions of the 'burials' at Lesser Kelco, the most likely candidates for this activity being Romano-British visitors to the cave (Lord 2004). In the case of Sewell's Cave, Keith (1936, 203) did question 'the absence of all traces of limb bones' but suggested that successive burial and clearance may have caused this phenomenon. Keith and subsequent authors never considered the exclusive deposition of cranial material as an alternative hypothesis.

Earlier Neolithic Treatment of the Dead

Fundamental social and economic changes occurred during the Earlier Neolithic and, while it is generally now agreed that these changes were for the most part gradual, they were certainly profound. In the British Isles these changes occurred at c. 4000 BC (Thomas 1991; Pollard 1997; Whittle 1999), with the introduction of horticulture, domestic livestock and pottery together with the construction of monuments, representing the first attempt to alter the earth (Harding 2003). Earlier Neolithic communities are considered to have been small and largely egalitarian, maintaining a mobile lifestyle and exploiting a range of resources both wild and domestic. These communities may also have been part of larger social alliances, meeting seasonally at specific locations in the landscape, for example, at the causewayed enclosures in the south of England. The changes not only related to their physical world and secular matters, but fundamental changes in ideology and belief systems are also evident in the archaeological record. Evidence suggests that the communities placed considerable importance on their ancestry and a collective identity.

Parker Pearson (2000) considers the funerary practices witnessed in the archaeological record to have been associated with ancestor worship and a collective supernatural identity of the deceased. He sees the journey from living individual through the afterlife into ancestorhood symbolised by the actions of decomposition and disarticulation of the human remains (Parker Pearson 2000, 204); the removal of individual human identity and its replacement with community spirits. The construction of long barrows and chambered tombs, containing mostly disarticulated and often manipulated human remains, and the deposition of commingled human remains in the ditches of causewayed enclosures are considered to represent this new ideology. This behaviour differed from anything that had gone before. As Pollard (1997, 50) has stated, from their material remains, it would seem that these Earlier Neolithic communities had an obsession with death; time, effort and resources were used to construct the mortuary monuments in which the human corpse was manipulated and transformed. Mortuary rituals involved complex and protracted sequences of behaviour, with the fragmentation of the body appearing to be of prime concern. The reduction or transformation of a fleshed corpse to skeletal elements deposited singularly or in commingled groups would appear to be the norm of Early Neolithic mortuary activity. Nevertheless, articulated remains do occur in the burial record, within causewayed enclosure ditches, tombs and barrows, often intermingled with disarticulated remains.

Although there appears to have been central themes or ideologies with regard to the treatment of the dead, there also seems to have been local or regional variations in ritual practice and corpse management. At Fussell's Lodge, Wiltshire, for example, the skeletal evidence suggests that the corpse was excarnated prior to inclusion in the tomb; the disarticulated bones were then transported to this location (Ashbee 1966; Pollard 1997). At Wayland's Smithy in Oxfordshire, West Kennet in Wiltshire and Hazleton North in Gloucestershire, the skeletal evidence suggests that the corpse was deposited in the chamber and allowed to decompose *in situ*; the bones were then manipulated and some elements, skulls for example, transported from this location as there were disparities in the representations of skeletal parts (Thomas and Whittle 1986; Saville 1990; Whittle 1991; Pollard 1997). At Hazleton North, only two skeletons – located in the north entrance – demonstrated a degree of articulation (Rogers 1990, 182). One skeleton was virtually complete, and was a male aged 30–45 years at death, and exhibited extensive osteoarthritic degenerative changes in his spine and hips, together with evidence of healed fractures in his lower limbs (Rogers 1990, 184).

The ditches of causewayed enclosures also contained human remains, where a diversity of depositional practices is witnessed in the archaeological record (Mercer 1990; Whittle *et al.* 1999). Deposits have included pottery, flints, carved chalk artefacts, organic materials, charcoal, animal bones – ranging from highly processed bone fragments, semi-articulated limbs to fully articulated carcasses – and human remains which are usually disarticulated, but occasionally represent articulated burials with a bias towards infants (Mercer 1990; Whittle *et al.* 1999). Although enacted in different contexts, Whittle *et al.* (1999, 357) were of the opinion that common themes may have linked the various depositional practices, these revolved around ideas of renewal and concerns for mediating points of physical and spiritual transition and transformation. Human remains were present in the outer ditches of the Windmill Hill causewayed enclosure. The skeletons were mostly disarticulated, and perhaps originated from local chambered tombs such as West Kennet (Whittle *et al.* 1999, 357).

Articulated burials were also present at the Windmill Hill causewayed enclosure; two complete infants were buried in the ditch of the outer circuit, one of whom rested on the solid chalk base, and an adult male had been deposited in an oval pit dug into the chalk under a bank during the early phase of the site's development (Whittle *et al.* 1999, 80). Whittle *et al.* (1999, 385) considered this latter burial to have been unusual – they noted the degree of separation from other human and cattle remains and questioned the reason for the lack of fragmentation of the individual. The skeleton was that of a taller than average, robust man, aged approximately 35–45 years at death (Brothwell 1999, 344). The skeletal remains exhibited evidence of both well healed, possibly childhood, and recent trauma, and he had suffered severe osteoarthritic changes in his neck vertebrae and left hip (Brothwell 1999, 344). The head of the left femur displayed significant degenerative changes in the form of eburnation and osteophyte development, this change also extending along the neck of the bone. Brothwell (1999, 344) considered that the changes represented an advanced state of degeneration, probably associated with significant pain and mobility problems. This situation can be considered as premature and unusual in a man of his age; in modern clinical circumstances, the hip would require replacement (Brothwell 1999, 344). An isolated cranium of a young child was also retrieved from an outer ditch deposit at Windmill Hill. It was found in association with a cattle skull and the calibrated radiocarbon dates for these two individuals were almost identical, ranging between 3640–3380 BC. Skulls of children and adults have also formed primary ditch deposits in other causewayed enclosures, such as Hambledon Hill and Maiden Castle (Mercer 1990). At Whitehawk Camp, Brighton, two articulated burials of young women and that of an infant were found in the outer ditches; the younger woman was considered to have possibly died in childbirth, although some doubt exists with regard to the age at death of the infant (Roberts and Cox 2003, 56).

Reilly (2003, 135) undertook a study of human remains deposited in the tombs of Orkney during the Earlier to Later Neolithic to determine how they treated and processed the corpse during this period. He suggested that the fate of the body was a long and complicated affair. The skeletal remains of the Neolithic tombs in Orkney frequently exhibited a degree of deliberate disarticulation and manipulation, involving specific spatial patterning within the tombs, and disparate representation of elements most often concerning the skull (Reilly 2003, 148). Richards (1988) has suggested this disparity in skeletal representation is indicative of the practise of the circulation of remains across the landscape. In the Knowe of Yarso, for example, a minimum number of 29 individuals was identified from the scattered remains in the tomb, and the fragmentary skulls of five adults had been lined up along the western wall of the tomb. The greatest concentration of human remains, however, occurred in the deepest part of the tomb (Reilly 2003, 139–41). Here a minimum number of 17 adults was represented, their crania lined up against the walls of the chamber and, as they lacked mandibles, it is considered that they represented the final stage of a process of corpse curation (Reilly 2003, 139–41). As Reilly (2003, 150) has stated, however, the processing of the dead involved and implied a great deal more than simple disposal and movement of remains; the deceased entered a long, ritual journey, during which the body was gradually fragmented and dispersed into its constituent parts where the body and the identity of the individual were distilled into the skull. Earlier Neolithic mortuary practices involved journeys of transformation.

The representation of human remains in the archaeological record is low for the proposed population of this period (Roberts and Cox 2003), and it is likely that the arenas for human deposition discussed above did not contain or represent the entire community from which it was derived. Diversity of treatment of remains has also been highlighted. What has remained unclear from discussion so far are the reasons that might explain why individuals were selected for deposition in these various contexts and the basis on which a corpse was left whole or subjected to mortuary fragmentation and circulation. After death, some individuals were left complete and buried in a context that may suggest their deposition was of a permanent nature, while others were subjected to a protracted mortuary regime. What was the basis of the selective process? Was it purely random, or based on functional necessities, including location and timing of the death of the individual? Or were other factors involved, perhaps based on aspects of the individual's life or manner of death or how their community perceived them? Were the 'non-fragmented' able to retain their individual identity for their journey into the afterlife or was this perhaps a sign of exclusion from the collective ancestral community? Perhaps examination of the bones of certain of these Earlier Neolithic individuals can enable us to suggest possible answers to some of these questions.

Human Skeletal Evidence

The human skeletal remains relating to the five sites are held in a private collection at Lower Winskill belonging to Tom Lord. Details of the anthropology, taphonomic and methodological approaches used during the reanalysis are provided in Leach (2005, 60–1) and further details relating to the sites and their death assemblages can be found in Leach (2007). Age at death for the adults was estimated using macroscopic anthropological standards including pubic symphysis transformations (Katz and Suchey 1986), auricular surface degeneration (Lovejoy *et al.* 1985) and sternal rib end appearance (Iscan and Loth 1986). Dental attrition provided a broad indication of age and wear stages were recorded (Smith 1984). Estimations of subadult age at death were primarily based on dental development and eruption stages (Moorees *et al.* 1963a; 1963b; Smith 1991); in the absence of dentition or to supplement this evidence, the appearance of centres of ossification and fusion (McKern and Stewart 1957; Suchey *et al.* 1984; Krogman and Iscan 1986) and diaphyseal length (Fazekas and Kosa 1978; Hoffman 1979; Scheuer *et al.* 1980) were also utilised.

The chronological sequence and mode of deposition of the human remains for the five sites is given in Table 3.1. Differential, yet seemingly contemporary, deposition of the human remains occurred at the sites, with Sewell's Cave and Lesser Kelco Cave having been used exclusively for the deposition of human cranial material.

Sewell's Cave

At Sewell's Cave the nature of the human cranial material was indicative of the presence of two adults and two children in the death assemblage. With the exception of one mandible, excavated from the entrance area, the human remains were situated at the back of the rock shelter, against the northern wall. All of the elements exhibited a high degree of postmortem fragmentation, but only one cranium displayed evidence of weathering or exposure to the elements. The most complete cranium and mandible represented a male, possibly aged 25–45 years at death based on dental attrition, and had extremely rugged characteristics with a very pronounced brow ridge and square prominent jaw. Further fragmentary remains suggested the presence of a second adult individual, possibly female. The crania of two children were also present; based on dental development and eruption, their ages at death were three years, plus or minus six months and 18 to 24 months respectively. No evidence for human processing in the form of cuts marks was noted and cervical vertebrae were absent. It would appear likely that these remains had been transported to the site as skeletal elements.

Lesser Kelco Cave

The human osteological profile from Lesser Kelco Cave is similar to that of Sewell's Cave, but consisted entirely of adult material, and mandibles were absent from the site. The crania were similarly fragmented, but did not exhibit evidence of having been exposed to the elements. One female and two males were present in the assemblage, and based on dental attrition, two appear to have been mature adults but it was not possible to associate the fragments of maxilla and dentition with a particular male or female cranium. A small fragment of cranial vault exhibited a healed depressed fracture, close to the bregma (top of the head), but it was not possible to associate this specimen with a particular individual or determine whether the trauma was the result of accidental injury or a violent confrontation.

Cave Ha 3

Four individuals were represented in the death assemblage from this rock shelter. As stated above, the majority of bones had been excavated from pockets of relic tufa and over half of the specimens were coated in, or surrounded by, this substance. In some instances the tufa had preserved anatomical articulations which strongly supports the idea that the remains were deposited within this substance while soft tissues still adhered to the bones (Figure 3.3), or that the tufa had formed rapidly around the body, or body parts, before decomposition could progress. The remains of two infants and a young child were recovered from natural recesses in the far wall of the shelter; the mandible of the oldest of the three was submitted for radiocarbon dating and produced the most recent date for the group – 3520–3100 cal. BC. The two babies were found together in an alcove, one was aged approximately nine months to one year at death, based on dental development, epiphyseal fusion and diaphyseal lengths; the second baby represented the remains of a neonate. The third child was aged approximately two years at death. Although the rock shelter was incompletely excavated and extraction of the fragile bones from the hard tufa deposits represented a challenge to the excavators (Tobin 1955), it would appear that the infants and young child had been deposited as complete, or relatively complete, corpses. Cause of death could not be ascertained for any of the subadults and evidence of disease or trauma was absent from their remains.

The most complete remains recovered from the site were of an adult male, with an age at death of 40–55 years. Musculoskeletal markers on the bones indicate that the individual would have had a relatively active lifestyle and evidence of severe wear and tear was present in his lower spine. Eburnation, the pathognomonic symptom of osteoarthritis, was present in the lumbar and thoracic vertebrae. An extremely unusual lesion was noted on the mandible of the individual (Figure 3.5). The exact cause has yet to be determined, but the development of a large haematoma with secondary infection, or actinomycosis infection are among the possible aetiologies (C. Knüsel 2005, pers. comm.; A. Ogden 2005, pers. comm.). The disease processes would have been visible in the soft facial tissues and would have caused some degree of disfigurement. Associated infection may have also caused a general debility in the individual and he certainly would have experienced problems when chewing the rough unprocessed diet of the Earlier Neolithic.

Figure 3.5. Mandibular lesion evident in the remains of a 40–55 year old male recovered from Cave Ha 3 (S. Leach).

The individual's left tibia displayed evidence of having undergone deliberate processing. This appears to have occurred soon after death, while the bone was still fresh. It had been split longitudinally, with spiral and V-shaped fractures with smooth oblique surfaces and a percussion notch or scar clearly visible on the strike zone, which is indicative that a blow had been dealt to the bone to open up the inner medullary cavity (Binford 1981; Lyman 1994; Outram 2002). No other modification or form of deliberate processing was noted on the bones of this individual or on the remains of the children present at Cave Ha. The individual's bones submerged in tufa represented an articulated foot, which suggests that at least a proportion of his body had been articulated when the remains were deposited. The reason for the breakage of his tibia remains unclear.

Thaw Head Cave

The remains of a young adult female and an infant were recovered from the cave; several of the woman's skeletal elements had been coated in tufa, but the substance was not as prolific at this site as it was within the Cave Ha Complex. Analysis of the skeletal part representation taken in conjunction with the data contained within the site plan would tend to suggest that she had been deposited as a complete corpse at the back of the cave. It would appear, however, that carnivores had gained entry to the cave and caused much disturbance to the inhumation, chewing and scattering her remains. The infant was only represented by a few cranial elements; a density of these fragments located within the region of the woman's thoracic and pelvic cavity might suggest that she died during childbirth. It was not possible to more precisely estimate the age of the infant, however, due to a lack of dental remains or long bones. The fragments appeared a little too robust to represent a perinatal infant. Skeletal evidence suggests the young woman was approximately 17–18 years old when she died; this finding is based on the state of epiphyseal fusion, dental eruption and attrition and the lack of closure of the spheno-occipital synchrondrosis. Her pelvic bones had developed pronounced female characteristics despite her young age at death. Lesions apparent in her skeletal remains suggested that she had engaged in high levels of physical activity. These comprised pronounced cortical defects or stress lesions on the left and right clavicles and upper humeri, which may suggest that chronic mechanical stress had been placed on the muscles and bones of her shoulders and upper arms. Degenerative changes were evident in her hand bones; specifically distinct marginal osteophytic lipping surrounding the proximal and distal articular surfaces of the left and right first metacarpals and several of the phalanges. The physiological stress noted in the upper body of this individual may relate to this early osteoarthritic development.

The cranium of the young woman was well preserved and the facial bones exhibited slight asymmetry, however, it is unlikely that this anomaly would have produced an obvious or noticeable facial deformity. Her left eye socket was slightly malformed and may be an indication that she would have suffered from vision impairment (C. Knüsel 2005, pers. comm.). Similar facial deformities were noted in the skeletal remains of a woman discovered deep in an extensive series of fissures in Littondale, approximately 15 miles to the east of this site (Hill 1907). Unfortunately it was not possible to re-examine these remains as their current location is unknown. Hill (1907, 224) described the facial anomalies and suggested that '... by our standards, her appearance would not have been attractive'.

A perimortem spiral fracture was noted in the lower left leg bones of the Thaw Head Cave burial; no evidence of healing was present at the site of the fracture, which may indicate that death had occurred soon after the injury. This sort of trauma is consistent with a fall and twisting or torsion of the foot and ankle. The nature of the fracture may imply that she died shortly after sustaining an injury consistent with a fall. Alternatively, it is equally feasible that the trauma could have arisen as a consequence of damage attained shortly after death.

Jubilee Cave

The main burial excavated from the cave represented a taller than average, robust male, aged 40–50 years at death. A fact that is manifestly evident from his skeletal remains is that the individual must have suffered an extremely painful existence, predominantly in his later years, with a corresponding lack of mobility. Severe and diffuse degenerative joint changes were noted; the knee joints exhibited the most extreme development of osteoarthritis (Figure 3.6), but eburnation was also present in his upper and lower spine, left shoulder and left hand (right side bones were absent or eroded). This form of knee osteoarthritis – within the condyles of the joint – is rare in prehistoric and even recent historical collections (Baetsen *et al.* 1997, 628; Waldron 2001, 87). The degenerative changes would have

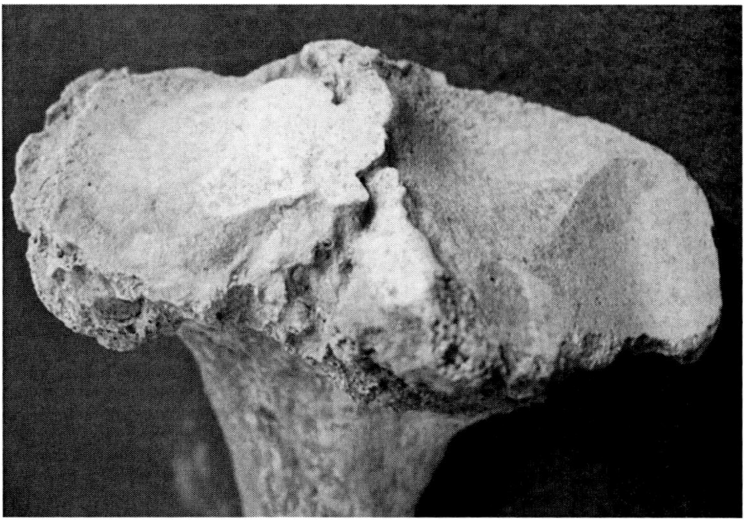

Figure 3.6. Degenerative joint disease of the knee apparent in the remains of a 40–50 year old male retrieved from Jubilee Cave. Two thirds of the articular area of the condyles exhibited eburnation, while the joint surface was surrounded by prolific marginal osteophytes and the tubercles of the intercondylar eminence have been almost entirely lost due to bone attrition (S. Leach).

resulted in a loss of joint stability and function and a varus deformity of the knees. The man would probably have become progressively bow legged and it is likely that this would have caused significantly restricted mobility and severe pain.

Muscle attachment sites on the pelvis, those related to the hamstrings, all exhibited pronounced cortical lesions suggesting evidence of over-exertion. These muscles are used during the action of flexing the knee and the external and internal rotation of the hip and knee. As such, their presence may provide a further indication of anomalous loading and mechanical pressures, having resulted from the degenerative changes in the knee joints and deformity, leading to an abnormal gait. Stress lesions were also noted on muscle attachment sites on the clavicles and upper arm bones; these may relate to an extremely active lifestyle or perhaps their formation may have been due to the loss of effective use of the knee joints, and subsequent use of some form of crutch to aid mobility, thereby placing additional mechanical loading on the shoulder and upper arms. This situation, however, remains a matter of conjecture. Diffuse periosteal reactive new bone formation on the skeletal elements – left and right metatarsals, tarsals, tibiae, pelvic bones and left humerus – also indicated the occurrence of an inferior immune response to some form of systemic infection.

Discussion

It is likely that Earlier Neolithic communities lived quite mobile, semi-nomadic lifestyles, with seasonal movements linked with livestock husbandry (Whittle 1997; Cowell 2000). This movement was perhaps orientated by a network of paths and significant locations within the natural landscape that were repeatedly visited, becoming foci for local communities who still maintained a transient way of life (Harding 1999, 37). Barclay and Hey (1999, 67) have suggested that the Earlier Neolithic cultural landscape contained a network of paths that connected natural places, living sites and monuments. In this upland region, caves and rock shelters could have played a significant role as such foci for community activities and meeting places. The Cave Ha Complex could have had a similar role to the causewayed enclosures of the south of England, while remote caves such as those of Jubilee and Thaw Head may have acted as markers of routes through this upland terrain. The deposition of human remains at these locations might be viewed, therefore, as a highly significant part of community life and ritual negotiations.

The range and variation noted in the treatment of the human corpse witnessed in the death assemblages excavated from these subterranean sites might simply relate to random occurrences, season of death and other such practical issues; differential postmortem treatment relating to mundane matters of death and disposal of the corpse. Alternatively, it could relate to deeper community concerns and deliberate, meaningful manipulation of the remains of specific individuals.

The deposition of human cranial material at Lesser Kelco and Sewell's Cave might represent 'foundation' deposits on the periphery of this group of Earlier Neolithic sites, representing the collective ancestral community and functioning in a similar way to the 'final stage' tombs in Orkney and the primary deposits of the outer ditches of causewayed enclosures. The cave sites on Giggleswick Scar can be perceived as a cohesive and interrelated group of sites. Parker Pearson (2000, 208) has suggested a strong association between the cult of the ancestors and the qualities of stone, representing the hardening of the life-death cycle. The placing of skulls, the distilled essence of the ancestral community, in rock shelters and caves to mark specific and important locations in the cultural landscape would seem in accord with this ideology.

Why were the bodies of other individuals, deposited at these sites, left complete and not subjected to lengthy transformation processes, marking their journey from living individuality to an ancestral collective? Was it merely fate or a deliberate act that maintained their corporeal identity? Perhaps these individuals were considered special in some way, relating to aspects of their life, their health or their manner or timing of death, and in need of individual treatment. Burial in tufa-forming rocky locations may have been a deliberate act or choice. Davies and Lewis (2005) have observed that an area of tufa formation associated with a stream in a Somerset valley formed the focus of activities relating to votive deposition in the Early Neolithic. Within the tufa they found a series of deposits including animal bones, charcoal and worked flint and, in one pit on the periphery of the tufa formation area, they discovered a hand-formed ball of tufa that possibly represented a votive deposit (Davies and Lewis 2005, 8). Davies and Robb (2002, 182) have suggested that tufa deposits may have been viewed as 'magical' in the past; the source of tufa formation forming a special and significant place in the landscape. Tufa may have been perceived in a similar way to chalk; deposition into tufa and the manufacture of tufa balls, might represent similar activities to the cutting of deep ditches and pits into chalk and the manufacture of chalk artefacts recovered from the ditches of the causewayed enclosures of southern England. It is perhaps of significance that the robust arthritic man at Windmill Hill who had not been subjected to mortuary fragmentation was deposited in a pit dug into the chalk (Whittle *et al.* 1999).

The deposition of individuals in tufa, a form of living rock, may symbolise ideas relating to ancestry or perhaps rebirth; the premature death of infants requiring special treatment or perhaps marking the sad loss of valued members of a community. Conversely, the petrifying quality of tufa may have acted to separate these individuals from the collective dead, to hold them apart. The individuals at Cave Ha 3 were sealed in stone; there is a finality or permanence about this resting place, the end of the mortuary and perhaps spiritual line.

Lack of fragmentation might imply an aspect of spiritual exclusion; the individuals whose remains were not commingled, in some way remained separate from the ancestral community of the dead. Perhaps due to circumstances in their life, or their manner or timing of death, they were considered in some way unfit or a bad omen for the collective caretakers of the community. The robust adult male from the chalk pit burial under the bank at Windmill Hill had suffered injuries and severe degenerative changes to his hip joint, mostly likely causing mobility problems (Brothwell 1999). The robust man buried at Jubilee Cave had also suffered from extreme degenerative joint disease and mobility in this upland region would have been a challenge. The articulated male from the north entrance at Hazleton North suffered similar hip arthropathies (Rogers 1990). Perhaps those who suffered mobility problems in a society that maintained a semi-nomadic lifestyle were considered unsuitable to join the collective ancestral guardians? As Finlay (1999, 2) has stated, however, definitions of disability are not universal; the experience of impairment and cultural ideas of what constitutes disability will vary greatly from our modern perceptions. They were still afforded burial or ritual deposition in a significant location, but they were held apart from the others. Their postmortem treatment or journey appears to have followed a divergent route to those whose remains were amalgamated into the collective dead.

Conclusions

The amount of excavated human remains derived from Earlier Neolithic contexts is low compared to the proposed population size during this time period. The individuals whose remains were deposited at these significant locations within the landscape therefore represent a select group – deliberate meaningful deposition of specific members of the community. Variations noted in the mode of deposition of these individuals may be equally significant. By looking at the bones of the Earlier Neolithic people we might gain further understanding of their mortuary rituals and, by implication, the beliefs and concerns of the living. The discussion above is based on a small sample of remains, however, and the ideas formulated must remain tentative. It should also be noted that not all physical impairment will be visible in the osseous record and psychological disorders or mental impairment will leave no trace in the remains of the deceased.

Unfortunately, this sample represents the only known Earlier Neolithic remains from the Craven upland region. No details survive relating to the skeletal remains excavated from two chambered tombs in the vicinity – the Druid's Altar on Malham Moor and the Giant's Grave at Penyghent. Comparison must therefore be made with material derived from further afield, however, as Roberts and Cox (2003) have noted, anthropological details, for example pertaining to health and lifestyle indicators, are often vague or absent from many skeletal reports which lack the necessary detail required for comparative analysis. Nevertheless, by allowing the bones to speak, rather than merely 'pattern-fitting' the evidence according to our preconceptions, the human remains do appear to be providing diverse, fascinating and unique information relating to prehistoric cultural practices.

Acknowledgements

Tom Lord kindly allowed access to the material held in his private collection, including an extensive paper archive of reports, plans and correspondence of the excavators of the cave sites. In addition, he granted permission for the bones to be sampled for dating purposes.

He also shared valuable information and discussion relating to the sites, based on his extensive knowledge of the archaeology of the area in general and the caves in particular. The University of Winchester provided funding for the radiocarbon dates and the research studentship. Stuart Hey, MB ChB FRCS (Orth), is to be thanked for his discussions relating to the knee arthropathy at Jubilee Cave. I am also grateful to Nick Thorpe for comments on the text and proof reading and to Robin Bendrey for his assistance with the production of a number of the photographs and proof reading.

References

Ashbee, P. 1966. The Fussell's Lodge Long Barrow excavations 1957. *Archaeologia* 100, 1–8.

Baetsen, S., Bitter, P. and Bruintjes, T. J. D. 1997. Hip and knee osteoarthritis in an eighteenth century urban population. *International Journal of Osteoarchaeology* 7, 628–30.

Barclay, A. and Hey, G. 1999. Cattle, cursus monuments and the river: the development of ritual and domestic landscapes in the Upper Thames Valley, pp. 67–76 in Barclay, A. and Harding, J. (eds), *Pathways and Ceremonies. The Cursus Monuments of Britain and Ireland* (Neolithic Studies Group Seminar Papers 4). Oxford: Oxbow Books.

Binford, L. R. 1981. *Bones: Ancient Men and Modern Myths.* New York: Academic Press.

Bronk Ramsey, C. 1995. Radiocarbon calibration and analysis of stratigraphy: the OxCal program. *Radiocarbon* 37, 425–30.

Bronk Ramsey, C. 2001. Development of the radiocarbon program OxCal. *Radiocarbon* 43, 355–63.

Brook, A., Brook, D., Davies, G. M. and Long, M. H. 1976. *Northern Caves. Volume 2. Penyghent and Malham.* Clapham: Dalesman Publishing.

Brothwell, D. 1999. Human remains, p. 344 in Whittle, A., Pollard, J. and Grigson, C., *The Harmony of Symbols. The Windmill Hill Causewayed Enclosure.* Oxford: Oxbow Books.

Cameron, D. 1950. Report on the human skulls from Lesser Kelco Cave, p. 262 in Simpson, E., The Kelcow Caves, Giggleswick, Yorkshire. *Cave Science* 2, 258–62.

Cowell, R. 2000. The Neolithic and Bronze Age in the lowlands of North West England, pp. 111–30 in Harding, J. and Johnston, R. (eds), *Northern Pasts. Interpretations of the Later Prehistory of Northern England and Southern Scotland* (BAR British Series 302). Oxford: Archaeopress.

Davies, P. and Lewis, J. 2005. A Late Mesolithic/Early Neolithic site at Langley's Lane, near Midsomer Norton, Somerset. *Past* 49, 7–8.

Davies, P. and Robb, J. G. 2002. The appropriation of the material of places in the landscape: the case of tufa and springs. *Landscape Research* 27, 181–5.

Fazekas, I. G. and Kosa, F. 1978. *Forensic Fetal Osteology.* Budapest: Akademiai Kiado.

Finlay, N. 1999. Disabling archaeology: an introduction, pp. 1–6 in Finlay, N. (ed.), Disability and archaeology. *Archaeological Review from Cambridge* 15, 1–6.

Gilks, J. A. 1976. Excavations in a cave on Raven Scar, Ingleton, 1973–5. *Transactions of the British Cave Research Association* 3, 95–9.

Gilks, J. A. 1985. A bone whistle from Raven Scar Cave, North Yorkshire. *Antiquity* 59, 124–5.

Gilks, J. A. 1988. The Cave Burial Research Project. *British Archaeology* 6, 6–7.

Gilks, J. A. 1989. Cave burials in Northern England. *British Archaeology* 11, 11–15.

Gilks, J. A. 1995. Later Neolithic and Bronze Age pottery from Thaw Head Cave, Ingleton, North Yorkshire. *Transactions of the Hunter Archaeological Society* 18, 1–11.

Harding, J. 1999. Pathways to new realms: cursus monuments and symbolic territories, pp. 30–8 in Barclay, A. and Harding, J. (eds), *Pathways and Ceremonies. The Cursus Monuments of Britain and Ireland* (Neolithic Studies Group Seminar Papers 4). Oxford: Oxbow Books.

Harding, J. 2003. *Henge Monuments of the British Isles*. Stroud: Tempus.

Hill, C. A. 1907. Notes on a prehistoric skeleton found in a cave in Littondale, Yorkshire. *Journal of Anatomy and Physiology* 41, 221–30.

Hoffman, J. M. 1979. Age estimations from diaphyseal lengths: two months to twelve years. *Journal of Forensic Sciences* 24, 461–9.

Hughes, T. M. 1874. Exploration of Cave Ha, near Giggleswick, Settle, Yorkshire. *Journal of the Royal Anthropological Institute* 1, 383–7.

Iscan, M. Y. and Loth, S. R. 1986. Estimation of age and determination of sex from the sternal rib, pp. 68–89 in Reichs, K. J. (ed.), *Forensic Osteology: Advances in the Identification of Human Remains*. Springfield: Charles C. Thomas.

Jackson, J. W. 1933. *Letter to Dr Lovett, Austwick*. Unpublished letter, Lord Cave Archive.

Jackson, J. W. 1962. Archaeology and palaeontology, pp. 252–346 in Cullingford, C. H. D. (ed.), *British Caving: An Introduction to Speleology*. London: Routledge and Kegan Paul Ltd.

Jackson, J. W. n.d. *Report Excavation Notes, Lesser Kelco Cave*. Unpublished archive notes, Lord Cave Archive.

Katz, D. and Suchey, J. M. 1986. Age determination of the male os pubis. *American Journal of Physical Anthropology* 69, 427–36.

Keith, A. 1936. Human remains, pp. 202–3 in Raistrick, A., Excavations at Sewell's Cave, Settle, W. Yorkshire. *Proceedings of the University of Durham Philosophical Society* 9, 191–204.

King, A. 1970. *Early Pennine Settlement. A Field Study*. Lancaster: Dalesman Publishing Co. Ltd.

King, A. 1974. A review of archaeological work in the caves of North-West England, pp. 182–200 in Waltham, A. C. (ed.), *The Limestones and Caves of North West England*. Newton Abbot: David and Charles.

Krogman, W. M. and Iscan, M. Y. 1986. *The Human Skeleton in Forensic Medicine* (second edition). Springfield: Charles C. Thomas.

Leach, S. 2005. Heads, shoulders, knees and toes. Human skeletal remains from Raven Scar Cave in the Yorkshire Dales, pp. 59–68 in Zakrzewski, S. and Clegg, M. (eds), *Proceedings of the Fifth Annual Conference of the British Association for Biological Anthropology and Osteoarchaeology* (BAR International Series 1383). Oxford: Archaeopress.

Leach, S. 2007. *Going Underground: Taphonomic and Anthropological Reanalysis of Human Skeletal Remains from Caves in Northern Yorkshire*. Unpublished Ph.D. thesis, University of Winchester.

Lord, T. C. 2004. *Site Archival Notes, Lord Cave Archive*. Unpublished notes.

Lovejoy, C. O., Meindl, R. S., Pryzbeck, T. R. and Mensforth, R. P. 1985. Chronological metamorphosis of the auricular surface of the ilium: a new method for the determination of age at death. *American Journal Physical Anthropology* 68, 15–28.

Lyman, R. L. 1994. *Vertebrate Taphonomy* (Cambridge Manuals in Archaeology). Cambridge: Cambridge University Press.

Manby, T. G., King, A. and Vyner, B. E. 2003. The Neolithic and Bronze Ages: a time of early agriculture, pp. 35–116 in Manby T. G., Moorhouse S. and Ottaway, P. (eds), *The Archaeology of*

Yorkshire: An Assessment at the Beginning of the 21st Century (Yorkshire Archaeological Society Occasional Papers No. 3). Leeds: Yorkshire Archaeological Society.

McKern, T. and Stewart, T. D. 1957. *Skeletal Age Changes in Young American Males, Analyzed from the Standpoint of Identification* (Technical Report EP-45). Natick, Massachusetts: Quartermaster Research and Development Command.

Mercer, R. J. 1990. *Causewayed Enclosures* (Shire Archaeology No. 61). Princess Risborogh: Shire Publications Ltd.

Moorees, C. F. A., Fanning, E. A. and Hunt, E. E. 1963a. Formation and resorption of three deciduous teeth in children. *American Journal of Physical Anthropology* 21, 205–13.

Moorees, C. F. A., Fanning, E. A. and Hunt, E. E. 1963b. Age formation by stages for ten permanent teeth. *Journal of Dental Research* 42, 1490–502.

Outram, A. K. 2002. Bone fracture and within-bone nutrients: an experimentally based method for investigating levels of marrow extraction, pp. 51–63 in Miracle, P. and Milner, N. (eds), *Consuming Passions and Patterns of Consumption* (McDonald Institute Monographs). Cambridge: McDonald Institute for Archaeological Research.

Parker Pearson, M. 2000. Ancestors, bones and stones in Neolithic and Early Bronze Age Britain and Ireland, pp. 203–41 in Ritchie, A. (ed.), *Neolithic Orkney in its European Context* (McDonald Institute Monographs). Cambridge: McDonald Institute for Archaeological Research.

Pierpoint, S. J. 1984. Cave archaeology in Yorkshire. *Studies in Speleology* 5, 7–14.

Pollard, J. 1997. *Neolithic Britain* (Shire Archaeology No. 75). Princess Risborough: Shire Publications Ltd.

Raistrick, A. 1936. Excavations at Sewell's Cave, Settle, W. Yorkshire. *Proceedings of the University of Durham Philosophical Society* 9, 191–204.

Reilly, S. 2003. Processing the dead in Neolithic Orkney. *Oxford Journal of Archaeology* 22, 133–54.

Reimer, P. J., Baillie, M. G. L., Bard, E., Bayliss, A., Beck, J. W., Bertrand, C. J. H., Blackwell, P. G., Buck, C. E., Burr, G. S., Cutler, K. B., Damon, P. E., Edwards, R. L., Fairbanks, R. G., Friedrich, M., Guilderson, T. P., Hogg, A. G., Hughen, K. A., Kromer, B., McCormac, G., Manning, S., Bronk Ramsey, C., Reimer, R. W., Remmele, S., Southon, J. R., Stuiver, M., Talamo, S., Taylor, F. W., van der Plicht, J. and Weyhenmeyer, C. E. 2004. IntCal04 terrestrial radiocarbon age calibration, 0–26 cal kyr BP. *Radiocarbon* 46, 1029–58.

Richards, C. 1988. Altered images: a re-examination of Neolithic mortuary practices in Orkney, pp. 42–55 in Barrett, J. C. and Kinnes, I. A. (eds), *The Archaeology of Context in the Neolithic and Bronze Age: Recent Trends* (Volume 3). Sheffield: Department of Archaeology and Prehistory, University of Sheffield.

Roberts, C. A. and Cox, M. 2003. *Health and Disease in Britain from Prehistory to the Present Day*. Stroud: Sutton.

Rogers, J. 1990. The human skeletal material, pp. 182–9 in Saville, A., *Hazleton North, Gloucestershire, 1979–82: The Excavation of a Neolithic Long Cairn of the Cotswold Seven Group* (English Heritage Archaeological Report No. 13). London: English Heritage.

Saville, A. 1990. *Hazleton North, Gloucestershire, 1979–82: The Excavation of a Neolithic Long Cairn of the Cotswold Seven Group* (English Heritage Archaeological Report No. 13). London: English Heritage.

Scheuer, J. L., Musgrave, J. M. and Evans, S. P. 1980. The estimation of late foetal and perinatal age from limb bone length by linear and logarithmic regression. *Annals of Human Biology* 7, 257–65.

Simpson, E. 1938. *Preliminary Report of Excavation of a Neolithic Burial Site at Lesser Kelco Cave, Giggleswick by Members of the Settle Naturalist and Antiquarian Society*. Unpublished report, Lord Cave Archive.

Simpson, E. 1950. The Kelcow Caves, Giggleswick, Yorkshire. *Cave Science* 2, 258–62.

Smith, B. H. 1984. Patterns of molar wear in hunter-gatherers and agriculturalists. *American Journal of Physical Anthropology* 63, 39–56.

Smith, B. H. 1991. Standards of human tooth formation and dental age assessment, pp. 143–68 in Kelly, M. A. and Larsen, C. S. (eds), *Advances in Dental Anthropology*. New York: Wiley-Liss.

Suchey, J. M., Owings, P. A., Wiseley, D. V. and Noguchi, T. T. 1984. Skeletal aging of unidentified persons, pp. 278–97 in Rathbun, T. A. and Buikstra, J. E. (eds), *Human Identification: Case Studies in Forensic Anthropology*. Springfield: Charles C. Thomas.

Thomas, J. 1999. *Understanding the Neolithic*. London: Routledge.

Thomas, J. and Whittle, A.1986. Anatomy of a tomb – West Kennet revisited. *Oxford Journal of Archaeology* 5, 129–56.

Tobin, J. 1955. *Excavation Reports 1954–1955, Cave Ha Excavations*. Unpublished Cave Ha Archive. Craven Museum, Skipton, Yorkshire.

Waldron, T. 2001. *Shadows in the Soil. Human Bones and Archaeology*. Stroud: Tempus.

White, R. 1997. *The Yorkshire Dales, Landscapes Through Time*. London: Batsford.

Whittle, A. 1991. Wayland Smithy, Oxfordshire: excavation of a Neolithic tomb in 1962–63 by R. J. C. Atkinson and S. Piggot. *Proceedings of the Prehistoric Society* 57, 61–101.

Whittle, A. 1999. The Neolithic period, c. 4000–2500/2200 BC, pp. 58–76 in Hunter, J. and Ralston, I. (eds), *The Archaeology of Britain. An Introduction from the Upper Palaeolithic to the Industrial Revolution*. London: Routledge.

Whittle, A., Pollard, J. and Grigson, C. 1999. *The Harmony of Symbols. The Windmill Hill Causewayed Enclosure*. Oxford: Oxbow Books.

4. The Value of Palaeoteratology and Forensic Pathology for the Understanding of Atypical Burials: Two Mediterranean Examples from the Field

Philippe Charlier

Abstract

Palaeopathology provides a direct vision of many diseases described in medical and literary texts. Some specialties of palaeopathology, including palaeoteratology and forensic pathology, may explain why some subjects were afforded deviant burial practices and provide information concerning the cause of death. In this paper two such recently analysed Mediterranean cases will be discussed – a trisomic girl who appears to have been sacrificed in Rome during the Late Bronze Age and deposed in a non-funeral area, and two women who appear to have been killed and possibly mutilated after exposition, prior to having been discarded in a cistern on Delos Island, Greece. In both cases, an attempt will be made to understand the historical background and the possible reasons why these individuals were excluded, possibly both during life and also in the world of the dead.

Introduction

Palaeopathology can be defined as a medico-scientific speciality that deals with the description and analysis of diseases apparent in archaeological human remains. The majority of specimens encountered comprise skeletal remains, although the discipline is of equal relevance to mummies (natural and artificial), pieces of bodies (e.g. relics) and human calcifications (e.g. gall stones, atherosclerosis, etc.). Anatomical depictions and human representations are also of relevance to palaeopathology and when used with caution they can enable the identification of many diseases that are impossible to identify in skeletal remains. One aspect of palaeopathology is the study of developmental defects or congenital malformations (e.g. Brothwell 1967; Turkel 1989; Barnes 1994; Murphy 2000). Another aspect is the use of forensic capacities during skeletal examinations, as is currently undertaken for modern cases (Byers and Myster 2004; Schmitt *et al.* 2006; Charlier 2008a). The following paper will discuss two archaeological cases from the Mediterranean World in which one individual with major developmental anomalies appears to have been accorded a form of burial that was atypical for her society. The second case involved the remains of two women who appear to have been killed using a special form of execution.

Case 1: Trisomic Girl from the Late Bronze Age in Rome

During the Late Bronze Age (1200–850 BC), a young girl appears to have been killed as a result of a blow from a hatchet. Her remains were then deposited in an isolated area of central Rome, near the actual Imperial forum. This place is absolutely atypical, because it is free of any cemeteries, funeral offerings, and is situated far from the necropolis. At that time it would have been a marshy area when all habitations would have been located on the Capitol and the Palatine, as well as the other hills of Rome (Coarelli *et al.* 2006). The skeleton was discovered by the Italian archaeologist Giacomo Boni at the beginning of the twentieth century and is still conserved within the reserves of the *Soprintendenza Archaeologica di Roma* (*Equus Domitiani* 2) (Figure 4.1). Radiocarbon dating has indicated that the burial

Figure 4.1. An upper view of the cranial vault from the skeleton from Equus Domitiani 2, showing evidence of perimortem trauma on the right parietal close to the sagittal suture (P. Charlier).

dated to between 1250 and 990 cal. BC (Catalano *et al.* 2003; Catalano *et al.* 2006). The author was invited by Paola Catalano, Head of the Anthropological Department of the *Soprintendenza Archeologica di Roma*, to undertake a reexamination of the palaeopathological features apparent in the body.

The dental age was calculated to be approximately 13–14 years, but the *in situ* length of the whole skeleton was 1.21 m, which corresponds more with the normal stature of a subadult of only 7–8 years! Furthermore, the diaphyseal lengths and state of epiphyseal fusions also corresponded to the trends expected for a 7–8 years old child (Reichs 1986; Charlier 2008a). In addition, many osteological anomalies were present. The anterior aspect of the skull had a jutting appearance (the frontal bone was prominent), with a slight brachycephaly, a flat face and a flat occipital bone with segmentation of the left occipital condyle (Figure 4.2). The cranial vault was abnormally thin, with many supernumerary (wormian) bones, a metopic suture and a unilateral right parietal foramen. The face was characterised by pronounced hypertelorism, a short hard palate, bilateral cribra orbitalia and a chronic inflammation of the nasal bones (rhinitis) (Figure 4.3). Dental examination showed malposition of the right third maxillary molar, many lines of enamel hypoplasia, asymmetrical degenerative joint disease of the temporomandibular joints and a complete absence of dental decay. The neck region appeared to have been abnormally short relative

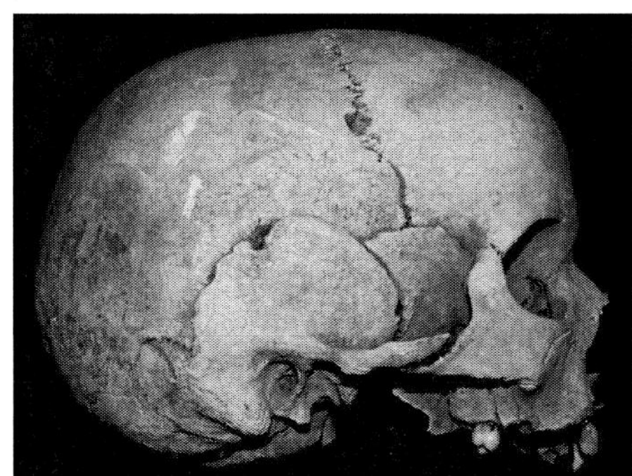

Figure 4.2. Lateral right view of the skull from Equus Domitiani 2. Note the slight brachycephaly and flattening of the face and occipital bone (P. Charlier).

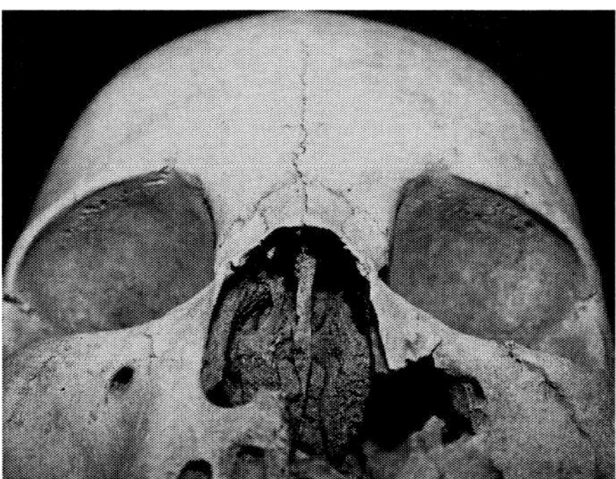

Figure 4.3. A close-up frontal view of the skull from Equus Domitiani 2. Note the chronic nasal inflammation, metopic suture and hypertelorism (P. Charlier).

to the remainder of the skeleton. Osteological analysis indicated that there were genuinely only ten left and eleven right ribs, as opposed to twelve on each side which is normally the case. The pelvis was hypoplasic, with an external flaring of the iliac wings. At least the first hand and foot phalanges were abnormally short and broad, particularly that of the second finger of the left hand.

The presence of a strong discordance between the osteological/statural age and the dental age would tend to suggest that the individual was stunted and had suffered major growth problems. A precise diagnosis of the cause is permitted, however, on the basis of the numerous osteological anomalies found in the skeleton. Indeed, the unusual features evident in the skull, ribs, iliac wings and the fingers, are particularly characteristic of Down's Syndrome. Indeed, all of the anomalies described above are apparent in over 50% of cases of the condition. The presence of only one or two of these features in a skeleton is absolutely not specific of the disease, but the association of all of them in only one subject is very evocative of a case of Trisomy 21, particularly the metrical modifications of the face and extremities (Stevenson *et al.* 1993; Lyons Jones 1997; Aufderheide and Rodríguez-Martín 1998).

The traumatic blow on the skull was located on the right parietal bone, adjacent to the sagittal suture. It measured some 3 cm in length and had a biconvex aspect which corresponds to the morphology of axes typically used during the Late Bronze Age in this region. The presence of many radiating fracture lines provides an indication that the axe blow had been dealt on 'fresh' bone, i.e. during the perimortem period. It is important to note that the injury has been known about since the original discovery of the skeleton by Giacomo Boni in the early twentieth century, thereby making it implausible that it was due to more recent damage.

When all of this data is considered it is possible to postulate that the girl may have been sacrificed as a consequence of her condition. Was this girl considered to be a *monster* or something/somebody one had to purify? Archaeological discoveries and palaeopathological examinations have revealed the presence of other later evidence for Early Iron Age human sacrifice. At the Carcer Tullianum, in the Roman Forum, for example, the skeleton of a strongly-built male, radiocarbon dated to 830–780 cal. BC, was discovered buried in a prone position with the hands behind the back. In addition, a massive perimortem blunt force trauma was evident on the skull. The nature of the injury and the unusual characteristics of the body position were considered highly suggestive that the man had been ritually sacrificed (Ottini *et al.* 2003).

Historical Background for Case 1

One may often read that during antiquity, disabled or malformed newborn infants were neither helped nor treated, particularly in societies devoted to certain kinds of eugenics, such as the Spartans (Bernand 1999). The malformed newborn infant in antiquity was often considered to have been a sign sent from the gods as an indication of their exasperation at human failings or to signal a forthcoming special event (Charlier 2003; 2004; 2008b). In many cases, the baby (and frequently the mother too, i.e. the 'monster maker') was identified as being impure, and were destined to be killed using a variety of methods, including fire, water or starvation. Infants with pronounced malformations could be immediately eliminated but, in a small number of cases, certain anomalies may have been ignored and thereby enabled to pass through generations.

But what were the causes, during antiquity and protohistory, that may account for the apparition of malformed subjects? They are numerous, but may be summarised into eight different groups (Table 4.1). It is important to understand that two teratogenic agents were predominant in this context – the enormous quantity and variety of infectious diseases (particularly parasites), and chronic poisoning from arsenic and lead due to the use of poor quality jewels, pollutant metal extractive methods and contaminated ceramics and water (Fornaciari *et al.* 1984). One might question the fact that if heavy metal poisoning was one of the main reasons for such defects, then why do not we see high levels of environmentally induced neoplasms among archaeological populations? In fact, a very short period of exposure to 'pollution' is necessary to induce malformations during pregnancy (i.e. the very early weeks *in utero*), with very quick and readily apparent consequences the

Genetic	(including endogamy practice)
Chromosomal	Familial or sporadic
Maternal illness	Nutritional trouble Endocrine disease Enzymopathy Immunological disease
Infectious disease	Virus Bacteria Fungus Parasites
Mechanical cause	Womb Membranes and amnios Twin
Physical agent	Natural radiation (radon, uranium) Temperature
Chemical agent	Element (e.g. heavy metals) Toxic substances (e.g. plants)

Table 4.1. Different teratogenic agents that would have been present in antiquity (revised from Fornaciari et al. *1984; Stevenson* et al. *1993; Thillaud 1996; Lyons Jones 1997; Aufderheide and Rodríguez-Martín 1998; Grmek and Gourevitch 1998; Charlier 2000; 2003; 2004; 2008a; 2008b).*

disabled baby. Chronic poisoning could indeed induce neoplasms that are invisible amongst archaeological remains for a number of reasons – the affected individual may die from another unrelated cause, such as an infectious disease or as a result of war or, alternatively, the resultant tumor may develop in the soft tissues (which is a common result of heavy metal poisoning), thereby killing the patient before it has time to invade the bone.

Even with modern eyes it is not easy to distinguish between infirmity and physical anomaly. As such, it is very difficult to appreciate the limit between these two entities from the perspective of the people who lived in antiquity. What is a slight anomaly to the modern world, such as polydactyly, limited hare-lip or neonatal teeth, could have been interpreted in the ancient world as a severe and *fatal* malformation, particularly because of the potential associated symbolic causes (e.g. the baby holds the evil eye). The incorporation of palaeopathological diagnosis with archaeological and historical data would tend to suggest that the interpretation of such defects may have varied according to the place and the historical period of birth, the social status of the parents and the accessibility to medical or surgical techniques.

Case 2: Two Dead in a Cistern

In 1960, Christian Le Roy, from the French School in Athens, discovered two skeletons in the cistern of the House of Fourni, Delos Island, Greece, one of which had been beheaded while the other only comprised the right side of the body (Figure 4.4; Daux 1961). On the basis of archaeological artifacts discovered near the corpses they have been dated to the end of the second century BC or the beginning of the first century BC. This is the time when some pirates and partisans of Mithridate would have been imprisoned and then killed by a number of the island's inhabitants (Pausanias, 3, 23, 5), which is quite exceptional due to the sacred character of the island which was devoted to the cult of Apollo and situated at the centre of the Aegean World (Bruneau and Ducat 2005). Anthropological examination was realised some years after the discovery (Ducrey and Ducrey 1973), but a palaeopathological and medico-legal study of the skeletons was only undertaken by the author in recent times.

Two different bodies were present. The first comprises a right hemi-skeleton – the lower limb without the foot, the upper limb without the hand, and the coxal bone. This fragmentation of the body seems to be secondary and due to a later renovation of the cistern rather than a deliberate segmentation of the corpse in the immediate postmortem period. The second individual is complete, with the exception of the first cervical vertebra and the skull. Both skeletons appear to have been primarily disposed of in the cistern, as indicated by the entire conservation of the smaller articulations. During the recent analysis of the remains it was no longer possible to determinate the sex of the hemi-skeleton, but anthropological analysis of the coxal bones from the complete body and examination of the original pictures of both skeletons indicated that they displayed female characteristics (Bruzek 2002). It should be noted that the archaeological evidence of torture, however, was considered to be an indication that the individuals were more probably male (Ducrey and

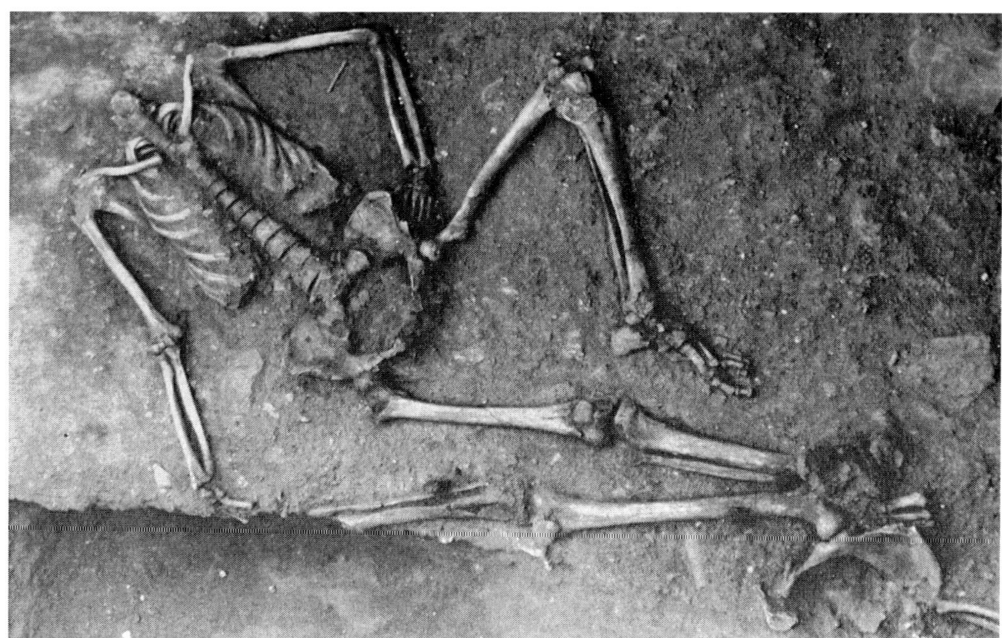

Figure 4.4. General view of the two skeletons discovered in the cistern at the House of Fourni on the Island of Delos (picture from Daux 1961; copyright of École Française d'Athènes).

Ducrey 1973)! Since no cranial fragments were present age determination was very difficult; the complete ossification of all long bones and the total absence of any degenerative joint disease provides an approximate age at death of 25 to 45 years.

Examination of both skeletons did not reveal any definitive signs of beheading or dismemberment, although it has to be said that the proximal extremity of the vertebral column is very fragmentary in the more complete skeleton and not present in the hemi-skeleton. The interpretation of decapitation for the complete individual is considered valid, however, since this part of the burial does not appear to have been subject to later disturbance and the first cervical vertebra and skull were clearly not present. Of particular interest was evidence for the presence of a number of iron nails close to both skeletons (Figure 4.5) – two were located on the lower limb of the hemi-skeleton, one of which was positioned on the lateral side of the proximal end of the right fibula (Figure 4.6), while the second was situated on the medial side of the right femoral diaphysis (Figure 4.7). A further three nails were associated with the complete skeleton – one in the inter-osseous space of the right leg (between the tibia and the fibula), while the remaining two were positioned on each hand between a number of phalanges. Another iron piece was discovered adjacent to the right ankle of the complete skeleton which had been made of a (now) 10 cm long cylindrical T-shaped piece that was articulated with a nail. The piece had measured some 14 cm when originally discovered.

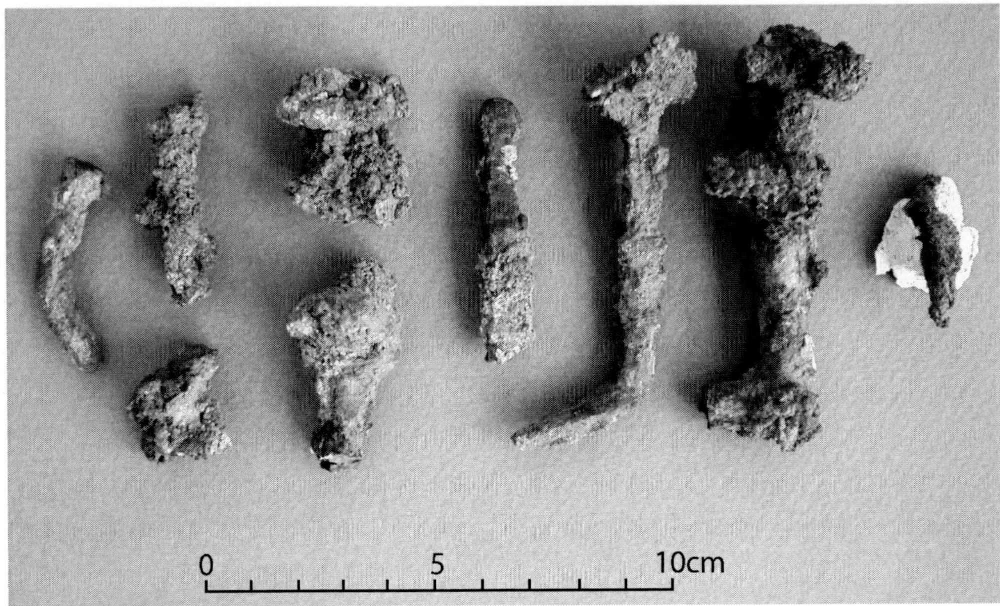

Figure 4.5. Iron nails discovered associated with the skeletons recovered from the House of Fourni, some of which were attached to the bones (P. Charlier).

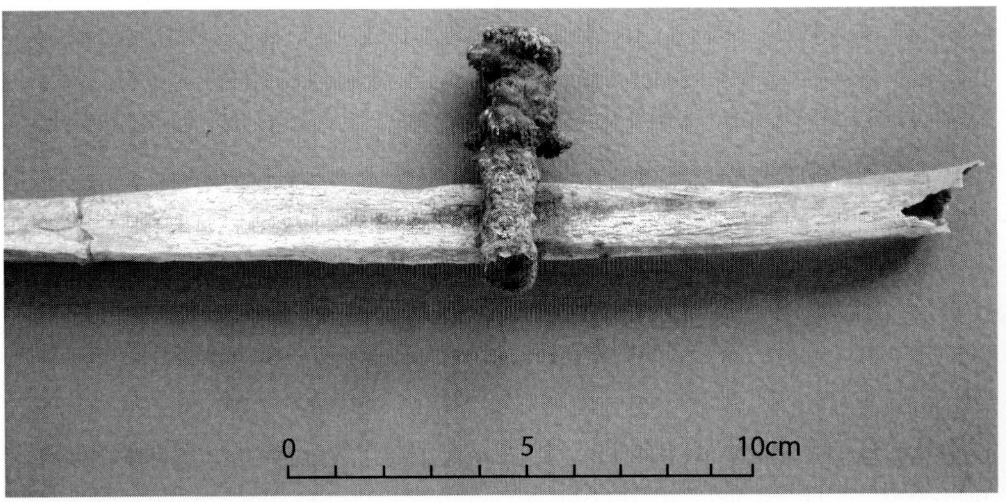

Figure 4.6. Right fibula of the incomplete skeleton from the House of Fourni; note the iron nail still attached to the bone (P. Charlier).

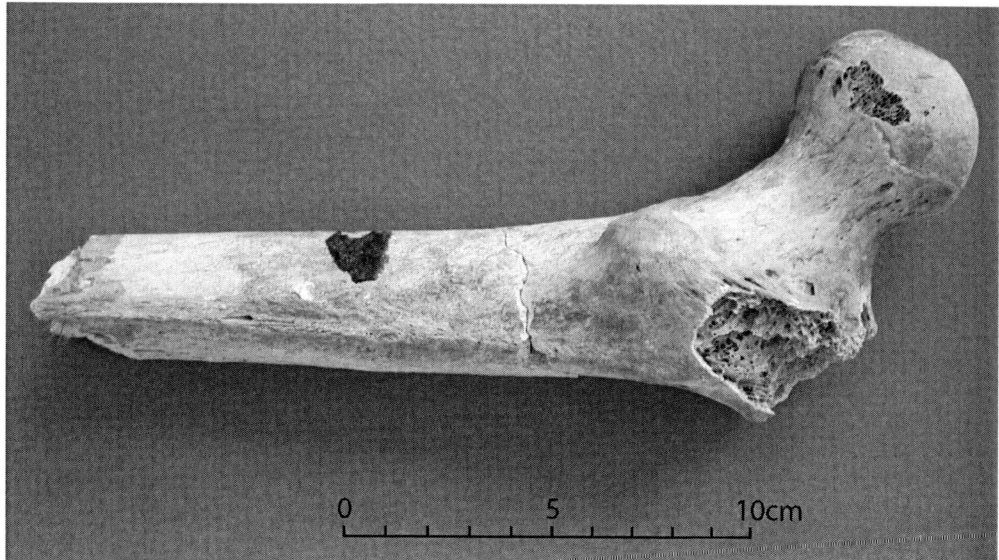

Figure 4.7. Right femur of the incomplete skeleton from the House of Fourni with rust traces still apparent on the cortical bone. When initially discovered in 1960 an iron nail was still attached to the bone

After the initial anthropological examination, Ducrey and Ducrey (1973) were of the opinion that the two individuals had been captured by Delians after Mithridate raids on the sacred island. They postulated that following their capture they had been tortured and killed (crucified) after which their bodies had been discarded within the cistern. This situation would have been quite exceptional since there had been a taboo on death and birth taking place on Delos since its purification by the Athenians in 426 BC (Bruneau and Ducat 2005). In fact, the palaeopathological examination showed that even if nails were associated with the skeletons, they are not necessarily evidence of crucifixion. To be useful and enable the *vertical* exposition of the body, the nails would have to have been inserted into the carpal bones, and not in the spaces between the metacarpals and phalanges. Insertion in the inter-osseous space of the leg, however, is quite uncommon but not impossible for a crucifixion; the insertion of nails in both superimposed ankles is more 'classical', as was apparent in the remains of a crucified individual discovered in Jerusalem. This individual also appeared to have had both legs broken in order to accelerate his death by suffocation – he would have been unable to support his body weight and subsequently may have suffered almost immediately from a fatal acute respiratory insufficiency (but it had to be said that a palaeopathological examination cannot determine whether such a practice would have taken place before or after the crucifixion process) (Haas 1970). There was no evidence for the deliberate breakage of the leg bones among the skeletons from Delos.

The study undertaken by the author indicated that the iron nail present on the right knee of the lower limb of the half-skeleton may have been in close contact with the individual for a substantial period of time during life. Possible support for this interpretation was the presence of a localised periostitis adjacent to the part of the nail that was fused to the bone surface (Figure 4.8). As such, it was considered more probable the iron piece was some form of device to limit movement that had been deliberately placed just below the right knee. It is unfortunate that the other half of the skeleton was not present since this could have greatly helped with the interpretation of the object. The iron piece discovered adjacent to the right ankle of the complete skeleton may have been a form of hobble and may originally have been similar to the object associated with the incomplete skeleton's right knee. Indeed, comparable inflammation (i.e. periostitis) has also been observed on the anterior surface of the distal extremity of the right tibia, a part of the bone in close proximity to the iron piece discovered near the right ankle of the complete skeleton.

Historical Background for Case 2

While the hypothesis of beheading is still accepted for the complete skeleton from Delos, it has been shown that crucifixion can no longer be considered as an explanation for either of the individuals. Other kinds of torture cannot be ruled out, however, such as the horizontal nailing of the body on a wooden board or its mutilation.

Figure 4.8. Detailed view of the surface of the right fibula presented in Figure 4.6. Note the new bone formation apparent in the vicinity of the iron nail which is indicative of chronic inflammation (P. Charlier).

But who were these two individuals? It would not appear to be acceptable to follow the logic of Ducrey and Ducrey (1973) that the individuals were male because of the possible evidence for torture when the morphology of their pelvic bones was considered to be female. So, who were these women and why were they treated in this manner? Were they considered to have been witches, women who engaged in piracy or prostitutes? Were they simply individuals who had profaned a sanctuary or who had given birth on the island despite the rule of purity that had been in place since 426 BC?

Information contained within texts and epigraphs would tend to suggest that the Classical mode of punishment for religious non-piety (*asebia*) was precipitation from a height (Cantarella 1996), which is theoretically not impossible on the Island of Delos. During Roman times, free women condemned to death were not killed in public but rather given over to their family, then killed inside the house by the male members of the family, particularly the *pater familias* (*in omnes cognati intra domos animadverterunt*: *Valerius Maximus*, 6, 3, 7, about women who profited of Bacchanals for committing impure actions in 186 BC, a period exactly contemporary to the two persons from Delos; see also *Titus Livus*, 39, 18, 6 for comparable procedures).

Ducrey and Ducrey (1973) have proposed that the two skeletons may have died as a result of an Athenian mode of execution – the *apotympanismos* or *apotympanizomenos* – which involved the condemned person having been solidly attached to a post or a board and then abandoned to a long, slow agonizing death. In cases where the process was considered too long death could be hastened by strangulation, decapitation or other means (Cantarella 1996). This type of death was reserved for criminals (*kakourgoi*), thieves (*kleptai*) and slave dealers (*andrapodistai*) amongst others (Cantarella 1996).

The House of Fourni, where both skeletons were discovered, displayed exceptional proportions for a private house on the island and strongly atypical artistic reliefs. These comprised depictions of two phalluses associated with the inscription 'this one for you, this one for me' (N° Inv. A 4020, Archeological Museum of Delos), a bust of Helios (N° Inv. A 2915, Archeological Museum of Delos), two Isiac symbols, and a hermaphrodite amongst others. This may indicate, for archaeologists, the siege of a religious association (Bruneau and Ducat 2005). Indeed, some supposed a mortal punishment for guilty members of this association, followed by the clandestine concealment of the bodies because of the law against death and burial on the island (Bruneau *et al.* 1996).

Furthermore, the decapitation apparent in the more complete skeleton may have been postmortem, undertaken for the purposes of mutilating a cadaver. It is known that this practice was often reserved for criminals or individuals who were considered to have the potential to be harmful. Xenophon, for example, related that the cadaver of King Cyrus was degraded by his brother Artaxerxes: 'His brother, a person born from the same mother, even after death, he cut his head and both hands, then nailed them to a cross' (*Anabase*, 3, 1, 17). A comparable Persian practice undertaken on the cadavers of enemies is noted by Strabo: 'Rebels are punished by death. One cut off his head and one his arm. [The] Remains of the body are given to animals' (*Geography*, 15, 3, 17). The Phoenicians are recorded as having undertaken similar practices during the capture of the city of Selinonte in Sicily by Hannibal in 409 BC: '[The] People of Selinonte, gathered in the public place in order to resist, were severely defeated. Barbarians were in all the city. Some pillaged houses and burnt inhabitants; others, penetrating the streets, pitilessly slit the throats of children, infants, women and old persons. According to their habit, they mutilated cadavers: some wear a belt made of enemies' hands, others put heads at the top of their javelins' (Diodorus of Sicily, 13, 57– 58). Similarly in Egypt, when Ptolemaos VIII Evegetus II Physkon killed the son he had born with his sister Cleopatra II in 144 BC, it is recorded that: 'Imitating the bloody cruelty of Medea, on the Island of Cyprus, he cut the throat of the boy named Mephites he had with her [his sister] and who was still young. The crime was already odious but he made it more so: he cut all his four limbs, put them in a box which he expedited to Alexandria. [The] Birthday of Cleopatra was approaching and Ptolemaos deposited at night, on the doors of the palace, the box containing parts of the victims' body' (Diodorus of Sicily, 34–35). When not placed within a box, such bodies could be stored within an animal skin, as was the case for a Seleucide (Achaios), whose remains were kept in Sardus in 213 BC by a mercenary of Antiochios III: 'When the council was open, they discussed for a very long time about the punishment they had to give to the captive. They decided to mutilate him firstly then, after having cut off his head, to crucify his body laid in a donkey skin' (Polybius, 8, 21).

Conclusion

Palaeopathological examination and the application of palaeoteratology or a forensic approach may help with the interpretation of skeletons recovered from atypical burials (e.g. Gejvall and Henschen 1968; Charlier 2000; 2003a; 2004; 2008a; 2008b; Charon 2002; Charlier *et al.* 2005), as is evident from the two cases discussed in the current paper. In the first case, a young girl associated with a sacred area dating back to the Late Bronze Age in Rome, appears to have been sacrificed by having had an axe blow dealt to the skull. The fact that she appears to have suffered from Down's Syndrome is probably no coincidence, and it may have been because of her condition that she was specifically selected for sacrifice. In the second case two middle-aged women discovered in a cistern of a building on the Island of Delos in Greece displayed injuries which appear to have been caused by torture and execution. Both women appear to have been hobbled to limit their physical movement and at least one of them was beheaded. This study has demonstrated the benefits of applying a multidisciplinary approach to help explain unusual burials – the combination of archaeological and documentary information with specialist palaeopathological knowledge has the potential to enable a clearer interpretation to be made concerning such burials.

Acknowledgements

The author would like to thank for their help the French School at Athens (Professor D. Mulliez, M. Brunet and C. Prêtre), the French School at Rome (Professor M. Gras, S.

Verger and Y. Rivière), the Soprintendenza Archeologica di Roma (P. Catalano and her team), the Ecole Pratique des Hautes Etudes (Professor D. Gourevitch and Dr Thillaud) and the Assistance Publique des Hôpitaux de Paris (Professor M. Durigon, Dr G. Lorin, Dr J. Ferrand and Dr I. Huynh-Charlier). A warm and special thanks to Anastasia Tsaliki and Dr Eileen Murphy who invited me to present this paper.

Note

All the translations used for the Classical texts (Pausanias, Valerius Maximus, Titus Livus, Xenophon, Strabo, Diodorus of Sicily, Polybius) are taken from the Collection des Universités de France (collection Guillaume Budé), Les Belles Lettres, Paris.

References

Aufderheide, A. C. and Rodríguez-Martín, C. 1998. *The Cambridge Encyclopedia of Human Paleopathology*. Cambridge: Cambridge University Press.

Barnes, E. 1994. *Developmental Defects of the Axial Skeleton in Paleopathology*. Colorado: Colorado University Press.

Bernand, A. 1999. *Guerre et Violence dans la Grèce Antique*. Paris: Hachette (collection Pluriel).

Brothwell, D. 1967. Major congenital anomalies of the skeleton. Evidence from the earlier populations, pp. 423–43 in Brothwell, D. and Sandison, A. T. (eds), *Diseases in Antiquity*. Springfield: Charles C. Thomas.

Bruneau, P. and Ducat, J. 2005. *Guide de Délos* (Sites and Monuments No. 1). Athens: Ecole Française d'Athènes.

Bruneau, P., Brunet, M., Farnoux, A. and Moretti, J. C. 1996. *Délos, Île Sacrée et Ville Cosmopolite*. Athens: Ecole Française d'Athènes.

Bruzek, J. 2002. A method for visual determination of sex, using the human hip bone. *American Journal of Physical Anthropology* 117, 157–68.

Byers, S. N. and Myster, S. N. 2004. *Forensic Anthropology Laboratory Manual*. Old Tappan (New Jersey): Allyn and Bacon.

Cantarella, E. 1996. *I Supplizi Capitali in Grecia e a Roma*. Milano: RCS Libri and Grande Opere S.p.A.

Catalano, P., Angeletti, L. R., Caldarini, C. and Charlier, P. 2003. Testimonianze di sacrifici umani nel Foro Romano in epoca protostorica: le sepulture del Carcer-Tulianum e dell'Equus Domitiani. Paper presented at the 15th Congress of the *Associazione Antropologica Italiana: Variabilità Umana e Storia del Popolamento*, Chieti, Italy.

Catalano, P., Caldarini, C., Charlier, P., Mariani Costantini, R., Minozzi, S. and Pantano, W. 2006. Analisi antropologica delle sepolture del Carcer-Tullianum e del c.d. *Equus Domitiani*. Paper presented at the international congress *Il Mostro e il Sacro. Coordinate Mitiche e Rituali della Difformità fra Emarginazione e Integrazione*, Rome, Italy.

Charlier, P. 2000. Nouvelles hypothèses concernant la représentation des utérus dans les ex-voto étrusco-romains. Anatomie et histoire de l'art. *OCNUS* 8, 33–46.

Charlier, P. 2003. Les malformations humaines dans l'Egypte ancienne (Egypte Pharaonique, Ptolémaïque et Romaine). Apport de la paléopathologie. *Egypte-Afrique-Orient* 31, 57–62.

Charlier, P. 2004. Ce que la paléopathologie apporte à la compréhension des individus malformés dans l'Antiquité gréco-romaine. *La Revue du Praticien (Monographie)* 54, 691–3.

Charlier, P. (ed.) 2008a. *Ostéo-archéologie et Techniques Médico-légales: Tendances et Perspectives. Pour un 'Manuel Pratique de Paléopathologie Humaine'*. Paris: De Boccard.

Charlier P. 2008b. *Les Monstres Humains dans l'Antiquité. Analyse Paléopathologique*. Paris: Fayard.

Charlier, P., Durand, R. and Huynh, I. 2005. Condyle aplasia in an 1800-year-old mandible from France. *Paleopathology Newsletter* 129, 16–20.

Charon, P. 2002. About anencephaly. *Paleopathology Newsletter* 119, 12–17.

Coarelli, F., Clauss, J. A., Clauss J. J. and Harmon, D. P. 2006. *Roma and Environs. An Archaeological Guide*. Berkeley: University of California Press.

Daux, G. 1961. Chronique des fouilles françaises à Délos. *Bulletin de Correspondance Hellénique* 85, 913–15.

Ducrey P. and Ducrey, N. 1973. Les suppliciés de Fourni. *Suppléments au Bulletin de Correspondance Hellénique* 1, 173–81.

Fornaciari, G., Menicagli Trevisiani, E. and Ceccanti B. 1984. Indagini paleonutrizionali e determinazione del piombo osseo mediante spettroscopia ad assorbimento atomico sui resti scheletrici di epoca tardo-romana (IV secolo d.C.) della 'Villa dei Gordiani' (Roma). *Archaeology, Anthropology and Ethnology* 114, 149–76.

Gejvall, N. G. and Henschen, F. 1968. Two late skeletons with malformations and close family relationship from ancient Corinth. *Opuscula Atheniensia* 8, 179–93.

Grmek, M. D. and Gourevitch, D. 1998. *Les Maladies dans l'Art Antique*. Paris: Fayard.

Guilaine, J. and Zammit, J. 2001. *Le Sentier de la Guerre, Visages de la Violence Préhistorique*. Paris: Seuil.

Haas, N. 1970. Anthropological observations on the skeletal remains from Giv'at ha-Mivtar. *Israel Exploration Journal* 20, 38–59.

Lyons Jones, K. 1997. *Smith's Recognizable patterns of human malformation* (fourth edition). Philadelphia: W. B. Saunders Company.

Murphy, E. M. 2000. Developmental defects and disability. The evidence from the Iron Age semi-nomadic peoples of Aymyrlyg, south Siberia, pp. 60–80 in Hubert, J. (ed.), *Madness, Disability and Social Exclusion* (One World Archaeology 40). London: Routledge.

Ottini, L., Angeletti, L. R., Pantano, W. B., Falchetti, M., Minozzi, S., Fortini, P., Catalano, P., Mariani-Costantini, R. 2003. Possible human sacrifice at the origins of Rome: novel skeletal evidences. *Medicina nei Secoli* 15, 459–68.

Reichs, K. J. 1986. *Forensic Osteology. Advances in the Identification of Human Remains*. Springfield: Charles C. Thomas.

Schmitt, A., Cunha, E. and Pinheiro, J. 2006. *Forensic Anthropology and Medicine: Complementary Sciences from Recovery to Cause of Death*. Totowa, New Jersey: Humana Press.

Stevenson, R. E., Hall, J. G. and Goodman, R. M. 1993. *Human Malformations and Related Anomalies* (Oxford Monographs on Medical Genetics 27). Oxford: Oxford University Press.

Thillaud, P. L. 1996. *Paléopathologie Humaine*. Sceaux: Kronos Editions.

Turkel, S. J. 1989. Congenital abnormalities in skeletal populations, pp. 109–27 in Iscan, M. Y. and Kennedy K. A. R. (eds), *Reconstruction of Life from the Skeleton*. New York: Alan R. Liss Inc.

5. Ritual Inhumations and 'Deposits' of Children among the Geto-Dacians

Valeriu Sîrbu

Abstract

There are more than 20 findings with the remains of over 100 children, spread throughout almost all the area inhabited by the Geto-Dacians and in a variety of site types – settlements, isolated pits or 'field of pits' cultic sites. The majority of the remains are those of young children – Infans I (0–7 years). The discoveries comprise whole skeletons, partial skeletons, skulls or isolated bones – cranial and post-cranial. They date from the fourth to third centuries BC, but most are of first century BC – first century AD date, a period when ordinary Geto-Dacian burials are practically missing. Special attention has been paid to the enclosure of Grădina Castelului in Hunedoara, where the remains of 39 children were discovered. These comprised 38 Infans I (0–7 years) and one Infans II (7–14 years), all of whom were inhumed. Their general features set these discoveries apart from contemporary ordinary tombs because they could be interpreted as the result of either human sacrifice or ritual inhumation.

Introduction

The following paper will focus on the Carpato-Danubian territory, which both the written sources and the archaeological findings indicate was the territory of the Geto-Dacians, namely the northern Thracians. The study will take into account discoveries that span almost five centuries (fourth century BC – first century AD), although particular attention will be paid to a period of two and a half centuries – from the middle of the second century BC to the conquest of Dacia by the Romans (AD 106). This period represents the so-called 'classic' period of the Geto-Dacian civilisation. The paper will consider children's burials in addition to 'non-cremated human bones in non-funerary contexts'. This phrase refers to all skeletons, parts of skeletons and isolated human bones recovered from non-funerary contexts (Sîrbu 2003, 21–2).

For a better comprehension of the phenomenon, it is necessary to provide a brief overview of the general funerary discoveries of the respective zone and period. The research undertaken to date has demonstrated the existence of major changes in the funerary beliefs and practices of the Geto-Dacians during this period, which were entirely different to either the preceding or succeeding periods (Sîrbu 1986, 91–108; 1993, 31–6, 86–100; 1997, 196–301; Babeş 1988, 13–16). In order to illustrate the dramatic nature of this change it is necessary to make only one comparison – more than 2000 graves, isolated or in necropoli, exist from the fifth to third centuries BC, whereas only 150 tombs date from the second century BC to the first century AD (Sîrbu 2002, 376).

An even more dramatic situation is apparent in the period from 50 BC–AD 106, when no necropoli or tombs of the common people have been found, and there are no more than 20 tumuli assigned to the aristocracy, in the main habitation area of the Geto-Dacians (Sîrbu 1986, 106–8; 1993, 39–40; 2006, 128–36; Babeş 1988, 5–22). This is the period between the reigns of Burebista and Decebalus, an epoch with a lot of settlements, cities and sanctuaries. Numerous excavations have been undertaken on these sites and it is not possible to explain the absence of burials as a result of a lack of excavation. The only reasonable explanation for the paucity of graves during this period would appear to be a major change in the Dacians' beliefs about the 'other world'. This seems to have involved funerary processing of the bodies of the dead, which left no physical traces detectable by traditional archaeological methods (Babeş 1988, 17–22; Sîrbu 1993, 38–40). The process of the drastic decrease in funerary vestiges began by the end of the third century BC and must have had its climax during the first century AD.

Analysis of the Findings

The current study will focus only on inhumations and deposits of children. The age categories Infans I (0–7 years) and Infans II (7–14 years) will be used throughout the current discussion. The first part of this section will discuss discoveries made in settlements, in isolated pits near settlements and in concentrations of pits from outside settlements – the so-called 'fields of pits', while the second part will concentrate on findings from the Grădina Castelului site in Hunedoara. Unfortunately, only summary data exist for some of the discoveries and anthropological analyses are available for less than half of the skeletons. As such, a lot of essential information is missing. Nevertheless, despite this situation a number of characteristics can be observed and it is possible to draw certain conclusions concerning this issue.

Settlements, Isolated Pits, 'Fields of Pits'

Diffusion Area

This sort of discovery appeared in almost all of the territory of the Geto-Dacians. They are more numerous in certain zones (Figure 5.1), but it is difficult to state whether they reflect a historical reality or are just a reflection of the early stages of the research (Sîrbu 1986, 91–108; 1993, 31–6, 86–100; 1997, 196–301; Babeş 1988, 13–16). Nevertheless, it is still possible to state that this was a general phenomenon for Geto-Dacian society during the period under study.

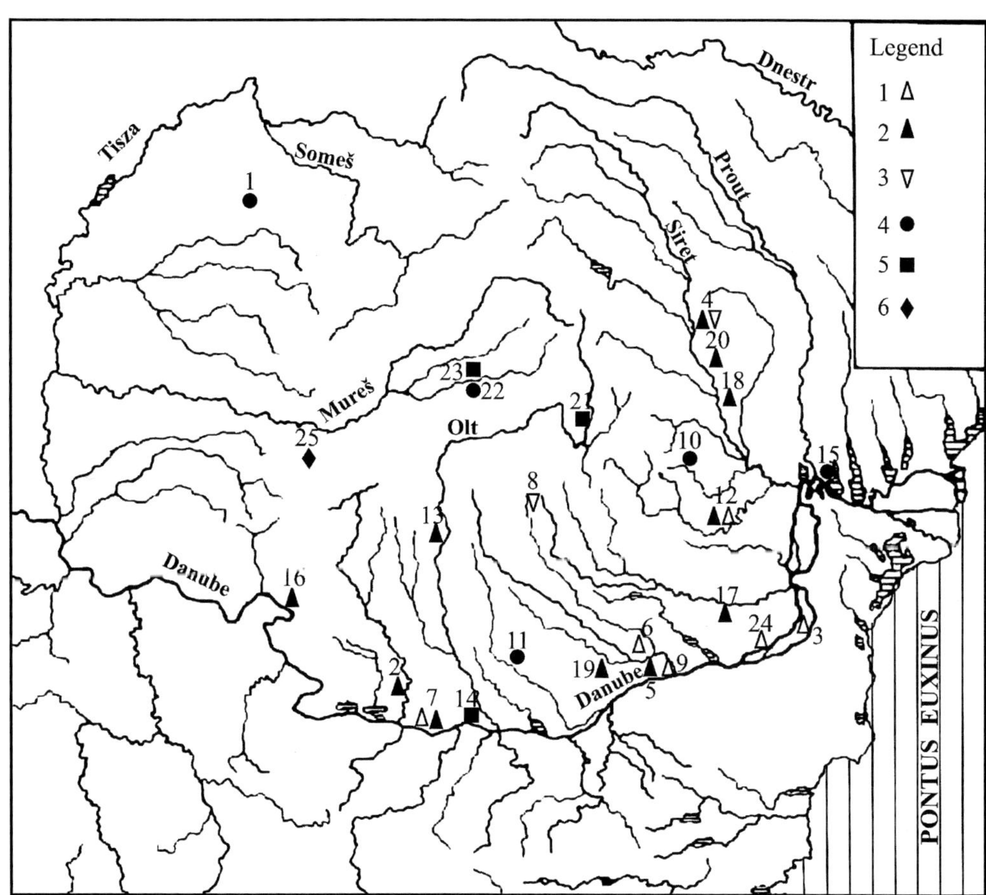

Figure 5.1. Ritual inhumations and 'deposits' of children at Geto-Dacian sites. The numbers in brackets correspond to those provided in the legend. a) in settlements – in dwellings (1), in pits (2), not specified (3), b) in isolated pits (4), c) in the 'fields of pits' (5), d) in the 'children's necropolis' from Hunedoara (6).

Locations: 1. Berea, 2. Bâzdâna, 3. Borduşani, 4. Brad, 5. Căscioarele, 6. Căţelu Nou, 7. Celei, 8. Cetăţeni, 9. Chirnogi, 10. Cândeşti, 11. Dulceanca, 12. Grădiştea, 13. Ocniţa, 14. Orlea, 15. Orlovka, 16. Ostrovul Şimian, 17. Piscu Crăsani, 18. Poiana, 19. Popeşti, 20. Răcătău, 21. Sf. Gheorghe-Bedehaza, 22. Sighişoara-Albeşti, 23. Sighişoara-Wietenberg, 24. Unirea, 25. Hunedoara.

Types of Sites and Archaeological Complexes

Most of the skeletons came from settlements (44), while 21 individuals were derived from 'fields of pits' and nine had originated from isolated pits (Sîrbu 1997, 197, figs 1, 3 and 4). The remains of nine children were recovered from dwellings or pit houses, deposited in pits or from under the stairs or the floor (Sîrbu 2001, 323–34). The majority of children (35) were recovered from pits inside settlements; usually, a single child was buried, but at

Brad (Ursachi 1980–1982, 12–116, 122–3) and Celei (see Figure 5.1; Sîrbu 1993, 88–9), multiple individuals are buried in the same place. 'The fields of pits' are concentrations of pits – sometimes tens of them – which can be circular, rectangular or clustered. They are generally located at great distances outside settlements and contain apparently cultic deposits, such as human and animal inhumations. In some cases they have also been found to contain the remains of children. There is usually more than one child in a single pit and, sometimes, one could also find remains of adolescents and adults in the same pit, near the subadult remains. In some cases, both the child and the adolescent or the adult remains show evidence for violence on their bodies, or certain skeletal elements are missing.

Human skeletons have neither been found beneath nor near sanctuaries – edifices in the Dacian society (Sîrbu 1993, 31–6) – with only one exception, at Cârlomăneşti, where a child's mandible was found (Babeş *et al.* 2005, 108). Parts of skeletons, even occasional skeletons or isolated bones, however, have been discovered in certain sacred enclosures throughout the different zones of the Geto-Dacian territory, such as Pietroasa Mică – Gruiu-Dării, Buzău County (Dupoi and Sîrbu 2001, 62–3, fig. 123; Sîrbu *et al.* 2005, 107) and Măgura Moigradului, Sălaj County (Sîrbu 1993, 97; Pop and Matei 2001, 253–77). They must have been linked to ritual acts and do not represent the ordinary graves of the communities.

Shape and Filling of the Pits

Most of the pits have a cylindrical or truncated shape. Those located in the interior of settlements are, as a rule, reused and do not seem to have been dug purely for the deposition of bodies. The pit fills usually have a domestic aspect, which means a random filling. In the part of the pit that contains the subadult skeleton(s), however, successive deposits of earthen layers or a certain arrangement of deposits are apparent which is suggestive of a deliberate sequence of deposition and intention.

Number of Skeletons in Pits

In the majority of cases (46) a single child skeleton was discovered within a pit, with the remains of two children having been found in seven pits and three or four children's skeletons having been present in a pit in five cases. In a number of situations the children had been buried with adolescents or adults so the total number of bodies within the pit was larger. At Sighişoara – Wietenberg, for example, the remains of seven individuals were retrieved from a pit (Horedt and Seraphim 1971, 18–19, 67–9; Sîrbu 1993, 98–9, figs 58–59; Andriţoiu and Rustoiu 1997, 71–6), while eight individuals had been interred within a pit at Orlea (Comşa 1972, 65–78; Figure 5.2), and sixteen individuals were identified in a pit at Berea (Zirra 1980, 68–9, fig. 56/1–2); in all these findings, children were buried together with adults and adolescents.

Position and Orientation of the Skeletons

Most of the children's skeletons were buried in an extended supine position, although quite a number of individuals were buried in a flexed position lying either on their right or left

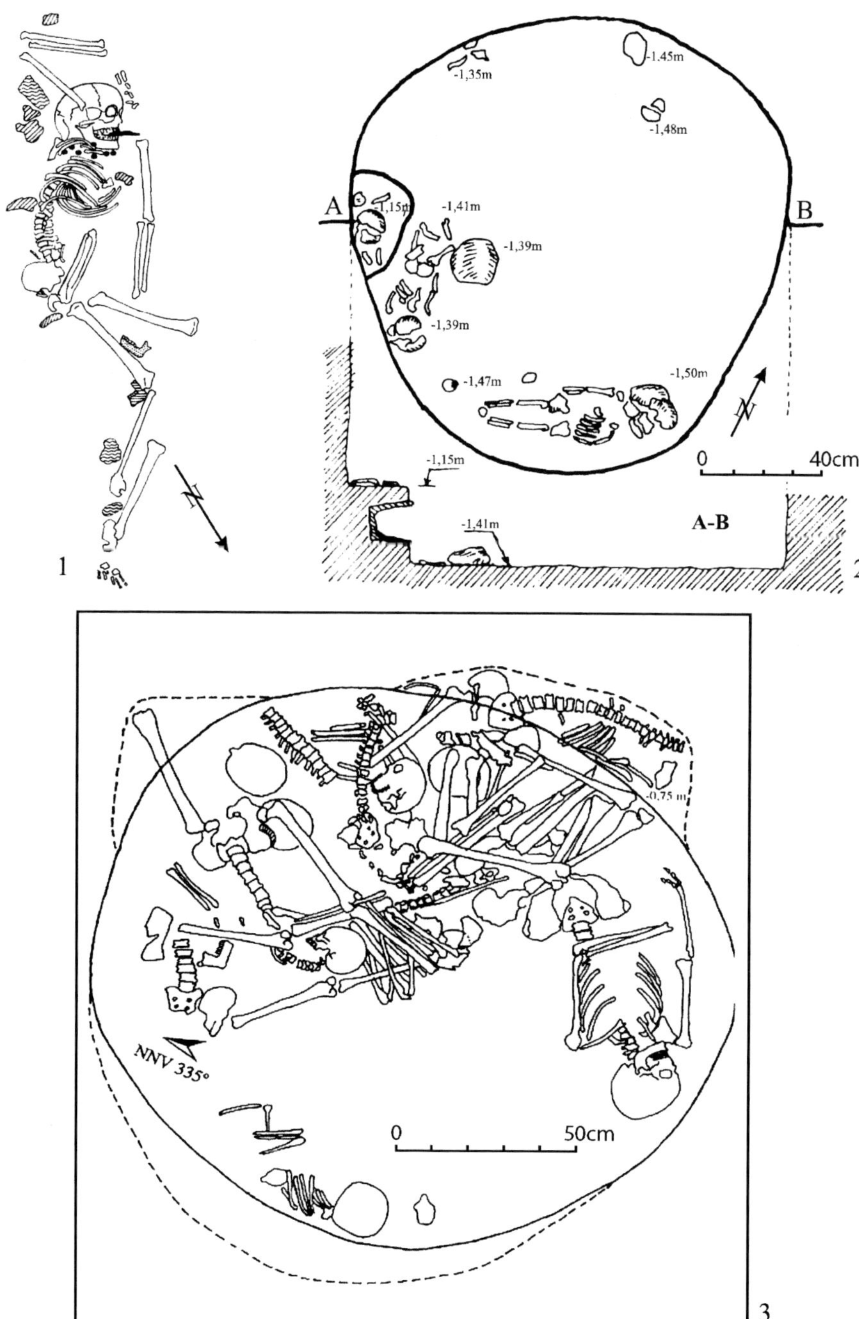

Figure 5.2. Children's inhumations in the settlement of Grădiştea (1), the 'field of pits' from Sf. Gheorghe-Bedehaza (2) and Orlea (3) (after Horedt 1956; Comşa 1972; Sîrbu 1993).

sides. In addition, in three cases the children had been buried crouched vertically. There does not appear to have been a preference for orientating the bodies towards particular cardinal points. In cases where only a single corpse was buried within a pit, it was usually positioned at its base. Where multiple individuals were interred within a single pit, they were positioned at different levels of the pit fill (Sîrbu 1986, 91–108). In some cases the children appear to have been buried very carefully within the pit, whereas in other examples their bodies have been simply thrown into the pits.

Condition of the Skeletons

Most of the skeletons were complete (c. 40), however, there were those that seemed to have been deliberately processed after death. In some cases, large portions of the body were missing and this did not appear to have been caused by taphonomic processes. In other situations only isolated cranial or post-cranial fragments were recovered (Sîrbu 1993, 32–3; 1997, 197, figs 1 and 3). Nevertheless, in many cases it was unclear whether the incomplete nature of the skeletons was due to taphonomic processes or if they were an accurate reflection of the nature of the original burial.

Age

Almost all of the cases comprised Infans I (0 to 7 years old) – 69 – while two cases were of Infans II (7 to 14 years old). Moreover, there were cases of babies, sometimes of twins, such as at Orlea, where we cannot determine if they were stillborn or died very soon after birth (Nicolăescu-Plopşor and Rişcuţia 1969, 69–73). In settlements, there were as a rule, only the burials of children (up to 14 years old), while in the 'fields of pits' the remains of teenagers and adults could also be present along with children within the same pit. More than 60% of the skeletons found in non-funerary contexts belong to children (Sîrbu 1997, 197, fig. 1).

Inventory and Offerings

Objects that could be clearly defined as part of the funerary inventory usually found within ordinary tombs, such as pottery, weapons and tools, did not accompany the skeletons of children. Only a few of the subadults had clothing pieces or accessories (fibulae, pendants, earrings, beads) and, exceptionally, other categories of objects and offerings (Sîrbu 1993, 32, 86–100).

Chronology

The children's skeletons are all dated from the fourth century BC to the first century AD, but a number of important differences were apparent concerning the number of individuals and the context of their discovery throughout this period. There are only six burial deposits which contain the remains of some 13–14 individuals from the fourth to the third centuries BC, while there are 18 discoveries associated with the remains of over 60 individuals from the second century BC to the first century AD (Sîrbu 1997, 206, fig. 1).

Although the earlier discoveries originated from different geographical areas it is evident that they derived from either settlements, or from pits near the settlements, but never from the 'fields of pits'.

Hunedoara

Grădina Castelului – 'The Children's Necropolis'

The children's burials are situated at the top of a dolomite plateau and are partially damaged by structures related to Corvin Castle (Figure 5.3). The work of the geologist Eugen Orlandea in 2004 indicated that the landscape would have taken the form of a rocky highland with peaks and crevices in ancient times. Furthermore, the fact that there is no evidence for the deliberate layout of the children's graves has been interpreted as an indication that those burying the children had made use of the crevices already present in the dolomite. The bodies were located in an area orientated south-west to north-east and have been organised into groups, probably set apart not just in terms of topography, but also in relation to the nature of the associated grave goods.

It was not always possible to determine the original position of the children's bodies as a consequence of disturbance or their young age. In general, however, they were either lying in a supine position or they had been buried in a flexed position on either their right of left sides. In many cases the burials had been covered with stones (Figure 5.4). No trends were apparent in terms of the orientation of the bodies. None of the burials appeared to have interfered with one another, which was interpreted as a potential sign that the inhumations had all been made over a short time span – the stone markers which overlay the burials must still have been in their original positions when other burials had been made. The skeletons were generally in a very poor condition. This situation arose because many of the burials were close to the surface and therefore exposed to environmental factors and also because the majority were those of infants, whose remains are particularly small and fragile (Sîrbu *et al.* 2006, 188–9; Sîrbu *et al.* 2007, 19–106).

To date, 31 deposits have been identified which contained the remains of 53 individuals. In terms of funerary rite, there are 48 inhumations and only five cremations. Nine of the deposits contained two to five individuals (amounting to 37 individuals), while 14 included the remains of a single individual and three of the deposits have not yet been subject to anthropological analysis (Sîrbu *et al.* 2006, 187–9).

The age categories for the 48 inhumed individuals are as follows: a) under one year – 20 individuals; b) 1–2 years – six individuals; c) 2–6 years – nine individuals; d) 0–7 years – three individuals; e) 7–14 years – one individual and f) over 14 years – nine individuals. Unfortunately, the sex of the inhumed dead was determined in only 22 cases, 12 of which are male and 10 female, of various ages. All five cremated individuals were adults.

The skeletons' poor state of preservation is problematic and it is probable that some of the bones have been entirely obliterated. Some skeletons had only partial skulls (e.g. G19

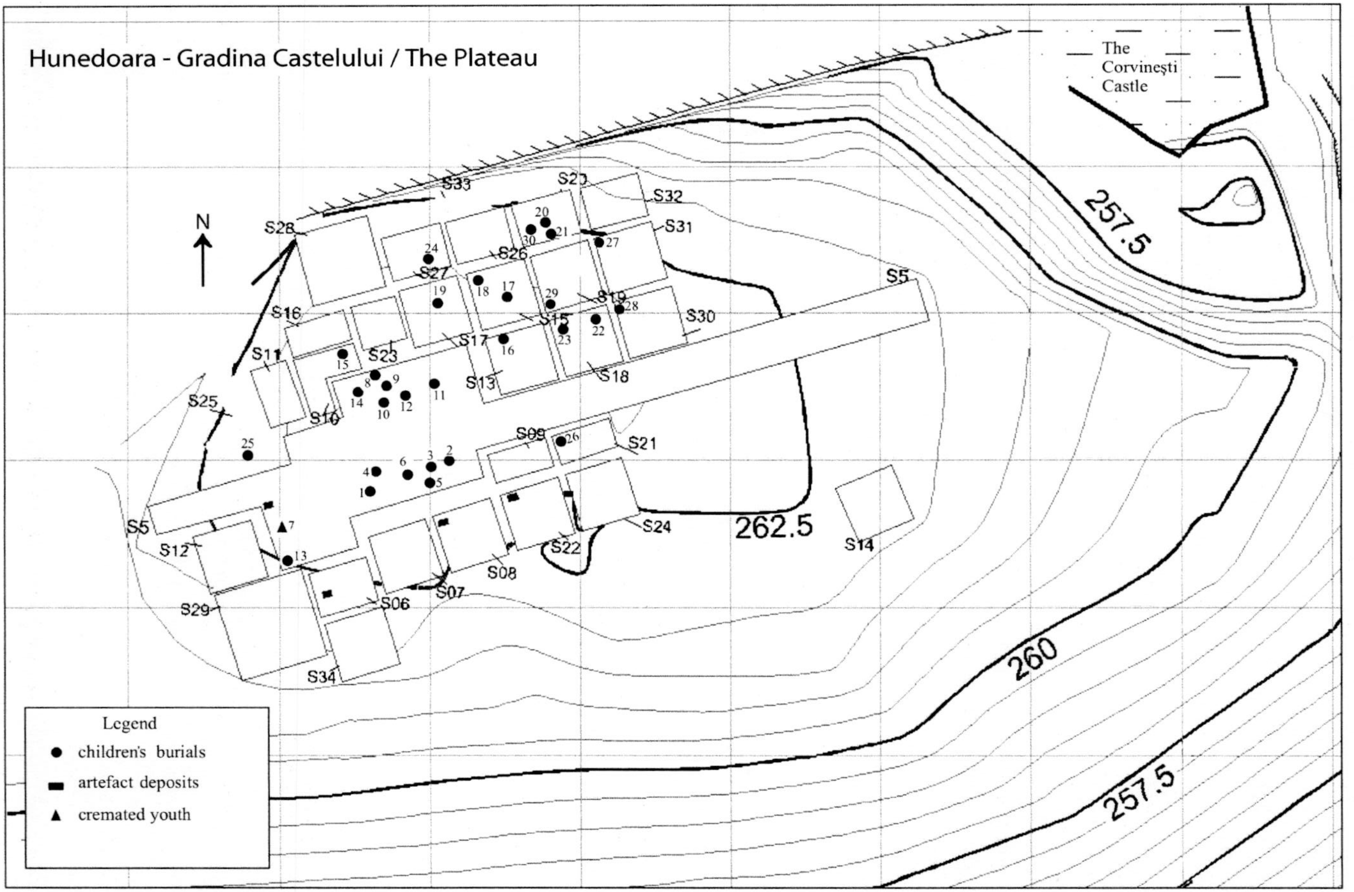

Figure 5.3. Hunedoara – Grădina Castelului/The Plateau (after Sîrbu et al. *2006).*

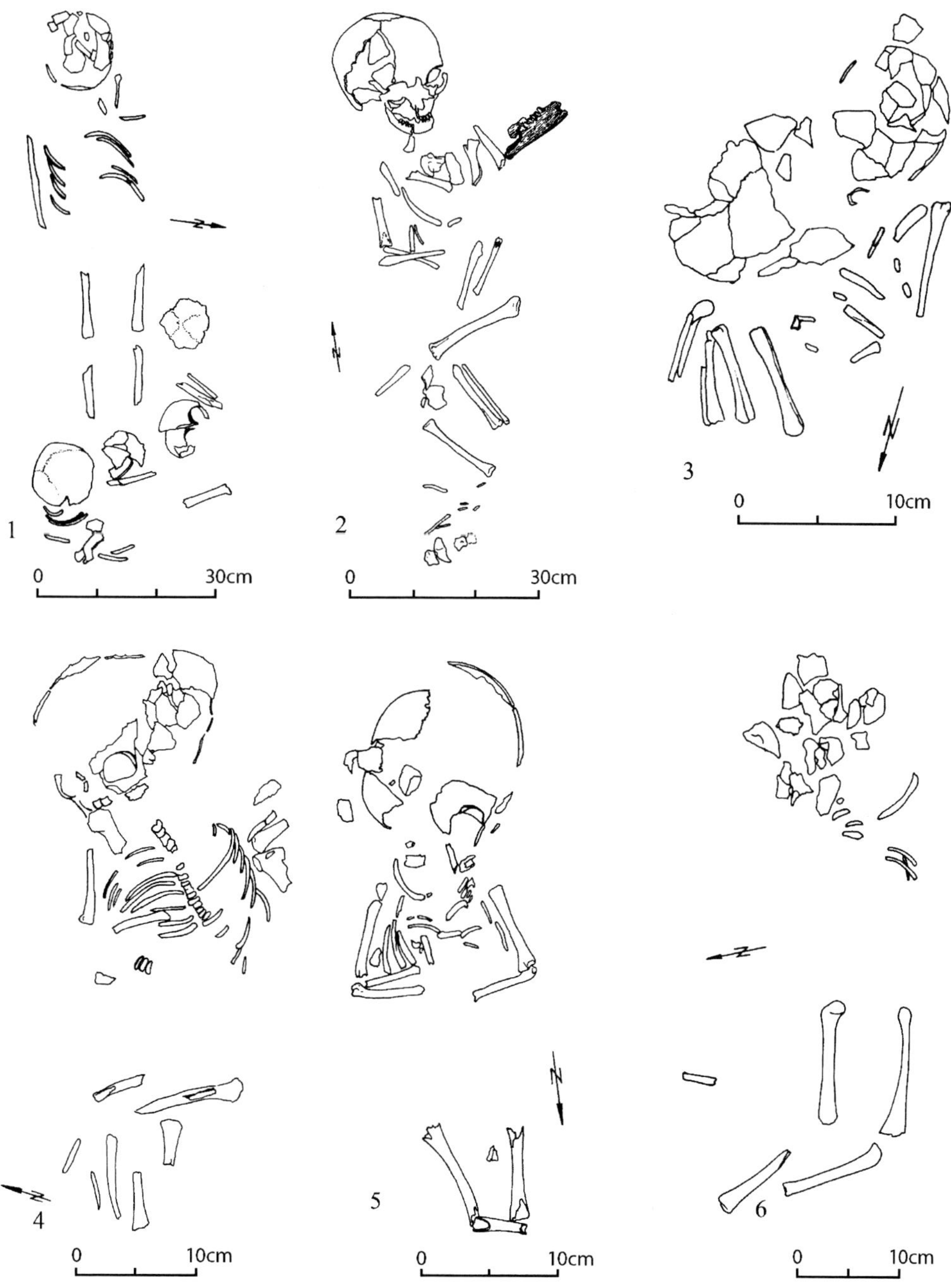

Figure 5.4. Hunedoara – Grădina Castelului/The Plateau. 1. Grave 1, 2. Grave 2, 3. Grave 4, 4. Grave 5, 5. Grave 6, 6. Grave 24 (after Sîrbu et al. *2006).*

and G20) or no skulls at all. As for the isolated bones, it is not possible to ascertain whether they represented isolated deposits originally or have become separated from the remainder of the skeleton as a result of later disturbance. However, the presence of skeletal remains, mostly isolated bones from various body parts, from two to five individuals, in 15 deposits, points to practices of exposing/decomposing the corpse and only then burying them here; it is difficult to explain it any other way, since this cannot be a case of re-inhumation. No signs of violence were observed in any of the skeletons but it should be remembered that it is possible to kill an individual in a manner that would not leave a trace on the skeleton, such as by strangulation or poisoning.

The rich and varied inventory is different not only depending on the individuals it accompanies, but also on the geographical grouping of the dead. The position of the objects also differs – some of the jewels and clothing accessories have been found lying next to the bodies in what appear to be normal positions, while others have been found under stones positioned around the skeletons (Figure 5.5). It is possible that some of the objects had shifted from their original positions over time. No pottery vessels of any kind were found near any of the children's burials (Sîrbu *et al.* 2006).

Based on the fibulae recovered from the Grădina Castelului burials it is possible to date them to the first century – beginning of the second century AD – the period prior to the Roman conquest of Dacia in AD 106. It was not possible to date all of the burials so precisely on the basis of their grave goods but it can be generally stated that they had all derived from the first century BC to the first century AD.

As it stands, one can conclude that the inhumations that have been recovered so far from Grădina Castelului – 31 burial deposits which contain the remains of at least 53 individuals – show several features which would appear to be unique among previous discoveries of human remains from the Geto-Dacian World (Protase 1971, 15–82; Babeş 1988, 3–32; Sîrbu 1993, 21–45; 1997, 193–221; 2002, 374–93). These unique characteristics can be summarised in the following manner:

- Most of the dead are children (39 out of 53).
- All of the small children (under seven years of age) were inhumed.
- In some cases, it is clear that the lack of certain skeletal parts and the presence of just isolated bones is due to the way the initial deposit was made and not related to environment factors or later interventions.
- There are no patterns in terms of body position and orientation.
- The graves were not deliberately dug but rather involved the use of natural rocky crevices and the covering of the bodies with stones.
- The wealth of the grave goods (fibulae, jewelry) appears to be in contrast with the absence of pottery vessels.

A total of five cremation burials were identified at Grădina Castelului. Tomb 7 is the only one where one cremated individual was found, a male aged 21 to 22 years of age and most likely a warrior. His grave goods were rich and diverse and a lack of evidence for burn-

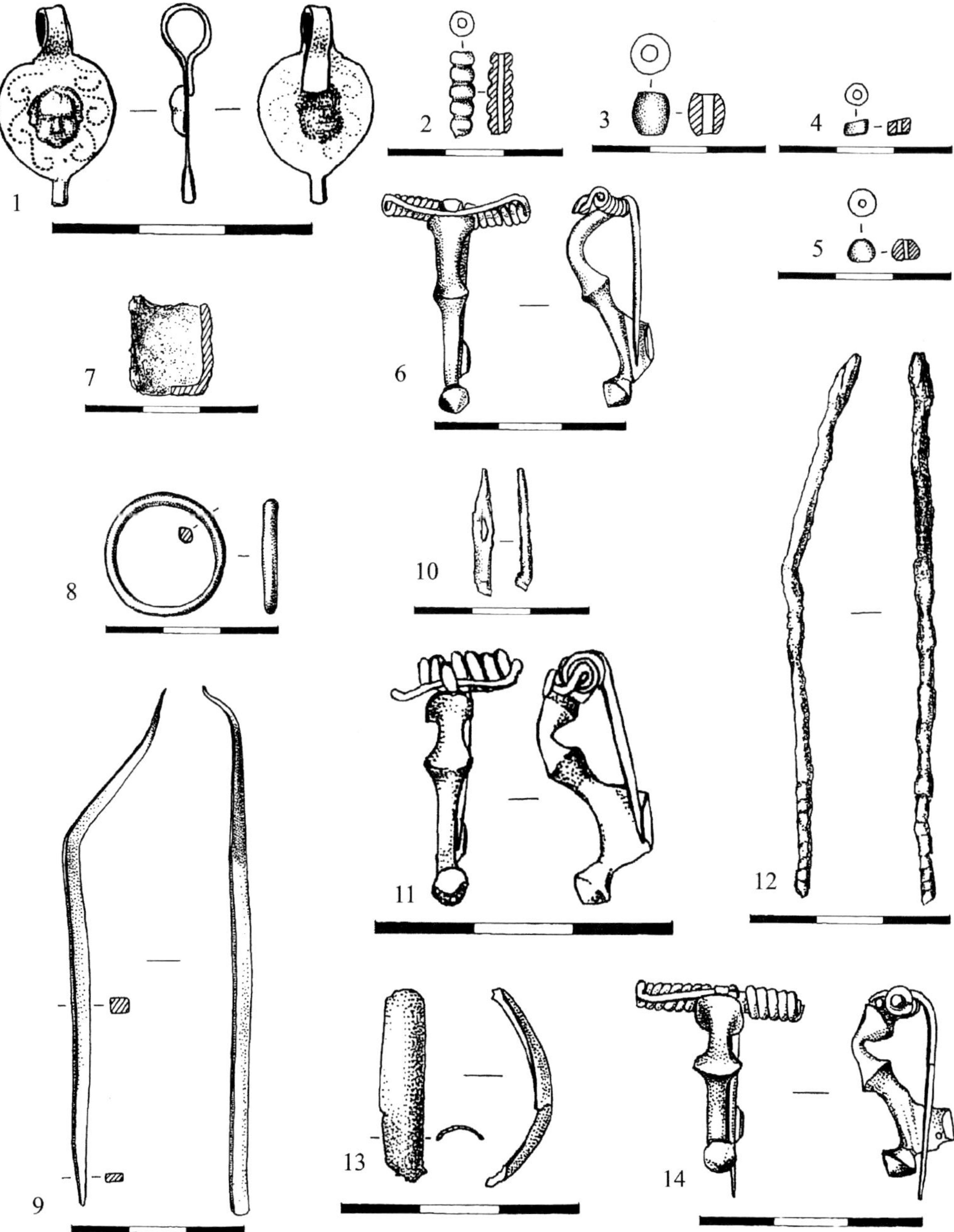

Figure 5.5. Hunedoara – Grădina Castelului (Hunedoara County). Artefacts derived from Grave numbers 8 (1–7), 9 (8), 10 (9), 11 (10–12), 12 (13 and 14). Objects made of gilded silver (1), glass (2–5), bronze (6, 8, 9, 11 and 14), iron (7, 10 and 12) and silver (13) (after Sîrbu et al. *2006). The scale bars are divided into centimetres.*

ing would tend to suggest that they had not accompanied him on the funerary pyre. The weapons comprised a curved dagger and spear head, but the grave good inventory also included a little bead, two items resembling round chain links, two fragmented clay cups and two decorated bone objects.

The site of Grădina Castelului appears to have held special significance and apparently votive deposits of both arefacts and animal remains have been recovered from certain areas of the site. The southern and southwestern sections yielded seven isolated clusters of objects. It is not possible to attribute the clusters to particular individuals but it is highly probable that they were in some way connected to the people who had been buried at the site. The northern and northwestern sectors of the sites produced several clusters of animal bones (bovines and caprovines etc.) that look like the remains of food. Some of these deposits also included rare fragments of Dacian pottery or fragments of children's skulls.

The area of the site where the skeletons were buried did not show any signs of habitation or other domestic activities. This may suggest that the pottery sherds and groups of animal bones may have originated as a result of funerary rituals. The dominant position of the plateau in the landscape would tend to suggest that it is unlikely they had become incorporated into the site accidentally, as a result of natural factors. It is more likely, that this situation arose because of intentional human actions since there is an ancient deep ravine positioned between the settlement of that time and the plateau with the human burials.

To summarise, there are four different kinds of deposit at Hunedoara – Grădina Castelului:

- Inhumed children (most of the deposits).
- Children's inhumations with grave goods.
- Artefact deposits.
- Animal bone deposits.

The inhumation burials at Grădina Castelului resemble those found in standard tombs where the dead have been deposited with care and the repertoire of associated grave goods was rich – particularly fibulae and jewelry, but also weapons. The burials are also similar to the non-funerary deposits described earlier in the paper – the majority of them are those of children; no set body positions or orientation have been followed and in some cases isolated body parts were present (Sîrbu *et al.* 2006, 187–207).

Possible Interpretations

It is clear that we must be very cautious with our interpretations because the phenomenon of child burial is very complex, we do not have sufficient data from the field and as yet very few anthropological analyses have been undertaken. In addition, the adolescent and adult skeletons that are often recovered from the same contexts as those of the infants must be considered. It is necessary to compare the children's burials with apparently ordinary contemporary funerary findings to gain a better understanding of the similarities and differences between these burials. In addition, there are no written sources and no iconographical representations that can help elucidate the nature of these children's burials.

Collections of child inhumations are no stranger to several peoples and epochs, and the different traditions and reasons behind them have yielded both similarities and particularities (Mahieu 1982–83, 137–54; d'Aude 1995; Fabre 1995, 403–14). It would be outside the scope of the current paper to go beyond Thracian discoveries, and only brief mention will be made of relevant findings from their contemporary neighbouring peoples.

Fourth to Third Centuries BC

The situation is most straightforward for the fourth to third centuries BC as there are numerous ordinary necropoli which can be compared with the child inhumations. There are only six child burials with some 13–14 individuals for this period, all of which originate from either settlements or isolated pits. At Berea there is a somewhat 'macabre pit' in which 16 skeletons were discovered. Some of the individuals were complete, but with the bones not in correct anatomical order, and others were missing bones or displayed signs of violence. Four children's skeletons had been buried separately, but there were also children within the 'macabre pit' along with the remains of men, women and adolescents. It has been assumed that the individuals buried within the pit had been the victims of a conflict between the Dacians and the Celts since the pit was located at the periphery of a Dacian settlement (Zirra 1980, 68–9, fig. 56/1–2).

The isolated post-cranial bones of a child were recovered from within a pit at Căscioarele. They had been positioned near the skulls of a man and a young girl who were considered to have been deliberately arranged in a sexual position and were interpreted as a sacrificial burial (Sîrbu 1993, 88; Figure 5.6). Two other remarkable pits have been discovered from this period – one at Celei, which contained the remains of three children, and the other at Orlovka, where the remains of two children and an adult were found (Sîrbu 1993, 95–6).

A total of 2000 tombs are known from the period, either in necropoli or as isolated burials. More than 95% of the burials are cremations, most of which are contained within urns. The few inhumation burials are largely those of adults whose remains are located within wealthy tumular graves, although there are also some children's graves (5%) (Sîrbu 2002, 376–7). The only exception is the Stelnica necropolis, where the number of inhumations of men, women and children, is almost equal to the number of cremations (Conovici and Matei 1999, 99–144).

When all of their characteristics are taken into consideration, it is possible to suggest that the burials of children in non-funerary contexts from this period are not ordinary graves. They would rather appear to represent the burials of deliberately selected individuals – the reasons for which are hard to decipher. It should also be considered possible that they represent human sacrifices.

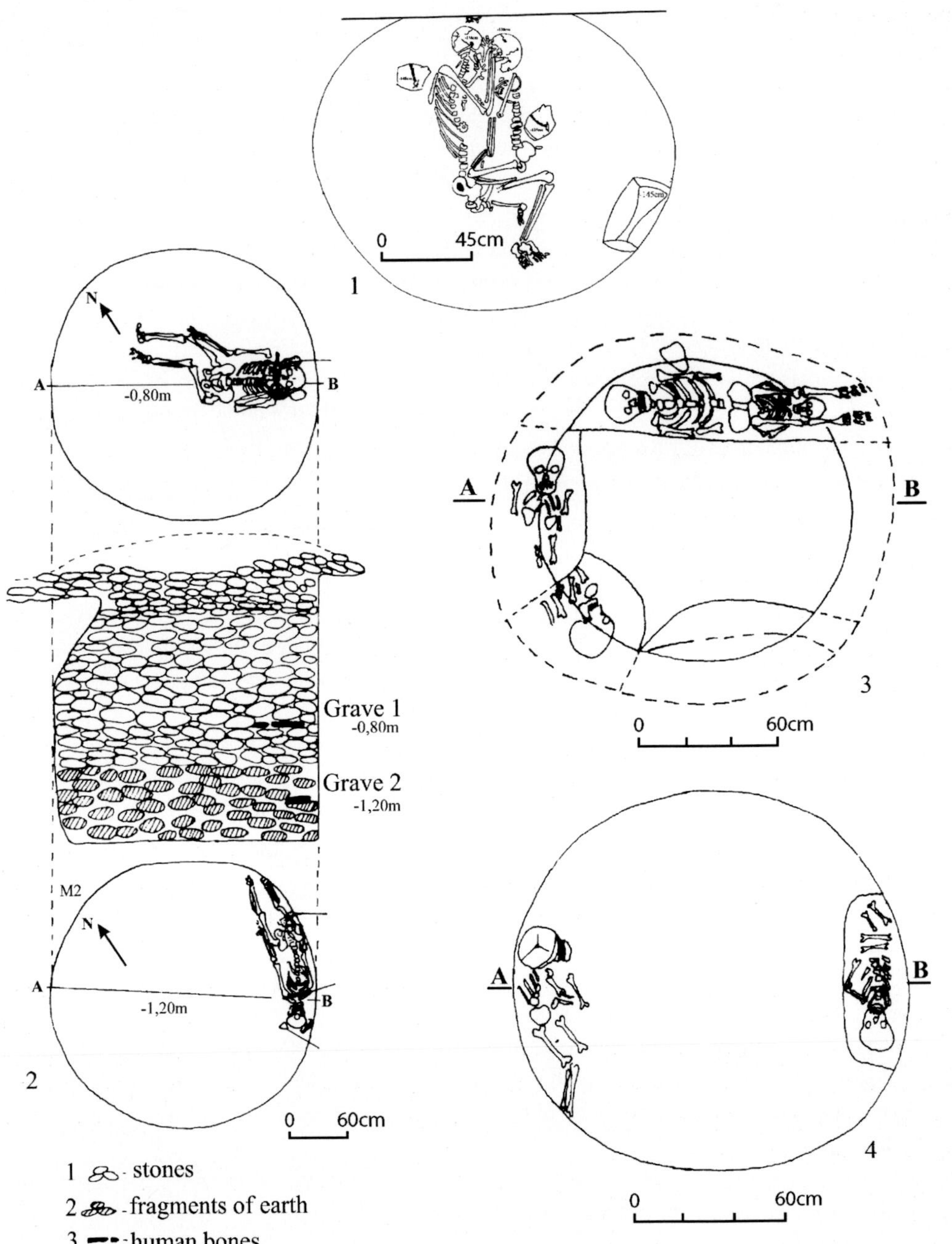

Figure 5.6. Children's inhumations in the settlements of Căscioarele (1), Ocnița (2) and Brad (3 and 4) (after Ursachi 1980–82; Berciu 1983; Sîrbu 1993).

Second Century BC to First Century AD

The situation is much more complicated for the second century BC to the first century AD, when there are very few ordinary graves available for comparative purposes and many more and varied skeletons recovered from non-funerary contexts. While the common funerary vestiges were drastically diminishing, the non-cremated human bones in non-funerary contexts (settlements, isolated pits, 'fields of pits') appear to have been significantly increasing. There are approximately 25 discoveries associated with some 200 individuals – children, adolescents, men and women – from this period (Sîrbu 1997, 196, fig. 1). It is also worth noting that specialised analyses have been made on bone assemblages recovered from settlements of this period, which has resulted in the identification of isolated human bones from different parts of the body, in particular the proximal or distal ends of the limbs, the cranium, and the mandible.

Isolated graves and necropoli are known only in the hinterland of the Dacian territory, in certain areas and following contacts with other populations. In southwestern Romania, there are 40 discoveries (most of which were fortuitous) with some 70 burials either isolated or in small groups (Sîrbu and Rustoiu 1999, 77–91). It is only possible to refer to a true necropolis in one case – Spahii (Gherghe 1978, 15–31). All of the burials at this site are flat cremation tombs, the majority of which are located within pits. The funerary inventory consists of spear and javelin heads, swords, daggers, shields, bridles, jewelry, clothing accessories and the occasional pottery vessel. The characteristics of the burials would tend to suggest that they were warrior graves, probably those of knights, and they are dated to between 170/160 BC and 50 BC. There is no information as to how the remainder of the population was treated in death. Indeed, for a period of one and a half centuries (50 BC – AD 106) in this region there is no evidence of any specific funerary remains. When the evidence from Padea-Spahii was compared to the settlement burial evidence it was concluded that the individuals were Dacian warriors, but we cannot rule out the presence of isolated Scordiscian Celts (Sîrbu and Arsenescu 2006, 163–86). In conclusion, the presence of regular Dacian tombs in the Padea-Spahii group can be considered a result of Scordiscian influence.

Only in northwestern Romania, in the tumular and flat cremation necropolis of Zemplin, would it appear that the Dacians continued their traditional funerary customs during this period with its general 'lack of tombs'. It is possible, however, that the presence of graves from the Germanic Przeworsk Culture is indicative of external influences (Budinský-Krička and Lamiova-Schmiedlova 1990, 245–354). On the other hand, in the northeastern part of the Dacian territory, the Upper Dniester Valley, the Lipica group continued, during the first and second centuries AD, to bury their dead according to their traditional customs. The remains were interred in tumular or flat graves and were either cremated or inhumed, although the latter rite has been particularly used for adults. It is interesting to note that a lot of the burials in this area also seem to belong to the Germanc Przeworsk Culture (Čigilik 1975, 70–8).

The only clear funerary remains for the entire period are the cremation tumular graves assigned, on the basis of the grave goods, to the Dacian warrior aristocracy. Here too, however, number of important changes may be observed (Vulpe 1976, 193–215; Moscalu 1977, 329–40; Babeş 1988, 5–8; Sîrbu 1993, 22–3, 71–4). The funerary customs became degraded while the associated grave goods became poorer and even disappeared. In addition, one could say that over time the tradition of using tumuli for burials 'migrated' from the south-west (datable to the 1st century BC) to the east (datable to the 1st century AD).

From this brief presentation of the normal funerary findings, it is clear they do not illustrate the treatment of the majority of the Dacian population, over the entire habitation area, during the three centuries prior to the Roman conquest. It is difficult to ascertain whether there is a 'Geto-Dacian phenomenon', with its own origin, or some thing that developed as a consequence of foreign influences – similarities have been found in groups throughout the Celtic World from as far apart as Central Europe and southwestern England (Waldhauser 1979, 124–56; Wilson 1981, 127–69). Nevertheless, we consider the idea of external Celtic influence as being less probable since the earliest manifestations of the phenomenon are known from the late third and early second centuries BC, in the outer Carpathian region, where there are no Celtic discoveries.

The remains of men, women, adolescents and children have been recovered from non-funerary contexts, even the so-called 'macabre pits' dating from the earliest Iron Age, particularly in the Babadag Culture of the Low Danube region (tenth to eighth centuries BC). The 'fields of pits' date from the fifth to the third centuries BC and are known from the right bank of the Danube, mainly in the southern Balkans, although they also date from the second to the first centuries BC (Bonev and Alexandrov 1996, 39–41, fig. 8; Tonkova 1997, 592–611; 2003, 479–505; Georgieva 2003, 313–22).

So that is how one can presently interpret the findings that are referred to as 'non-cremated human bones in non-funerary contexts'. These findings are clearly not ordinary burials – there are quite a few finds of isolated bones and skeleton parts; the complete skeletons are often buried in unusual positions; many of them are children; there are no old people (Senilis – more than 60 years old) and there are no patterns of orientation or body position or traditional inventories of grave goods (Babeş 1988, 13–16; Sîrbu 1993, 31–6).

Trying to decipher the reasons behind such major changes in funerary beliefs and practices or explanations for the special treatment of certain individuals is no easy task. Sometimes, there is enough evidence to suggest that the burials represent human sacrifices or ritual inhumations. Certain human remains – isolated human bones or skeleton parts recovered from inside settlement boundaries or in nearby pits – can be explained as the result of exposure/decomposition practices (Sîrbu 1997, 199–201). Further field observations and anthropological examinations might be able to elucidate more about the nature of these burials.

Children represent over 60% of the inhumations and for them too, the motivations that lay behind each burial may be different. Complete skeletons of children associated with fragments of clothing and carefully deposited beneath houses or in nearby pits could be considered as ritual inhumations, deeply rooted in Thracian society. The care for premature babies and their burial under or near the house is a well known phenomenon, in different times and among different populations (Mahieu 1982–83, 137–54; d'Aude 1995; Fabre 1995, 403–14), and the discoveries made in the Dacian World confirm it (Sîrbu 2001, 323–34). On the other hand, it would seem to be the case, when the remains of several children are recovered from a single pit, with the bones in unusual positions or showing signs of violence, then human sacrifice is the most appropriate explanation. It should be remembered that a violent death may not always leave evidence on skeletal remains and that some of these young individuals could have died as a result of drowning, strangulation, or poisoning.

It is worth mentioning that we are not aware of the remains of children having been deposited in settlements or nearby pits with domestic contents. It is interesting to note that inhumations of children from before (fifth to third centuries BC) or after (second to third centuries AD) the time under study display different features. As mentioned before, there are not many cases of inhumation (below 5% of the total) during the fifth to third centuries BC and the majority of these are adults. The few children's graves that do exist are in flat necropoli, and have poor inventories of grave goods or none at all (Protase 1971, 76–82; Sîrbu 1993, 41–2). These necropoli also include the cremated remains of children, but the lack of anthropological analysis means that it is not possible to specify the number of individuals, their ages at death, or suggest why they were deposited in non-funerary contexts (settlements or pits).

The situation is clearer when it comes to the province of Dacia and the free Dacians during the second to third centuries AD. There are no child inhumations outside necropoli and no 'macabre pits' (Sîrbu 1993, 35). There is only one exception to this rule, namely a newborn baby who was deposed in a garbage pit inside a *villa rustica* (Roman farm) from Seusa (Sonoc *et al.* 2005, 121–38). In addition, inhumation appears to have been practiced almost exclusively for children – only ten of 250 inhumation burials of the free Dacians in the Eastern Carpathians were those of adults (Bichir 1973, 29–44; Ioniță and Ursachi 1988, 84–9; Sîrbu 1993, 43–4). The proportions are approximately the same for those under Roman rule – 112 out of 116 inhumations were those of children (Sîrbu 1993, 45). Although children's inhumations existed both before and after the second century BC to the first century AD, they were never so numerous, located in such a variety of contexts and connected with a distinct lack of ordinary burials.

Conclusions

To conclude, the more the Romans dominated their territory, the more the Dacian populations appear to have returned to normal funerary practices, both inside and outside the province of Dacia. At the same time traces of possible human sacrifices and ritual burials disappeared (Sîrbu 1993, 35–6). After analysing all the funerary remains, it is possible to suggest that the Romans had overturned the Dacian priests responsible for these earlier belief systems. All of the Dacian sanctuaries, without exception, appear to have been demolished either by the Dacians themselves, or by the Roman army, and there is no trace of any cultic activity after the Roman conquest of Dacia (Sîrbu 2006, 80–2).

References

Andrițoiu, I. and Rustoiu, A. 1997. *Sighişoara-Wietenbereg. Descoperirile preistorice şi aşezarea dacică.* Bucureşti: Bibliotheca Thracologica XXIII.

Babeş, M. 1988. Descoperirile funerare şi semnificația lor în contextul culturii geto-dace clasice. *Studii şi Cercetări de Istorie Veche şi Arheologie* 39, 3–32.

Babeş, M., Motzoi-Chicideanu, Măgureanu, D., Sîrbu, D. and Matei, S. 2005. Cârlomăneşti, com. Verneşti, jud. Buzău. Punct: Cetățuie, pp. 107–9 in Angelescu M. V., Oberlander-Târnoveanu I. and Vasilescu, F. (eds), *Cronica Cecetărilor Arheologice din România 2004*. Bucureşti: S.C.DAIM P.H. s.r.l.

Bichir, M. 1973. *Cultura Carpică.* Bucureşti: Editura Academiei.

Bonev, Al. and Alexandrov, G. 1996. *Bagačina. Selišče ot Kăsnata, Kamenno – Medna Epoha i Trakijski Kultov Centăr (III – I Hiljadoletie pr. Xp.)*. Montana: Polimona.

Budinský-Krička, V. and Lamiová-Schmiedlova, M. 1990. A Late 1st century BC–1st century AD cemetery at Zemplin. *Slovenská Archeológia* 38, 245–354.

Čigilik V. M. 1975. *Naselennja Verh'ogo Podnistrov'ja Pershv Stolit'nčesoj ery.* Kiev: Naukova Dumka.

Comşa, E. 1972. Contribuție la riturile funerare din secolele II–I î.e.n. din sud-estul Olteniei (Mormintele de la Orlea). *Apulum, Acta Musei Apulensis* 10, 65–78.

Conovici, N. and Matei, Gh. 1999. Necropola getică de la Stelnica-Grădiştea Mare (jud. Ialomița). Raport general pentru anii 1987–1996. *Materiale şi Cercetări Arheologice, Serie Nouă* 1, 99–144.

d'Aude, S. 1995. Nouveau-nés et nourrissons Gallo-Romains, pp. 9–146 in Duday, H., Laubenheimer, F. and Tillier, A.-M. (eds), *Annales Littéraires de l'Université de Besançon* (Centre de Recherches d'Histoire Ancienne, vol. 144). Besançon.

Duday, H., Laubenheimer, F. and Tillier A.-M. 1995. Sallèles-d'Aude. Nouveau-nés et nourrissons Gallo-Romains, pp. 9–146 in *Annales Littéraires de l'Université de Besançon* (Centre de Recherches d'Histoire Ancienne vol. 144). Paris: Les Belles Lettres.

Dupoi V. and Sîrbu, V. 2001. *Incinta dacică fortificată de la Pietroasele-Gruiu Dării, Județul Buzău* (I). Buzău: Editura Alpha.

Fabre, V. 1995. L'inhumation des enfants en milieu domestique comme critère d'identification culturelle, pp. 403–14, in Duday, H. and Laubenheimer, F. (eds), *L'Identité des Populations Archéologiques* (Actes de XIV Rencontre Internationale d'Archéologie et d'Histoire d'Antib). Besançon: Édition APDCA, Sophia Antipolis.

Georgieva, R. 2003. Sépultures insolites de Thrace (fin du IIe–Ier mill. av. J.-C.). *Thracia* 15, 313–22.

Gherghe, P. 1978. Cercetările arheologice de salvare efectuate în necropola şi aşezarea geto-dacicăde la Turburea-Spahii. *Litua* 1, 15–31.

Horedt, K. and Seraphim, C. 1971. *Die Prähistorische Ansiedlung auf Wietenberg, bei Sighişoara-Schaburg.* Bonn.

Ioniță, I. and Ursachi, V. 1988. *Văleni. O mare necropolă a dacilor liberi.* Iaşi: Editura Junimea.

Mahieu, E. 1982–83. Foetus et nouveau-nés préhistoriques: études et problèmes d'interprétation. *Bulletin du Musée d'Anthropologie Préhistorique de Monaco* 28, 137–54.

Moscalu, E. 1977. Sur les rites funéraires des Géto-Daces de la Plaine du Danube. *Dacia (Nouvelle Série), Revue d'Archéologie et d'Histoire Ancienne* 21, 329–40.

Nicolăescu-Plopşor, D. and Rişcuţia, C. 1969. Caracterizarea antropologică şi morfologică a scheletelor din complexul funerar de la Orlea. *Revista Muzeelor* 1, 69–73.

Pop, H. and Matei, Al. V. 2001. Măgura Moigradului, zonă sacră (sec. I î.. Hr.) şi aşezare dacică fortificată (sec. I d. Hr.), pp. 253–77 in Crişan V., Florea G., Gheorghiu G., Iaroslavschi E. and Suciu, L. (eds), *Studii de Istorie Antică. Omagiu Profesorului Ioan Glodariu.* Deva: Astra.

Protase, D. 1971. *Riturile funerare la daci şi daco-romani.* Bucureşti: Editura Academiei.

Sîrbu, V. 1986. Rituels et pratiques funéraires des Géto-Daces (IIe siècle av. n. è.–Ier siècle de n. è.). *Dacia (Nouvelle Série), Revue d'Archéologie et d'Histoire Ancienne* 30, 91–108.

Sîrbu, V. 1993. *Credinţe şi practici funerare, religioase şi magice în lumea geto-dacilor.* Brăila-Galaţi: Editura Porto-Franco.

Sîrbu, V. 1997. Sacrifices humains et pratiques funéraires insolites dans l'aréal thrace du Hallstatt et La Tène, pp. 193–221 in Simion, G. and Jugănaru, G. (eds), *Actes du Colloque International, Premier âge du Fer aux Bouches du Danube et dans les Régions Autour de la Mer Noire,* Tulcea, 1993. Bucureşti: Arti Grafiche Giacone Romania SA.

Sîrbu, V. 2001. Sacrifices et dépôts d'hommes et d'animaux dans/sous les demeures dans le monde Thrace, pp. 323–34 in Draşovean, F. (ed.), *Festchrift für Gheorghe Lazarovici, Zum 60.* Geburtstag : Timişoara.

Sîrbu, V. 2002. Funeral and sacrificial beliefs and practices with the Geto-Dacians (5th c. BC – 1st c. AD), pp. 374–93 in Boşnakov, K. and Boteva, D. (eds), *Sbornic v čest na Prof. Margarita Tačeva.* Sofia: Sv. Kliment Ohridski.

Sîrbu, V. 2003. *Funerary Archaeology and Sacrifices: A Unifying Terminology (dictionary, lexis, branching).* Brăila: Editura Istros.

Sîrbu, V. 2006. *Man and Gods in the Geto-Dacian World.* Braşov: Editura C2 Design.

Sîrbu, V. and Arsenescu, M. 2006. Dacian settlements and necropolises in Southwestern Romania (2nd c. B.C.–1st c. A.D.), pp. 163–86 in Luca, S. A and Sîrbu,V. (eds), *Proceedings of the 7th International Colloquium of Funerary Archaeology*, Sibiu, 17 October 2005. Sibiu: Editura ALTIP.

Sîrbu, V. and Rustoiu, A. 1999. Découvertes funéraires géto – daces du sud – ouest de la Roumanie (±150 – ±50 av. J.-C.), pp. 77–91 in Vasić, M. (ed.), *Le Djerdap/Les Portes de Fer à la deuxième moitié du Premier Millénaire av. J.-Ch. jusqu'aux Guerres Daciques.* Kolloquium in Kladovo-Drobeta-Turnu Severin (September–October 1998). Beograd: Grafomarket.

Sîrbu, V., Matei, S. and Dupoi, V. 2005. *Incinta Dacică Fortificată de la Pietroasa Mică-Gruiu Dării, com. Pietroasele, jud. Buzău* (II). Buzău: Alpha MDN.

Sîrbu, V., Luca, S. A., Roman, C., Purece, S. and Diaconescu, D. 2006. Dacian settlement and children necropolis of Hunedoara. A unique discovery in the Dacian World. Archaeological approach, pp. 187–207 in Luca, S. A and Sîrbu, V. (eds), *Proceedings of the 7th International Colloquium of Funerary Archaeology*, Sibiu, 17 October 2005. Sibiu: Editura ALTIP.

Sîrbu, V., Luca, S. A., Roman, C., Purece, S., Diaconescu, D. and Cerişer, N. 2007. *Vestigiile dacice de la Hunedoara/The Dacian Vestiges in Hunedoara.* Sibiu: Editura ALTIP.

Sonoc, Al. Gh., Ciută, M.-M. and Gall, S. S. 2005. Eine kindesbeerdigung im fundort von Şeuşa -,La cărarea morii' (Gem. Ciugud, Kr. Alba), pp. 121–38 in Gaiu, C. and Găzdac, C. (eds), *Fontes Historiae. Studia in Honorem Demetrii Protase.* Bistrita-Cluj-Napoca: Accent.

Tonkova, M. 1997. Un champ de fosses rituelles des Ve–IIIe s. av. J.-C. près de Glédacevo, Bulgarie du Sud, pp. 592–611 in Roman, P. (ed.), *The Thracian World at the Crossroads of Civilisations I. Proceedings of the Seventh International Congress of Thraco*logy, Mangalia-Tulcea- Bucharest. Bucharest: Vavila Edinf SRL.

Tonkova, M. 2003. Late Iron Age pit-sanctuaries in Thrace: the contribution of the studies at Gledaceco. *Thracia* 15, 479–504.

Ursachi, V. 1980–82. Rituri şi ritualuri de înmormântare la populaţia dacică din cetatea de la Brad, com. Negri, judeţul Bacău. *Memoria Antiquitatis, Acta Musei Petrodavensis* 12–14, 105–51.

Vulpe, Al. 1976. La nécropole tumulaire gète de Popeşti. *Thraco-Dacica* 1, 193–211.

Waldhauser, I. 1979. Beitrag zum studium der keltischen Siedlungen oppida und Gräbefelder in Böhmen, pp. 117–56 in *Les Mouvements Celtiques du Ver au Ier Sièle Avant Notre Ere.* Paris.

Wilson, C. E. 1981. Burials within settlements in southern Britain during the Pre-Roman Iron Age. *Bulletin of the Institute of Archaeology, London* 18, 129–69.

Zirra, V. 1980. Locuiri din a doua epocă a fierului în nord-vestul României (Aşezarea contemporană cimitirului La Tène de la Ciumeşti şi habitatul indigen de la Berea, jud. Satu Mare). *Studii şi Comunicări, Muzeul Judeţean Satu Mare, Satu Mare* 4, 39–84.

6. Aspects of Deviant Burial in Roman Britain

Alison Taylor

Abstract

Burials in Roman Britain followed a variety of rites derived from native, European, Classical and Eastern traditions. These mostly demonstrate respect and care for the corpse together with a desire to keep burials undisturbed and well away from settlements. However, there is evidence for different attitudes to small numbers of the dead. This evidence includes sacrifice, infanticide, execution, mutilation after death, disinterment, and fear of ghosts and revenants. In the archaeological record we commonly recognise decapitated, prone, controlled and mutilated skeletons. Can we link this physical evidence with attitudes and behaviour we would not expect in a normal burial context? This paper uses mixed (and admittedly rather random) sources to look at various ways that we might. It dismisses some as unlikely, but in accepting that superstitious fear of ghosts and witches is probably the most common explanation, it is also argued that no single explanation will fit all. It is the archaeologist's job to leave twenty-first-century preconceptions behind and to consider many possibilities.

Introduction

The Romans are often used as a byword for civilization. Few would argue with their military success, architectural achievements, economic efficiency or literary merits, but why should we also expect humane or rational treatment of fellow human beings? Nothing in the written texts, even though written by Romans, leads us to expect high standards in this respect (e.g. Caesar's accounts of the fate of prisoners of war and non-combatants during the Gallic Wars). Other great civilizations of the Mediterranean World, including Greece, accepted, usually without criticism, practices such as human sacrifice, macabre execution ceremonies, infanticide and postmortem manipulation of human remains, just as scholars of the Iron Age say we must recognise in the archaeology of that period. Classicists seem to have few problems with accepting that the Romans were as violent, vindictive and plain superstitious as any other culture, but modern archaeologists may go to great lengths to avoid explanations for anomalous burials that touch on attitudes we might regard as deviant in our world. The objective of this paper is to look at some of the possible explanations that may account for the evidence we observe in Roman burial records.

Firstly, we need to remember that the keynote for normal Roman burials from the first through to the fourth century was care for the integrity of the body, whether in a thorough cremation or protected inhumation, and concern for future well-being, especially on the immediate postmortem journey. This is expressed in provision of food, drink, lamps, money for the fare and boots for a long walk. Healthy respect for the dead included keeping burials outside urban areas and the use of secure coffins to ensure peace and a hygienic environment for the living. Cremation, often urned, as the normative rite, was succeeded by neatly laid-out bodies, usually wrapped in shrouds and often interred in coffins. A few burials, however, show a different and darker attitude to corpses. These have often been written off as careless but we know, for example, from work in Rome that the poor and those who did not deserve formal burial were summarily dealt with. According to Valerie Hope (2000, 110–11) many hundreds each year were at best just dumped in communal pits, but most were left exposed for scavenging animals and official street-cleaners to dispose of. This is in contrast to those I would categorise as 'deviant' since these tend to be careful and deliberate, to follow patterns and to include surprising levels of violence.

Such burials include indications of human sacrifice, execution, *poena post mortem* (punishment after death), which is often linked to the 'triple death' phenomenon, fear of ghosts, a cult of relics, and infanticide. In archaeological terms, 'deviant' forms of burial are apparent as decapitation, prone burial, unusually secure graves, signs of unusual violence unconnected with warfare, and dismembered remains (especially heads).

My interest in deviant burials arose from looking for meanings behind the normative rites, especially what they can tell us about religious beliefs, and realising that some did not follow accepted patterns, even in the most highly Romanised contexts (Taylor 2001). Unfortunately, though the evidence is plentiful, it is almost always ambiguous. Archaeologists will usually know if there is something unusual, but providing a definitive explanation is a bit trickier. Furthermore, the categories are not watertight – how should we classify the sacrifice of prisoners of war or criminals who face death anyway, can we separate normal infanticide from babies who died in religious contexts, and surely gladiators were a barely sanitised version of human sacrifice? Can archaeologists ever differentiate heads displayed for abuse and punishment from those preserved for veneration? Accepting that archaeology rarely deals in unambiguity, it is worth questioning why few burials depart so blatantly from the norm.

Human Sacrifice

Human sacrifice is well documented in Iron Age Europe, and also throughout the Classical World. Miranda Aldhouse Green (2001), as part of wider studies of this phenomenon, documents traditional sacrifice in Etruscan and Roman traditions BC, as well as in many Mediterranean cultures such as Greece (with notable examples, such as Iphigenia, sacrificed by her father before he led the Greeks to Troy; Achilles' own sacrifices of Trojans at the burial mound of Patroclus; and a sixth-century BC Greek vase which Aldhouse Green (2001, 31) illustrates, depicting a Trojan princess having her throat cut over the tomb of Achilles). Gladiatorial displays and ritualised execution of prisoners of war are linked with this tradition, without hints of disapproval, and the sacrifice of Iphigenia was apparently only upsetting for her mother.

Burial alive is occasionally suggested for some strange graves, especially if large stones have been dropped on the back or there are other signs of coercion. This can be seen as punishment or sacrifice. There are certainly parallels for this amongst the civilised people of the ancient world. Herodotus described burial alive as 'the Persian custom' (de Selincourt 1954, 479), and the Persians heavily influenced the Greeks as the Greeks did the Romans. The examples he gives are high-born youths (male and female), and the reasons for the sacrifice vary. In some it is undertaken as punishment (even 'for some trifling charge'; de Selincourt 1954, 218), sometimes for good luck (as before the invasion of Greece), or to keep young (Xerxes' ageing wife buried 14 boys alive to persuade the god of the underworld not to take her; de Selincourt 1954, 479). Erring Vestal Virgins could be buried alive as punishment, the idea being that no one was responsible for actually killing them.

In Britain at the time of the Conquest Tacitus and Cassius Dio, as well as Julius Caesar in the century before, tell of sacrifices in the woods and drowning in miry swamps. Methods include burning, strangulation, stabbing, drowning and dismemberment, and sacrifice was used both for propitiation and to tell the future through death throes. Such practices are well known in German and Scandinavian contexts, seen for example on the Danish Gundestrup cauldron and in innumerable bog burials. Victims of such burial were of every age, social class and sex, but an exceptional proportion had a physical impairment of some kind (e.g. Aldhouse Green 2001, 160). Isabella Mulhall's (2005, 108) description of recent Irish bog body discoveries is a graphic confirmation of these issues (see Kelly 2006 for further information).

In Britain human sacrifice was supposed to stop with the Romans. Killing *adults* for religious reasons was actually banned by Augustus throughout the Empire, and was also a special complaint against druids. Although it was officially disapproved of, however, it was certainly not uncommon for the Romans to engage in human sacrifice. Raphael Isserlin (1997) has produced considerable evidence for the existence of human sacrifice in Roman Britain, including direct reference on a curse tablet from Brandon and evidence of several bog bodies with Roman dates. Aldhouse Green (2001) documents some of the increasing evidence for human sacrifice in Roman times, and Richard Turner (1995) describes how bog bodies include examples, such as Lindow III and the body from Grewelthorpe Moor, Yorkshire, that are dated within Roman times. The multiple and excessive violence typically practiced on these bodies reminds us of the 'triple death' phenomenon recognised in Celtic rituals, in Roman Christian martyrdoms, and in other ancient societies, and which may be linked to the 'overkill' we see in decapitated or mutilated Roman burials. Human remains may be found disarticulated in ditches especially around temple complexes and in ritual shafts/wells. At Folly Lane, Verulamium, a boy's defleshed skull, thought to have been exposed on a spike, was recovered from the base of a ritual shaft, along with dog skulls. In addition, a high incidence of stray human bone was noted on the site (Niblett 1999, 319, 415). Certain animals, especially dogs and horses, were defleshed and exposed in similar ways to humans. Ritual shafts positioned around a comparable shrine in Cambridge contained babies buried in rush baskets along with small dogs and shoes (Alexander and Pullinger 1999, 53–7). Such shafts with sacrifices and burials seem to be part of regular contact with the otherworld. Simon Mays (1993) also argues that there is evidence for child sacrifice among the 14 babies at Springhead Temple, Kent; two pairs of decapitated babies by a wayside temple at Ware, Hertfordshire; and perhaps under a fourth-century basilica in York. There are innumerable other infant burials that are arguably foundation sacrifices but could simply be home burials for those who suffered an early but natural death. This evidence from Roman Britain ties in with recognition of 'special deposits' of infants, dogs and horses that Helena Hamerow (2006, 27) recognises as prominent in Anglo-Saxon settlements across the whole of the North Sea Zone 'as well as in Roman and Iron-age Britain: indeed … back to the Bronze Age'.

Infanticide

Infanticide, usually by exposure, was undoubtedly a sad fact of Roman (and Greek and many other cultures') life, regretted by some moralists but accepted in law. Christian church fathers preached against the practice and in AD 374 it was officially banned (for what this was worth) though the need even then was still accepted for poor families on humanitarian grounds. It was apparently regarded rather like modern abortion, an unfortunate necessity, especially for those in difficult circumstances. Simon Mays' (2000) review of the archaeology and history of infanticide (Roman and otherwise) indeed demonstrates the reality that killing unwanted babies at or soon after birth has been practiced on every continent and at every date, whatever the religious objections.

In Roman times it was the father who had the right to decide if a child should be exposed or live. Pliny, in his *Natural History*, states that a child is not fully human until teething and defends infanticide because of a need to limit the population – despite the fact that the Romans were suffering a decline in population (e.g. Shelton 1998, 29). The dramatic rescue by a wolf of the exposed twins, Romulus and Remus, is one of the most famous Roman tales, with the underlying assumption that this was a normal thing to do to babies. There are even private letters such as the Oxyrhynchus Papyri 744 in which the callous instructions 'if it is a girl, expose it' are included in an otherwise affectionate letter written by a husband in Alexandria to his wife, in 1 BC (as quoted in Shelton 1998, 28). Apuleius tells a story involving a man, who when setting out on a journey, ordered his pregnant wife to kill the baby when born if it was a girl (Graves 1950, 257). In this case, the soft-hearted mother smuggled the child to a neighbour and later had her adopted into her son's household, with disastrous results. We usually only hear these tales when there is some extraordinary outcome in later years. As a result there were observable shortages of women in Roman society, even amongst the upper classes. Augustus, for example, legislated on various occasions to encourage an increase in the birth rate (giving priority to consuls with more children was one way), yet had to change laws to allow upper class men to marry freed women because there were not enough girls of their own rank (Shelton 1998, 29).

It is impossible to tell how common this attitude was in Britain, but the evidence is that in urban cemeteries there was a fairly consistent imbalance of sexes, with too many males for a normal population profile (Mays 2000, 184, gives a ratio of 1.46:1 in favour of males, aggregated from 2,400 adults from assorted Romano-British cemeteries). In the countryside girls had more of an economic function and most cemeteries are more evenly balanced. The fourth century coincides with the regular appearance of infant burials in ordinary cemeteries, rather than the home burial that had been the normal practice. However, it was noted at Poundbury, Dorset (Farwell and Molleson 1993), that there were no congenital anomalies that would have been recognised at birth, and thus selective killing of infants was highly likely. In contrast, one particularly careful burial of tiny bones from an embryotomy demonstrates the extreme of a different viewpoint, with an unborn infant apparently regarded in a way that would not be normal in Britain until the late twentieth century. The explanation of female infanticide as inherently unlikely is regularly proposed (e.g. Davison 2000), but alternative explanations such as the burial of women elsewhere and misidentification of the sex of skeletons in this period so far lack archaeological or literary evidence. The predominance of men in Roman towns, however, was compared by Katie Meheux (Richard Reece 2006, pers. comm.) with a similar predominance in Georgian towns. In the latter case the predominance arose because it was necessary for men to move to the urban environment for work purposes. As such, it is possible that a similar phenomenon could also explain the situation during Roman times.

Mutilation after Death

Mutilation of the body after death can be seen as an extra punishment added to execution, or after normal death for some perceived fault, or to prevent ghosts walking. Alternatively, it could have been a ritual reserved for selected members of society, although not chosen for age, sex or particular wealth/poverty, trends which should otherwise be perceptible to archaeologists. Prone burial may also have been seen as a form of punishment, or at least penitence, echoed in the Merovingian King Pepin, who wanted to be buried face down 'for the sins of his fathers' (as quoted in Gilchrist and Sloane 2005, 154).

Poena post mortem, punishment after death, was in fact the worst punishment of all in Imperial Rome and could run to the full panoply of the *damnatio memoriae* whereby the whole memory of the deceased was defiled. This could involve mutilation of facial features on statues and other images, disposal of damaged statues into rivers and eradication of written works, and through attacks on properties. All such acts attempted to prevent the individual's afterlife by destroying their memory – rather a forlorn hope in the cases of emperors, such as Caligula and Nero, who were subject to this fate but who tend to be the ones best remembered. Corpses of serious criminals could be mutilated and dragged to the Tiber or its sewers, or they could be left for dogs to eat – unspeakably awful fates with eternal consequences (discussed in Hope 2000, 104–27).

Decapitation after death was often part of the mutilation and is recorded for example in the cases of the Emperors Elagabalus, Maximin, Maximus and Gallienus as well as various would-be usurpers. So ubiquitous is the phenomenon that a massive compendium of severed heads in Roman literature has been compiled by Keith Jones at the Department of Greek and Latin, Ohio State University (http://omega.cohums.ohio-state.edu/mailing_lists/LATIN-L/2003/04/0000.php). Numerous classical texts demonstrate that decapitation was a common act of mutilation after death as much as it was a form of execution, with recognisable heads being suitable for display and abuse (Hope 2000). Even the respected Cicero's head and hand were put on display for some time (Hope 2000, 113–4). These were evidently not supposed to be exceptional punishments, but rather to degrade their victims to the level of the worst common criminals, for whom such treatment was normal.

Certainly too a cult of the head persisted in Britain as in Gaul, and this includes the most Romanised areas. The topic is widely explored by Anne Ross (e.g. 1974), who remarks that although it was a universal Celtic cult to venerate the head as the seat of the soul (Ross 1974, 162), it was in fact under the Romans that most of the surviving British cult heads originated (Ross 1974, 106). As in Gaul, several cases of bones, especially loose skulls, occur on temple sites, including those in Roman towns. One particularly peculiar find is the top and front of a skull, cut to detach it from the rest of the head and carefully drilled as if for suspension, from Gill Mill, Oxfordshire (Paul Booth 2006, pers. comm.). This was found in ditch fill in a second-century settlement context. We can safely dismiss head-hunting as a motive for decapitated burials, however, for nearly all include the head in the grave. Skulls recovered from non-burial contexts, such as in a legionary ditch outside a fortress gate at Colchester and in a fort ditch at Vindolanda (Loe 2003), however, may well indicate display of the heads of enemy dead.

Throughout human history beheading has been used as an addition to, as well as a means of, execution. The practice carries the heavy symbolism of dehumanisation as well as having been a conveniently portable and dramatic way of proving death in the days before photo-journalism. For the Scythians, for example, Herodotus informs us that it was a case of 'no head, no loot' (de Selincourt 1954, 291). In more modern times we are familiar with great reverence for the heads of saints preserved in Catholic and Orthodox Christian churches, but also with displays of traitors' heads, for example in Tudor England, and macabre internet displays of beheading as a symbol of power and terror during the current conflict in Iraq.

Witchcraft and the Fear of Ghosts

Witches and ghosts, both associated with cemeteries in Roman times as in most cultures (including modern Britain), were much feared. They were closely linked, for witches could commune with, and even temporarily raise, the dead as well as use them for fortune telling (necromancy). Educated opinions might scoff, but from slaves to emperors there was recognition that these were powers that needed control. Ovid describes an annual ritual to dispel ghosts from houses (Ovid, *Fasti: V*). Apuleius has many tales, including one which involved a student exploring Thessaly who ran out of money and agreed to stand guard over a corpse at night to prevent witches gnawing flesh from the dead man's face for use in magical concoctions (Graves 1950, 64). Jock Macdonald (1977, 36) stresses the importance of the fear of ghosts as a driver for Roman burial rituals and the placatory festivals that followed.

Martin Henig (1984, 203) has to admit that the Romans could be guilty of 'the grossest superstition', giving the example of an amphora-burial in London battened down with tiles and pot lids to prevent the ghosts of a mother and child walking. Many 'secure' graves and restrictive forms of burial (see below) are perhaps best explained in this necrophobic way and there certainly seems to be a strong link between these burial rites and the 'vampire burials' for the dangerous dead that Edeltraud Aspöck (this volume) describes from folklore and archaeology in Eastern Europe and which resonate with world wide traditions. Anastasia Tsaliki (2006; this volume) explores issues surrounding the world-wide phenomenon of necrophobia. She concentrates especially on those individuals who were seen as deviant because of particular sorts of sickness or disability or who had suffered a violent death, and demonstrated how this could result in restricting or disabling forms of burial. In a forthcoming paper her discussion of two 'vampire burials' from post-Byzantine Turkey (incidentally, one Christian and one Muslim, demonstrating the irrelevance of official religion in this behaviour) demonstrates how physical disabilities could predispose victims to this treatment (Tsaliki and Takis forthcoming). Elsewhere she demonstrates how the concept of necrophobia has dominated burial customs of the Greek World since the Neolithic period, and can be observed to have had a world-wide impact (Tsaliki 2001). In particular vampirism, a form of necrophobia involving a bloodsucking ghost, has a long tradition in Greece, from Homer to the Greek Orthodox church which, under Slavic influences, accepted folklore legends of the undead corpse, restless because of excommunication, suicide, lack of baptism, lycanthropy (where victims believe they are turned into wolves) or witchcraft. In Scandinavia too the need for the dead to be killed again to restore social order is a common refrain that has been explained by Terje Gansum from Norway. He has provided me with information about saga stories, such as Thorseff Half-foot, where the dead might terrorise the living until dug up and buried elsewhere. New religions such as Christianity increased tensions and problems, which we might easily be seeing in fourth-century Britain (Terje Gansum 2005, pers. comm.).

Execution

The Roman *ius gladii* is taken to mean beheading, although there were plenty of other forms of capital punishment, often involving the greatest possible suffering and degradation (e.g. crucifixion). Beheading was actually quite a privilege if no other torments were included. Among the Gallic martyrs under Verus, Marcus Aurelius' co-Emperor, 'all who appeared to possess Roman citizenship were beheaded and the rest were sent to the beasts' (Eusebius I; Lake 1925, 429). Accounts of the deaths of Christian martyrs are a rather good source for gaining an understanding of execution practices which involve unnecessary violence and overkill and even take us back into the Celtic World of triple death, especially for high born and virtuous youths. During the third century, famous examples include St. Sebastian, who was shot with arrows, beaten on the head and then beheaded, and St. Cecilia (Figure 6.1), who was suffocated/burned in her own bathhouse, stabbed in the breast and then decapitated. She was so virtuous that, on exhumation centuries later, it was reported that her perfectly-preserved body had the head back in place and only a scar remaining, a feat of preservation echoed during exhumations of later saints, especially virginal women such as Aethelthryth (Etheldreda) of Ely and her sister Withburh, both of whom appeared as if sleeping and with 'rosy cheeks' (Fairweather 2005, 59–60, 279–80). Eusebius gives us a run-down of local customs:

> sometimes they were slain with the axe, as was the case with those in Arabia. At other times they had their legs broken – as happened to those in Cappodocia. On some occasions they were suspended on high downwards while a slow fire was kindled beneath ... as in Mesopotamia; on others noses, ears, and hands were mutilated, and other parts of the body cut up – as was done in Alexandria (Eusebius II; Oulton 1923, 287–9).

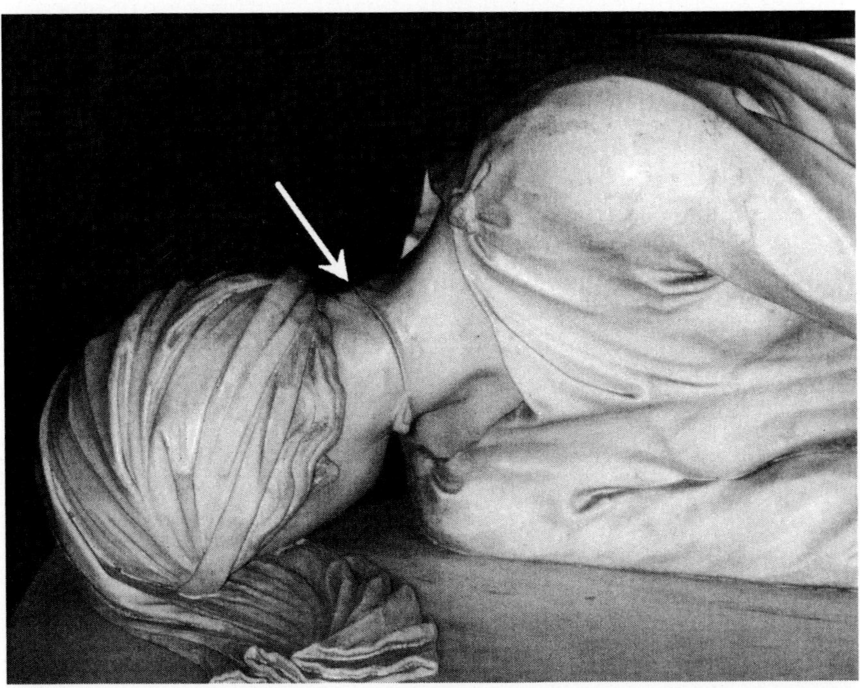

Figure 6.1. St. Cecilia suffered triple death, including decapitation, as a Christian martyr. This replica of the effigy made after her exhumation in the sixteenth century is in the Basilica di Santa Cecilia in Trastevere, Rome, and shows the scar left on her neck (A. Taylor).

Roman Britain of course had the beheading of St. Alban. As part of their punishment criminals were generally left exposed for animals to eat, or were dragged to rivers, however, and thus the evidence will generally be lost to archaeology, whereas decapitated burials are in other respects indistinguishable from normal ones. In the case of martyrs the authorities went to great lengths to prevent bodies being collected by their followers. An example given by Eusebius (I; Lake 1925, 437) runs:

> thus the bodies of the martyrs, after having been exposed and insulted in every way for six days, and afterwards burned and turned to ashes, were swept away by the wicked into the river Rhone which flows nearby, that not even a relic of them might still appear upon the earth.

We know this often failed and the burial places of such bodies became cult centres that then became early churches (St. Albans is a well known British example, and the practice was common in Rome and Gaul). Jesus himself is another example of an execution where the body was, exceptionally, taken for burial within a normal tomb. It is therefore possible that some decapitated or mutilated skeletons were execution victims who were rescued by a devoted family or friends, or simply came under another judicial regime.

In his exploration of Anglo-Saxon deviant burials Andrew Reynolds (1998; forthcoming) shows that decapitated burials of this date are indeed usually executions and postulates that in Early Anglo-Saxon cemeteries 'the possibility that certain offences were punished by beheading, as they were in the middle and late Anglo-Saxon periods, must not be discounted, but even in these instances a superstitious motive seems likely'. In this case we should remain alert to the possibility of execution as an explanation for the more common Roman decapitations and other deviant forms. In fact, his list detailing the characteristics of execution cemeteries – 'prone burials, multiple interments, decapitation, evidence of restraint, shallow and cramped burial and mutilation' – relate closely to Roman practices. Such burials may have grave goods and other normal characteristics, but in many cases liminal aspects 'reveal a geographically widespread application of the concept of burial at the edge of cemeteries and at the limits of clusters of graves usually interpreted as family plots' (Reynolds forthcoming).

Salutary evidence too includes the latest results derived from executed bodies at Sutton Hoo, East Anglia (Carver 2005, 315–59). The bodies exhibit cases of beheading, hanging, binding of feet and wrists, trussing up (in a sack?) and display until the corpse rotted. They date to between the eighth and eleventh centuries and represent judicial killings. Surviving as stains ('sand bodies') and not as skeletons they cannot be compared directly with most excavated evidence, but images of the body positions are a vivid reminder of what we could be looking for (Carver 2005, 330). It is notable that some have coffins and other 'respectful' traits, some are supine and quite normal, and of course they share what was previously a royal burial ground. Of Reynold's (forthcoming) examples of legal executions within a Christian context, a significant number are decapitated, about 30% lie prone, 75% have hands tied behind the back and some are represented by partial bodies. Most are from the usual criminal class – young men – and they were probably also poor as most crimes, even murders, could be paid for with blood money.

Forms of Deviant Burial

Roman prone, headless, bound and secure burials are found in small numbers within many third and fourth-century cemeteries. They appear to be more common in the countryside than towns, rarely form more than a few percent of the buried total and are currently best known in southern and eastern England. They very occasionally occur in earlier contexts such as an example from Cuxton, Kent, associated with pots dating to AD 50–100 (Tester 1963, 81–2), and the decapitated infants which appear to have been foundation deposits discovered within the Springhead temple, also in Kent (Penn 1960, 113). Some large Roman cemeteries in London contain hardly any deviant burials, although recent work by AOC Archaeology in the Roman working class suburb of Southwark has produced some examples which will be discussed below. In their seminal work Harman *et al.* (1981) demonstrate that that both decapitation and prone burial are common in small numbers in cemeteries of the Upper Thames Valley during Romano-British times and that the two rites are connected and sometimes apply to the same individual.

Some rural, probably pagan, cemeteries are now being examined which have a high proportion of deviant forms assimilated amongst normal graves. At Horcott Pit, Fairford, in Oxfordshire excavations undertaken in 2006 demonstrated that 13 (20%) out of 61 burials were prone. One of the individuals was also decapitated, as were five other burials (Paul Booth 2006, pers. comm.). Kempston, Bedfordshire, is a well organised rural example that contained 12 decapitated and 12 prone burials amongst 88 inhumations (Boylston *et al.* 2000). Decapitation victims, one of whom was a child, had modest grave goods and five were in coffins, but the prone burials had no grave goods and only one was buried in a coffin. The latest six decapitations (late fourth century) were also dignified with an individual ditched enclosure around the grave, although a similar enclosed cemetery at Biddenham, about 100 m distant on the opposite side of the river, has only one decapitation and two burials that are prone and crouched, itself a distinctive ritual (Mike Luke 2006 pers. comm.). Philpott (1991, 80) also notes cemeteries at Chignall St. James, Essex, and Winterbourne Down, Wiltshire, where the percentages of decapitated bodies are each around 20%.

The pagan aspect is emphasised at Ashton, Northants, where there were four decapitations amongst backyard burials but none within the large formal cemetery. In highly organised cemeteries such as Poundbury, Dorset, where there is segregation by class and religion, deviant burials only occur in certain areas of the cemetery. For example, only one prone burial was discovered amongst some 1000 individuals buried in the main (probably Christian) cemetery, in addition to just two decapitations, both of whom were mature women. In contrast, outside the main cemetery there was a disorderly layout which included several examples of prone, crouched and decapitated bodies, associated with hob nails and grave goods, as in rural areas (Farwell and Molleson 1993). The late date (fourth century) of the numerous decapitated and prone burials at Kempston, Bedfordshire, shows that nominal Christianity had no effect, even where formalisation of the undertaking process occurred.

Large urban cemeteries, with a high percentage of unusual forms of burial include working-class Bath Gate, Cirencester (see below), and the extreme example of Driffield Road, York, where current excavations are continuing to produce nearly 90% of burials as decapitations (Richard Hall 2006, pers. comm.; see below). Rare burial within walled towns, which is a deviant practice in itself, could have an unusual form, for example, a man in Cambridge who was buried in a sprawled prone position with one of his feet removed and the space covered by a pot sherd (Alexander and Pullinger 1999, 73; Figure 6.2).

Overall, the impression is that decapitated burials are deposited in otherwise normal graves with respect to grave goods, coffins, position in cemetery and body layout. Prone and bodies in otherwise unconventional positions, however, tend to be liminal or located entirely outside cemeteries, have few grave goods and generally display evidence for less respectful treatment (with plenty of exceptions to these generalisations). Though decapitation and prone burial are linked, and can both be evident in a single individual, they appear to be two distinct rites, both a violation of the integrity usually accorded a corpse and both indicating a need for extra control.

There are marked differences too in the precedents and antecedents of prone and decapitated bodies. Despite the well known cult of the head, specifically decapitated bodies

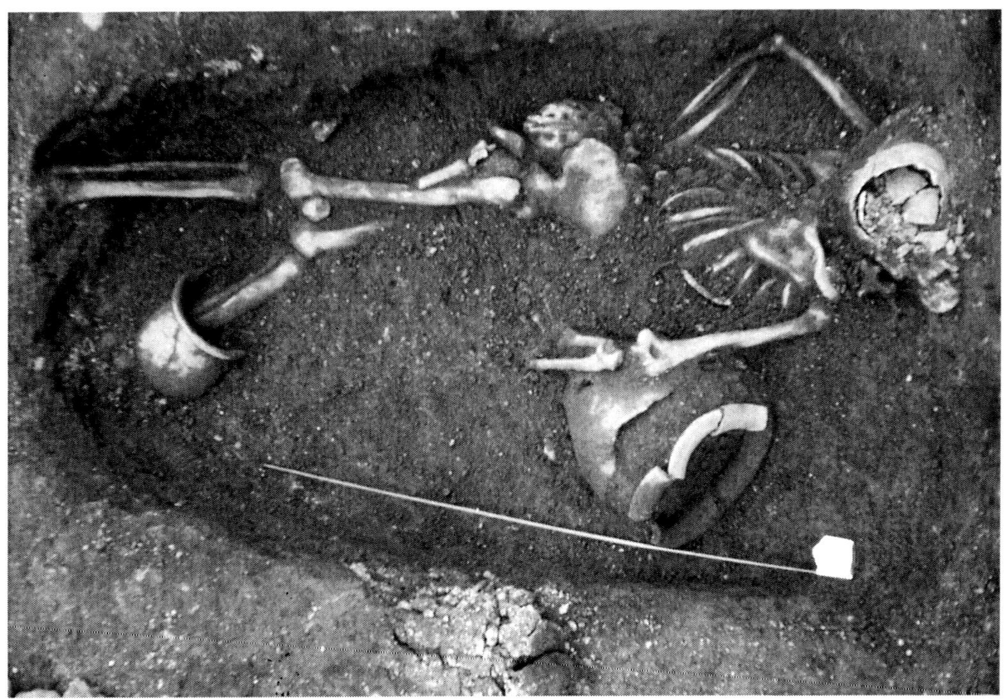

Figure 6.2. A man buried prone within the walled Roman town of Cambridge, with a potsherd where his foot had been removed (copyright Cambridge Antiquarian Society).

do not seem to appear in formal Iron Age graves in Britain (Gerry Wait 2006, pers. comm.) and (*pace* Harman *et al.* 1981) they are scarce in Early Anglo-Saxon cemeteries. Sam Lucy (2000, 75–7) provides evidence of a few fairly reliable cases and the subject is addressed in detail by Andrew Reynolds (forthcoming). Out of the entirety of fifth to seventh century burials in Britain he is able to give 54 possible examples, but in the majority of these cases either the head or the body is simply missing. There are only nine cases where the head is placed near or between the legs in the Roman style. In Later Anglo-Saxon England both decapitation and prone burial seem to be specifically linked to executions (Reynolds 1998; forthcoming; Buckberry, this volume). Despite folk memories for the efficacy of removing heads to lay ghosts, decapitations are rare in Medieval contexts, and these too can sometimes be attributed to executions (Gilchrist and Sloane 2005, 73).

Prone burials, however, occur regularly as sprawled and often mutilated bodies in Iron Age pits and ditches, and in the Early Anglo-Saxon period they are commonly assimilated in normal cemeteries, in small numbers, much as in Roman Britain. The difficulty for archaeologists of explaining these burials in the Anglo-Saxon period are similar to those encountered when dealing with Roman Britain, and again there is no single explanation (Lucy 2000, 80). The impression is that, apart from very occasional examples where live burial is suggested, prone bodies at this time were not treated significantly differently to others in a cemetery. In Later Medieval Britain prone burial is rare, and again cases can be identified as the remains of executed criminals (e.g. at St. Margaret in Combusto, Norwich, where they also had bound hands and might be incorrectly oriented), unbaptised infants, victims of violence or individuals with some abnormality (see Gilchrist and Sloane 2005, 153–4 for examples). This list, leaving nearly all possibilities open, is hardly helpful to those seeking explanations in earlier periods.

Decapitation

Methods

Decapitations, especially those with the head placed between the legs, are often careful and respectful burials within normal cemeteries. The bodies often have cut or chop marks on neck vertebrae, with the top few vertebrae articulated with the skull. Most are front to back and are often described as quite surgical, generally thought to have been carried out after death and not to have been the cause. A few are violent however, with evidence of multiple and/or powerful blows, and may be back to front, although still buried within an otherwise normal cemetery. Sometimes the cutting involved extra effort and care, as for example a case recovered from a cemetery at Baldock where Jacqueline McKinley (1993, 41–4) noted the presence of six blows made by a narrow blade, probably a short sword, all stabbed with precision from the front so that the neck could be snapped off when pushed back. The burial was otherwise normal and quite rich, accompanied with beads, bone pins and finger rings. Anthea Boylston and Charlotte Roberts include a particularly helpful description and discussion of the cemetery at Kempston, Bedfordshire (2000, 241–54), where their forensic analysis was able to prove that cut marks were made at or immediately after death. Some of the blows demonstrated evidence of considerable violence – one blow at the front went through the neck and into the clavicle, and another skeleton had six cuts to the bone, as at Baldock. One man may possibly have died in combat but in others throats were cut with care down to the vertebrae, which were then prised apart to remove the head.

As Richard Reece (2006, pers. comm.) has pointed out, it is impossible to slice neatly through the tissue and hit exactly between the third and fourth cervical vertebrae, and all variations will leave clear cut marks, and so perimortem damage remains the best explanation for the majority of cases. In addition, Harman *et al.* (1981, 167) refer to literary evidence which indicates that the sacrificial victim had their throats cut before the head was removed. Several cases of other injuries to the head, especially the mandibles, are noted by Harman *et al.* (1981, 165) and at Kempston, Bedfordshire, three individuals displayed additional cuts to the mandible which had possibly been attained as a result of throat-cutting. As such, we cannot discount a dark side to some of these burials too, even if the normality otherwise surrounding most decapitations discourages too much lurid interpretation. Modern parallels such as internet evidence from Iraq as well as ancient attitudes suggest we should not be put off by the idea that execution by cutting off a head from the front using a knife was too bloody and brutal to be possible.

Dating

The majority of decapitated burials are Late Roman, although the frequent lack of grave goods makes precise dating difficult. Furthermore, McKinley (2004) has identified three early Roman headless *cremations* at Brougham, Cumbria. Theresa Hawtin (2004), in a thoughtful discussion of decapitation in general, notes other cremation records deficient in skull fragments. It is therefore possible, as she suggests, that the practice of decapitation was always present and only becomes obvious as inhumation became the more common mode of burial. At Kempston it was evident that a small number of decapitations were present within the cemetery in every phase from the mid-third to late fourth century (Boylston *et al.* 2000).

Variations

Philpott's (1991) magisterial summation of evidence for Roman decapitation provides figures which indicate that the vast majority of skulls were placed between the knees and feet or between or beside the feet. Occasionally extra heads are included within otherwise normal burials, such as the recovery of a skull on a girl's knees at Southwark, London (Melikian forthcoming) (Figure 6.3). In some cases the decapitated head was occasionally replaced with something else – for example, an area of burning in a burial at Horcott Pit, Fairford, Oxfordshire (Louise Loe 2006, pers. comm.) and a pot in a burial in Oxford (Bradly *et al.* 2005). In some cases there is no evidence for cutting on the bones and it would seem that the head may have been removed at some stage after the original burial. Quite a few have been discovered in a prone position, and other forms of mutilation are not uncommon in decapitated bodies, such as the amputation of the arms of a woman at Foxton, Cambridgeshire (Price *et al.* 1997, 34) and a man at Alington Avenue, Dorchester (Davies *et al.* 2002, 152). At Dunstable, Bedfordshire, a decapitated woman had her legs chopped, while the foot of a decapitated lame man was removed (Matthews 1981). Similar examples can also be found in the work of Harman *et al.* (1981, 165).

Among unusual funerary practices noted at Guilden Morden, Cambridgeshire, were the charred remains of a decapitated probable male. The individual's arms and lower legs also appear to have been removed and his skeleton was discovered lying in thick layers of charcoal. The latter finding was interpreted as an indication that his body had been burnt *in situ*. A nearby burial contained a disabled woman whose head had been severed as a consequence of a sideways cut and placed at her feet (Figure 6.4). Another woman from the cemetery had her head removed in a similar way and placed in her lap. It is too tempting to quote Lethbridge's (1936, 117) own words:

> I suggest, though this may appear fanciful, that this lame woman had been decapitated after her death to ensure that her spirit – perhaps bad-tempered owing to her infirmity – should not walk and haunt her relatives. The method of laying a ghost by decapitating the corpse was of course well known in later times, and is often mentioned in the sagas … one wonders if both of these women had been witches.

Figure 6.3. An extra skull placed on a girl's knees in Southwark, London (copyright AOC Archaeology).

A decapitated man had been buried prone, with his arms crossed beneath him 'as if bound' (Lethbridge 1936, 109–20). This is an unusual cemetery in many ways. It began in the pre-Roman first century AD (*pace* the title of the article), has many well furnished early cremations and was used into the fourth century. Unfortunately the deviant burials have no grave goods and cannot be dated, other than having been stratigraphically later than cremations and some other inhumations.

Executions?

Occasionally there are sites where execution may account for the decapitated burials. Three decapitated men in a cemetery just outside the walled town of Cambridge included one who displayed contemporary sword cuts around his head, with the lethal blow having been delivered from behind (Alexander *et al.* 2004), while at Dunstable, Bedfordshire, eleven individuals appear to have been decapitated from behind and were interpreted by the excavator as possible victims of execution (Matthews 1981). Admittedly, however, definitive evidence for the practice of deliberate execution is extremely slight. Dunstable is a confusing site with many anomalies, and an example that Philpott (1991) suggests as an execution site – Walkington Wold, Humberside – is indeed an execution site but of Anglo-Saxon date (see Buckberry, this volume). Another possible execution site is King's Dyke, Whittlesey, Cambridgeshire, where, out of eight male burials four had been decapitated, three of whom had also lost feet, while another was prone and footless, and one displayed evidence of having received a heavy blow to the head (Challands 1977). The dating evidence and osteological report are weak, however, and there could well have been disturbance during soil stripping. In addition, the methods of rescue excavation undertaken in a brick pit during 1961 do not inspire confidence as to the validity of the results, although the recovery of a skull near the lower legs of one individual does appear to fit the normal burial pattern for a decapitated individual.

Decapitations from Driffield Terrace, York

The majority of cemeteries which contain a percentage of decapitated bodies are small and rural. The small number of urban cemeteries with decapitated burials display a notably different pattern. The most extreme results are the discoveries at Driffield Terrace, York. Work is ongoing on this extensive cemetery and it is not possible to make conclusive statements about the findings, but some elements appear to separate it from the norm. In recent (2006) phases of work 49 out of 56 excavated individuals were adult males, 30 of whom had been decapitated with a 'very sharp blade' (presumably a sword) (Gore and Tucker 2006; Hunter-Mann 2006) (Figure 6.5). Two methods had been used for decapitation – a single clean cut (which takes practice) and hacking into the neck from front and back. Three burials had grave goods, including pots of late second to early third century date. The most extraordinary decapitated man was recovered from a double grave and his ankles had been bound with heavy iron shackles (Figure 6.6). Signs of infection caused by the shackles had affected the underlying bone, indicating that they had been worn for a substantial period of time. Further excavations of the site have added more complications.

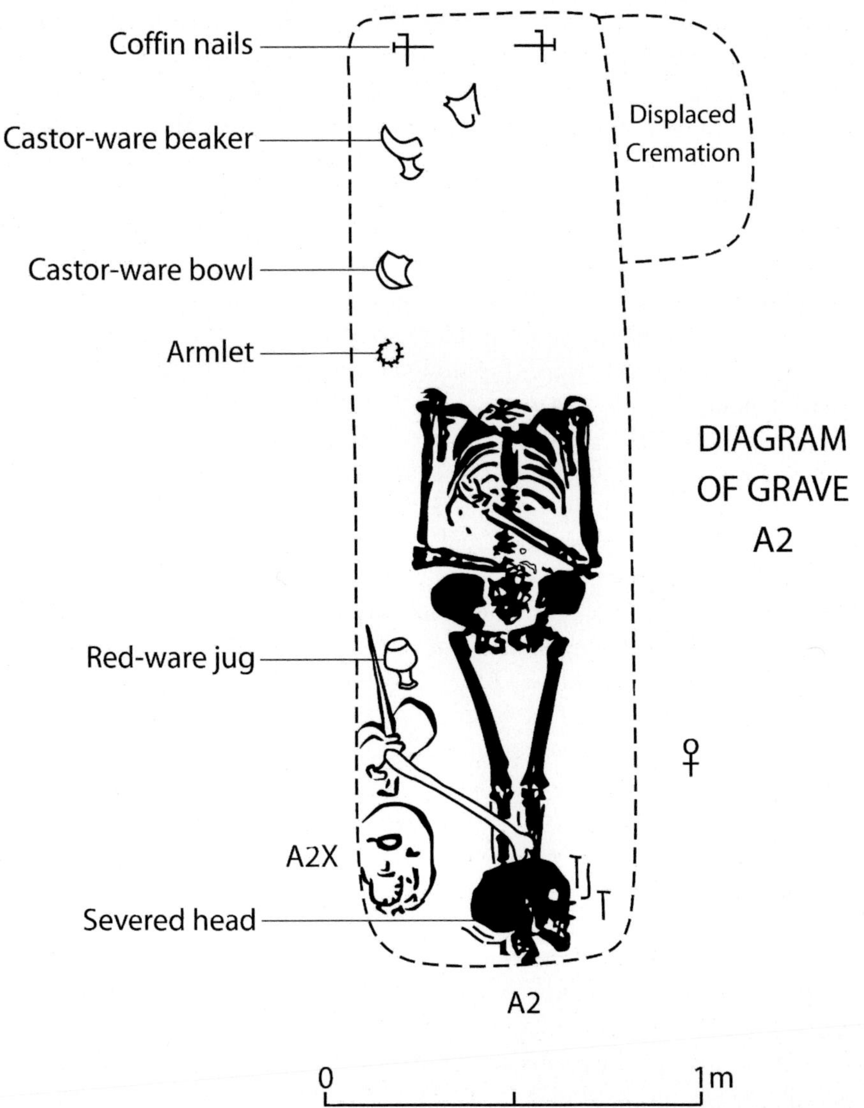

Figure 6.4. An elderly arthritic woman excavated at Guilden Morden, Cambridgeshire, her head had been severed by a sideways cut and then placed over the ankles (copyright Cambridge Antiquarian Society).

Here 16 out of 18 burials were decapitated, some were multiple burials (Figure 6.7) and some were associated with horse bones. It became clear that the burials had taken place over several decades and were not the result of a single violent event (or at least not from just one). The military context of York is clearly significant for interpretation here, both as an army with its emperor (Septimius Severus) present then dying in residence, with violent succession by Caracalla, and for the many foreign troops brought in from the Mediterranean and other parts of Europe and Africa. As such, there would have been plenty of scope for the introduction of foreign burial rites as well as the potential for finding evidence of the brutality of army life and imperial vengeance.

Prone

Prone (face down) burials tend to be located on the edge, or just to the exterior, of cemeteries and are thought to indicate outcasts of some sort. Few have evidence of proper grave goods or coffins, although there are exceptions and many are recovered from otherwise

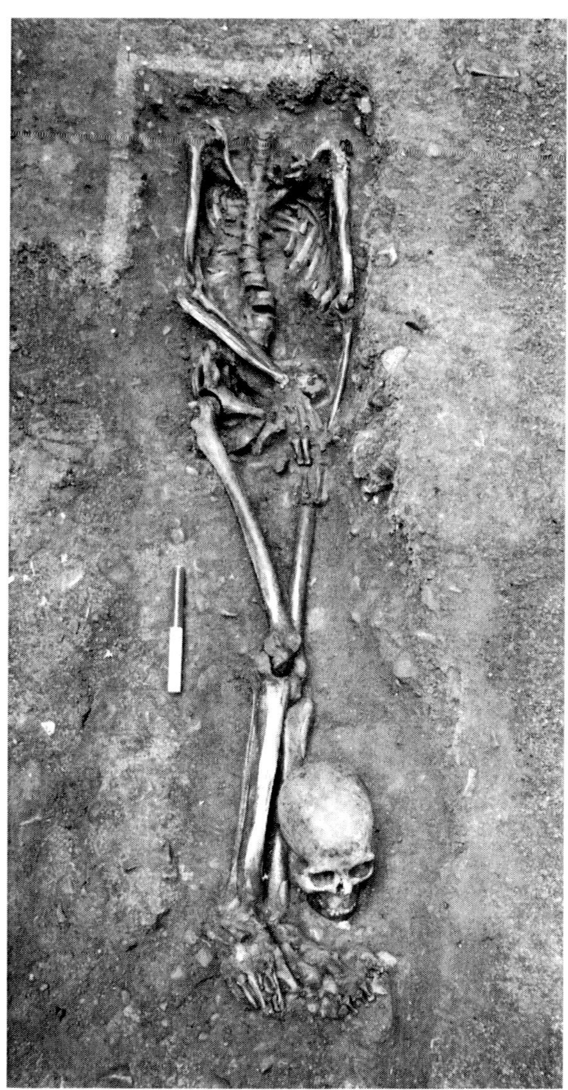

Figure 6.5. Decapitated male from Driffield Terrace, York, buried in a coffin (copyright York Archaeological Trust).

Figure 6.6. Man buried in York, with his feet shackled (copyright York Archaeological Trust).

normal graves. Robert Philpott (1991, 71–6) divides prone burials into four categories – those with signs of coercion, careless examples, simultaneous double burial, and formal burials. He quite reasonably concludes that 'no single all-embracing interpretation' can explain their disparate features.

It is unlikely that prone burials indicate something careless and hurried, however, since one would expect such burials to have been too shallow to survive in the ground in normal conditions. Adequate burial in the Roman World could be achieved with just a handful of earth. One story by Apuleius describes how, in the aftermath of a sudden death, a man had buried his friend: 'After a hurried funeral service I scraped away a sandy soil and laid him in his eternal resting place, there by the brookside' (Graves 1950, 40). One can imagine how long a body in such an environment would remain undisturbed by animals and erosion.

Careless undertakers, especially if dealing with shrouded bodies at night, might have been responsible for a few prone burials, although patterns are too standard for this to be a common explanation. In cemeteries such as Bath Gate, Cirencester, where 33 prone bodies displayed many signs of disrespect and one probably had his arms tied behind his back, the degree of negligence seems to mark them as outcasts. This finding is echoed in their liminal position within many cemeteries. In the case of the Bath Gate cemetery the authors plausibly argued that the individuals were gladiators (McWhirr *et al.* 1982). The

Figure 6.7. Excavation of a multiple grave with sprawled skeletons at Driffield Terrace, York (copyright York Archaeological Trust).

site is also notable for the presence of six decapitated burials. In Colchester the burials of two men located outside the cemetery boundary lay prone, with their wrists and ankles bound and the bones gnawed as if they had been left exposed at some stage. All of these findings may be an indication of criminal status, and are in notable contrast to the remains buried within the well organised cemetery in a supine and extended position (Crummy *et al.* 1993, 105–6, 194). More normal cases on the perimeter, or just outside the limits of cemeteries, include the unremarkable options at Huntingdon, near Roman Godmanchester where, out of 72 burials within an organised cemetery, there was just one prone woman who was otherwise no differently treated than the supine bodies around her. The remains of a second prone woman however lay outside the cemetery, with her limbs positioned at unnatural angles. She was elderly and suffered severe osteoarthritis and pseudoarthritis (Nicholson 2006). Prone burial therefore *may* indicate disapproval, but even in a single community there could be inconsistency.

A number of other examples of prone burials appear to have had their hands bound (e.g. Guilden Morden, Cambridgeshire, Lethbridge 1936), or were deliberately weighed down with large stones (e.g. the Eastern Cemetery of the Roman London Cemetery, Barber and Bowsher 2000). An interesting example is currently being investigated at Welwyn, Hertfordshire, by Tony Rook (2006, pers. comm.). Here the prone burial of an adult male had rocks positioned on his back and a cremation located on his legs. His body lay above and at right angles to that of a man who was lying on his side at the edge of a pit. Another prone male burial, with a rock overlying the head, was recovered from the bottom of the pit. A later, apparently normal, burial had cut this grave, while another body lay awry at the bottom of the pit. A range of possibilities demonstrated at recent AOC Archaeology excavations at Southwark, London, revealed that some burials had been carefully deposited within coffins, while others had been roughly thrown into uncoffined graves. Some display an unusual combination of burial features. A girl, for example, had a clearly visible coffin but her body was positioned in an ungainly manner, her arms beneath her head and shoulders (Figure 6.8; Melikian forthcoming).

Different need not mean inferior. One prone burial from Poundbury, Dorset, for example was associated with a coffin and quite wealthy grave goods, in itself marking him out in this apparently Christian cemetery where grave goods were rare. Ongoing work on one of the three small enclosed cemeteries at Boscombe Down, Wiltshire, has produced just one prone burial – a woman who again was exceptional since hers was the only burial to contain grave goods (Andrew Fitzpatrick 2006, pers. comm.).

Unusually Secure

It is worth noting that there are also examples of very secure burials, often of children with disabilities, in unusually careful and respectful graves. We cannot know the motive for this treatment, but it is more for the archaeologist to bear in mind. At Poundbury, Dorset, a six year old child who was considered to have been congenitally deaf, was buried prone in a coffin that was made of, and covered by, stone roof tiles (Farwell and Molleson 1993). At Arrington in Cambridgeshire a hydrocephalic infant, surprisingly kept alive to about nine months of age, was buried in an oversized lead-lined coffin that lay a good 2 m deep in heavy clay. The baby had been wrapped in a coloured shawl, with aromatic resin packed around its face and a box of pipe clay figurines placed on top of the coffin (Taylor 1993). Loving care may have been demonstrated here, but care too was taken that the soul would pass safely to the afterlife and would not escape to trouble the living. The phenomenon of feared burials being abnormally secure is explored by Tsaliki (this volume).

Conclusions

We know how important it was for the Romans to separate their dead from the living by a series of rituals – as Valerie Hope describes it: 'to send the soul on its journey to the next world, to placate restless spirits, to remove a potential source of infection and to reintegrate the survivors into the world of the living'. Proper burial was so important that funeral costs had to be covered even if other debts went unpaid, with clubs to provide co-operative

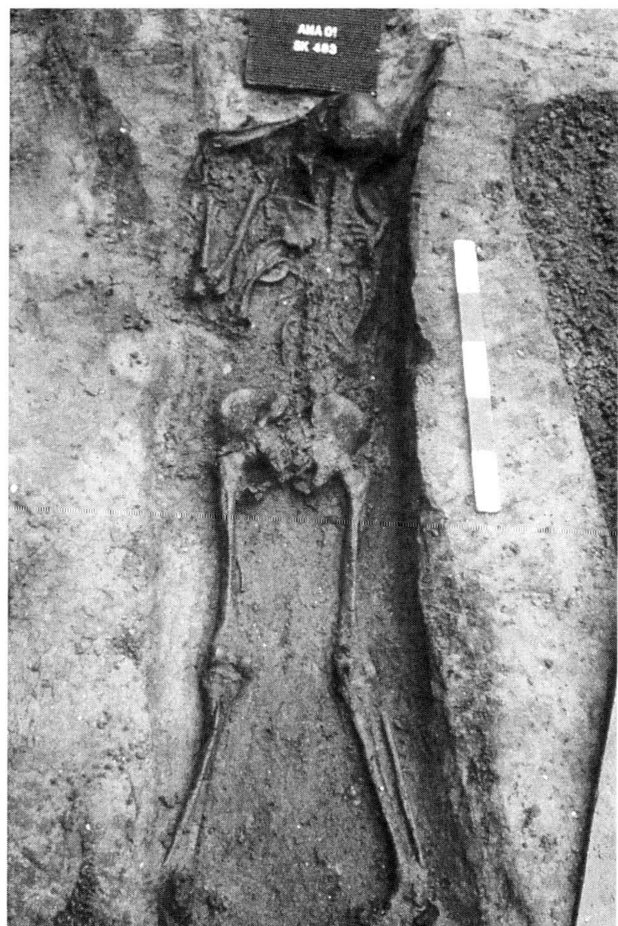

Figure 6.8. Girl buried in a prone and ungainly position but in a coffin, at Southwark, London (copyright AOC Archaeology).

assistance when needed. It was only those at the extremes of honour and disgrace who would expect dramatically different treatment (Hope 2000, 104–27).

As discussed above, explanations for 'deviant burials' include prevention of witchcraft/ghosts, punishment after death for some perceived fault, execution, or simply a differential rite considered appropriate for individuals who were somehow different from their neighbours (though so far family groups have not been identified). These explanations can of course overlap, and the evidence is that causation in any case varied over time – from military brutality in second century York to extra respect in late fourth century Kempston, for example? As such, it is highly unlikely that archaeologists will find one explanation to account for all such unusual burials. Prevention of witchcraft and of ghosts walking, which is seen again in the Middle Ages and seems to be a constant fear at a certain level of all societies, is probably the most common explanation and fits with other signs of constraint, but evidence for execution too, however, has close parallels in better documented periods and is not inherently unlikely.

So there is plentiful evidence in archaeology, as in literature, for a range of strange and brutal practices, none of which should surprise a twenty-first century citizen anywhere in the world. As I said at the beginning of the paper, however, most of this evidence is ambiguous. To start tracing patterns, and then to provide motives and explanations will require at least a proper database for all Roman burials and a greater appreciation of Continental European evidence. Furthermore, it also needs archaeologists to keep their minds open to all possibilities when interpreting such unusual burials.

References

Aldhouse Green, M. 2001. *Dying for the Gods: Human Sacrifice in Iron Age and Roman Europe.* Stroud: Tempus.

Alexander, J. and Pullinger, J. 1999. Roman Cambridge: excavations on Castle Hill 1956–1988. *Proceedings of the Cambridge Antiquarian Society* 88.

Alexander, M., Dodwell, N. and Evans, C. 2004. A Roman cemetery in Jesus Lane, Cambridge. *Proceedings of the Cambridge Antiquarian Society* 93, 67–94.

Barber, B. and Bowsher, D. 2000. *The Eastern Cemetery of Roman London: Excavations 1983–1990* (MoLAS Monograph 4). London: MoLAS.

Boylston, A., Knüsel, C. J., Roberts, C. A. and Dawson, M. 2000. Investigation of a Romano-British burial ritual in Bedford, England. *Journal of Archaeological Science* 27, 241–54.

Bradly, P., Charles, B., Hardy, A. and Poore, D. 2005. Prehistoric and Roman activity and a Civil War ditch: excavations at the Chemistry Research Laboratory, 2–4 South Parks Road. *Oxoniensia* 70, 141–202.

Carver, M. O. H. 2005. *Sutton Hoo: A Seventh-century Princely Burial Ground and its Context* (Report of the Society of Antiquaries of London 69). London: The British Museum Press.

Challands, A. 1977. The Kings' Dyke burials. *Durobrivae* 5, 27–30.

Clarke, G. 1979. *Winchester Studies 3: Pre-Roman and Roman Winchester. Part II: The Roman Cemetery at Lankhills.* Oxford: Oxford University Press.

Crummy, N., Crummy, P. and Crossan, C. 1993. *Excavations of Roman and Later Cemeteries, Churches and Monastic Sites in Colchester, 1971–88* (Colchester Archaeological Trust Report 9). Colchester: Colchester Archaeological Trust.

Davies, S. M., Bellamy, P. S., Heaton, M. J. and Woodward, P. J. 2002. *Excavations at Alington Avenue, Fordington, Dorchester, Dorset, 1984–87.* Dorchester: Trust for Wessex Archaeology Ltd and Dorchester Natural History and Archaeological Society.

Davison, C. 2000. Gender imbalance in Romano-British cemetery populations, pp. 231–7 in Pearce, J., Millett, M. and Struck, M. (eds), *Burial, Society and Context in the Roman World.* Oxford: Oxbow Books.

de Selincourt, A. (translator). 1954. *Herodotus – The Histories.* Harmondsworth: Penguin.

Fairweather, J. (translator). 2005. *Liber Eliensis: A History of the Isle of Ely from the Seventh Century to the Twelfth.* Woodbridge: The Boydell Press.

Farwell, D. E. and Molleson, T. I. 1993. *Excavations at Poundbury 1966–80. Vol II: The Cemeteries* (Monograph series No. 11). Dorchester: Dorchester Natural History and Archaeological Society.

Gilchrist, R. and Sloane, B. 2005. *Requiem: The Medieval Monastic Cemetery in Britain.* London: Museum of London Archaeology Service.

Gore, E. and Tucker, K. 2006. Romans lose their heads in York. *Yorkshire Archaeological Society Roman Antiquities Section* 22, 3–7.

Graves, R. (translator). 1950. *Apuleius – The Golden Ass.* Harmondsworth: Penguin.

Hamerow, H. 2006. 'Special deposits' in Anglo-Saxon settlements. *Medieval Archaeology* 50, 1–30.

Harman, M., Molleson, T. I. and Price, J. 1981. Burials, bodies and beheadings in Romano-British and Anglo-Saxon cemeteries. *Bulletin of the British Museum (Natural History) Geology Series* 35, 145–88.

Hawtin, T. 2004. *Losing your Head: The Significance of Decapitation in Romano-British Burials.* Unpublished B.A. dissertation, Birkbeck College, London.

Henig, M. 1984. *Religion in Roman Britain.* London: Batsford.

Hope, V. M. 2000. The treatment of the corpse in ancient Rome, pp. 104–27 in Hope, V. M. and Marshall, E. (eds), *Death and Disease in the Ancient City.* London: Routledge.

Hunter-Mann, K. 2006. More Roman lose their heads in York. *Yorkshire Archaeology Today* 10, 8–11.

Isserlin, R. M. J. 1997. Thinking the unthinkable: human sacrifice in Roman Britain, pp. 91–100 in *TRAC 96, Proceedings of the Sixth Annual Theoretical Archaeology Conference, Sheffield 1996.* Oxford: Oxbow Books.

Kelly, E. P. 2006. *Kingship and Sacrifice* (Archaeology Ireland Heritage Guide No. 35). Bray: Wordwell.

Lake, K. (translator). 1925. *Eusebius: Ecclesiastical History Vol I.* London: Heinemann.

Lethbridge, T. C. 1936. Further excavations in the Early Iron Age and Romano-British cemetery at Guilden Morden. *Proceedings of the Cambridge Antiquarian Society* 36, 109–20.

Loe, L. 2003. *Specialist report on the human skull (8658) from Vindolanda, Northumberland.* Unpublished report prepared for The Vindolanda Trust.

Lucy, S. 2000. *The Anglo-Saxon Way of Death.* Stroud: Sutton publishers.

Macdonald, J. 1977. Pagan religions and burial practice, pp. 35–8 in Reece, R. (ed.), *Burial in the Roman World* (CBA Research Report No. 22). London: Council for British Archaeology.

Matthews, C. L. 1981. A Romano-British inhumation cemetery at Dunstable. *Bedfordshire Archaeological Journal* 15, 3–73.

Mays, S. 1993. Infanticide in Roman Britain. *Antiquity* 257, 883–8.

Mays, S. 2000. The archaeology and history of infanticide, and its occurrence in earlier British populations, pp. 180–90 in Sofaer-Derevenski, J. (ed.), *Children and Material Culture.* London: Routledge.

McKinley, J. I. 1993. A decapitation from the Romano-British cemetery at Baldock, Herts. *International Journal of Osteoarchaeology* 3, 41–4.

McKinley, J. I. 2004. The human remains and aspects of pyre technology and cremation rites, pp. 283–309 in Cool, H. E. M., *The Roman Cemetery at Brougham, Cumbria* (Britannia Monograph 21). London: Society for the Promotion of Roman Studies.

McWhirr, A., Viner, L. and Wells, C. 1982. *Romano-British Cemeteries at Cirencester.* Cirencester: Cirencester Excavation Committee.

Melikian, M. forthcoming. *2 America Street, London Borough of Southwark. Post excavation assessment.* Unpublished report produced for AOC Archaeology.

Mulhall, I. 2005. Abstract – The National Museum of Ireland Bog Bodies Project, p. 108 in the *Book of Abstracts of the European Association of Archaeologists 11th Annual Meeting, Cork 2005.*

Niblett, R. 1999. *The Excavation of a Ceremonial Site at Folly Lane, Verulamium* (Britannia Monograph series No. 14). London: Society for the Promotion of Roman Studies.

Nicholson, K. 2006. A late Roman cemetery at Watersmeet, Mill Common, Huntingdon. *Proceedings of the Cambridge Antiquarian Society* 95, 57–90.

Oulton, J. E. L. (translator). 1923. *Eusebius: Ecclesiastical History Vol II.* London: Heinemann.

Oxford Archaeology. 2006. *118–120 London Road, Gloucester: Post-excavation Assessment and Updated Project Design.* Unpublished report.

Penn, W. S. 1960. Springhead Temples III & IV. *Archaeologia Cantiana* 74, 113.

Philpott, R. 1991. *Burial Practice in Roman Britain: A Survey of Grave Treatment and Furnishing A.D. 43–410* (BAR British Series 219). Oxford: Tempus Reparatum.

Price, J., Brooks, I. P. and Maynard, D. J. 1997. *The Archaeology of the St Neots to Duxford Gas Pipeline 1994* (BAR British Series 255). Oxford: Archaeopress.

Reynolds, A. 1998. Anglo-Saxon Law and the Landscape. An Archaeological Study of the Old English Judicial System. Unpublished Ph.D. thesis, University College London.

Reynolds, A. forthcoming. *Anglo-Saxon Deviant Burial Customs.* Oxford: Oxford University Press.

Ross, A. 1974. *Pagan Celtic Britain.* London: Cardinal.

Shelton, J. A. 1998. *As the Romans did: A Sourcebook in Roman Social History* (second edition). Oxford: Oxford University Press.

Taylor, A. 1993. A Roman lead coffin with pipe clay figurines from Arrington, Cambs. *Britannia* 24, 191–225.

Taylor, A. 2001. *Burial Practice in Early England.* Stroud: Tempus.

Tester, P. J. 1963. A decapitated burial at Cuxton. *Archaeologia Cantiana* 78, 181–2.

Tsaliki, A. 2001. Vampires beyond legend: a bioarchaeological approach, pp. 295–300 in la Verghetta, M. and Capasso, L. (eds), *Proceedings of the XIII European Meeting of the Paleopathology Association, Chieti, Italy, 18–23 Sept. 2000.* Teramo: Edigrafital S.p.A.

Tsaliki, A. 2006. *An Investigation of Extraordinary Human Body Disposals, with Special Reference to Necrophobia: A Multi-disciplinary Analysis with Case Studies from Greece and Cross-cultural Comparisons.* Unpublished Ph.D. thesis, University of Durham.

Tsaliki, A. and Takis, F. forthcoming. *Disease and Deformity as Factors of Fear and Social Exclusion: The Case of Two Vampire Burials.* Paper presented at the International Congress of Anthropology. November 21–23 2003, Athens, Greece.

Turner, R. C. 1995. The Lindow bog bodies: discoveries and excavations at Lindow Moss 1983–8, pp. 10–18 in Turner, R. C. and Scaife R. G. (eds), *Bog Bodies: New Discoveries and New Perspectives.* London: The British Museum Press.

7. Normal, Deviant and Atypical: Burial Variation in Late Saxon Wessex, c. AD 700–1100

Annia Kristina Cherryson

Abstract

At what point should a burial be considered deviant? This study uses the burial evidence from Late Saxon Wessex to address this question. The paper first considers what may have constituted normal burial practices for the period by examining the development of churchyard burial and the increasing evidence for the persistence of interment away from the new churchyards. Then the evidence for Late Saxon execution cemeteries in Wessex is considered. The burial practices seen in these cemeteries provide a marked contrast to those interred in the region's community burials grounds, be they churchyards or field cemeteries, and few would hesitate to describe these burials as deviant. Finally, those burials which are less easily classified are examined. All are clearly atypical, differing from usual practices in either the mode or location of the burial. Yet should they be considered deviant or simply an unusual variation in acceptable mortuary practices? This paper demonstrates that there is no simple or single answer to that question.

Introduction

The term deviant is applied to burials not accorded whatever mortuary rites deemed appropriate and acceptable by contemporary society. Yet at what point should a burial be considered deviant as opposed to representing unusual but acceptable mortuary behaviour. In some cases, the burial rites accorded to an individual are so far removed from the accepted practices of that time that the label deviant can be assigned with little hesitation. With other burials, the situation is less simple. These inhumations are clearly atypical differing from the vast majority of contemporary burials in either burial practice or burial location. Should such burials be seen as representative of a minority rite or as deviant? This paper examines those inhumations which fall in the no-man's land between normal and deviant burial practices by considering burial variation in Late Saxon Wessex. For the purposes of this paper, Wessex is defined as the pre-1974 counties of Devon, Somerset, Dorset, Wiltshire, Hampshire, Berkshire and the Isle of Wight. By reviewing the Wessex evidence, it hoped to obtain a greater understanding of what might be considered to be deviant burial practices during this period and some of the factors which may have resulted in individuals being accorded atypical mortuary rites.

The Development of Churchyard Burial in Early Medieval Wessex

Before considering the evidence for atypical and deviant burial practices in Late Saxon Wessex it is worth briefly describing the normal mortuary rites of the period. This in itself is not entirely straight-forward as the period saw a marked transition in burial practices, notably with the development of churchyard burial. Christianity was present in the eastern part of the study area from the early seventh century in the form of Christian missionaries (Sherley-Price 1990, 153) and there was an earlier Christian tradition in the west of the study area (Morris 1989, 6). Traditionally, the arrival of Christian missionaries in eastern Wessex was thought to have acted as a catalyst for the rapid transition to churchyard burial, which is believed to have occurred over a few generations during the seventh and eighth centuries (Meaney and Hawkes 1970, 51). However, the validity of this assumption has been increasingly questioned, with recent work demonstrating that the transition to churchyard burial was far from rapid or as straightforward as initially thought (Hadley 2000a, 160; 2000b, 199; Blair 2005, 245).

Indeed, there is little evidence for churchyard burial in seventh and early eighth-century Wessex. The Christian missionaries in Wessex, as in the other Anglo-Saxon kingdoms, initially targeted the royalty and the nobility (Morris 1989, 91). As such, it can be assumed that some, but not necessarily all, of the newly converted elite may have been interred within churchyards. This supposition is supported by a few documentary sources, such as the twelfth-century *Annales monasterii de Wintonia*, which refers to the seventh-century West Saxon kings, Cenwalh, Aescwine and Centwine, having been interred at the Old Minster in Winchester (Deliyannis 1995, 119).

The archaeological evidence for early churchyard burial is equally fragmentary. Within the study area, only three sites – SOU 13 in Hamwic, Hampshire (Morton 1992); Beckery Chapel, Somerset (Rahtz and Hirst 1974) and Wells Cathedral, Somerset (Rodwell 2001) – have produced evidence for possible seventh-century churchyard burials. All three sites have burials that have produced radiocarbon dates which indicate they may have been interred during the seventh century (Table 7.1), but it should be remembered that radiocarbon dating often provides a relatively broad date range. This means that while the burials may have been interred during the seventh century, in the majority of cases they are equally likely to have been buried during the eighth, ninth or even tenth centuries. For example, the only radiocarbon date from the monastic cemetery at Beckery Chapel has a date range of AD 660–980 at a two sigma level of confidence and may represent a seventh-century burial, but may equally be of a much later date (Rahtz and Hirst 1974). Only two examples – one of the bones from the charnel at Wells Cathedral and Burial 40 from SOU 13 – produced date ranges which predate the beginning of the eighth century at a two sigma level of confidence, while Burial 257 from Wells Cathedral has a range of AD 619 – 690 at a one sigma level of confidence. Yet while there is little evidence for interments in

Site	Grave No.	Laboratory reference	Uncalibrated radiocarbon date (BP)	Calibrated date with a confidence level of		Reference
				1σ (AD)	2σ (AD)	
Beckery Chapel	HB 18	Birm 69	1220±80	690–900	660–980	Rahtz and Hirst 1974
Wells Cathedral	B115	HAR-3397	1220	685–889	660–980	Rodwell 2001
	B294	GU-5014	1260	677–790	660–890	
	B257	GU-5016	1360	619–690	550–853	
	F1493	GU-5018	1210	680–953	640–1020	
		GU-5019	1450	553–652	450–670	
		GU-5154	1230	685–883	660–950	
SOU 13	31	OxA-12041	1260±26	690–780	675–865	Cherryson 2005, 48
	40	OxA-12042	1475±26	560–640	540–645	
	59	OxA-12043	1239±26	690–860	685–885	
	64	OxA-12044	1290±25	685–770	665–780	

Table 7.1. Churchyard burials within Wessex which may date to the seventh century.

churchyards in Wessex prior to AD 700, there is substantial evidence for seventh-century burial in the region. These burials occur not adjacent to a church but in field cemeteries, such as Winnall II (Meaney and Hawkes 1970) and Snell's Corner in Hampshire (Knocker 1955), or in the form of isolated burials, often under barrows, such as at Swallowcliffe Down in Wiltshire (Speake 1989) and Lowbury Hill in Berkshire (Atkinson 1916; Fulford and Rippon 1994). Indeed, the archaeological evidence suggests that during the seventh and early eighth century churchyard burial should be seen as a minority rite.

By the mid-eighth century there is a marked change in the archaeological evidence from Wessex with the vast majority of burials from the mid-eighth to eleventh centuries being found adjacent to ecclesiastical buildings, such as at Wells Cathedral, Somerset (Rodwell 2001); Exeter Cathedral, Devon (Henderson and Bidwell 1982), the Old and New Minsters in Winchester, Hampshire (Kjølbye-Biddle 1992) and Bath Abbey, Somerset (Bell 1996). These churchyard burials were, with a few exceptions, orientated west-east with the body interred in a supine extended position and the grave goods, which had characterised the burials of preceding centuries, were virtually absent (Cherryson 2005). Late Saxon churchyard burials were traditionally seen as very homogenous but recent work has demonstrated a far great variation in the funerary practices of the period than once thought (Hadley 2000a; 2000b; 2001; Buckberry 2004; 2007; Cherryson 2005). Common variations observed in the region include evidence for the use of wooden coffins, in the form of nails, wood stains and more unusually coffin fittings, and the use of partially or complete stone grave linings (Cherryson 2005). Less common variations included the use of stones to support the head, lining the grave with a bed of charcoal (see Holloway, this volume) and the use of structural features, such as ledges in the sides of the grave and head niches (Cherryson 2005).

While the archaeological evidence suggests that the major shift to churchyard burial occurred after the beginning of the eighth century, the speed at which churchyard burial was adopted is less clear. The main problem lies in the way that many of these churchyards are dated. The usual methods involve either stratigraphy or the radiocarbon dating of a few burials, with both methodologies tending to provide a relatively wide chronological range. This situation makes it difficult to detect changes in the frequency of burial within a churchyard over time. For example, the churchyard at Wells Cathedral was in use from the eighth century to the end of the Early Medieval period and beyond. It is possible that large numbers of the lay population were interred in this cemetery from its earliest days, thereby making the transition to churchyard burial very rapid. However, it is equally possible that it was only in the tenth and eleventh centuries that large numbers of the laity were interred within the churchyard. The existing archaeological evidence allows no distinction to be made.

Regardless of the speed at which churchyard burial was adopted, there must have been a transitional period when both churchyard and non-churchyard burial would have been considered acceptable modes of burial. Indeed, there is evidence for the persistence of non-churchyard burial within Wessex into the ninth and tenth centuries (Tables 7.2 and 7.3). A number of field cemeteries founded in the seventh century appear to have continued in use into the Late Saxon period. The nature of the grave goods and/or radiocarbon dating has indicated that the cemeteries of Bevis' Grave in Hampshire and Templecombe in Somerset were founded in the seventh century, but in both cases there is evidence for the continued use of the site into the ninth century. At Bevis' Grave, Hampshire, a strap-end dated stylistically to the ninth or tenth century accompanied one of the burials, while a radiocarbon date from another gave a tenth-century date (Rudkin 2001; Cherryson 2005). Similarly at Templecombe, Somerset, a radiocarbon date from one of the inhumations suggests that burial at the site continued into the ninth century (Newman 1992).

<table>
<tr><th>Type of site</th><th>Site</th><th>Date</th><th>No. of burials</th><th>Basis of dating</th></tr>
<tr><td rowspan="4">Long lasting 7th century cemeteries</td><td>Bevis Grave (Ha)</td><td>7th–10th century</td><td>88</td><td>Grave goods & radiocarbon dating</td></tr>
<tr><td>SOU 862 (Ha)</td><td>7th–11th</td><td>16</td><td>Radiocarbon dating</td></tr>
<tr><td>Wembdon (So)</td><td>7th–9th century</td><td>At least 22</td><td>Radiocarbon dating</td></tr>
<tr><td>Templecombe (So)</td><td>7th–11th century</td><td>11</td><td>Radiocarbon dating</td></tr>
<tr><td rowspan="3">Cemeteries founded post-c. 700 AD</td><td>Six Dials (Ha)</td><td>9th century</td><td>11</td><td>Stratigraphy</td></tr>
<tr><td>St. Mary's Stadium II (Ha)</td><td>8th–9th century</td><td>8</td><td>Radiocarbon dating</td></tr>
<tr><td>Staple Gardens, Winchester (Ha)</td><td>c. 850–1000 AD</td><td>288</td><td>Radiocarbon dating</td></tr>
</table>

Table 7.2. Post-eighth century non-churchyard community burial grounds within the study area.

Site	Grave No.	Laboratory reference	Uncalibrated radiocarbon date (BP)	Calibrated date with a confidence level of		Reference
				1σ (AD)	2σ (AD)	
Bevis Grave	3	OxA-12182	1237±32	690–865	685–890	Cherryson 2005
	59	OxA-12193	1075±33	900–1020	890–1020	
SOU 862	22	GU-7595	1160±70	770–980	690–1020	Southern Archaeological Services 1998
Templecombe	282	GU-3124	1190±70	720–960	680–990	Newman 1992
	288	GU-3123	1090±60	890–1020	770–1040	
Wembdon	4	GU-5149	1300±90	650–860	580–970	Chris Webster 2002, pers. comm.
	8	GU-5150	1240±70	690–890	660–970	
	12	GU-5151	1060±90	780–1160	770–1190	
St. Mary's Stadium II	7380	NZA-14941	1245±70	680–880	650–960	Birbeck 2005
Staple Gardens, Winchester	203	GrN-26184	1040±25	988–1018	900–1030	Bayliss 2001
	219	GrN-26815	1130±25	890–975	780–990	
	276	GrN-26186	1145±25	780–980	780–980	
	327	GrN-26187	1140±25	885–975	780–990	
	355	GrN-26188	1175±25	780–900	770–960	
	380	GrN-26189	1165±25	780–950	770–970	
	536	GrN-26190	1130±25	890–975	780–990	
	546	GrN-26191	1105±25	895–985	890–995	
	549	GrN-26192	1170±25	780–940	770–960	

Table 7.3. Post-800 AD radiocarbon dates for non-churchyard burial grounds.

The dating evidence from two other sites – Wembdon, Somerset (Woods n.d.) and SOU 862, Hampshire (Southern Archaeological Services 1998) – is less clear-cut but may also be indicative of the persistence of burial into the Later Saxon period. Radiocarbon dates from burials at both sites have produced relatively wide date ranges, which may indicate a post-800 AD date for the burials. Although, the radiocarbon date ranges are so wide that the burials could equally have been interred during the seventh or eighth centuries.

Traditionally, poorly furnished field cemeteries with predominantly extended west-east burials have been dated to the seventh and early eighth centuries either on the basis of datable grave goods or, if the grave goods cannot be closely dated, are often assumed to be of that date. It seems likely that many of these cemeteries were relatively short-lived and did not persist beyond the eighth century. However, sites like Templecombe and Bevis' Grave raise the possibility that other large seventh- and eighth-century cemeteries, such as Winnall II, Hampshire (Meaney and Hawkes 1970), may contain later burials that can only be identified using radiocarbon dating. As such, the phenomenon of long-lived burial grounds with seventh-century origins may be more prevalent than current evidence from Wessex would suggest.

Non-churchyard burials in Later Saxon Wessex were not just confined to those cemeteries that originated during the seventh century. There is evidence within the study area for the foundation of two, possibly three, cemeteries with no associated ecclesiastical buildings during the eighth and ninth centuries (Tables 7.2 and 7.3). Two of these cemeteries lie in the northern part of the Middle Saxon emporium of Hamwic. The small cemetery of St. Mary's Stadium II consisted of eight unaccompanied west-east burials, and has been dated to the eighth, and possibly ninth, century (Birbeck 2005, 107). A second cemetery of eleven unaccompanied west-east burials at Six Dials lay approximately 400 m to the north-west of the St. Mary's Stadium site (Andrews 1997, 198) and is thought to have been in use during the second half of the ninth century (Andrews 1997, 203). The third possible site is the cemetery at Staple Gardens in Winchester (Kipling and Scobie 1990). Two hundred and eighty-eight burials thought to date to c. AD 850–1000 have been excavated from the cemetery (Winchester Museums Service Archives SG84 and SG89; Bayliss 2001), which lies within the city's Roman walls but some distance from the minster church (Kipling and Scobie 1990, 8). Although no evidence for any buildings has been uncovered at any of these cemeteries the possibility that there were associated ecclesiastical structures at one or both of the sites cannot be completely eliminated (Winchester Museums Service Archives SG84 and SG89). However, these cemeteries raise the possibility that not all burial grounds founded during the eighth and ninth centuries were associated with churches. In fact, there is already archaeological evidence for churches in both Hamwic and Winchester, all with associated churchyards. In Hamwic, the churchyard associated with the church at SOU 13 dates to the eighth and ninth centuries (Morton 1992; Cherryson 2005) and that associated with St. Mary's Church was in use at least by the ninth century and probably earlier (Smith 1995, 258–9). Similarly, in Winchester burial was occurring from the seventh and tenth centuries at the Old and New Minsters respectively (Kjølbye-Biddle 1992, 222, 226). As such, there were contemporary churchyards in the vicinity of all three cemeteries that lack any evidence for associated ecclesiastical buildings. This second category of non-churchyard burial is important as it raises the possibility that not only did burial continue in older burial grounds founded during the seventh century, but that new cemeteries without any associated buildings were being founded away from the minster churches during the eighth and ninth centuries. Moreover, this practice was not occurring in remote areas away from any ecclesiastical influence. All of the examples of possible later non-churchyard cemeteries in Wessex lie in large settlements containing churchyards of a contemporary date.

The evidence from Wessex suggests that what was considered to be a suitable location for burial between the mid-eighth and early eleventh century is far more diverse than traditionally assumed. The period saw increasing numbers of individuals having been interred in the new churchyards, but also the persistence of non-churchyard burial through the continued use of earlier cemeteries and the foundation of new cemeteries away from churches. Indeed, the archaeological evidence from Wessex suggests that it is only during the tenth and eleventh centuries that burial was completely concentrated around minster or manorial churches and that the scattered cemeteries and burials disappear (Cherryson

2005). This process may, in part, be linked to the challenges to the minster's rights posed by the new manorial and urban churches, which resulted in an increasing pressure on the population to inter their dead adjacent to the local minster church (Blair 2005, 463–5). Another factor may have been the consecration of cemeteries. This practice is first referred to in documentary sources from the latter part of the ninth century, although references are uncommon until the tenth century (Gittos 2002, 201). Consecration was used to separate the sacred from the secular and required an increasing need to define churchyard boundaries (Gittos 2002, 202). It was easier to enclose a single centralised cemetery adjacent to a church as opposed to a series of scattered satellite cemeteries. Also, as ever greater numbers were interred adjacent to or within churches, burial in field cemeteries may have increasingly been seen as inappropriate (Thompson 2004, 179–80). Finally, it is important to realise that burial away from the church does not necessarily equate with freedom from ecclesiastical control. There is increasing evidence for the diffuse nature of ecclesiastical institutions during this period and many non-churchyard cemeteries may have been part of religious complexes, with burials in these cemeteries being interred under the auspices of the church (Blair 1992, 257).

There is marked uniformity in the burial rites accorded to those interred in community burial grounds during the Late Saxon period regardless of whether the cemetery was by a church or not. The burials are west-east orientated, the body is usually supine with legs extended and there are few grave goods. Some variations, such as charcoal burials and the use of stones to support the head, are less common among the non-churchyard burials. This may be in part due to chronological factors. Charcoal burials, and to some extent the use of stones to support the head, appear from the available evidence to become more common during the tenth and eleventh centuries (Cherryson 2005). Given that the tenth and eleventh centuries saw the increased centralisation of burial around churches, it is perhaps not particularly surprising that there are only a few examples of charcoal burials and the use of stone head supports outside the churchyards of Wessex.

Deviant Burials in Wessex: The Execution Cemeteries

The uniformity in the burial practices seen in the community burials, be they churchyards or field cemeteries, is in direct contrast to the interments in three cemeteries in Hampshire. Burials at Old Dairy Cottage (Winchester Museum Archive ODC89), Meon Hill (Liddell 1933) and Stockbridge Down (Hill 1937), are characterised by the lack of care shown in interring the deceased. Many burials from both sites were not supine but lay on their sides or in a prone position, often with their limbs akimbo, giving an overall impression that many had been thrown and not carefully placed within the grave (Liddell 1933, 137; Hill 1937, 247–8, 253–4). Instead of the west-east orientated burials which characterise the cemeteries of this period, the orientation of the burials at Old Dairy Cottage and Stockbridge Down is highly variable (Hill 1937, 248; Winchester Museum Archive ODC89), while those at Meon Hill are interred with their heads to the south (Liddell 1933, 132). In addition, a number of those interred in the three cemeteries had been decapitated and/or interred with bound hands (Liddell 1933, 132, 137; Hill 1937, 248; Winchester Museum Archive ODC89).

These features are characteristic of execution cemeteries, burial grounds used to inter those denied a churchyard burial, including criminals, the unbaptised and suicide victims (Reynolds 1997, 37; Buckberry, this volume). Prior to the eighth century, criminals appear to have been interred within community cemeteries judging by the incidence of decapitations, amputations and prone burials found in many Early and Middle Saxon cemeteries (Horne 1933, 55, 58, 63; Reynolds 1997). It is possible that the earliest churchyards were also initially more inclusive as six prone burials were found in the monastic cemetery at Beckery Chapel, Somerset, which has been dated from the eighth to tenth centuries (Rahtz and Hirst 1974). It has been postulated that these individuals may have been guilty of having committed some form of mortal sin, although the possibility that prone burial in this context may represent some form of penance cannot be excluded (Rahtz 1993, 121). The period between the eighth century and the end of the Early Medieval period saw a marked shift in attitude towards the treatment of the corpses of criminals. The early tenth century saw the first specific ordinance excluding criminals from churchyard burial in Edmund's first set of laws (Robertson 1925, 7). It seems likely that this legislation may have served to reinforce existing practices (Reynolds 1997, 38). One of the two radiocarbon-dated burials from Old Dairy Cottage provided a range of AD 775–965 (Cherryson 2005) and it may well have been interred prior to Edmund's legislation. It is possible that initially some of those executed by decapitation or hanging for their crimes were simply interred close to gallows to avoid having to transport the body to the community burial ground. As the practice became more commonplace, it became the custom to exclude those guilty of certain crimes from community burial grounds, with the practice being subsequently formally codified in the law codes.

Atypical Burial: Isolated Burial in Late Saxon Wessex

While few would hesitate to describe those interred in the execution cemeteries as deviant burials, another group of Later Saxon inhumations are less easy to classify. The last few years have seen the identification of a growing number of isolated burials in Late Saxon Wessex (Tables 7.4 and 7.5). Isolated burials of this date have traditionally been seen as having been individuals excluded from community burial grounds, for whatever reason (Zadora-Rio 2003, 7). Yet should these burials by their very location be considered deviant, particularly given the increasing evidence for the persistence of burial outside churchyards? In some cases, the nature of the burial or the liminal location of the interment means that the burials could be considered deviant. For example, the position of the eighth- to tenth-century skeleton recovered from a Saxon ditch at Bugle Street, Southampton, suggests little care was taken when burying this individual (Southampton City Museum Archive SOU 124). This lack of care, similar to that seen in the execution cemeteries, may indicate that the individual had been excluded from the community burial ground or that perhaps this

Type of site	Site	Date	No. of burials	Basis of dating
Long lasting 7th century cemeteries	Bevis Grave (Ha)	7th–10th century	88	Grave goods & radiocarbon dating
	SOU 862 (Ha)	7th–11th century	16	Radiocarbon dating
	Wembdon (So)	7th –9th century	At least 22	Radiocarbon dating
	Templecombe (So)	7th–11th century	11	Radiocarbon dating
Cemeteries founded post-c. 700 AD	Six Dials (Ha)	9th century	11	Stratigraphy
	St. Mary's Stadium II (Ha)	8th–9th century	8	Radiocarbon dating
	Staple Gardens, Winchester (Ha)	c. 850–1000 AD	288	Radiocarbon dating
Execution cemeteries	Old Dairy Cottage (Ha)	Late 8th–early 11th century	18	Radiocarbon dating
	Stockbridge Down (Ha)	11th century	43	Coins
Isolated burials	Shepton Mallet II (So)	8th–9th century	3	Radiocarbon dating
	Bugle Street, Southampton (Ha)	Late 8th–early 10th century	1	Radiocarbon dating
	The Brooks, Winchester (Ha)	Late 10th–11th century	2	Stratigraphy
	Westgate, Southampton (Ha)	9th–10th century	3	Radiocarbon dating
	Lower High Street, Southampton (Ha)	9th–10th century	At least 2	Radiocarbon dating
	Eggardon Hill-fort (Do)	7th–10th century	3	Radiocarbon dating
	Ogbourne St. Andrews (Wi)	Late 9th–10th century	1	Coffin fittings
	Play Hatch, Sonning (Bk)	Late 9th–10th century	2	Grave goods
	Reading I (Bk)	Early 9th century	1	Grave goods

Table 7.4. Late Saxon isolated burials in Wessex.

was an illicit burial. Similarly, the location of two supine extended burials from The Brooks in Winchester, interred on marginal marshy ground close to the river within Winchester's Roman walls, may point to these individuals having been ostracised from the rest of society in death (Scobie *et al.* 1991, 34–7).

Other isolated burials, while not exhibiting the lack of care or marginal location seen in the examples above, do exhibit some very atypical features. This may be indicative of the differential treatment of these individuals, yet is this sufficient for them to be described as deviant? For example, the isolated furnished burials from Reading, Berkshire (Meaney 1964, 50; East 1986) and Play Hatch, Sonning, Berkshire (Evison 1969), are unusual, not because they are furnished, but because of the type of grave goods. The swords that accompany the isolated burials from Reading and Play Hatch, Sonning, provide a marked

Site	Grave No.	Laboratory reference	Uncalibrated radiocarbon date (BP)	Calibrated date with a confidence level of		Reference
				1σ (AD)	2σ (AD)	
Shepton Mallet II	HB 33	GU-5267	1160±50	780–960	720–990	Leach 2001
Bugle Street, Southampton	N/A	OxA-12076	1169±22	780–940	775–960	Cherryson 2005
Westgate, Southampton	Sk. 3558	OxA-12115	1075±24	900–1000	895–1020	Cherryson 2005
	Sk. 3425	OxA-12195	1066±32	900–1020	895–1025	
Lower High Street, Southampton	3933	OxA-5941	1135±60	780–990	770–1020	Andy Russel 2002, pers. comm.
Eggardon Hill-fort	Unknown	HAR-6251	1260±90	670–880	640–980	Bill Putnam 2002, pers. comm.

Table 7.5. Radiocarbon dates of the isolated burials discussed in the text.

contrast to the grave goods seen in other late burials, which are invariably small personal items such as knives, or items of dress such as buckles and strap-ends (Cherryson 2005). The Reading burial has been dated to the early ninth century (East 1986, 6), while grave goods accompanying the Play Hatch, Sonning, burial, which included a knife, arrowheads and a bronze pin, suggest a ninth- to tenth- century date (Evison 1969, 333). The presence of grave goods, particularly weapons, in post-eighth century burials has traditionally been equated with pagan practices and, in particular, has been thought to have been indicative of a Scandinavian presence (Richards 2000, 142). Indeed, the closest stylistic parallels to the gripping beast design on the Reading sword come from Danish and Norwegian contexts, which may be indicative of a Scandinavian origin for this item, although a Carolingian manufacture cannot be completely eliminated (East 1986, 4). The Reading burial, also, reportedly contained the skeleton of a horse (Meaney 1964, 50). This is the only known example of an Early Medieval burial containing a horse within Wessex. The practice is seen elsewhere in Early Medieval England, notably in East Anglia, such as the example from Sutton Hoo (Carver 1998, 86), but it appears to have been confined to the sixth and seventh centuries. Yet horse burials are seen in Scandinavia during the ninth and tenth centuries (Richards 2000, 142), so it is possible that those who interred this individual had Scandinavian connections. The Sonning burial exhibits less obvious Scandinavian influences, accompanied as it is by a 'Celtic' ring-headed pin (Evison 1969, 330), and with the inlaid blade of the sword possibly having been of English origin (Halsall 2000, 269). However, the number and type of grave goods that accompanied the burial do find parallels with contemporary Scandinavian practices. The Viking army was known to have been in Berkshire in AD 870–871 and it is possible that these burials were interred at that time (ASC A and E 871(870) – Swanton

2000, 70–1; Graham-Campbell 2001, 115). The burials from Reading and Sonning have no parallels with any contemporary churchyard or non-churchyard burials within the study area, but they should not necessarily be classified as deviant. Both exhibit Scandinavian influences and may be linked to known Viking incursions into Wessex during the ninth century. Should that be the case these burials, although atypical for Wessex, would fall within the accepted norms of contemporary Scandinavian mortuary practices.

Unlike the burials at Reading and Sonning, the isolated burial from Ogbourne St. Andrews, Wiltshire, with a supine extended body enclosed within the remains of a fir coffin would not have been out of place in any Late Saxon churchyard (Cunnington 1885, 346). However, this burial was interred within a prehistoric burial mound (Cunnington 1885, 346). The re-use of prehistoric barrows was a common practice in the study area during the Early Medieval period, but one which is thought to be mainly confined to the period between the late fifth and early eighth centuries (Williams 1998, 95). The coffin fittings associated with the Ogbourne St. Andrews burial possess stylistic features comparable to those seen at the Old Minster in Winchester, St. Oswald's Priory, Gloucestershire and York Minster, North Yorkshire (Semple 2003, 79). Stylistic comparisons suggested a ninth- or tenth century date for this burial, making it the latest known example of a barrow burial within the study area. So should this burial be described as deviant? There was a significant investment of both time and expense involved in the interment of the individual at Ogbourne St. Andrews. This differs markedly from the lack of care shown to those interred in the execution cemeteries, suggesting caution should be exercised in assuming the individual has been excluded from community burial grounds. However, there is evidence that barrows acquired malevolent connotations as the haunts of evil spirits and creatures during the Late Saxon period (Semple 1998, 121, 123). The question is at what point barrows cease to become an acceptable location for burial and acquire more sinister connotations? The lack of examples of post-eighth-century barrow burials suggest that barrow burial had ceased to become an acceptable burial location by the ninth century and it is possible that the change in attitude to barrows may have occurred about the same time.

Yet although the burial at Ogbourne St. Andrews is the only barrow burial that definitely post-dates the eighth century within Wessex, there may be another possible example of a barrow containing later burials within the study area. Three unfurnished west-east extended inhumations were discovered during the excavation of a prehistoric barrow, which lies on a ridge to the south of Eggardon Hill-fort, Dorset (Putnam 1982, 181; B. Putnam 2002, pers. comm.). Radiocarbon dating of one of the burials provided a wide date range, AD 670–880 and AD 640–980 at a one sigma and two sigma level of confidence respectively, which may indicate a post-eighth-century date for the burials, although a seventh- or eighth-century date is equally possible. Furthermore, given that there are many barrows in the study area that contain unfurnished undated burials, it is possible that there may be other examples of ninth- or tenth-century barrow burials in Wessex. Whether the burial at Ogbourne St. Andrews should be considered to be deviant, atypical or an example of a minority burial rite is largely dependant on how long barrow burial persisted into the Later Saxon period and at what point attitudes to barrows changed. These questions may in part be answered by radiocarbon dating some of the undated unfurnished barrow burials in Wessex.

So far the isolated burials considered above have differed from the majority of contemporary burials either through the lack of care involved in the deposition of the body or because they exhibited atypical features, but this is not always the case. The three supine extended west-east inhumations discovered during the excavations at Fosse Lane, Shepton Mallet, Somerset, would not have looked out of place in a contemporary churchyard (Leach 2001, 31). Yet this group of isolated burials, one of which had a radiocarbon date of AD 720–990 at a two sigma level of confidence, were interred in graves cut into the remains of a Roman building. A similar situation exists with the row of three west-east burials, two supine extended and the other partially crouched, which were uncovered from the Westgate site in Southampton (Webster and Cherry 1980, 251). Radiocarbon dating of two of the skeletons gave a tenth-century date for both burials. The burials lie some distance from any known churchyard in Early Medieval Southampton and there are no associated contemporary structures, although it should be noted that only part of the site was excavated. It has been postulated that these burials may form the southern extremity of a larger cemetery (Southampton City Museum SOU 25 Archive), but as there is currently no evidence for any other burials in the vicinity of these graves, they are being considered as isolated burials in this study. The partially crouched burial at Westgate is unusual for the Late Saxon period, but there is nothing about these burials which is inherently deviant or suggestive of an outcast status for them. Elsewhere in Southampton, disarticulated bone from at least three individuals was recovered during the excavation of the Lower High Street (Platt 1975; A. Russel 2002, pers. comm.). The bones were radiocarbon-dated to between the eighth and eleventh centuries (Platt 1975; A. Russel 2002, pers. comm.) and may be indicative of the existence of another small cluster of isolated burials within the Late Saxon town (Southampton City Museum Archive SOU 161). Scattered burials have been observed in Early Medieval settlements, especially in France (Zadora-Rio 2003, 3), and it appears the burials from Southampton may also be an example of this phenomenon. It is also worth noting that many towns in Wessex contain isolated undated burials. Unfurnished burials are always difficult to date, with radiocarbon dating often being the only option. Unfortunately, this technique is not cheap and it is often only used to date larger cemeteries, and not small numbers of isolated burials. As such, it is possible that isolated burial is not as uncommon during the Later Saxon period as the evidence currently suggests. Indeed, it is possible that at least up until the tenth century some isolated burials, especially those discovered in settlements, should simply be seen as a part of the normal range of funerary practices, particularly if they exhibit no atypical features other than their location.

Conclusion

This paper has attempted to address the difficulties in determining exactly what may have been perceived to be deviant burial practices by contemporary society and what may simply have constituted an unusual but acceptable variation. Looking at the evidence for burial in Later Saxon Wessex, the majority of the inhumations can easily be classified as falling within the realm of acceptable burial practices or as deviant burials. However, there are always going to be some burials that fall in the no-man's land between what is considered to be normal and what is clearly not. In Wessex, the majority of these examples are isolated burials, but these burials are far from a homogenous group. They range from burials which would not look out of place in a contemporary churchyard to bodies dumped in ditches. Some could be described as deviant, others are definitely atypical and others may well represent acceptable funerary practices. Each case needs to be examined individually against the wider context of burial practices during this period. However, the greatest problem may actually lie in our definition of 'normal' mortuary practices during this period. It may be because the focus has tended to be on churchyard burial that our perception of what constitutes acceptable burial practices is too narrow. Just as recent work has demonstrated that non-churchyard burial persisted much later than traditionally thought, further work, especially on barrow burials and isolated burials, may serve to redefine what may have been considered to be acceptable burial practices during this period.

Acknowledgements

Thanks are due to the following individuals who have generously provided information on unpublished sites and additional information on published sites: Phil Andrews – Wessex Archaeology; Duncan Brown – Southampton City Museum; Peter Davenport – Bath Archaeological Trust; Matt Garner – Southampton Archaeological Unit; John Hawthorne; Bruce Howard – Hampshire SMR; Alan Morton – Southampton City Council; Bill Putnam – University of Bournemouth; Andy Russel – Southampton Archaeological Unit; Graeme Scobie – Winchester Museums Service; Roland Smith – Wessex Archaeology; Jenny Stevens – Portsmouth City Museum; Nick Stoodley – University of Winchester; Steve Teague – Winchester Museums Service; Karen Wardley – Southampton City Museum; Chris Webster – Somerset SMR. Thanks too to Dawn Hadley and Jo Buckberry for many helpful discussions. This research was funded by a University of Sheffield studentship. Funding for the radiocarbon dating was obtained through the NERC ORADS scheme.

Note

All radiocarbon dates have been recalibrated using OxCal version 3.8.0.1 (Bronk Ramsey 2003). The only exception was for Wells where insufficient information was provided to enable the recalibration of any of the radiocarbon dates.

References

Andrews, P. 1997. *Excavations at Hamwic. Volume 2: Excavations at Six Dials* (Council for British Archaeology Research Report 109). York: Council for British Archaeology.

Atkinson, D. 1916. *The Romano-British Site on Lowbury Hill in Berkshire.* Reading: University College Reading.

Bayliss, A. 2001. *Letter Containing a Model of the Chronology for the Staple Gardens Cemetery.* Winchester Museum Service Archive SG89.

Bell, R. 1996. Bath Abbey: some new perspectives. *Bath History* 6, 7–24.

Birbeck, V. 2005. *The Origins of Middle Saxon Southampton.* Salisbury: Wessex Archaeology.

Blair, J. 1992. Anglo-Saxon minsters: a topographical review, pp. 226–66 in Blair, J. and Sharpe, R., *Pastoral Care Before the Parish.* Leicester: Leicester University Press.

Blair, J. 2005. *The Church in Anglo-Saxon Society.* Oxford: Oxford University Press.

Buckberry, J. L. 2004. *A Social and Anthropological Analysis of Conversion Period and Later Anglo-Saxon Cemeteries in Lincolnshire and Yorkshire.* Unpublished Ph.D. thesis, University of Sheffield.

Buckberry, J. L. 2007. On sacred ground: social identity and churchyard burial in Lincolnshire and Yorkshire, c. 700–1100 AD. *Anglo-Saxon Studies in Archaeology and History* 14, 117–29.

Carver, M. O. H. 1998. *Sutton Hoo. Burial Ground of Kings?* London: British Museum Press.

Cherryson, A. K. 2005. *In the Shadow of the Church: Burial practices in the Wessex Heartlands, c. 600–1100 AD.* Unpublished Ph.D. thesis, University of Sheffield.

Cunnington, W. 1885. Barrow at Ogbourne St. Andrew's, Wiltshire. *Wiltshire Archaeological and Natural History Magazine* 22, 345–8.

Deliyannis, D. M. 1995. Church burial in Anglo-Saxon England: the prerogative of kings. *Fruhmittelaterliche Studien* 29, 96–119.

East, K. 1986. A lead model and rediscovered sword, both with gripping beast decoration. *Medieval Archaeology* 30, 1–7.

Evison, V. 1969. A Viking grave in Sonning, Berks. *Antiquaries Journal* 49, 330–45.

Fulford, M. and Rippon, S. J. 1994. Lowbury Hill, Oxon: a re-assessment of the probable Romano-Celtic temple and Anglo-Saxon barrow. *Archaeological Journal* 151, 158–211.

Gittos, H. 2002. Creating the sacred: Anglo-Saxon rites for consecrating cemeteries, pp. 195–208 in Lucy, S. and Reynolds, A. (eds), *Burial in Early Medieval England and Wales* (Society for Medieval Archaeology Monograph 17). Leeds: Manley Publishing.

Graham-Campbell, J. 2001. Pagan Scandinavian burial in the central and southern Danelaw, pp. 105–23 in Graham-Campbell, J., Hall, H., Jesch, J. and Parsons, D. N. (eds), *Vikings and the Danelaw.* Oxford: Oxbow Books.

Hadley, D. 2000a. Equality, humility and non-materialism. *Archaeological Review from Cambridge* 17, 149–79.

Hadley, D. 2000b. Burial practices in the Northern Danelaw, c. 650–1100 AD. *Northern History* 36, 199–216.

Hadley, D. M. 2001. *Death in Medieval England.* Stroud: Tempus.

Halsall, G. 2000. The Viking presence in England? pp. 259–76 in Hadley, D. and Richards, J. D. (eds), *Cultures in Contact: Scandinavian Settlement in England in the Ninth and Tenth Centuries.* Turnhout: Brepols.

Henderson, C. G. and Bidwell, P. T. 1982. The Saxon minster at Exeter, pp. 145–75 in Pearce, S.

M. (ed.), *The Early Church in Western Britain and Ireland* (BAR British Series 102). Oxford: British Archaeological Reports.

Hill, N. G. 1937. Excavations on Stockbridge Down 1935–36. *Proceedings of the Hampshire Field Club and Archaeological Society* 13, 247–59.

Horne, E. 1933. Anglo-Saxon cemetery at Camerton, Somerset. *Proceedings of the Somersetshire Archaeological and Natural History Society* 79, 39–63.

Kipling, R. and Scobie, G. 1990. Staple Gardens 1989. *Winchester Museum Service Newsletter* 6, 8–9.

Kjølbye-Biddle, B. 1992. Dispersal or concentration: disposal of the Winchester dead over 2000 years, pp. 196–209 in Bassett, S. (ed.), *Death in Towns*. Leicester: Leicester University Press.

Knocker, G. M. 1955. Early burials and an Anglo-Saxon cemetery at Snell's Corner near Horndean. *Proceedings of Hampshire Field Club and Archaeology Society* 19, 117–70.

Leach, P. 2001. *Fosse Lane, Shepton Mallet 1990. Excavation of a Romano-British Roadside Settlement* (Britannia monograph 18). London: Society for the Promotion of Roman Studies.

Liddell, D. M. 1933. Excavations at Meon Hill. *Proceedings of the Hampshire Field Club and Archaeological Society* 12, 126–62.

Meaney, A. 1964. *A Gazetteer of Early Anglo-Saxon Burial Sites*. London: Allen and Unwin.

Meaney, A. L. and Hawkes, S. C. 1970. *Two Anglo-Saxon Cemeteries at Winnall* (The Society for Medieval Archaeology Monograph No. 4). London: Society for Medieval Archaeology.

Morris, R. 1989. *Churches in the Landscape*. London: Phoenix.

Morton, A. 1992. *Excavations in Hamwic: Volume 1: Excavations 1946–83, excluding Six Dials and Melbourne Street* (Council for British Archaeology Research Report 84). London: Council for British Archaeology.

Newman, C. 1992. A late Saxon cemetery at Templecombe. *Proceedings of Somerset Archaeological and Natural History Society* 136, 61–7.

Platt, C. 1975. *Excavation in Medieval Southampton, 1953–1969*. Leicester: Leicester University Press.

Putnam, B. 1982. Eggardon. *Proceedings of Dorset Natural History and Archaeological Society* 105, 181.

Rahtz, P. 1993. *Glastonbury*. London: B.T. Batsford Ltd.

Rahtz, P. and Hirst, S. 1974. *Beckery Chapel, Glastonbury, 1967–8*. Glastonbury: Glastonbury Antiquarian Society.

Reynolds, A. 1997. The definition and ideology of Anglo-Saxon execution sites and cemeteries, pp. 27–32 in De Boe, G. and Verhaegle, F. (eds), *Death and Burial in Medieval Europe – Papers of the Medieval Europe Brugge 1997 Conference* (Volume 2). Zelik: Instituut voor het Archeologisch Patrimonium.

Richards, J. D. 2000. *Viking Age England. Life and Landscape*. Stroud: Tempus.

Robertson, A. J. (translated and edited) 1925. *The Laws of the Kings of England from Edmund to Henry I*. Cambridge: Cambridge University Press.

Rodwell, W. 2001. *Wells Cathedral Excavations and Structural Features, 1978–93* (English Heritage Archaeological Reports 21). London: English Heritage.

Rudkin, D. 2001. *Excavations at Bevis' Grave, Camp Down, Bedhampton, Hants*. Unpublished manuscript, Fishbourne Roman Palace Museum.

Scobie, G. D., Zant, J. M. and Whinney, R. 1991. *The Brooks, Winchester. A preliminary Report on the Excavations, 1987–8* (Winchester Museums Service Archaeology Report 1). Salisbury: Winchester Museums Service.

Semple, S. 1998. A fear of the past: the place of the prehistoric burial mound in the ideology of middle and late Anglo-Saxon England. *World Archaeology* 30, 72–91.

Semple, S. 2003. Burials and political boundaries in the Avebury Region, North Wiltshire. *Anglo-Saxon Studies in Archaeology and History* 12, 72–91.

Sherley-Price, L. (translator) 1990. *Bede's Ecclesiastical History of the English People.* London: Penguin.

Smith, M. 1995. Excavation of two Saxon burials beneath Chapel Road, Southampton (SOU 630). *Proccedings of Hampshire Field Club and Archaeological Society* 51, 255–60.

Southern Archaeological Services. 1998. *Interim Report on an Archaeological Watching Brief at 75 Bitterne Road, Southampton SAS108/SOU 862.* Unpublished document, Southampton SMR.

Southampton Museum of Archaeology Archive SOU 25.

Southampton Museum of Archaeology Archive SOU 124.

Southampton Museum of Archaeology Archive SOU 161.

Speake, G. 1989. *A Saxon Bed Burial on Swallowcliffe Down* (English Heritage Archaeological Report No. 10). London: Historic Buildings and Monuments Commission for England.

Swanton, M. (translated and edited) 2000. *The Anglo-Saxon Chronicles.* London: Phoenix Press.

Thompson, V. 2004. *Dying and Death in Later Anglo-Saxon England.* Woodbridge: The Boydell Press.

Webster, L. E. and Cherry, J. 1980. Medieval Britain in 1979. *Medieval Archaeology* 24, 218–64.

Williams, H. 1998. Monuments and the past in early Anglo-Saxon England. *World Archaeology* 30, 90–108.

Winchester Museums Service Archive ODC89.

Winchester Museums Service Archive SG84.

Winchester Museums Service Archive SG89.

Woods, H. n.d. *Excavations at Wembdon Hill 1984–90.* Unpublished manuscript, Somerset SMR.

Zadora-Rio, E. 2003. The making of churchyards and parish territories in the early medieval of France and England in the 7th–12th centuries. A reconsideration. *Medieval Archaeology* 47, 1–39.

8. Charcoal Burial: A Minority Burial Rite in Early Medieval Europe

James Holloway

Abstract

'Charcoal burial' is a type of Early Medieval burial in which the body is laid on, or under, a layer of wood charcoal. Burials of this type are found in England, Ireland, Scotland and Scandinavia, mainly from tenth-to-twelfth century contexts. Similar rites are known from Merovingian French cemeteries. Although burials of this type have been known about for over 100 years, very little about them is understood. A number of competing theories exist, which explain them as everything from a sanitary practice to a symbolic comfort for the deceased. Very little attention has been focused on the role of this burial type in constructing identities. This paper presents a brief overview of the types, distribution and chronology of charcoal burials. Five sample cemeteries from five different areas are discussed, and future avenues are suggested for research into this common, but little-understood, burial practice.

Introduction

'Deviant' burial practices include special treatment given to 'criminals, women who died during childbirth, unbaptised infants, people with disabilities, and supposed revenants' (Murphy 2005). Archaeologists have applied this concept to a wide variety of places and periods, usually in cases where the archaeological record shows a number of significant variations from a majority or 'standard' burial practice. When we discuss these burial practices, then, we usually think in terms of excluded or marginalised groups. In Early Medieval England, for example, Andrew Reynolds (1999, 105) has identified specific interments as being the burials of executed criminals. Osteological analysis of some of the remains derived from these sites has supported this identification (see Buckberry, this volume; Buckberry and Hadley 2007). These burials are found outside the 'normal' Christian burial area – the churchyard. They are located on administrative boundaries and buried in unusual positions, often prone. These are very much what we expect to find when we look for deviant burials – distinguished by location and burial practice, they appear to represent a group on the margins of society.

We understand the concept of 'deviant' burial in opposition to an idea of 'normal' burial. If deviant burials embody concepts of difference and marginalisation, we assume that 'normal' burials represent community and inclusion. However, even within the bounds of 'normal' burial practice, we can observe significant variation. In some cases, it is possible to identify and interpret these variations within the 'normal' burial rite. For instance, in the Medieval period the majority of burials in England are within churchyards or church buildings, and the deceased is buried in a shroud or wooden coffin, orientated west-east, with no grave goods. However, a number of burials with shoes, wooden staves, or pilgrim badges are known from Medieval British burial grounds, the most famous of these being the 'Worcester Pilgrim' (Lubin 1990). Although buried in the 'normal' location of churches or churchyards, these burials vary from the norm by the inclusion of clothing and grave goods. They have been interpreted as representing pilgrimage although whether they represent pilgrimages undertaken in life, or a symbolic pilgrimage in death, is unclear (Gilchrist and Sloane 2005, 173–6).

There are a wide variety of other variant or minority burial rites, however, which remain enigmatic. While it is evident that these burials are being marked as special in some way, it is not clear whether the normally negative connotations of 'deviant' burial apply. This paper will discuss one such burial practice, found across northern Europe during the Early Medieval period.

Charcoal Burial

The term 'charcoal burial' refers to a range of burial types in which a layer of charcoal is found in association with the body. The burial may include a coffin, in which case the charcoal is normally positioned below the coffin on the floor of the grave cut. In addition to a layer of charcoal on the floor of the grave, charcoal may be packed around the sides of the coffin as at Winchester (Biddle 1968, 321), or placed in a layer on top of the coffin. Some burials, both with and without coffins, have been 'encased' in charcoal (Dawes and Magilton 1980, 16).

In addition to the presence of charcoal in the grave other burial practices vary. Charcoal burials are known in stone-lined graves (Fowler 1880, 388), with pillow or 'earmuff' stones (Shoesmith 1980, 24), in wood-lined graves (Hurley *et al.* 1997) and in furnished burials (Fowler 1880, 388; Young 1984, 124). In some burial grounds, the practice appears to correlate with other funerary rites. At Winchester, for example, the excavators suggested a correlation between charcoal burial and the presence of 'elaborated' coffins with iron fittings (Biddle 1969, 322). In other burial grounds, there appears to be a negative correlation between charcoal burial and other rites. An example of this from Lund is discussed below.

Charcoal samples from several sites in Britain have been analysed (Kjølbye-Biddle 1992, 229; Cormack *et al.* 1995, 34; Heighway and Bryant 1999, 218). The English examples have been found to comprise oak from mature trunks or branch wood, with small amounts of other plant species also represented. By contrast, the Scottish examples represent alder, oak, ash and hazel, probably reflecting variations in the wood used to make local charcoal. There is no evidence to suggest that the charcoal was burnt *in situ*.

A number of practices found in Early Medieval or Medieval burial grounds resemble charcoal burial in some ways. Ash burial, for example, is common in the High Medieval period. In such cases a layer of ash is found, usually under the body. In the known examples, the ash had preserved the outline of a coffin, suggesting that the layer of ash was placed inside the coffin itself, in direct contact with the body. This ash contains elements of charcoal, animal and plant matter, pottery and other domestic refuse, demonstrating that it may have 'originated from a domestic fireplace of some form' (Gilchrist and Sloane 2005, 121–2). Early Anglo-Saxon burials are sometimes found with charcoal in the grave fill, perhaps suggesting that a fire had been lit at the grave (Adams 1996, 165). Similarly, burials in Merovingian Gaul often contain charcoal, ash, burnt stone or other traces of *feux rituels* (Young 1975, 118). These burials are discussed further below. Some Early Medieval English burials have also been found to contain carbonised wood; this has been interpreted as the remains of coffins which had been charred before being buried (Rodwell 1981, 150). Lastly, Medieval Scandinavian burials sometimes include *gravpotter*, small pottery vessels filled with charcoal (Kieffer-Olsen 1993, 169). Although the preceding burials all involve the presence of charcoal or other burning residue within the grave, none of these are 'charcoal burials', the key element of which is a layer of charcoal associated with the body.

This, then, is our 'normal' or 'standard' charcoal burial – a layer of charcoal is found on the floor of the grave cut, not as a residue derived from a burning process but rather as an intentional deposit. Charcoal burials from all over northern Europe have this in common. However, the rites associated with such burial also have a number of important variations; burials which are similar in their physical layouts may differ in terms of their location within the cemetery, in the types of cemeteries they are found in, and in numbers within a cemetery (Figures 8.1 and 8.2).

Charcoal burials are currently known from dozens of burial grounds in northern Europe and the North Atlantic region. There are far too many sites and burials to cover in the current paper. As such, the text will describe and compare examples from five Early Medieval and Medieval burial grounds in England, Scotland, France, Ireland and Sweden. These examples can only provide a general overview of the practice, but the similarities and differences between the burials can provide important information about the ways in which minority rites were used to construct identities in varied communities across northern Europe (Figure 8.3).

Charcoal Burial in Ireland

Only one charcoal burial site is known from Ireland; this is derived from St. Peter's Church in Waterford, which was excavated between 1986 and 1992. The church is first mentioned in historical records in the fourteenth century, but excavation revealed the presence of an earlier stone structure on the site. The earliest phase of this stone church was constructed in the early twelfth century, but 62 Phase I burials were found to have predated the structure and are tentatively dated to the eleventh century (Lanting 1997, 818). The evidence for a

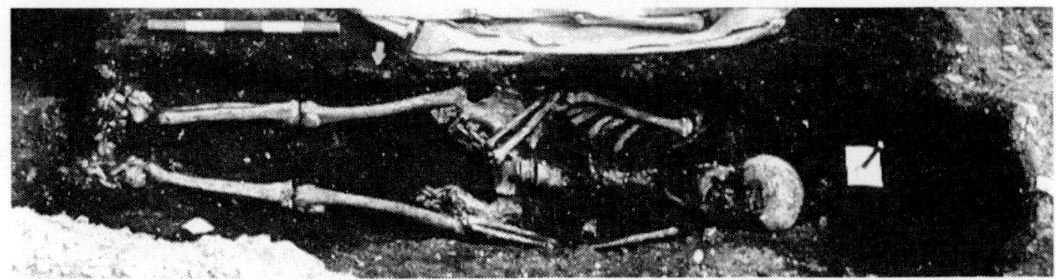

Figure 8.1. A charcoal burial from Staple Gardens, Winchester (courtesy of Winchester City Council).

Figure 8.2. Cross-section of a charcoal burial from Staple Gardens, Winchester, clearly showing the layer of charcoal positioned beneath the skeleton (courtesy of Winchester City Council).

wooden church in Phase I is considered to be 'equivocal' (Hurley *et al.* 1997, 190). Two of the graves associated with the possible wooden church contained layers of charcoal. Both of these were located beneath the stone church, and the individuals' legs had been cut by the foundations for the eastern nave wall.

The two graves, B3041 and B3071, were positioned less than 2 m apart. In both cases the body lay on a layer of charcoal, but the amounts of charcoal within the layer were very different. Grave B3071 contained a charcoal layer c. 12 mm thick, while the body in B3041 rested on a charcoal layer c. 50 mm thick and was covered by a layer with a depth of 19 cm in places (Hurley *et al.* 1997, 196). The large amount of charcoal in this latter burial would be highly unusual in a British or Scandinavian charcoal burial. No conclusive evidence for coffins was found in either burial.

The Irish charcoal burials are similar in some ways to the rite as known in England, and

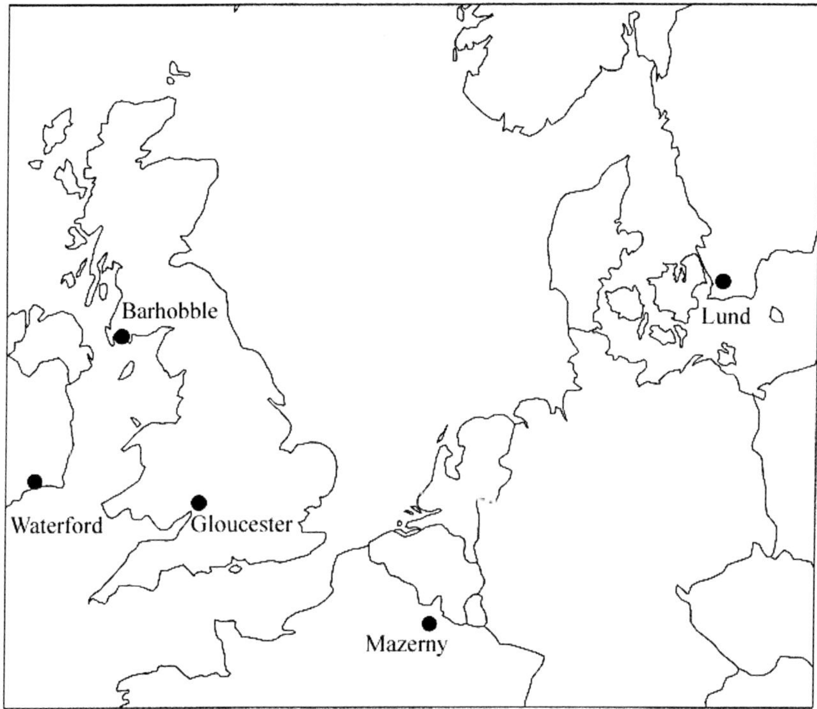

Figure 8.3. Location map showing the five examples of burial grounds containing charcoal burials mentioned in the text.

it is tempting to say that this is simply a transplanted English practice. It is certainly true that Medieval Waterford had significant commercial and cultural ties to England. Later expansions to the stone church on this site included the construction of a semi-circular apse, an uncommon feature in contemporary Irish churches, but well-known in England (Hurley *et al.* 1997, 191). Malchus (Mael Iosa Ó h-Ainmire), the first Bishop of Waterford, was consecrated in Canterbury in AD 1096 and had been a monk at Winchester (Gwynn and Hadcock 1970, 100), which has the largest number of excavated charcoal burials of any English church. The charcoal burials which predate the stone church at Waterford may date from around this period. There is no conclusive link, however, between the arrival of a bishop with English connections and this brief appearance of a rite also known in England.

Another possible influence is Scandinavian burial practice. As we shall see, charcoal burial was known both in contemporary Denmark and in at least one 'Celto-Norse' cemetery from western Scotland. Waterford was a Viking town, and appears to have had a significant population with a distinct Scandinavian identity as late as the twelfth century (Hurley *et al.* 1997, 14). However, there is no other evidence to connect the Irish and Scandinavian practices of charcoal burial.

Although an English origin for the practice of charcoal burial in Ireland seems likely, it is interesting to note that the Irish examples have some unusual characteristics compared to their English counterparts, notably the very heavy charcoal layer in grave B3041. The contemporary burials also differed from contemporary English burials, placing the Waterford charcoal burials in a very different context. Of the 62 graves in the Period I burial ground, 34 were wood-lined, an 'unusual feature' in Irish burials (Hurley 1992, 54). Wood-lined graves are not common in Medieval England, although a number are known from Medieval Scottish contexts (Stones 1989, 117–8). At St. Peter's the excavators interpreted them as having been related to the later stone-lined graves in the Period II burial ground. While it seems likely that cultural contact with Britain or Scandinavia introduced the practice of charcoal burial to Waterford, the rite is found in a different context; it appears to have been used in a different way.

Charcoal Burial in England

The single charcoal burial site in Ireland, with only two charcoal burials, is in direct contract to the situation in England where over 30 sites have produced evidence for over 300 excavated examples of the practice. Many of these burials come from large urban minster graveyards, such as the 96 cases found in the burial grounds of the Old and New Minsters at Winchester (Kjølbye-Biddle 1992, 230), the 61 examples found in the graveyard of the Saxon Minster at Exeter (Henderson and Bidwell 1982, 154), or the 15 cases found at York Minster (Philips and Heywood 1995, 88–93) (Figure 8.4).

One such site is the Anglo-Saxon minster of St. Oswald in Gloucester, which was founded around AD 900 by Ealdorman Æthelred of Mercia and his wife, the famous Æthelflæd, daughter of Alfred the Great. It housed the relics of St. Oswald, translated from Danish-held Bardney in AD 909. Æthelflæd and her husband favored the cult of St. Oswald, possibly as a means of legitimising their rule in Mercia (Thacker 1981, 211). Although it was 'the principal church established at the highest level of patronage available in Mercia' (Heighway and Bryant 1999, 7), St. Oswald's was not the only important church in Gloucester. An older minster – St. Peter's – stood within the *burh* and was still receiving burials during this period. This church's graveyard has not been systematically excavated, and it is therefore unknown whether it contained any charcoal burials.

A total of 34 charcoal burials were excavated at St. Oswald's Minster between 1975 and 1983. These burials amount to less than 10% of the total burials for the periods in which they were found. However, most of the charcoal burials were contained in 'generations' that were identified by the excavators as occurring between approximately AD 900 and AD 1120. In Generations B–E, which covered a period from the early-to-mid tenth to early twelfth centuries, charcoal burials comprised 20% to 30% of the burial population. They appeared in very small numbers for brief periods both before AD 900 and after AD 1120 (Heighway and Bryant 1999, 202). The longevity and prevalence of the rite at St. Oswald's is remarkable, which may suggest that the rite had been institutionalised. The small number of charcoal burials at Waterford might represent the preference of single individuals, but at St. Oswald's we are clearly dealing with an established, traditional practice. Compared

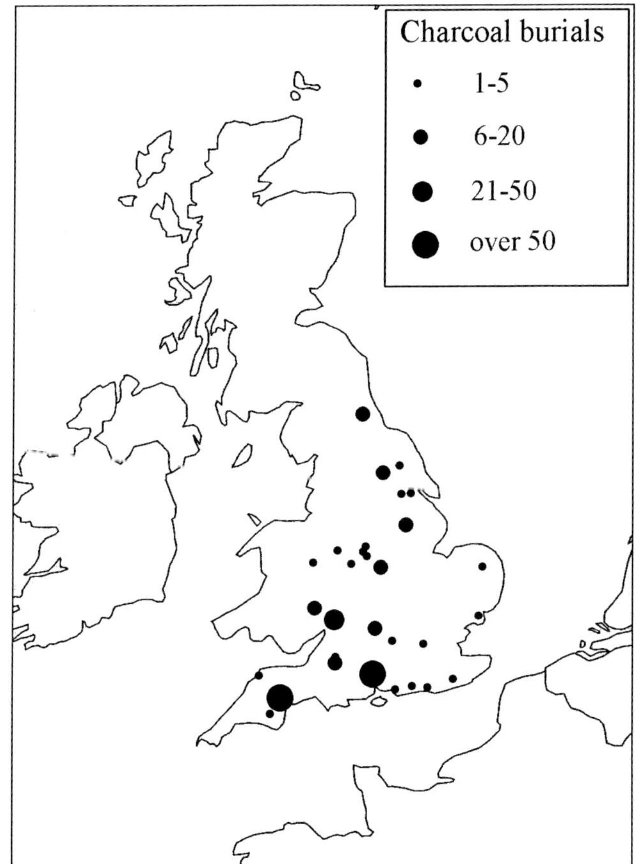

Figure 8.4. Distribution map of charcoal burials in England. Note that multiple burial grounds within the same city may overlap.

to burials without charcoal, a high percentage of the charcoal burials were located to the north of the church and all, but one, were positioned in close proximity to the church. Of the 34 charcoal burials at St Oswald's, 12 contained adult skeletons which could be sexed. Of these, seven were male or probably male and five were female or probably female.

Charcoal Burial in Sweden

A series of excavations that occurred from the 1960s to the 1980s revealed the buildings and graveyards of four churches in the centre of Medieval Lund (Cinthio 1997, 114). The Drotten or Trinitatis Church, built in stone in the mid-eleventh century, is the largest of these. Two other wooden structures, to the south-west and east, were contemporary with the stone church, while a tenth-century wooden structure located to the north is believed to have been replaced by the stone church (Andrén 2000, 11). All four structures were surrounded by burial grounds; most of the area had been used for burial during the late tenth and eleventh centuries, but the central area surrounding the stone church was used for burial for over 500 years. Charcoal burials were found in proximity to all four church structures, but their distribution varied depending on the part of the excavated area and the period in question. The coffins of the charcoal burials were found to have rested on layers of charcoal between 3 cm and 6 cm in depth. In some cases, small quantities of charcoal were also found inside the coffin and above the lid of the coffin (Blomqvist and Mårtensson 1963, 93).

The distribution of charcoal burials in Lund paints a fascinating picture of the role of variant burial rites in this part of Early Medieval Denmark (Lund became part of Sweden in AD 1658). Over 1200 burials from before AD 1100 are known from the graveyards of these churches. These graves fall into five main types – unaccompanied burial, charcoal burial, burial with lime in the grave, burial in log coffins, and burial with hazel sticks. With the exception of burials in log coffins, burials of these types may be found with or without coffins. Stone-lined cuts are also found in some later examples.

The hazel sticks, or *hasselkäppar*, found in many graves will reward further examination. These thin, unbarked hazel sticks, which were sometimes almost as long as the grave cut, were laid on the grave floor beneath the coffin, or under or alongside the body. This practice was also known in Germany and in the Slavic World (Cinthio 1999, 33), and it also occurred in a small number of English graveyards (Morris 1989, 80).

A small number of charcoal burials have been found to contain *hasselkäppar* (Blomqvist and Mårtensson 1963, 93), but in general the two rites are found in separate areas of the burial grounds. In the earliest phases of the Trinitatis graveyard (T1 and T2), in use from around AD 990 to 1050, the excavated area around the original wooden church contained 22 charcoal burials and 16 burials with lime, but only two log coffin burials and two burials with hazel sticks (Arcini 1999, 34; Cinthio 2002, 88). In contrast, the other trenches, further to the north and east of the church, contained dozens of log coffin burials and over 100 *hasselkäppar* burials, but no charcoal burials (Cinthio 2002, 88).

In the later period, from around AD 1050–1100, three churches were active in the area. The large stone Trinitatis Church contained burials of all types in its graveyard. Burials dated to the period c. AD 1050–1100 included three burials with sticks, seven charcoal burials and three log coffin burials. Unaccompanied inhumation was the dominant rite. During the same period, the church to its south, labeled D, had 28 charcoal burials and no burials at all with sticks, lime, or log coffins. Charcoal burials made up 21% of the excavated burials in this cemetery. The church to the east, labeled K, had over 100 burials with *hasselkäppar*, a few log coffins, and 16 charcoal burials, mainly to its south. Only 5% of the excavated burials contained charcoal, while 40% contained sticks (Cinthio 2002, 125). It is clear that these churches – located only around 10 m apart – practiced burial according to different sets of rules. Maria Cinthio (1997) has suggested these may represent the burial practices of different ethnic or immigrant communities in Lund, while Anders Andrén (2000, 14) has argued that this separation may have been more closely connected with status. Osteological analysis has also detected a much higher number of bodies showing signs of leprosy and periostitis among the graves in the main area of *hasselkäppar*, surrounding the eastern church (Cinthio 2002, 128). It is possible that these individuals were treated differently in death because of their infectious conditions. If we accept that burial near the church implies higher status than burial near the edge of the cemetery, this may be evidence of a marginalised group receiving a marginalised burial rite, or of a low-status population more vulnerable to illness (Figures 8.5 and 8.6).

It is certainly true that during this period Lund would have had an extensive English presence. During the early eleventh century, it was 'the most important mint' in Denmark (Pederson 2004, 64–6), with many of its moneyers having also struck coins for the English king, Æthelred II. Other artefacts, either of English origin or crafted in an English style, have been found in Lund, and a mid-eleventh century church bears a dedication to St. Botulf (also Botwulf or Botolph), a common dedication in eastern England but rare elsewhere (Blair 2005, 425).

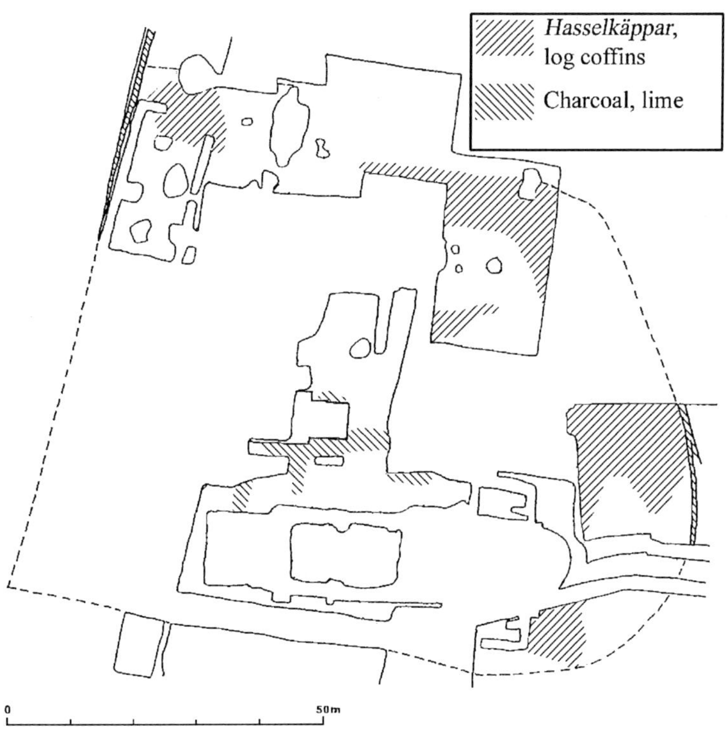

Figure 8.5. Trinitatskyrkan, Lund: the period T1 and T2 cemeteries, c. AD 990–1060 (after Cinthio 1999; Andrén 2000).

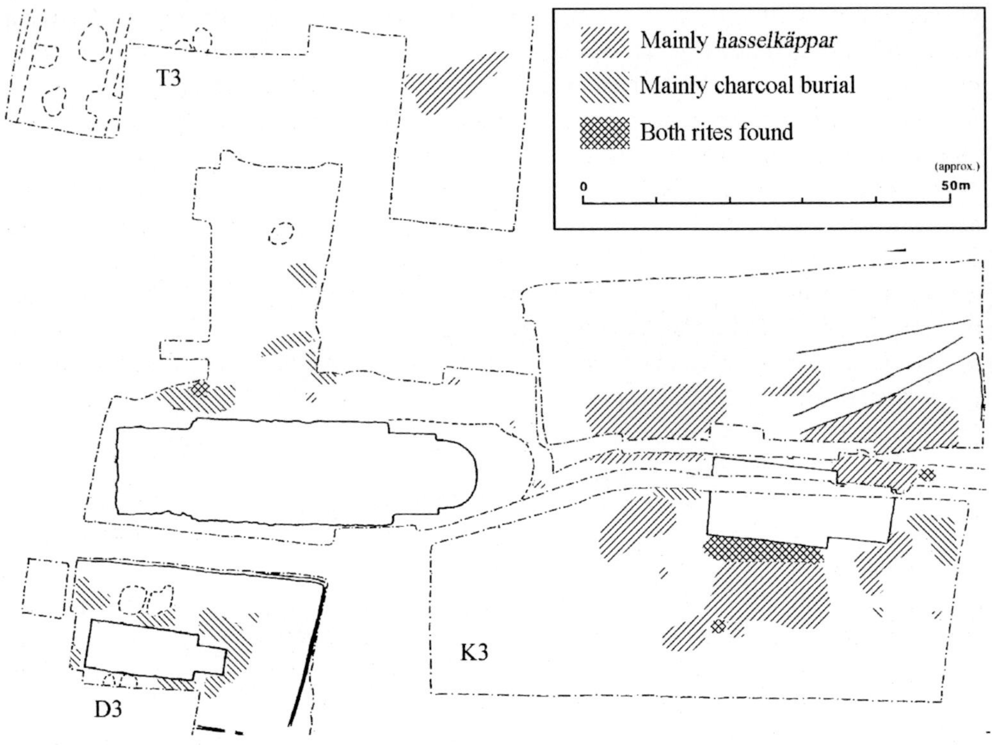

Figure 8.6. Trinitatskyrkan, Lund: the later cemeteries, c. AD 1050–1100 (after Cinthio 1999).

Charcoal Burial in Scotland

The site of a stone church at Barhobble in Galloway, western Scotland, was excavated between 1984 and 1994 by W. F. Cormack. Over 130 burials were found to have surrounded and underlay this structure, which appears to have been preceded by an earlier timber-built structure. The possible earlier structure was 'closely associated' with one of two groups of charcoal burials (Cormack *et al.* 1995, 24). Radiocarbon dating of charcoal samples produced dates of AD 1036–1256 and AD 1027–1192 at one sigma.

A total of 12 charcoal burials and possible charcoal burials were excavated at Barhobble. Structurally, some of these charcoal graves differ from their English and Irish counterparts – in four cases, charcoal had been laid both over and under the body, creating 'a D shape in section' (Cormack *et al.* 1995, 35). One more burial had a layer of charcoal only beneath the body. In the remaining cases, sections of the burial were not obtained. Many of the graves had extensive stone elaboration, including capstones. Six of the 12 charcoal burials and possible charcoal burials contained this type of elaboration. Among burials without charcoal in the same areas, by contrast, graves without stone elaboration were around twice as common. When burials within the church itself and burials outside the church are separated, the proportions change slightly. Within the church, in Area A, four charcoal burials have stone elaboration as opposed to two without. Outside the church, in Area E, only one charcoal burial has stone elaboration; five do not. In both areas, the proportions for burials without charcoal are similar – about one third have stone elaboration.

Pebbles, found in several of the other burials at the site, were also found in three of the charcoal burials. One of these, Burial I, contained a piece of 'exotic porphyry'. This type of find is known from other graves in Galloway, as well as graves in Caithness, primarily from pagan contexts (Cormack 1989; Cormack *et al.* 1995, 40).

The presence of charcoal in the graves at Barhobble appears to be a unique finding in Scottish archaeology. The contemporary monastic town of Whithorn, located on the same peninsula and less than 25 km from Barhobble, had no charcoal burials, although few graves from the same periods as the Barhobble charcoal graves have been excavated (Hill 1997, 187, 234).

Charcoal Burial in France

The final burial ground to be included in the current study provides a marked contrast to the preceding four cases. Despite their many differences, St. Oswald's, St. Peter's, Trinitatis and Barhobble all appear to be churchyard burial grounds, with at least some burials dating from the tenth to twelfth centuries. By contrast, the burial ground of Mazerny, in the French *Département* of Ardennes-sur-Meuse, dates to the sixth to eighth centuries. There is no physical evidence of an accompanying church, but Bailey K. Young (1986, 396) has argued that the varying orientation of one group of graves may be due to their having been aligned on a now lost timber building. This is a common type of burial ground for the Merovingian period; although burial in urban mortuary churches was becoming increasingly common, rural burial grounds typically remained outside settlements, 'away from centres of habitation' (James 1979, 60).

Mazerny was excavated in the period between 1963 and 1967, although the results have never been fully published. A total of 273 graves were excavated, of which nine contained 'véritables lits de charbon de bois' (Young 1984, 123). These graves with 'beds of charcoal' were not the only burials in the burial ground which contained charcoal, however, and 58 of the graves displayed evidence of fire, in the form of traces of charcoal, ash or burnt stones, while 10% of the graves were recorded by the original excavators as having contained no charcoal. The situation for the remaining graves, where the presence of charcoal is not mentioned, is unclear.

From these remarks, we can see that the charcoal burials at Mazerny occurred among a number of other, possibly related burial practices involving the use of charcoal and burning residues. These are the so-called *feux rituels*, which Bailey Young has divided into two types. Type I refers to burials in which there is evidence of burning having occurred within the grave cut itself, while Type 2 refers to burials in which ash or charcoal are found either in the fill or in association with the body. Charcoal burials as they appear in Britain, Ireland and Scandinavia fall under Type 2.

At Mazerny, charcoal burial coincided in two of the nine cases with other evidence of fires having occurred in the grave. It also tended to appear in graves with no, or limited, grave goods. Young describes the rite as appearing 'seldom in the graves of men and not at all in the graves of women' (Young 1984, 125). This description refers only to grave goods, not skeletal sexing; 'beds of charcoal' appear in only two graves with 'typically masculine' grave goods. In the other seven cases, the assemblage does not indicate gender.

Charcoal burial at Mazerny, then, occurred within a context of rites related to fire. This is an important contrast with charcoal burial in Gloucester, Waterford, Mochrum and Lund, which appears to be a distinct rite, one of a range of discrete practices. The connection between Frankish charcoal burial and the rite as practised elsewhere is unclear. Frankish connections played an important role in the conversion of the English (Blair 2005, 61). However, during the conversion period, there are no known charcoal burials in Britain (Geake 1997). Any connection between the two must therefore remain a matter for speculation.

It may make sense to view Mazerny as an outlier, but given the cultural contacts between Ireland, Britain and Scandinavia during the tenth, eleventh and twelfth centuries, we must assume that the rites practiced at the other sites covered in this paper are related. We have here an example of a variant burial rite found across northern Europe. In each case, however, the rite has been adapted to its new setting.

Interpretation of Charcoal Burial

Archaeologists have proposed a wide range of interpretations for this burial rite. Charcoal burial has been identified as a sanitary practice designed to absorb fluids from the decomposing body (Thompson 1979, 178). It has also been called an act of penance, with the charcoal substituting for penitential ash (Daniell 1996, 160). Victoria Thompson (2004, 120) has suggested that charcoal burial might have served to identify members of a community who failed to die 'with decency', while Jacob Kieffer-Olsen (1993, 188) has identified charcoal burial as one of a variety of practices intended to make the grave 'as pleasant as possible'. Blomqvist and Mårtensson (1963, 54) believed that the charcoal may have represented 'a symbolic hint of the hope of the soul's purification after worldly, sinful living'. Fleming (1993, 26) has suggested that charcoal burial is indicative of high status, but like many early writers is reluctant to suggest a possible symbolic or liturgical interpretation. J. T. Fowler, who excavated nine examples of charcoal burial from beneath the chapter house of Durham Cathedral in 1876, suggested that the practice might derive from incense-burning, or have been used to mark the location of a grave (Fowler 1883, 245). It has been suggested that the Merovingian *feux rituels* contained 'pre-Christian elements', derived either from late antique or 'barbarian' customs such as feasting by the side of the grave or even cremation (Effros 2003, 165). The evidence for some of these practices is better than others – it is hard to imagine, for example, how charcoal would have functioned to absorb bodily fluids in cases where the charcoal was positioned in direct contact with a coffin rather than a body.

Contemporary written sources are silent on the subject of charcoal burial. Indeed, we know comparatively little about Early Medieval funerary practice in general from the written sources. Medieval written sources do discuss the laying out of dying individuals, particularly monks, on a bed of ash. A connection has been suggested between this practice, which first appears in the *Life of St. Martin of Tours*, written by Sulpicius Severus in AD 396, and charcoal burial (Thompson 2002, 240). While dying, St. Martin rested on a bed of sackcloth and ashes (Roberts 1894, 23). King Louis IX of France, later St. Louis, was laid out in a similar manner 'en un lit couvert de cendre' (Joinville DCCLVII – Corbett 1977). There is no direct connection between the use of ash described in these sources, however, and the use of charcoal in charcoal burials. The liturgical significance of the practice remains unclear.

If we do not understand the exact symbolic content of charcoal burial, what *do* we know about it? The appearance of charcoal burials at a wide number of sites tells us that it cannot have been a local variation. The diversity of rites within each churchyard is also suggestive. A vocabulary of Christian burial practices appears to have existed; a number of different rites were known, all having been seen as appropriate for people receiving Christian burial. Each of the burial grounds in this brief survey has a different vocabulary, but all have at least one element in common. How were these elements communicated, and why were some adopted and others not? In the face of the silence of the written sources, we can only answer these questions by examining the burials themselves.

In England, for instance, we are dealing with a rite in use over a long period of time and over a wide area. Charcoal burial is never a majority rite, but it is found in a large number of Late Saxon burial grounds and a smaller number of post-Conquest ones; four separate cemetery excavations in Oxford have produced charcoal burials (Lambrick and Woods 1976; Boyle 2001; Tyler *et al.* 2001; Dodd 2003). The high percentage of charcoal burials at St. Oswald's is consistent with findings at other high-status English churches, such as Durham and the Old and New Minsters of Winchester. Even in smaller burial grounds, however, one or two charcoal burials are sometimes found (Rodwell and Rodwell 1982, 301; Corbishley 1984, 21), and even quite small churches, such as St. Mark's, Lincoln, may be associated with a comparatively large number of these burials (Gilmour and Stocker 1986, 16). English charcoal burial is a widespread, institutionalised rite, one that was understood as acceptable for Christian burial – albeit for a minority of Christians – by clerics or laypeople all across England for several hundred years.

In Ireland and Scotland, by contrast, the picture is less clear. At Waterford, charcoal seems to have been used either for a very short period or in very limited circumstances. Possibly the rite was in use among one family or community in this cosmopolitan environment, or by members of a particular religious group. In any case, it does not appear to be a widespread, institutionalised practice along the same lines as the English model. Further excavation may clarify this situation. The same is true for the Scottish examples, which are even more puzzling. Charcoal burial appears to have been common during at least one phase at Barhobble, but is not known from other sites.

The examples from Trinitatis and the other unidentified churches in Lund provide a striking example of a rite similar, and almost certainly connected, to the English practice but being used in very different ways. Although an individual charcoal burial from Lund may appear similar to an individual charcoal burial from St. Oswald's, the distribution of rites within the two burial grounds is completely different. Communities with different identities employed similar rites differently, interpreting them in the context of an existing vocabulary of burial rites and constructing new interpretations and oppositions for them.

Barring some remarkable new discoveries, we will never be able to say with certainty what charcoal burial meant to the communities that practiced it. A number of interpretations have been discussed above, but the evidence for any remains slight. We are on firmer ground matching the burial rite with demographic patterns, both within graveyards (Kjølbye-Biddle 1992, 231; Heighway and Bryant 1999, 202) and on a larger scale (Holloway 2003). Within England, comparison of data from excavated sites has allowed us to see how the application of the rite differed from church to church and from region to region. The full range of sites in Scandinavia also awaits a more comprehensive study, examining both variations of the rite within Scandinavia and the connections between Scandinavian and English Christian burial practice.

Conclusions

A concept of Medieval burial that fails to take into account the wide variety of burial practices is inadequate. This paper provides a brief overview of one of many such variant rites, a rite well within the boundaries of what is usually considered 'normal' Medieval Christian burial practice. This rite and others like it require further study, but perhaps the variety of burial practices and combinations of burial practices encountered even in this brief survey may begin to suggest that we should view Medieval burial practice not as an opposition between normal and deviant burials but rather as a vocabulary of symbolic elements from which a range of rites are produced and reproduced.

Acknowledgements

The author wishes to thank Conny Johansson Hervén of Kulturen Museum, Lund, for his assistance and comments. Thanks are also due to Lisa Donel of Gloucester City Museum and Art Gallery, for assistance with excavation records. Winchester City Council generously gave permission to use photographs from the Staple Gardens excavations. Alison Klevnäs helped with Swedish translations and Dr Robert Dewar assisted with cartography. Dr Catherine Hills provided comments on early versions of the paper, while Dr Andrew Nicholson and Dr David Bowler gave advice on Scottish and Irish burials. The assistance of all these individuals and organisations has been invaluable. Funds to attend the conference at which this paper originated were generously provided by the H. M. Chadwick Fund of the Department of Anglo-Saxon, Norse and Celtic at Cambridge University.

References

Adams, M. 1996. Excavation of a Pre-Conquest cemetery at Addingham, W. Yorkshire. *Medieval Archaeology* 40, 151–91.

Andrén, A. 2000. Ad sanctos – de dödas plats under medeltiden. *Hikuin* 27, 7–26. (*Ad sanctos* – the place of the dead in the Middle Ages).

Biddle, M. 1968. Excavations at Winchester, 1967: 6th interim report. *Antiquaries Journal* 48, 250–84.

Biddle, M. 1969. Excavations at Winchester, 1968: 7th interim report. *Antiquaries Journal* 49, 295–329.

Blair, J. 2005. *The Church in Anglo-Saxon Society*. Oxford: Oxford University Press.

Blomqvist, R. and Mårtensson, A. W. 1963. *Thulegrävningen 1961* (Archaeologica Lundensia. Investigationes de Antiquitatibus Urbis Lundae, II) Lund: Kulturhistoriska Museet. (Thule Excavation, 1961).

Boyle, A. 2001. Excavations in Christ Church Cathedral graveyard, Oxford. *Oxoniensia* 66, 338–68.

Buckberry, J. L. and Hadley, D. M. 2007. An Anglo-Saxon execution cemetery at Walkington Wold, East Yorkshire. *Oxford Journal of Archaeology* 26, 309–29.

Cinthio, M. 1997. Trinitatiskyrkan i Lund – med engelsk prägel. *Hikuin* 24, 113–34. (The Church of the Trinity in Lund – with English influence).

Cinthio, M. 1999. The archaeological context, pp. 18–46 in Arcini, C., *Health and Disease in Early Lund* (Archaeologica Lundensia. Investigationes de Antiquitatibus Urbis Lundae, VIII). Lund: Lund University Department of Community Health Services.

Cinthio, M. 2002. *De Första Stadsborna: Medeltida Gravar Och Människor I Lund*. Stockholm: Brutus östlings Bokförlag Symposion. (The first town-dwellers: Medieval graves and people in Lund).

Corbett, N. L. (ed.) 1977. J. de Joinville – *La Vie de Saint Louis. Le temoignage de Jehan, Seigneur de Joinville. Texte du XIVe siècle*. Quebec: Editions Namaan de Sherbrooke. (The Life of St. Louis. The accout of Jehan, lord of Joinville, fourteenth-century text).

Corbishley, M. J. 1984. Excavations at St Mary's Church, Little Oakley, Essex, pp. 15–27 in Essex County Council, *4 Church Excavations in Essex* (Essex County Council Occasional Papers 4). Chelmsford: Essex County Council.

Cormack, W. F. 1989. Two recent finds of exotic porphyry in Galloway. *Transactions of the Dumfriesshire and Galloway Natural History and Antiquarian Society* 64, 43.

Cormack, W. F., Barnetson, L., Clark, J., Gabra-Sanders, T., Habeshaw, D., Holmes, N., Hunter, F., Home Lorimer, D. and Pirie, E. 1995. Barhobble, Mochrum. Excavation of a forgotten church site in Galloway. *Transactions of the Dumfriesshire and Galloway Natural History and Antiquarian Society* 70, 5–106.

Daniell, C. 1996. When penance continued into the grave. *British Archaeology* 19, 7.

Dawes, J. D. and Magilton, J. R. 1980. *The Cemetery of St Helen-on-the-Walls, Aldwark, York* (Archaeology of York 12/1). London: Council for British Archaeology.

Dodd, A. 2003. The town: detailed studies of sites within the Late Saxon and Medieval town, pp. 201–70 in Dodd, A. (ed.), *Oxford Before the University*. Oxford: Oxford Archaeology.

Effros, B. 2002. *Caring for Body and Soul: Burial and the Afterlife in the Merovingian World*. Pennsylvania: Pennsylvania State University Press.

Effros, B. 2003. *Merovingian Mortuary Archaeology and the Making of the Early Middle Ages*. Berkeley: University of California Press.

Fleming, R. 1993. Rural elites and urban communities in Late-Saxon England. *Past and Present* 141, 3–37.

Fowler, J. T. 1880. An account of excavations made on the site of the chapter-house of Durham Cathedral in 1874. *Archaeologia* 45, 385–404.

Geake, H. 1997. *The Use of Grave-goods in Conversion-period England, c. 600–c. 850* (BAR British Series 261). Oxford: British Archaeological Reports.

Gilchrist, R. and. Sloane, B. 2005. *Requiem: The Medieval Monastic Cemetery*. London: Museum of London Archaeology Service.

Gilmour, B. J. J. and Stocker, D. A. 1986. *St Mark's Church and Cemetery* (Archaeology of Lincoln XIII–1). London: Council for British Archaeology.

Gwynn, A. and Hadcock, R. N. 1970. *Medieval Religious Houses: Ireland.* London: Longman.

Heighway, C. and Bryant, R. 1999. *The Golden Minster: The Anglo-Saxon Minster and Later Medieval Priory of St. Oswald at Gloucester* (CBA Research Report 117). York: Council for British Archaeology.

Henderson, C. G. and Bidwell, P. T. 1982. The Saxon minster at Exeter, pp. 145–76 in Pearce, S. M. (ed.), *The Early Church in Western Britain and Ireland: Studies Presented to C. A. Ralegh Radford, Arising from a Conference Organised in his Honour by the Devon Archaeological Society and Exeter City Museum* (BAR British Series 102). Oxford: British Archaeological Reports.

Hill, P. 1997. *Whithorn and St Ninian: The Excavations of a Monastic Town, 1984–91*. Stroud: Sutton.

Holloway, J. 2003. *Charcoal Burials in Early Medieval Northern England.* Unpublished M.A. thesis, University of Durham.

Hurley, M. 1992. Late Viking age settlement in Waterford city, pp. 49–72 in Nolan, W. and Power, T. P. (eds), *Waterford: History and Society: Interdisciplinary Essays on the History of an Irish County*. Dublin: Geography Publications.

Hurley, M. and Sheehan, C. M. 1995. *Excavations at the Dominican Priory, St Mary's of the Isle, Cork.* Cork: Cork Corporation.

Hurley, M., Scully, O. M. B. and McCutcheon, S. J. 1997. *Late Viking Age and Medieval Waterford, Excavations 1986–1992.* Waterford: Waterford Corporation.

James, E. 1979. Cemeteries and the problem of Frankish settlement in Gaul, pp. 55–90 in Sawyer, P. H. (ed.), *Names, Words, and Graves: Early Medieval Settlement.* Leeds: University of Leeds.

Kieffer-Olsen, J. 1993. *Grav Og Gravskik I Det Middeladerlige Danmark.* Højberg: Afd. for Middelalder-arkæologi: Middelalder-arkæologisk Nyhedsbrev. (Grave and burial customs in Medieval Denmark).

Kjølbye-Biddle, B. 1992. The disposal of the Winchester dead over 2000 years, pp. 210–47 in Bassett, S. (ed.), *Death in Towns*. Leicester: Leicester University Press.

Lambrick, G. and Woods, H. 1976. Excavations on the second site of the Dominican Priory, Oxford. *Oxoniensia* 41, 168–231.

Lanting, J. 1997. Radiocarbon dating, p. 818 in Hurley, M., Scully, O. M. B. and McCutcheon, S. J., *Late Viking Age and Medieval Waterford, Excavations 1986–1992.* Waterford: Waterford Corporation.

Lubin, H. 1990. *The Worcester Pilgrim* (Worcester Cathedral Publications 1) Worcester: West Mercian Archaeological Consultants.

Morris, R. 1989. *Churches in the Landscape.* London: Dent.

Murphy, E. 2005. Session abstract – Deviant burial practices in the archaeological record, p. 107 in the *Book of Abstracts of the European Association of Archaeologists 11th Annual Meeting, Cork 2005.*

Pederson, A. 2004. Anglo-Danish contact across the North Sea in the eleventh century: a survey of the Danish archaeological evidence, pp. 43–68 in Adams, J. and Holman, K. (eds), *Scandinavia and Europe 800–1350: Contact, Conflict, and Coexistence*. Turnhout: Brepols.

Philips, D. and Heywood, B. 1995. *Excavations at York Minster Vol. 1*. London: HMSO.

Reynolds, A. 1999. *Later Anglo-Saxon England: Life and Landscape*. Stroud: Tempus.

Roberts, A. 1894. *The Works of Sulpitius Severus*. Oxford: Parker.

Rodwell, W. 1981. *The Archaeology of the English Church: The Study of Historic Churches and Churchyards*. London: Batsford.

Rodwell, W. and Rodwell, K. 1982. St Peter's Church, Barton-Upon-Humber: excavation and structural study 1979–81. *Antiquaries Journal* 62, 283–315.

Shoesmith, R. 1980. *Hereford City Excavations 1: Excavations at Castle Green*. London: Council for British Archaeology.

Thacker, A. T. 1981. Chester and Gloucester: early ecclesiastical organization in two Mercian burhs. *Northern History* 18, 199–211.

Thompson, A. 1979. St. Nicholas-in-the-Shambles. *Current Archaeology* 65, 176–9.

Thompson, V. 2004. *Dying and Death in Later Anglo-Saxon England* (Anglo-Saxon Studies 4). Woodbridge: Boydell.

Tyler, R., Boyle, A. and Challinor, D. 2001. Archaeological investigations during refurbishment of St. Aldate's Church, Oxford. *Oxoniensia* 66, 369–410.

Young, B. K. 1975. *Merovingian Funeral Rites and the Evolution of Christianity: A Study in the Historical Interpretation of Archaeological Material*. Ann Arbor, Michigan: University Microfilms International.

Young, B. K. 1984. *Quatre Cimitières Mérovingiens de l'Est de la France* (BAR International Series 208). Oxford: British Archaeological Reports. (Four Merovingian Cemeteries in the east of France).

Young, B. K. 1986. Exemple aristocratique et mode funéraire dans La Gaule Mérovingienne. *Annales ESC* 41, 379–408. (Aristocratic example and funerary fashion in Merovingian Gaul).

9. Off With Their Heads: The Anglo-Saxon Execution Cemetery at Walkington Wold, East Yorkshire

Jo Buckberry

Abstract

From the seventh century AD onwards, execution cemeteries began to appear in England. These are typically located away from normal community cemeteries. The burials are usually of adult males, sometimes arranged in unusual positions, occasionally with evidence that their hands were tied, or that individuals were decapitated (Reynolds 1997). However, the osteological evidence to back this up was often lacking, particularly for cemeteries that were excavated in the eighteenth or early nineteenth centuries.

The execution cemetery at Walkington Wold, East Yorkshire, was excavated in the 1960s, and the burials were initially interpreted as having resulted from a massacre that took place during the Late Roman period (Bartlett and Mackey 1973). The site was subsequently identified as a probable Anglo-Saxon execution cemetery (Reynolds 1997). The present research has provided three radiocarbon dates securely dating the cemetery to the Mid to Late Anglo-Saxon period, together with a detailed osteological analysis of the skeletal remains. This paper will discuss the osteological evidence for execution at Walkington Wold, and will place the site in its archaeological and social context.

Introduction

The term 'deviant' was first used to describe a discrete type of seventh- and eight-century burial by Helen Geake in 1992, in her wider discussion of the range of burial practices employed in the Mid Anglo-Saxon period (Geake 1992, 87–8). Geake highlighted that not all seventh-century burials were of the 'Final Phase' type, characterised by west–east aligned burials, often arranged in rows, many of which contained grave goods, although these were typically both fewer in number and selected from a narrower range of artefacts that in the earlier burials of the fifth and sixth centuries (Morris 1983, 53–4; Boddington 1990, 181; Geake 1992, 84–8). Geake defined 'princely' burials as those that were characterised by a large number of high quality grave goods and frequently marked by a barrow, for example the mound burials at Sutton Hoo, (Suffolk), Taplow (Taplow), Caenby (Lincolnshire) and Cuddesdon (Oxfordshire). Finally she defined 'unfurnished' burial sites, as those which are similar to 'Final Phase' burials, other than the fact that all or most of the graves were unfurnished (e.g. Kemp Howe, Yorkshire), with only small items such as knives or pins present, if at all (Geake 1992, 85–6).

The fourth type of Mid Anglo-Saxon burial defined by Geake was 'deviant' burials, and it is this group of burials that is the focus of the present paper. Seventh- and eighth-century 'deviant' burials are characterised by 'a scarcity or complete lack of grave goods, and by an unusual way of positioning both the grave and the body in the grave' (Geake 1992, 87). Geake described how many of these burials may have been decapitated, buried prone, show evidence of tied hands and/or feet, or were buried in various positions 'indicating that some sort of ritual abuse or mutilation was carried out just before or just after death' (Geake 1992, 87). Geake noted that, in many examples, it is difficult to ascertain the date of these burials in the absence of radiocarbon dates but more 'deviant burials' are known for the Mid Anglo-Saxon than the Early Anglo-Saxon period (Geake 1992, 87). These 'deviant' burials have been interpreted as both battlefield cemeteries, for example Ocklynge Hill in Sussex (Meaney 1964, 252) and execution cemeteries, for example at Sutton Hoo in Suffolk, Cuddesdon in Oxfordshire and South Acre in Norfolk (Dickinson 1974; Wymer 1996; Carver 2005).

Recent work by Andrew Reynolds has recognised that many Mid Anglo-Saxon deviant burials are from execution cemeteries. Separate execution cemeteries were first founded in the seventh century, and continued to be used throughout the Later Anglo-Saxon period and sometimes as late as the twelfth century, for example at Staines in Surrey (Reynolds 1997, 34–5; Hayman and Reynolds 2006; Reynolds forthcoming). Many of these cemeteries were located close to Hundred boundaries, away from community cemeteries and settlements.[1] Prior to this development, during the fifth and sixth centuries AD, deviant burials were usually found within normal community cemeteries, rather than in liminal locations (Geake 1992, 87; Reynolds 1997, 37).

The introduction of separate execution cemeteries during the seventh and eighth centuries has been linked to the conversion to Christianity in the seventh century and the rise of churchyard burial from the eighth century onwards (Reynolds 1997, 37). From this time onwards it was no longer the norm to include wrongdoers in community cemeteries (see Cherryson, this volume). This has been linked to the influence of the church, however, it is generally agreed that the early English church showed little interest in enforcing churchyard burial, at least in the centuries immediately following the conversion (Bullough 1983, 186; Morris 1983, 50; Geake 2002, 153; Gittos 2002, 202). Indeed, the first law code referring to the exclusion of criminals from burial in consecrated ground (II Æthelstan 26) dates to the early tenth century (Wormald 1999, 307–8, 339–40; Gittos 2002, 201). Churchyards appear to have been consecrated from the tenth century onwards (Gittos 2002, 208), and from this date it is legitimate to argue that the unbaptised, suicide victims and criminals were excluded from burial in *consecrated* ground, however, in practice they were buried away from churchyards and other community cemeteries at a much earlier date (Reynolds 1997, 38). The foundation of execution cemeteries in the seventh and eighth centuries suggests that the process of state formation, rather than the influence of the Church, governed their development (Reynolds 1997; Reynolds forthcoming).

Later Anglo-Saxon execution cemeteries have been defined as having several of the following characteristics (Wymer 1996, 89; Reynolds 1997; Reynolds forthcoming):

- Varied burial alignments
- Unusual burial positions
- Prone burials
- Evidence of decapitation or other trauma (for example amputation of hands or feet)
- Evidence of tied hands and/or feet
- Shallow and undersized graves
- Evidence of intercutting graves
- Multiple internments
- Presence of low status dress fittings
- Predominantly adult male populations
- Pre-existing earthworks, especially prehistoric barrows
- Location close to boundaries, especially of Hundreds
- Proximity to routeways

This introduction to deviant burial in the Later Anglo-Saxon period is necessarily very brief, and serves only to provide a context for the following discussion of the cemetery at Walkington Wold in East Yorkshire (Figure 9.1).

Walkington Wold

Before discussing the cemetery at Walkington Wold in detail, it is necessary to briefly discuss the excavation, initial interpretation and subsequent reinterpretations of the cemetery. John Bartlett and Rod Mackey excavated two Bronze Age barrows at Walkington Wold between 1967 and 1969 (Bartlett and Mackey 1973). Both barrows produced the expected Bronze Age burials, however the excavation also revealed evidence of re-occupation of Barrow 1 during the Late Roman period (Bartlett and Mackey 1973, 27). A group of 12 burials, ten of which were buried without their crania articulated with the remainder of the skeleton, and eleven disarticulated crania (some of which were articulated with mandibulae and occasionally vertebrae) were also discovered around Barrow 1 (Figure 9.2). These burials were deposited in an apparently random manner and included one 'triple burial' and skeletal evidence of decapitation (Bartlett and Mackey 1973, 25). The stratigraphy of the site only allowed the burials to be dated to between the fourth century and the Later Middle Ages. However, the presence of several small bronze objects of Post-Roman 'Germanic manufacture' close to the burials led the excavators to speculate that the burials were probably fifth century in date (Bartlett and Mackey 1973, 10, 21, 26). Bartlett and Mackey suggested

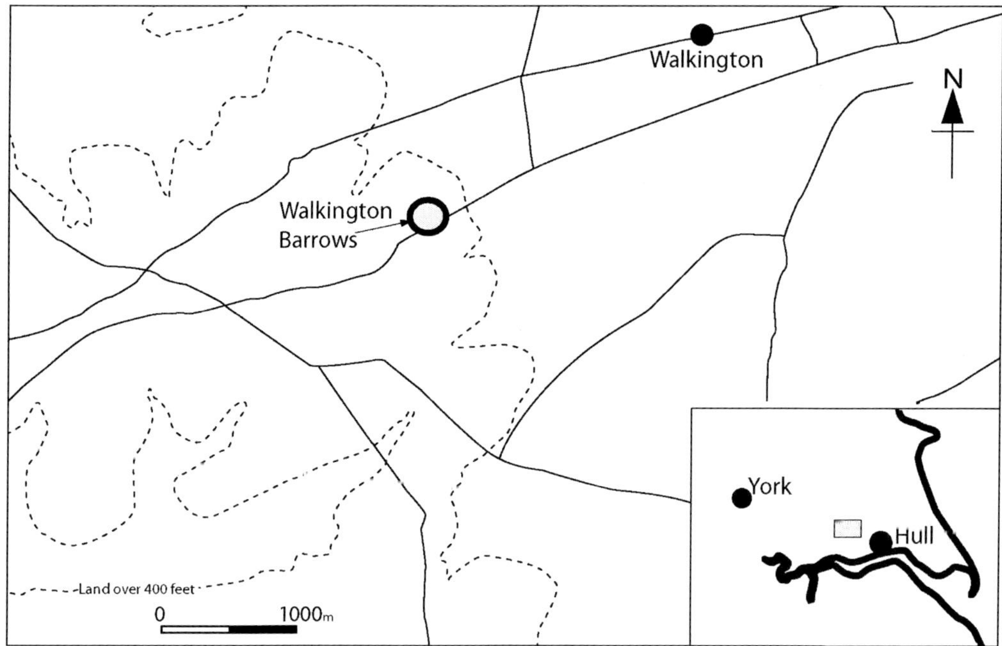

Figure 9.1. Map showing the location of Walkington Wold, East Yorkshire (drawn by Oliver Jessop).

that the cemetery represented 'a massacre or a series of executions' (Bartlett and Mackey 1973, 3), on the basis of the apparently haphazard manner of the burials combined with the evidence for decapitation among the skeletal remains. They surmised that this event marked the end of occupation of an inland signal station. However, the date and nature of the cemetery remained uncertain, and therefore G. B. Bailey reinterpreted the site as a shrine pertaining to a 'Celtic' head cult, which had survived into the Roman period elsewhere in east Yorkshire (Bailey 1985). More recently, Andrew Reynolds proposed that Walkington Wold may be an Anglo-Saxon execution cemetery, as it has many features in common with identified execution cemeteries of this period elsewhere in England and because of its location close to the Hundred boundaries of Welton and Cave (Reynolds 1997, 36; Reynolds 1998, 155–6). Radiocarbon dates were obtained for the cemetery by the present author and Dawn Hadley, confirming that the cemetery did, indeed, date to the Mid to Late Anglo-Saxon period (Buckberry and Hadley 2007).

Osteology

A full re-analysis of the osteological material was undertaken by the present author, in order to assess the findings of Jean Dawes in light of recent osteological developments (Dawes 1973). It should be noted that the skeleton numbers and skull numbers used in the archive

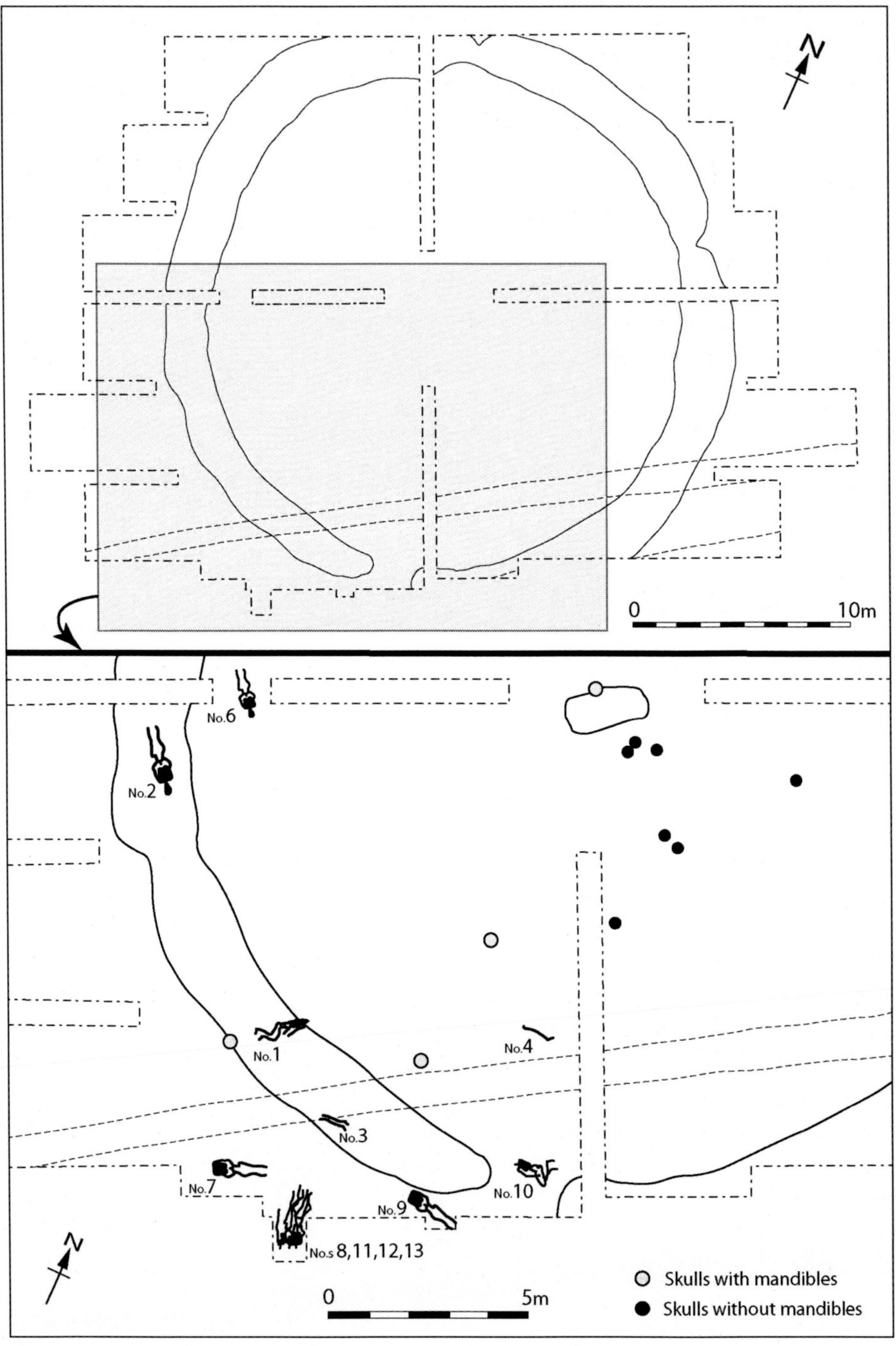

Figure 9.2. Plan of the Walkington Wold cemetery (drawn by Oliver Jessop).

at Hull and East Riding Museum are different from the skeleton numbers and skull numbers used in the 1973 publication (see below). The sex of the individuals was assessed using standard morphological features of the pelvis and skull, with particular emphasis on the morphology of the pubic bone (Phenice 1969; Buikstra and Ubelaker 1994). Age-at-death was estimated using standard osteological methods, many of which have been developed or revised since the initial osteological report (Miles 1962; Meindl and Lovejoy 1985; Webb and Suchey 1985; Suchey *et al.* 1988; Scheuer and Black 2000; Buckberry and Chamberlain 2002). Stature was estimated using the equations provided by Trotter and Gleser (1952). Cribra orbitalia was recorded using a revised version of the method described by Stuart-Macadam (1991), with Type 2 described here as slight cribra orbitalia, Type 3 as moderate, Type 4 as severe and Type 5 as very severe. Capillary impressions (Stuart-Macadam Type 1) were not recorded as cribra orbitalia.

A partially complete list relating archive numbers to skeleton numbers was provided to the author by Rod Mackey and the remaining skeletons and skulls were identified with their publication number by comparing the completeness of the skeleton, pathologies present and the state of their dentitions with the data presented in Jean Dawes' report (Table 9.1). For simplicity, and for the ease of any future researchers, the skeleton and skull numbers used in this paper relate to the archive numbers used on the boxes in the museum. The skeleton numbers refer to post-cranial remains (including cranial remains if these were found articulated with the body), and the skull numbers refer to the disarticulated cranial remains.

Skeleton 1

Skeleton 1 was located on top of a Roman rubbish level in the barrow ditch. There was no evidence of a grave cut, and it appeared that the body had been covered with a heap of earth. It was orientated north-east to south-west, flexed on its left side, and the cranium was not articulated with the post-cranial remains (Bartlett and Mackey 1973, 21–4).[2] A cranium, mandible and four cervical vertebrae were located 0.5 m from the feet of the skeleton. These bones were originally assumed to belong to Skeleton 1, however the present re-analysis has shown that they belong to a different individual, as the age-at-death estimates obtained for the skeleton (18 to 20 years) differ significantly to those derived for the cranial remains (26 to 35 years). Therefore the cranium, mandible and four cervical vertebrae are referred to as 'the Skull associated with Skeleton 1' throughout this paper.

The post-cranial remains reveal that Skeleton 1 was a young adult, aged between 18 and 20 years on the basis of an unfused medial clavicle and distal fibula, partial fusion of the ischial tuberosity and vertebral annular rings, and recent fusion of the proximal and distal tibiae (Webb and Suchey 1985; Scheuer and Black 2000). Although initially sexed as female by Jean Dawes (Bartlett and Mackey 1973, 21; Dawes 1973, 72), Skeleton 1 was found to be a probable male in the present study. Overall the skeleton was gracile, with many feminine features and a wide sciatic notch, however the pubic bone is characterised by a narrow pubic angle, no sub-pubic concavity and no ventral arc, indicating that this individual is male, with an accuracy level of 96% (Phenice 1969).[3] Despite the lack of an articulated

Archive Number	Original Publication Number	Notes
1	13	Cranium, mandible and cervical vertebrae boxed with this individual do not belong to this skeleton.
2	4	Complete skeleton with articulated cranium, numbers match the excavator's list.
3	11	Identification based on completeness of skeleton.
4	15	Identification based on completeness of skeleton.
5		Bronze Age skeleton, not discussed in this paper.
6	5	Complete skeleton with articulated cranium. Skeleton numbers match the excavator's list.
7	12	Skeleton numbers match the excavator's list.
8	9	Identification based on the pathologies present.
9	10	Skeleton numbers match the excavator's list.
10	14	Skeleton numbers match the excavator's list.
11	8	Skeleton numbers match the excavator's list.
12	7	Identification based on the pathologies present.
13	6	Skeleton numbers match the excavator's list.
Skull associated with Skeleton 1	Skull 1	Stored with Skeleton 1, but does not relate to this individual.
Skull I*	Skull 2	Identification based on dentition.
Skull 2**	Skull 3	Identification based on dentition.
Skulls 4–11	Skulls 4–11	Identification based on dentition confirms that the archive numbers and publication numbers for these Skulls were the same.

Table 9.1. Summary of the archive numbers used in the Hull and East Riding Museum and publication numbers used in Bartlett and Mackey (1973). The archive numbers are used throughout the present paper.

** This cranium is labelled as Skull I, not Skull 1, in the archive.*
***There is no Skull 3 in the archive, possibly this number was used to describe the 'Skull associated with Skeleton 1' before it was erroneously combined with Skeleton 1 in the archive.*

cranium, no perimortem trauma or skeletal pathology was evident on the skeleton. Stature could not be calculated.

Skeleton 2

Skeleton 2 was an extended and supine inhumation, with the cranium articulated with the remainder of the skeleton. It was interred in a shallow grave orientated south-east to north-west that was cut into the pre-Roman fill of the barrow ditch. A coin of Claudius Gothicus (AD 268 to 270) was located next to the shoulder and fourth-century pottery was found in the grave fill (Bartlett and Mackey 1973, 21). The individual was male, aged between 18 and 25 years, and was 1.75 m tall (± 2.99 cm). His third molars were congenitally absent. No perimortem trauma was present on this skeleton.

Skeleton 3

The distal femora, tibiae, fibulae and several foot bones were all that remained of Skeleton 3. The burial had been cut by a roadside ditch, just above the knees of the skeleton (Bartlett and Mackey 1973, 24). The burial was probably extended and was orientated west to east. The remains were of an adult of undetermined sex. No evidence of perimortem trauma or skeletal pathology was present.

Skeleton 4

The right lower limb (femur, tibia, fibula and some foot bones) was all that remained of Skeleton 4. The leg was slightly flexed and was located in the mound of the barrow (Bartlett and Mackey 1973, 21). The burial was orientated west to east. The remains were those of an adult, however sex could not be determined. No evidence of skeletal pathology or perimortem trauma was present on the bones, and there is no evidence that the leg had been deliberately removed from a body as a form of mutilation close to the time of death (contra Reynolds forthcoming).

Skeleton 5

Skeleton 5 was a crouched secondary burial dated to the Bronze Age, and therefore will not be discussed further here.

Skeleton 6

Skeleton 6 was buried in a shallow grave in the foot of the barrow mound. The burial was orientated south-west to north-east and fourth-century pottery was found in the grave fill. The skeleton was extended and supine, with the arms crossed over the torso (Bartlett and Mackey 1973, 21). The remains were those of a young adult male, aged 18 to 25 years. The cranium was articulated with the post-cranial remains, and there was no evidence of skeletal pathology or trauma.

Skeleton 7

Skeleton 7 was laid on the surface of the natural chalk, outside the barrow ditch. No trace of a grave cut could be identified at the time of excavation (Bartlett and Mackey 1973, 24). The burial was orientated south-west-west to north-east-east. The torso of the individual had been block-lifted, which made detailed examination of the vertebrae and ribs difficult. The skeleton was supine and extended, and no cranium was found with the post-cranial remains. This was the burial of a young to middle adult male (20 to 35 years), approximately 1.70 m ± 2.99 cm tall. Two parallel cut marks were present on the superior aspect of the first thoracic vertebra (Figure 9.3). The injuries were perimortem, had been delivered from the front and are consistent with blood-letting, throat slitting or decapitation from the front. Although the initial skeletal report suggested that the individual had suffered a stab wound to the back (Bartlett and Mackey 1973, 24), the present analysis indicated that postmortem taphonomic processes had caused the marks suggestive of further sharp force trauma. No other pathology was present on the skeleton.

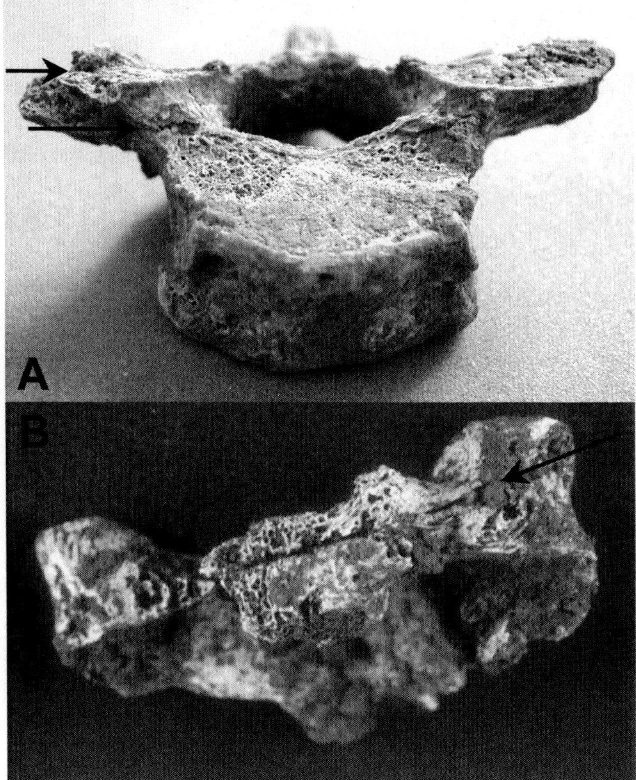

Figure 9.3. Evidence for decapitation on vertebrae from Skeleton 7 (A) and Skull 8 (B) (J. Buckberry).

Skeleton 8

Skeleton 8 was buried in the so-called triple grave positioned directly above Skeleton 11 (Bartlett and Mackey 1973, 24), although the excavation photograph reveals that a layer of soil separated the two skeletons (Figure 9.4). The burial was extended, supine, orientated south to west and was located between the spread lower limbs of Skeleton 11. No cranium was articulated with the post-cranial remains, and it was radiocarbon dated to 900–1030 cal. AD (two sigma). Skeleton 8 was a young middle adult male (25 to 35 years), 1.57 m ± 3.27 cm tall. There was no evidence of perimortem trauma, however this individual had suffered antemortem fractures to the midshaft of the right tibia and fibula. These were both well-healed, but malaligned. The distal portion of the tibia was displaced anteriorly and laterally, with an overlap of 2 cm. There was evidence of a non-specific osteomyelitic infection around the fracture site, with a rounded cloaca 0.7 cm in diameter on the lateral surface and a second cloaca 0.16 cm by 0.3 cm on the posterior of the bone. The distal end of the fibula was displaced medially and laterally and there was also callus present on the lateral side. The distal portion was angulated medially; there was no evidence of infection at this fracture site.

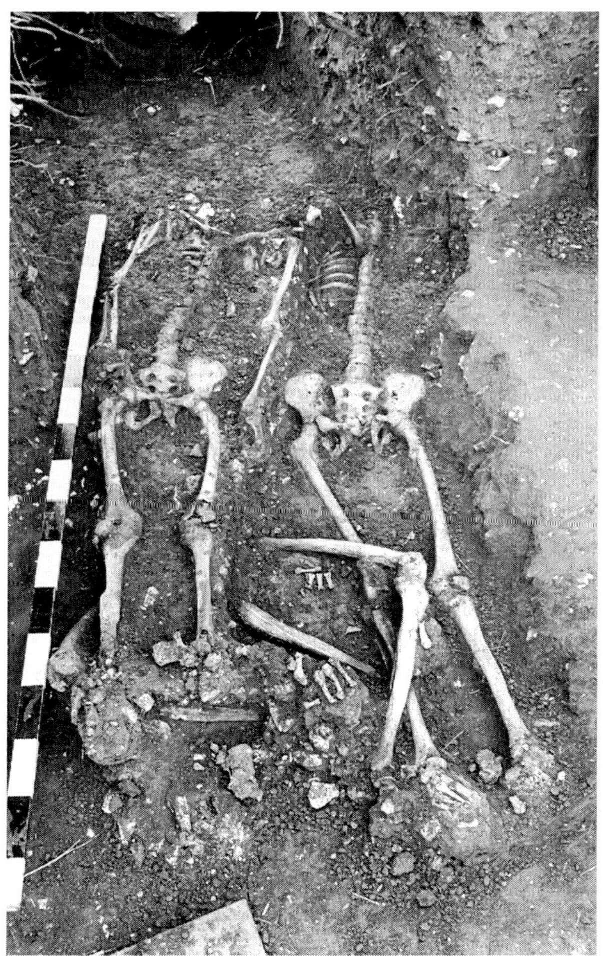

Figure 9.4. Skeleton 8 (left), Skeleton 11 with legs spread (underneath Skeleton 8) and Skeleton 12 (right) during excavation. There is a tibia, probably from the disturbed remains of Skeleton 13, located between the right lower limb of Skeleton 11 and the right tibia of Skeleton 8 (courtesy of Hull and East Riding Museum).

Skeleton 9

Skeleton 9 was an extended and supine burial located beyond the barrow ditch. It was orientated north-west-west to south-east-east. The cranium was not articulated with the remainder of the skeleton (Bartlett and Mackey 1973, 24). The individual was a young or middle adult male (18 to 45 years), 1.75 m ± 4.05 cm tall. No evidence of perimortem trauma or skeletal pathology was present on the skeleton.

Skeleton 10

Skeleton 10 had been buried on top of the prehistoric causeway of the barrow, flexed on the right side, with the left upper limb contorted under the back. It was deposited in a shallow depression in the chalk, suggesting a shallow grave had been dug, and was orientated west to east (Bartlett and Mackey 1973, 21). The remains comprised the post-cranial skeleton of a young middle adult male (26 to 35 years), approximately 1.77 m ± 3.27 cm tall. There was no evidence of perimortem trauma, however Schmorl's nodes were present in the lower thoracic spine.

Skeleton 11

Skeleton 11 was buried in the so-called triple grave positioned underneath Skeleton 8 and next to Skeleton 12 (see Figure 9.4). It was buried in a supine position, with the lower limbs flexed and spread apart and was orientated south to north (Bartlett and Mackey 1973, 24). No cranium was present. The individual was a young to middle adult male (20 to 35 years) and was 1.70 m ± 2.99 cm tall. A perimortem fracture was present on the base of the mandibular body (Figure 9.5). The posterior portion of the mandible was not present, and it is likely that the fractures were radiating from areas of sharp force trauma to the

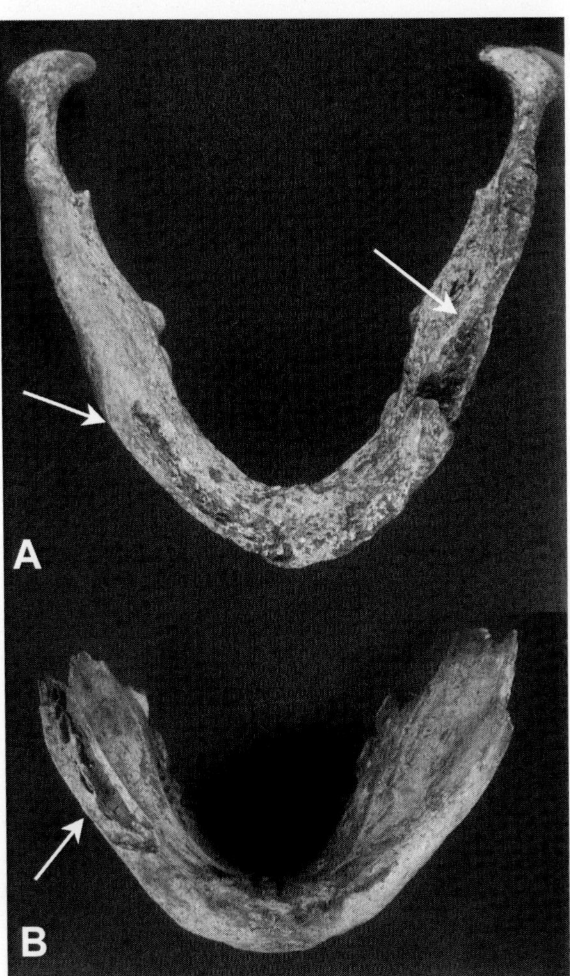

Figure 9.5. Sharp force trauma to the base of mandibles from the 'Skull associated with Skeleton 1' (A) and Skeleton 11 (B) (J. Buckberry).

inferior portion of the ascending ramus. This blow had been delivered from behind and is consistent with decapitation. The dens of the second cervical vertebra also appears to have been removed by this blow, however the presence of consolidant and adhering soil in this area has made this injury difficult to identify with confidence. Schmorl's nodes were present in the thoracic spine, and both mandibular third molars were congenitally absent. The skeleton was radiocarbon dated to 640–775 cal. AD (two sigma).

Skeleton 12

Skeleton 12 was buried in the so-called triple grave next to Skeleton 11 and was also orientated south to north (see Figure 9.4). It was in a supine and extended position, with the right femur located directly underneath the left femur of Skeleton 11 (Bartlett and Mackey 1973, 24; Rod Mackey 2006, pers. comm.). The individual was a young adult male (18 to 25 years) and was 1.78 m ± 3.27 cm in stature. No cranium was present, but there was no osteological evidence of decapitation. Schmorl's nodes were present in the lower thoracic spine.

Skeleton 13

Skeleton 13 had been badly disturbed by Skeletons 11 and 12, and was orientated in the opposite direction (north to south). The only bones present were foot bones at the north end of the grave and cervical vertebrae to the south (Bartlett and Mackey 1973, 24). The lack of disturbance of the cervical vertebrae indicates that this individual was buried without the head having been articulated with the body. A disarticulated humerus, radius, several carpals and a tibia in the grave fill were also thought to belong to the individual (see Figure 9.4). Only the location of the tibia in the grave fill was noted at the time of publication (Bartlett and Mackey 1973, 24; Dawes 1973, 65). The radiocarbon date obtained for the humerus (775–980 cal. AD at two sigma level) is later than the date derived for Skeleton 11 (640–775 AD), indicating that the humerus must belong to a different burial than the vertebrae and feet of Skeleton 13, and that it had probably been incorporated into the grave fill during the burial of Skeleton 8. Indeed, excavation photographs in the archive reveal that the humerus was in the layer of soil between Skeletons 8 and 11, thereby supporting this interpretation. The remainder of the disarticulated bones found throughout the grave fill and attributed to Skeleton 13 may have belonged to either the disturbed Skeleton 13 or the same burial as the humerus, which had been re-deposited into the grave during the burial of Skeleton 8. All of the bones described here are from one (or more) adult(s), and could not be sexed. There was no pathology or evidence of decapitation on any of the bones.

Skull Associated with Skeleton 1

As discussed above, the cranium, mandible and vertebrae that comprise this 'skull' do not belong to Skeleton 1, even though they were found just 0.5 m from the feet of the skeleton (Bartlett and Mackey 1973, 21). The remains are of a young middle adult (26 to 35 years) who was probably male. Sharp force trauma is present along the base of the mandibular body, with radiating fractures extending towards the chin (see Figure 9.5). The blow had been delivered from behind by a heavy weapon, such as an axe or sword. There is no sign of any injury to the cervical vertebrae, although these were poorly preserved. Dental pathology comprised a moderate level of calculus (Brothwell 1972, 150), antemortem loss of the upper left second premolar and lower right second premolar. Linear enamel hypoplasia was observed on the upper left second incisor.

Skull I

Skull I comprised the cranium of a young adult male (18 to 25 years). Linear enamel hypoplasia was observed on both upper first premolars. The cranium showed evidence of claw damage, most likely having been caused by badgers, which had probably occurred after the bone had degraded (Dawes 1973, 75; Terry O'Connor 2006, pers. comm.).

Skull 2

Skull 2 was represented by the cranium of a young adult male (18 to 25 years). Three incidences of sharp force trauma to the back of the head were apparent. These comprised a glancing blow which had exposed an area of diploic bone on the right parietal and occipital, crossing the lambdoid suture; a shallow blow, which had just cut into the occipital to the right of the midline; and a deep blow, which had exposed diploic bone and was associated with two radiating fractures in the centre of the occipital (Figure 9.6). All of the blows had been delivered in an upwards direction, indicating that the victim was most likely bent over with his head held in extreme flexion (i.e. with the chin resting on the chest), a position that is unlikely to have occurred had these injuries been the result of armed combat. The injuries are not consistent with decapitation, but the concentration of them on the occipital and the direction of the blows suggest that decapitation may have been attempted. A further blow or blows probably succeeded in removing the head at a lower level through the neck region, however no vertebrae or mandible were found with the cranium. Extensive porosity was observed on the ectocranial surface of the cranium, with large areas of woven new bone formation. This had probably been caused by a non-specific inflammatory condition.

Skull 4

Skull 4 comprised a cranium and mandible, and was from a young to middle adult male (20 to 35 years). The cranium was badly crushed taphonomically, and most of the right side was either damaged or missing. The only pathology was slight calculus (Brothwell 1972, 150).

Skull 5

Skull 5 was represented by the cranium of a young to middle adult male, aged 20 to 35 years. A large, penetrating blade injury was present on the right occipital (Figure 9.7). A second injury had sliced off the base of the left mastoid process and zygomatic bones, and would probably have succeeded in decapitating the individual. Both of the injuries had been delivered from behind. A possible third injury was present anterior to the large penetrating injury, on the inferior of the occipital.

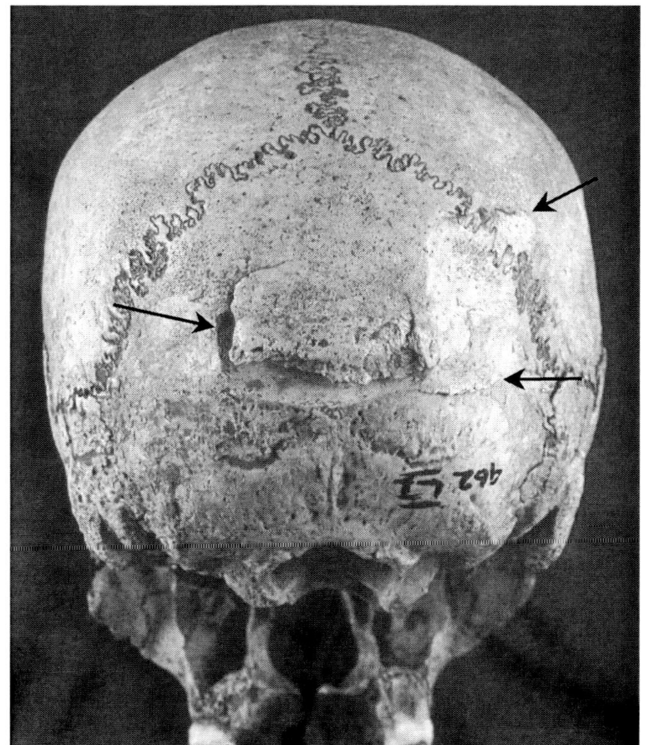

Figure 9.6. Posterior of Skull 2 showing three sharp force injuries to the occipital (J. Buckberry).

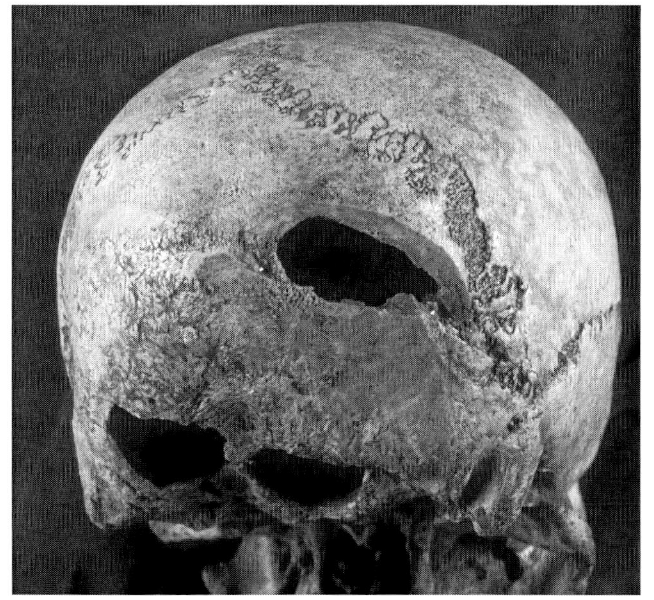

Figure 9.7. Large penetrating sharp force injury to the occipital of Skull 5 (J. Buckberry).

Overall the surface of the cranium was quite pitted and porous, indicating that this individual suffered from a non-specific inflammatory condition. He suffered from premature closure of the right occipitomastoid suture resulting in an asymmetric cranium. Linear enamel hypoplasia was observed on the upper right second and third molars. Although there was a large hole in the base of the cranium, this appears to have been caused by postmortem taphonomic damage, and not through the perimortem use of a head stake (see below).

Skull 6

The cranium was all that remained of Skull 6. This was of a young or middle adult male (18 to 45 years). Carious lesions were present on the upper right second molar and upper left third molar. The upper right third molar had been either lost antemortem or was congenitally absent. The surface of the cranium was porous. A small osteoma, 1.5 cm in diameter, was present on the left parietal.

Skull 7

Skull 7 consisted of a complete cranium. The individual was male and was a young or middle adult (18 to 45 years). Slight cribra orbitalia was present in the right orbit (Stuart-Macadam 1991, 109). Pitting was observed over much of the cranium, and was focussed around major muscle attachment sites, especially the supra-orbital ridges, where new bone had also been deposited. This is evidence of a non-specific inflammatory condition similar to, but less severe, than that seen in Skull 2. There was no evidence of decapitation.

Skull 8

Skull 8 consisted of a cranium, mandible and four cervical vertebrae. This was a young adult male, aged 18 to 25 years, although he was more likely at the lower end of this range. The very young age of the cranium may indicate that it belongs to Skeleton 1, but this was impossible to verify. Slight calculus was present on many of the teeth (Brothwell 1972, 150) and both lower second premolars had been lost antemortem. Sharp force trauma was observed on the anterior of the vertebral body of the fourth cervical vertebra (see Figure 9.3) and to the base of the fifth cervical vertebra. Both of these injuries had been delivered from the front by a thin-bladed weapon such as a fine sword or knife.

Skull 9

Skull 9 consisted of the complete cranium of a young middle adult male, aged 26 to 35 years. Linear enamel hypoplasia was present on both upper first premolars, and moderate cribra orbitalia was present in both orbits (Stuart-Macadam 1991, 109). The right occipitomastoid suture had closed prematurely, and the cranium was asymmetric. No evidence of decapitation was observed.

Skull 10

Skull 10 was represented by the cranium of a young middle adult male (26 to 35 years).

There was considerable torsion and asymmetry in the base of the cranium, indicating that he had suffered from torticolis. In addition, the frontal bone was asymmetric, possibly due to a small area of premature suture closure in the coronal suture. Overall the cranium was very porous. A carious lesion was present on the upper right first molar, slight calculus was observed on many teeth (Brothwell 1972, 150) and the upper left first molar had been lost antemortem. No evidence of trauma was observed on this cranium.

Skull 11

Skull 11 consisted of a fragmented cranium, mandible and three cervical vertebrae at the time of initial analysis (Dawes 1973, 85), however only the cranial elements (maxillae and temporal bones) were present at the time of re-analysis. Skull 11 is from a young to middle aged adult (26 to 35 years) and was probably male. No pathology or trauma was observed.

Summary of Demographic Data

By combining the data for individuals with associated crania with the data for the disarticulated crania (assuming that the disarticulated crania belonged to the skeletons buried without heads, and not to additional individuals), the demography and sex ratio of the excavated population can be derived. This reveals that a minimum of five individuals were young adults (18 to 25 years), two were aged between 20 and 35 years, and a further four were aged between 26 and 35 years. The age-at-death of the remaining two individuals could not be determined precisely; however, it is certain they were both adults who were no older than 45 years. Overall, the age and sex data for Walkington Wold show that the population consisted entirely of young to middle aged adults (18 to 45 years). The combination of data for skeletons and disarticulated skulls reveals that the cemetery population consists of a minimum of eleven males in addition to a further two probable males.

Discussion

Two of the post-Roman burials at Walkington Wold were buried with their heads articulated with their bodies. The burials (Skeletons 2 and 6) are set apart from the remainder of the burials, located several metres to the south. It is notable that these two burials contained the only datable material, a third-century coin and fourth-century pottery respectively. Both burials are supine and extended, and are orientated south-east to north-west. While these burials clearly date to at least the Roman period, it is not certain if they belong to the Late Anglo-Saxon execution cemetery. Indeed, the excavators suggest that they do not (Bartlett and Mackey 1973, 21, 25). However, in the absence of radiocarbon dates, it is still possible that these two individuals do relate to the execution cemetery and may represent either the victims of hanging, which would leave little or no trace on the skeleton, or that they are the burials of the unbaptised, suicide victims or social outcasts.

The remaining burials were interred in a variety of positions and orientations. Although potentially as many as six burials were supine and extended, the orientations were very random, with six different orientations recorded for the ten burials where orientation could be determined. In addition, one burial was flexed on the left side (Skeleton 1) and a further burial was probably flexed (side not known, Skeleton 4). Two more unusual positions were evident for Skeleton 10, which was flexed on the right with the left upper limb contorted under his back, and Skeleton 11, which was supine, but with the lower limbs flexed and spread apart at the knees. The latter two burials suggest hurried, careless interments and contrast to the many supine and extended burials.

The analysis of the human skeletal remains revealed six instances with evidence of perimortem decapitation. When the duplication of skeletal elements is considered, however, it is apparent that these instances relate to a minimum number of four individuals. The disassociation of crania from post-cranial skeletons in eleven cases strongly argues that all of these individuals had been decapitated. In four of these cases the cranium had been buried articulated with the mandible (three of which were also articulated with upper cervical vertebrae). These had presumably been buried before the soft tissue holding the different bones together had decayed. The remaining seven skulls, where only the cranium was present, had probably been displayed prior to burial thereby allowing the mandible and vertebrae to become separated from the crania. Indeed, it is significant that the remains of eight mandibles were present among the disarticulated material (Dawes 1973, 84). These heads may have been displayed on a gibbet at the top of the barrow, where a large posthole was found during the excavation (Bartlett and Mackey 1973, 25, 26; Rod Mackey 2006, pers. comm.). It is unlikely that they were displayed on *heafod stoccan* (head stakes), as there is no evidence for damage to the base of any of the crania.

The manner of decapitation varied within the six cases available for study. Two individuals had been decapitated from behind, with the sword or axe cutting through part of the mandible (Skeleton 11 and the 'Skull associated with Skeleton 1'). In two further cases, decapitation was attempted from behind, but the back of the cranium had been hit, at least initially. In the case of Skull 5, one blow had penetrated the right occipital while a second had clipped the base of the cranium and probably succeeded in decapitating the individual. Skull 2 had suffered three blows to the back of the head, none of which would have caused decapitation. Presumably a further blow succeeded in removing the head. These two cases of repeated blows to the back of the head may indicate that the victim was struggling, the executioner misaimed or a combination of both of these situations. The character of the injuries on all four of these individuals would suggest that the weapons used were probably heavy swords or axes.

The remaining two cases are more unusual. Both Skeleton 7 and Skull 8 appear to have been decapitated from the front. Skeleton 7 displayed two parallel cut marks to the anterior of the first thoracic vertebra and Skull 8 suffered sharp force trauma to the front of the third and fourth cervical vertebrae. It would appear that a thin blade, such as a knife, dagger or fine sword, was used in both of these cases.

The three radiocarbon dates obtained for Walkington Wold indicate that the cemetery was in use sporadically over a long period of time from the seventh or eighth century to at least the tenth century AD. Indeed, the radiocarbon dates indicate that the so-called 'triple burial' (which cut through Burial 13) does not represent a single grave, but rather that burial took place in this location on multiple occasions. The first burial was that of Skeleton 13, which was badly disturbed by the burial of Skeletons 11 and 12. The proximity of the left femur of Skeleton 11 and the right femur of Skeleton 12 strongly suggests that these two burials were contemporary. Skeleton 11 was radiocarbon dated to AD 640–775. Some time later Skeleton 8 was buried above and almost between the spread legs of Skeleton 11. The digging of this later grave did not disturb Skeleton 11, probably as a consequence of the shallow grave depth, which left a layer of soil between the two skeletons. Skeleton 8 was radiocarbon dated to AD 900–1030, indicating that a period of over 100 years had passed between the two burial events. It was presumably during the burial of Skeleton 8 that the humerus radiocarbon dated to AD 775–980 became incorporated into the grave fill positioned between Skeletons 8 and 11. The re-use of this specific location indicates that it may have been marked, although no evidence of a grave marker was identified at the time of excavation.

The skeletal population from Walkington Wold revealed evidence of a moderately high level of skeletal pathology. Of the ten individuals with observable orbits, two had cribra orbitalia, a true prevalence rate (TPR) of 20% (the crude prevalence rate, CPR, calculated using the total number of burials at the site was 15.4%). Of the six individuals with teeth for which the presence/absence of enamel hypoplasia could be recorded with confidence, four individuals had enamel hypoplasia, often affecting more than one tooth, giving a TPR of 66.7% (CPR = 30.8%).[4] In addition, five crania were extensively porous and one of these had extensive areas of new bone deposition, providing a TPR of 55.6% (CRP = 38.5%). These changes were present on most of the ectocranial surfaces, but were frequently more severe around the areas of muscle attachment, and are not similar to the discrete areas of porosity associated with porotic hyperostosis. The cause of these changes is unknown, but it is most likely a non-specific inflammatory condition. In sum, it is fair to say that the Walkington Wold population suffered from higher than normal levels of skeletal stress, which may indicate that these individuals came from the lower strata of society.

Overall, the cemetery location, around a Bronze Age barrow and close to the Hundredal boundary, the varied burial orientations, different body positions and the evidence of decapitation combined with that for the display of severed heads strongly indicate that Walkington Wold was an execution cemetery, similar to those found in the south of England. However, Walkington Wold is by far the most northerly example of an Anglo-Saxon execution cemetery (Buckberry and Hadley 2007), with the next most northern site identified in Andrew Reynold's survey located at Crosshill, on the boundary of Rushcliffe and Bingham Hundreds in Nottinghamshire (Reynolds forthcoming). The long period of cemetery use may account for the different styles of execution evidenced at the cemetery, with decapitation from behind having been replaced with decapitation from the front, or *vice versa*.

Notes

1. Hundreds were the basic administrative units during the Late Anglo-Saxon period and local judicial matters were usually settled at Hundred courts. For further discussion of the Anglo-Saxon Hundred see Reynolds (1999, 75–81).
2. Throughout this paper the first compass point given for grave orientation denotes the head end of the grave.
3. It should be noted that the Phenice method was only published shortly before Jean Dawes' analysis of the material from Walkington Wold, and was probably not used during her analysis.
4. The tooth surfaces of many individuals had been obscured by consolidant or excessive calculus, or had been eroded by the acidic soil.

Acknowledgements

I am grateful to Martin Foreman and Bryan Sitch of Hull and East Riding Museum for granting access to the Walkington Wold skeletons. Rod Mackey kindly discussed the site and provided help in selecting radiocarbon dating samples and allowed me to reproduce Figure 9.4. I would like to thank Dawn Hadley, Annia Cherryson and Andrew Reynolds for sharing their data and for many enlightening discussions on Walkington Wold. Andrew Reynolds kindly provided a copy of the paper on the Staines burials and chapters of his book in advance of publication. Thanks also to Rebecca Storm, Andrew Chamberlain, Christopher Knüsel, Anthea Boylston and Alan Ogden for their discussion on the osteological aspects of this study, and to Terry O'Connor for his description of the badger claw-marks. Oliver Jessop drew Figures 9.1 and 9.2. This research was funded by a White Rose Studentship, awarded by the Universities of Sheffield, York and Leeds, the Royal Society and The British Academy. The radiocarbon dates were funded by NERC.

References

Bailey, G. B. 1985. Late Roman inland signal station, or temple? Functional interpretation at Walkington Wold. *Yorkshire Archaeological Journal* 57, 11–14.

Bartlett, J. E. and Mackey, R. W. 1973. Excavations on Walkington Wold 1967–1969. *East Riding Archaeologist* 1, 1–93.

Boddington, A. 1990. Models of burial, settlement and worship: the final phase reviewed, pp. 177–99 in Southworth, E. (ed.), *Anglo-Saxon Cemeteries: A Reappraisal*. Stroud: Sutton.

Brothwell, D. R. 1972. *Digging up Bones*. London: British Museum Press.

Buckberry, J. L. and Chamberlain, A. T. 2002. Age estimation from the auricular surface of the ilium: a revised method. *American Journal of Physical Anthropology* 119, 231–9.

Buckberry, J. L. and Hadley, D. M. 2007. An Anglo-Saxon execution cemetery at Walkington Wold, East Yorkshire. *Oxford Journal of Archaeology* 26, 309–29.

Buikstra, J. and Ubelaker, D. H. 1994. *Standards for Data Collection from Human Skeletal Remains*. Arkansas: Arkansas Archeological Survey.

Bullough, D. 1983. Burial community and belief in the early medieval west, pp. 177–201 in Wormald, P. (ed.), *Ideal and Reality in Frankish and Anglo-Saxon Society*. Oxford: Basil Blackwell.

Carver, M. 2005. *Sutton Hoo: A Seventh-century Princely Burial Ground and its Context*. London: British Museum Press.

Dawes, J. 1973. Human skeletal remains, pp. 59–93 in Bartlett, J. E. and Mackey, R. W. (eds), Excavations on Walkington Wold 1967–1969. *East Riding Archaeologist* 1, 1–93.

Dickinson, T. M. 1974. *Cuddesdon and Dorchester-on-Thames, Oxfordshire: Two Early Anglo-Saxon 'Princely' Sites in Wessex* (BAR British Series 1). Oxford: British Archaeological Reports.

Geake, H. 1992. Burial practice in 7th and 8th century England, pp. 83–94 in Carver, M. (ed.), *The Age of Sutton Hoo*. Woodbridge: The Boydell Press.

Geake, H. 2002. Persistent problems in the study of conversion-period burials in England, pp. 144–55 in Lucy, S. J. and Reynolds, A. (eds), *Burial in Early Medieval England and Wales*. London: The Society for Medieval Archaeology.

Gittos, H. 2002. Creating the sacred: Anglo-Saxon rites for consecrating cemeteries, pp. 195–208 in Lucy, S. J. and Reynolds, A. (eds), *Burial in Early Medieval England and Wales*. London: The Society for Medieval Archaeology.

Hayman, G. and Reynolds, A. 2006. A Saxon and Saxo-Norman execution cemetery at 42–54 London Road, Staines. *Archaeological Journal* 162, 215–55.

Meaney, A. L. 1964. *A Gazetteer of Early Anglo-Saxon Burial Sites*. London: George Allen and Unwin Ltd.

Meindl, R. S. and Lovejoy, C. O. 1985. Ectocranial suture closure: a revised method for the determination of skeletal age at death based on the lateral-anterior sutures. *American Journal of Physical Anthropology* 68, 57–66.

Miles, A. E. W. 1962. Assessment of the ages of a population of Anglo-Saxons from their dentitions. *Proceedings of the Royal Society of Medicine* 55, 881–6.

Morris, R. K. 1983. *The Church in British Archaeology* (CBA Research Report 47). London: Council for British Archaeology.

Phenice, T. W. 1969. A newly developed visual method of sexing the os pubis. *American Journal of Physical Anthropology* 30, 297–301.

Reynolds, A. 1997. The definition and ideology of Anglo-Saxon execution sites and cemeteries, pp. 33–41 in De Boe, G. and Verhaege, F. (eds), *Death and Burial in Medieval Europe*. Zellick: I. A. P. Rapporten.

Reynolds, A. 1998. *Anglo-Saxon Laws in the Landscape: An Archaeological Study of the Old English Judicial System*. Unpublished Ph.D. thesis, University College London.

Reynolds, A. 1999. *Later Anglo-Saxon England. Life and Landscape*. Stroud: Tempus.

Reynolds, A. forthcoming. *Anglo-Saxon Deviant Burial Customs*. Oxford: Oxford University Press.

Scheuer, L. and Black, S. 2000. *Developmental Juvenile Osteology*. London: Academic Press.

Stuart-Macadam, P. 1991. Anaemia in Roman Britain: Poundbury Camp, pp. 101–13 in Bush, H. and Zvelebil, M. (eds), *Health in Past Societies. Biocultural Interpretations of Human Skeletal Remains in Archaeological Contexts* (BAR International Series 567). Oxford: British Archaeological Reports.

Suchey, J. M., Brooks, S. T. and Katz, D. 1988. *Instructions for use of the Suchey-Brooks system for age determination of the female os pubis. Instructional materials accompanying female pubic symphyseal models of the Suchey-Brooks system*. Colorado: Distributed by France Casting.

Trotter, M. and Gleser, G. C. 1952. Estimation of stature from long bones of American whites and negroes. *American Journal of Physical Anthropology* 10, 436–514.

Webb, P. A. O. and Suchey, J. M. 1985. Epiphyseal union of the anterior iliac crest and medial clavicle in a modern multiracial sample of American males and females. *American Journal of Physical Anthropology* 68, 457–66.

Wormald, P. 1999. *The Making of English Law. Volume I: King Alfred to the Twelfth Century*. Oxford: Blackwell.

Wymer, J. J. 1996. The excavation of a ring ditch at South Acre, pp. 58–89 in Wymer, J. J. (ed.), *Barrow Excavations in Norfolk, 1984–88* (EAA Report No. 77). Dereham: East Anglian Archaeology.

10. Unusual Life, Unusual Death and the Fate of the Corpse: A Case Study from Dynastic Europe

Estella Weiss-Krejci

Abstract

This article explores how deviant behaviour in life, deviant circumstances of death, and young age at death affected mortuary treatment among historically documented individuals from Medieval and Post-Medieval European dynasties. The study is based on an investigation of 868 individuals who are members of the Habsburg and Babenberg Dynasties or affiliated with these two houses. From this sample a group of 221 individuals as well as an additional 36 individuals, whose lives or deaths may be considered deviant, were selected for a closer investigation. The results show that 'social deviants' as well as people who died during warfare and in battle, victims of murder and disease, as well as young children have been afforded differential mortuary treatment. On the other hand, individuals who died during childbirth or from accidents were usually treated according to the norm.

Introduction

Several years ago I conducted an analysis of elite burials in Medieval and Post-Medieval Europe. I especially investigated historic sources concerning the mortuary treatment of 868 individuals belonging to two Austrian dynasties: the Babenbergs and the Habsburgs. The purpose of the study was to gain a better understanding of the reasons for variability in mortuary treatment and to develop more appropriate methods of burial analysis. During my research I came across a variety of individuals whose mortuary treatment not only differed from those afforded to other people but was directly caused by circumstances relating to their lives or death. Being accorded differential treatment these individuals and their burials can be classified as 'deviant', in the sense that they diverge from the burial norm. I have already partially touched upon this issue by discussing the nature of so called 'secondary burials', the formation of collective burial deposits and the causes for variation in the treatment of the corpse (Weiss-Krejci 2001; 2004; 2005). The current paper will provide a more complete and condensed summary of the relationship between unusual life, unusual death and the fate of the corpse amongst these groups.

Archaeologists always run the risk of misinterpreting evidence derived from bones, burial position, grave goods and the kind and location of the burial. To be able to infer that a specific dead person in an archaeological deposit did not receive mortuary treatment in accordance with his/her normal social persona but rather in relation to deviant behaviour in life, or deviant circumstances of death, one must understand the nature of the society that produced the deposit. It is also necessary to understand its death symbolism, rituals, ideology and ideas about what constitutes a proper burial. In a prehistoric context this is not easy. The present analysis of a historic sample forms a contribution to this ongoing discussion (e.g. Ucko 1969; Shay 1985; Duncan 2005; Forgey and Williams 2005).

The Sample

For this investigation I have selected historically documented individuals whose lives or deaths may be considered deviant and compared the characteristics of their mortuary treatment to those that followed the norm. I started with an investigation of 868 individuals who died between AD 994 and 1993 (see Weiss-Krejci 2001). I then split the sample into three successive patrilineal groups: the Medieval Babenberg Dynasty (ruled AD 976–1246), the Medieval and Post-Medieval House of Habsburg (AD 1273–1740), and the House of Habsburg-Lorraine (AD 1740–1918). The House of Habsburg and the House of Habsburg-Lorraine form one dynasty, but two patrilineal groups. When the House of Habsburg died out in the male line in AD 1740, political survival was only possible through the female line. The descendants of Maria Theresa of Habsburg and Francis of Lorraine again followed rules of patrilineal descent (Hamann 1988).

In the sample 136 people from ten generations are affiliated with the Babenberg Dynasty (dates of death range from AD 994–1333), 389 individuals from 15 generations are connected to the House of Habsburg (dates of death range from AD 1256–1780) and 343 individuals derived from six generations of the House of Habsburg-Lorraine (dates of death range from AD 1740–1993). The total sample includes 505 patrilineal blood relatives (58 Babenberg, 237 Habsburg, and 210 Habsburg-Lorraine), 120 affinal relatives (23 Babenberg, 52 Habsburg, and 45 Habsburg-Lorraine) and 243 non-dynasty members (55 Babenberg, 100 Habsburg, 88 Habsburg-Lorraine). Patrilineal blood relatives are women and men who were born into one of the two dynasties as well as several children from morganatic marriages. Affinal relatives are women who were married to male dynasty members at some point in their lives. The founder of the House of Habsburg-Lorraine, Maria Theresa's husband Francis of Lorraine, also belongs to this group. The group of non-dynasty members consists of men who married patrilineal female blood relatives, children of female blood relatives who were members of other dynasties but were buried with the Habsburgs, morganatic wives whose status was too low to be accepted as full members of the dynasty, morganatic husbands, and – if married more than once – men who were married to female affinal relatives, and the women who were married to these men.

Proper Burial

From a large group of archaeologically visible variables of mortuary practices (see Binford 1971; O'Shea 1984, 39–44; Carr 1995, 130–2) I have selected three practices for this comparative analysis – the treatment of the corpse, the location of the burial, and the association of individuals with each other (Table 10.1).

Treatment of the Corpse

Almost all people in the sample were members of the aristocracy and were therefore treated differently from the rest of society. The proper treatment of the corpse was to leave it in the flesh or to embalm it. Originally, evisceration (also called exenteration) of the internal organs was practiced in Central Europe only when corpses needed to be transported. Gradually, in Medieval France, England and Scotland, it also became a practice independent from the necessity to transport a corpse (Bradford 1933; Brown 1981; Dodson 1994). In large parts of the German-Roman Empire evisceration remained predominantly functional until the end of the Middle Ages (Meyer 2000, 212). From the late sixteenth century onwards a high percentage of corpses were eviscerated without need for preservation. At this time it became customary in the House of Habsburg to extract and separately bury the internal organs, especially the heart (Gerbert *et al.* 1772; Hawlik-van de Water 1989; Weiss-Krejci 2001, 778). At least 117 people in the sample were eviscerated (five from the Babenberg sample, 67 Habsburg, 45 Habsburg-Lorraine), and their entrails buried in separate places or within containers. In the sample only nine eviscerations are known to date before AD 1500.

In Medieval times noblemen and women often died during journeys to southern Europe and to the Holy Land. Since burial in foreign, hostile and heathen lands was out of the question for a high noble of the Middle Ages the remains of the deceased needed to be

	Corpse treatment	Grave location	Association of individuals
FREQUENT/ PROPER	corpse in the flesh, evisceration, embalming	cathedral, church, monastery, castle church	with dynasty members (close affinal or blood relatives)
LESS COMMON/ ACCEPTABLE	boiling, defleshing, skeletal mutilation		with distant patrilineal relatives, without relatives (alone)
RARE/ IMPROPER	cremation	churchyard	with matrilineal relatives, with members of an unrelated group

Table 10.1. Proper and improper mortuary behaviour in three categories of mortuary practices in dynastic Europe.

transported back home. An excarnation method was invented that became known as *mos teutonicus*. The corpses were eviscerated, boiled in water, wine or vinegar and then defleshed and wrapped in animal skins (Brown 1981; Finucane 1981; Weiss-Krejci 2001; 2005). Three people in the sample of 868 individuals had received this treatment.

An additional selection of processed nobles, bishops, kings and queens from various other European dynasties as detailed in Figure 10.1 shows that excarnation was the preferred treatment for individuals who had died far from their homeland and in the Mediterranean region. Evisceration was used for transport over shorter distances. The map includes two excarnated Babenbergs (Frederick I, † 1198 and Leopold VI, † 1230), two eviscerated people affiliated with the Babenbergs (Emperor Conrad II, † 1039 and Empress Gisela, † 1043), one excarnated Habsburg (Rudolph IV, † 1365) and two eviscerated Habsburgs (Queen Anna, † 1281 and Emperor Frederick III/V, † 1493).

Duke Frederick I died on a Crusade during April 1198. His excarnated skeleton (Figure 10.2) was brought to the monastery of Heiligenkreuz in Austria where it still rests today (Niemetz 1974; Lechner 1976, 193). Queen Anna (alias Gertrud), the founding ancestress of the House of Habsburg who died in Vienna in February 1281, was transported over a much shorter distance. Her corpse was first eviscerated and filled with sand and ash and it was then wrapped within a wax-soaked cloth and dressed in a silk gown. The body of the embalmed queen travelled 600 km to Basel where it was buried at the cathedral within 32 days (Schäfer 1920, 482; Gut 1999, 100). When Queen Anna's grave was opened in AD 1762 her corpse was found to have been partially mummified (see Figure 10.2).

Both excarnation and evisceration were banned by the pope in AD 1299 and again in AD 1300. In the aftermath of the ban alternative body processing techniques were sought. Henry VII from the House of Luxembourg was roasted over a fire in AD 1313. When the sarcophagus was opened in AD 1727 the bones were found to exhibit signs of burning (Meyer 2000, 55). Privileges were also granted by the pope, for example, to Philip the Fair in AD 1305 who was allowed to have his body treated as he wished (Brown 1981, 256). The pope's ban made body processing an even more desirable practice and a sure sign of status and distinction. Excarnation went out of fashion in the fifteenth century, but evisceration remained a popular practice among people of noble descent up until the twentieth century. In the House of Habsburg-Lorraine it was regularly practiced until AD 1878, and was then revived in 1922 (death of Emperor Karl I) and 1989 (death of Empress Zita) (Weiss-Krejci 2001; 2005).

Cremation of the corpse was construed as destructive to the soul and was considered to be highly improper (Finucane 1981). The ideology regarding cremation is the reason for the development of excarnation. Cremation is still unpopular among Roman Catholics to this very day. Only one person in the sample was cremated, and this occurred in 1958 and took place in the USA.

Passive excarnation (temporary storage of corpses) and postfuneral relocation (exhumation and reburial) were also very frequent in the sample (see Weiss-Krejci 2001; 2004; 2005 for details).

Location of Burial Place

The proper deposition places for members of aristocratic houses were ceremonial structures such as cathedrals, churches, monasteries, convents or castle churches. The dead were deposited in wooden, stone or metal monuments and buried in front of the altars, in side chapels, or within subterranean crypts (Vocelka and Heller 1997; Jahn 2001; Weiss-Krejci 2004; see also Boase 1972; Binski 1996; Störmer 1980 for other areas of Europe). Burial in a churchyard would have been considered highly improper for a member of a dynasty. The few graveyard burials in the sample either belong to morganatic spouses from the nineteenth and twentieth century, to infants, or to members of the House of Habsburg-Lorraine who had died after the abolishment of the monarchy in 1918.

Association of Individuals

The majority of people were buried or reburied with close relatives (i.e. patrilineal blood relatives and affinal house members) in collective burial vaults. Few individuals were buried with distant relatives and even fewer alone and away from other members of the dynasty. Burial with matrilineal relatives (e.g. the parents or grandparents of the mother), other non-dynasty members, or people of lower status was very rare (see Weiss-Krejci 2004). As in many other areas of the world where collective burial is practiced the mixing of unrelated people and people of unequal rank was regarded as improper (Waterson 1995, 210; Hutchinson and Aragon 2002, 32). Within the 15 House of Habsburg generations (AD 1273–1740) no adult non-dynasty member was ever buried in a Habsburg vault. In the House of Habsburg-Lorraine (AD 1740–1918) a few exceptions were made (see Weiss-Krejci 2004, 387–8).

Deviant Burial

From the sample of 868 individuals I have selected 221 people who stand out either because of circumstances surrounding their death, because of their ideological or political positions or because of their young age. I have separated them into three groups (Table 10.2) and compared the characteristics of their burials with the burial norms of the overall sample:

1. Unusual death is a characteristic of men who died during war expeditions (a), men who were killed in battle (b), people who died from communicable diseases (c), women who died in childbirth (d), and victims of accidents (e), suicide (f), and murder (g).
2. 'Social deviants' are defined as people who suffered political prosecution and were executed (h) and outlaws (i). Since members of the Babenberg and Habsburg Dynasties were Roman Catholic, excommunicated people (j) and non-Catholics (k) also belong in this group.
3. Children who died younger than five years of age are included in the third group. Some of these individuals were premature (l) or stillborn (m). The exact age for seven children of the Babenberg Dynasty (q) is not known.

A few individuals who contracted morganatic marriages and were buried away from their dynasty together with their spouses have been omitted from Table 10.2. Table 10.2 also

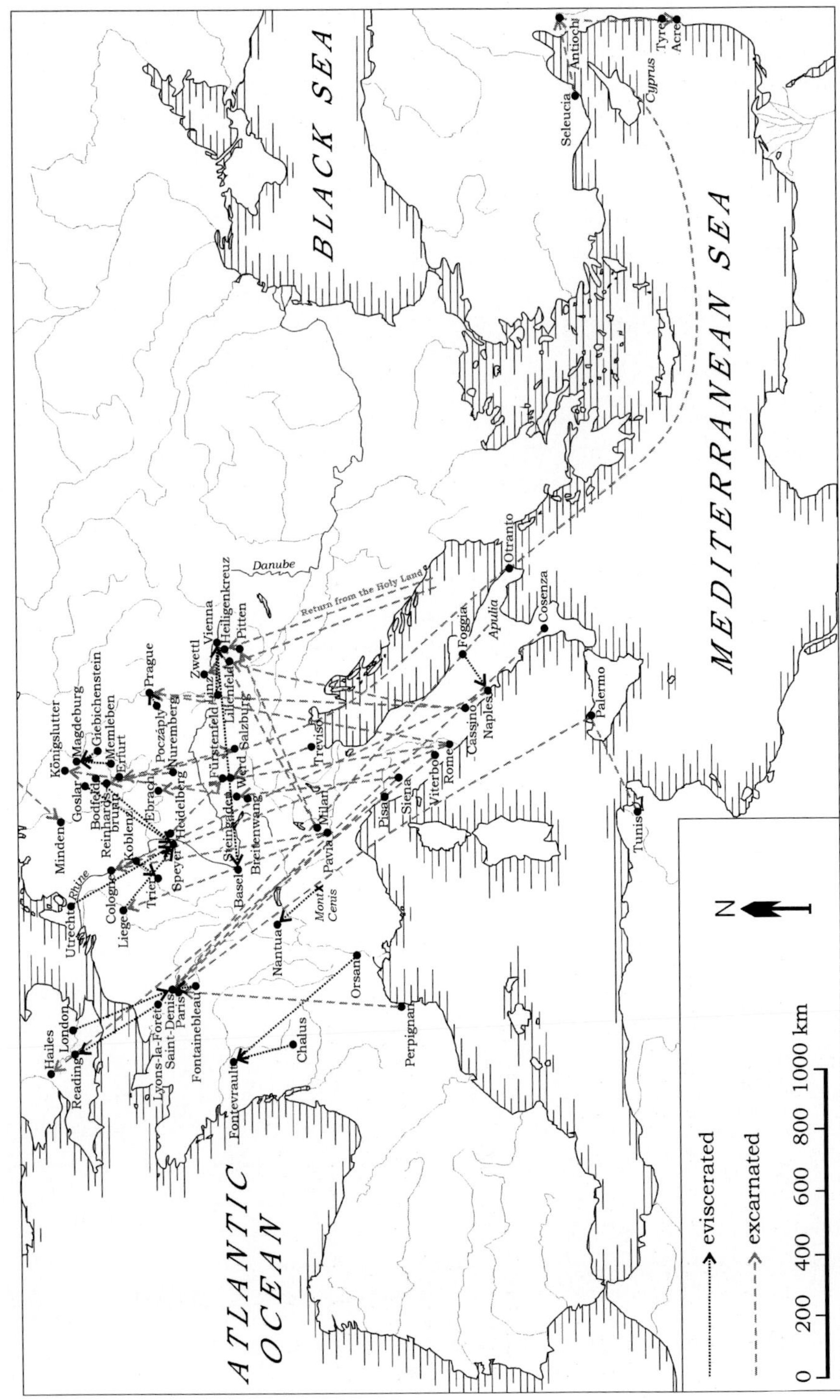
BLACK SEA
MEDITERRANEAN SEA
ATLANTIC OCEAN
Danube
Rhine
Return from the Holy Land
Hailes
Reading
London
Lyons-la-Forêt
Saint-Denis
Paris
Fontainebleau
Fontevrault
Chalus
Orsan
Perpignan
Utrecht
Liege
Cologne
Trier
Koblenz
Speyer
Minden
Reinhards-brunn
Bodfeld
Goslar
Königslutter
Magdeburg
Giebichenstein
Memleben
Erfurt
Ebrach
Heidelberg
Nuremberg
Począpły
Prague
Basel
Steinbaden
Breitenwang
Werd
Fürstenfeld
Salzburg
Linz
Lilienfeld
Zwettl
Vienna
Heiligenkreuz
Pitten
Nantua
Mont Cenis
Pavia
Milan
Treviso
Pisa
Siena
Viterbo
Rome
Cassino
Naples
Foggia
Apulia
Otranto
Cosenza
Palermo
Tunis
Seleucia
Antioch
Cyprus
Tyre
Acre
N
eviscerated
excarnated
0 200 400 600 800 1000 km

Figure 10.1. The relationship between place of death, transport distance and the treatment of the corpse from the ninth to the fifteenth century. The arrows point from the place of death to the place of burial.

Eviscerated: *Emperor Charles II the Bald († 877); Emperor Otto I († 973); Waltherdius, Archbishop of Magdeburg († 1012); Emperor Conrad II († 1039); Empress Gisela († 1043); Emperor Henry III († 1056); Emperor Henry IV († 1106); Robert of Abrissel († 1117); Emperor Henry V († 1125); Henry I, King of England († 1135); Albero, Archbishop of Trier († 1152); Richard I the Lion-hearted, King of England († 1199); Wenceslas I of Bohemia († 1253); Queen Anna († 1281); Charles I of Anjou, King of Naples and Sicily († 1285); Philip IV, King of France († 1314); Jean II, King of France († 1364); Emperor Frederick III/V († 1493).*

Excarnated: *Emperor Lothar II of Supplingenburg († 1137); Ekbert III, Count of Puntten († 1158); Frederick of Berg-Altena, Archbishop of Cologne († 1158); Henry, Bishop of Liege († 1164); Adolf II, Count of Holstein († 1164); Rainald of Dassel, Archbishop of Cologne († 1167); Frederick of Rothenburg, Duke of Swabia († 1167); Daniel, Bishop of Prague († 1167); Welf VII, Duke of Spoleto († 1167); Emperor Frederick I Barbarossa († 1190); Ludwig III, Landgrave of Thuringia († 1190); Conrad, Duke of Bohemia and Moravia († 1191); Philip of Heinsberg, Archbishop of Cologne († 1191); Frederick I, Duke of Austria († 1198); Hademar II († 1217); Luitold, Count of Plaien († 1219); Ludwig IV, Landgrave of Thuringia († 1227); Leopold VI, Duke of Austria and Styria († 1230); Louis IX the Saint, King of France († 1270); Isabelle, Queen of France († 1271); Alfonse of Poitiers († 1271); Henry of Almain († 1271); Pierre, son of Louis IX († 1283); Philip III, King of France († 1285); Rudolph, Archbishop of Salzburg († 1290); Ludwig III, Duke of Bavaria († 1294); Hermann, Count of Gleichen († 1345); Rudolph IV, Duke of Austria († 1365).*

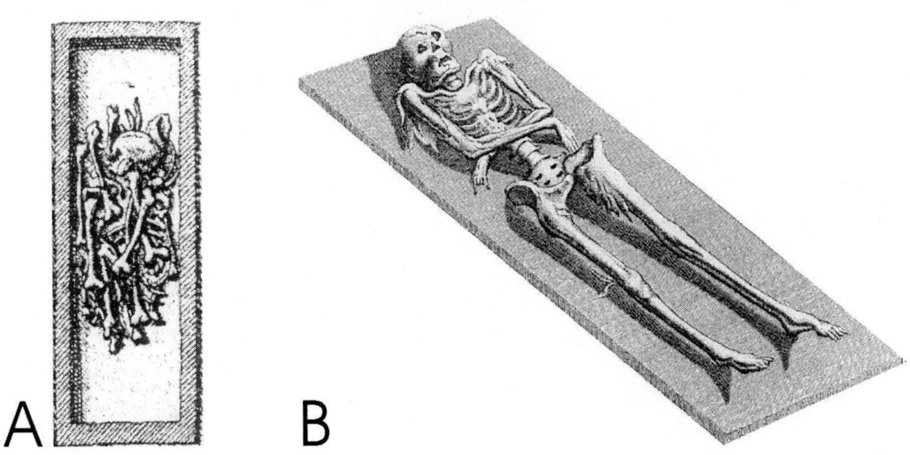

Figure 10.2. (A) – The excarnated skeleton of Duke Frederick I († 1198) in grave VIII of the chapter house at the monastery of Heiligenkreuz, Austria. The drawing was made by Salomon Kleiner in 1739 and engraved by Georg Nicolai (Gerbert et al. *1772, 4/2, plate VI). (B) – The mummified corpse of Queen Anna († 1281) at Basel Cathedral, Switzerland; drawn and engraved by Johann Baptist Haas (Gerbert et al. 1772, 4/2, plate II).*

shows that the number of Babenbergs and Habsburgs in the group 'Unusual Death', especially categories (a), (b), (f) and (g), and in the group of 'Social Deviants' is rather low. In order to better understand the relationship between 'deviants' and mortuary behaviour I have tried to increase my sample size. I have found 36 members of European dynasties who are not related to the Babenberg or Habsburg Dynasty but fit into one of the two groups [categories (a), (b), (g), (h), and (j)]. I added them on to the sample, which brings the total number up to 257. Among them are 20 Medieval kings and nobles who died during war expeditions (a) (e.g. Frederick Barbarossa † 1190), seven who died in battle (b) (e.g. Richard the Lion-hearted † 1199) and two who were murdered (g) (Archbishop Engelbert † 1225 and Henry of Almain † 1271). Five individuals were executed (h) (among them Mary, Queen of the Scots † 1587 and Tsar Nicholas II † 1918) and two individuals who were excommunicated (j) (Louis the Bavarian † 1347 and Emperor Henry IV † 1106).

Every individual in the list of 257 was only counted once. In some instances, multiple categories apply to one person and I have chosen the variable, which I consider most significant. Henrietta of Nassau-Weilburg died from scarlet fever, for example, but she also was a Protestant. The deviant burial treatment in her case was due to her having been a Protestant, not the fact that she died of a communicable disease. As such, Henrietta is counted in Category (k) of Table 10.2, and omitted from Category (c). Frederick Barbarossa drowned during the Crusades and was excarnated because his remains needed to be transported. As such, he is listed under Category (a), as a victim of a war expedition, and not as a victim of an accident [Category (e)].

		Babenberg	Habsburg	Habsburg-Lorraine	Other	Total
UNUSUAL DEATH (124)	a) death during war expedition	2	1	-	20	23
	b) death in battle	2	5	1	7	15
	c) communicable disease	-	13	17	-	30
	d) pregnancy/childbirth	1	17	8	-	26
	e) accident	7	3	6	-	16
	f) suicide	-	-	1	-	1
	g) murdered	3	5	3	2	13
'SOCIAL DEVIANTS' (14)	h) convicted/executed	1	-	3	5	9
	i) outlawed (murderer)	-	1	-	-	1
	j) excommunicated	1	-	-	2	3
	k) Protestant	-	-	1	-	1
SMALL CHILDREN (119)	l) premature	-	3	1	-	4
	m) neonate	-	19	8	-	27
	n) died during first year	-	35	8	-	43
	o) died age 1–2	-	16	12	-	28
	p) died age 3–4	-	3	7	-	10
	q) died under age 5	7	-	-	-	7
		24	121	76	36	257

Table 10.2. Selection of 257 people, whose circumstances of death, position in life or age diverges from the rest of the sample.

Results

The investigation revealed that individuals in some of these categories did receive differential treatment in death, whereas others did not.

Unusual Death

The circumstances of death did influence the treatment of individuals who died during war expeditions (a), in battle (b), who died, or were believed to have died, from communicable diseases (c) and were murdered (g).

War Expeditions (a) and Death in Battle (b)

Since the locations of wars (especially during the Crusades), and the warrior's homeland

and burial place were usually distant from each other, it was necessary for corpses to be processed for transport. Of 38 individuals who died during war expeditions or directly in battle (Table 10.2), 26 were boiled and defleshed, four were eviscerated, two were not eviscerated, and the treatment of six is unknown. Excarnation would appear to have been the proper treatment for high ranking persons who had died during a Crusade. All eleven Crusaders in the sample were excarnated. The corpse of Emperor Frederick Barbarossa, who drowned in Seleucia during the Third Crusade in AD 1190, was boiled and defleshed but subsequently lost somewhere in Palestine, probably at Acre (Prutz 1879, 30–3). His burial spot at Speyer Cathedral was occupied by Rudolph of Habsburg 100 years later (Klimm 1953, 55). Count Hermann of Gleichen died in AD 1345 in Nuremberg on his way back from the Holy Land (Schäfer 1920, 490). Despite the comparably low transport distance from Nuremberg to Erfurt, he was excarnated probably because he had died during a Crusade.

King Richard I, the Lion-hearted, was also a Crusader. His death at the siege of Chalus in AD 1199, however, was unrelated to the Crusades. He was not excarnated but eviscerated; his entrails, blood and brain were buried at Charroux, his heart at Rouen and his corpse at the abbey of Fontevrault (Giesey 1960, 20).

Don John of Austria, also known as Don Juan d'Austria, Governor General of the Netherlands and illegitimate son of Emperor Charles V with a woman from Regensburg, was eviscerated and cut into pieces. He died in AD 1578 during the war against William of Orange, most likely from typhus, although the cause of his death has been a matter of great speculation. His entrails and corpse were buried at Namur Cathedral with great pomp. In the year following the funeral the body was exhumed by order of his brother Philip II for removal to Spain. Because of the political conditions at the time it was decided to smuggle the body through France. In order to keep the transport secret, the corpse was disarticulated at the joints and packed into three leather bags, which were carried on the pack saddle of a horse (Petrie 1967, 326–8). The portions of the corpse were reassembled in Spain and Don John of Austria was buried in the dynastic vault of the Spanish branch of the House of Habsburg at El Escorial (Martínez Cuesta 1992). John's corpse was of interest to many parties and its fate can be considered to be directly related to his special status and political significance. He was the victorious commander of the Holy League and winner of the Battle of Lepanto in AD 1571, which saved Italy from the Turks. He was a native of Germany, the brother of the King of Spain and Governor of the Low Countries, but he was also the enemy of William of Orange and his allies.

Communicable Diseases (c)

The most common diseases in the sample are smallpox, tuberculosis, plague, influenza and typhus. They caused the death of 30 individuals. Those individuals who died from these diseases during war expeditions [Category (a)] are not included in this count. In the group of 30 disease victims, eleven individuals were eviscerated, nine were not eviscerated and the treatment of the rest is unknown. The eleven eviscerated individuals had died from smallpox (n=6), tuberculosis (n=3), typhus and influenza. Of the nine untreated individuals three had died from smallpox, three from tuberculosis, two were suspected to have died from plague and one is known to have died from influenza.

Two smallpox victims did not lie in state as usual because of the disease (Hawlik-van de Water 1989, 68). One was Maria Josefa, the 16 year old daughter of Emperor Leopold I who died in AD 1703, and the other was the young King Ferdinand IV († 1654). Both individuals had been eviscerated.

For the two suspected plague victims, Bohemian and Hungarian King Ladislas Postumus († 1457) and Duke Albert VI of Austria († 1463), there exists a direct relationship between mortuary treatment and the suspected cause of death. The doctors refused to eviscerate the corpse of Ladislas Postumus († 1457) although this was customary in Bohemia at that time (Bláhova 1997, 104). Duke Albert VI of Austria († 1463), who was also not eviscerated, was stored in a plague pit and later reburied (Mraz 1988, 43; Weiss-Krejci 2001; 2005). Such fear of the plague had not existed 300 years earlier. When the plague broke out in Frederick Barbarossa's army in Rome in the summer of AD 1167 six bishops and four dukes [in Category (a)] were eviscerated and also boiled and stripped of flesh (Schäfer 1920, 483).

Death during Pregnancy and Childbirth (d)

Five women died because of complications during pregnancy and 21 during, or shortly after, childbirth (Table 10.2). Ten women died together with their babies, while 12 babies (ten singletons plus a pair of twins) survived the death of their mothers. In the sample child bearing appears to have been a more frequent cause of death from the end of the fifteenth century onwards. Since this is the time of the development of medical sciences and breakthroughs in anatomy (Bergdolt 2000, 100) I would suggest that these deaths were directly caused by the doctors who – after dissecting bodies – caused infections in the women as a result of their unwashed hands.

In this group no relationship exists between the cause of death, the kind of treatment afforded to the corpse and the choice of burial location. When mothers and babies died together they were buried either in the same coffin or within the same monument or vault (Figure 10.3). It should be noted, however, that the presence of a woman and child in one monument does not always indicate simultaneous death. Queen Anna (see Figure 10.2) shared a grave at Basel Cathedral, for example, with her six month old son Karl who had died five years previously (Gut 1999).

Accidents (e)

Sixteen people, 13 of them male, had died as a result of accidents. The most frequent reasons for death were hunting accidents (n=4), riding accidents (n=4) and accidents involving a carriage (n=2). Other fatal accidents had been caused by an arrow (which went astray), a dress (which caught fire from a cigarette), drowning, a joust, a fall from a tree, and an explosion. As far as I can tell death as a result of an accident did not result in deviant mortuary treatment.

Figure 10.3. Blanche of France and her baby († 1305) at the Church of Friars Minor, Vienna. The monument was destroyed in the eighteenth century (Gerbert et al. *1772, 4/2, plate XI, drawn by Kleiner, engraved by Nicolai).*

Suicide (f)

The only person in the sample to have committed suicide was Crown Prince Rudolph, the only son of Emperor Franz Joseph and Empress Elizabeth. Rudolph shot his lover, the 17 year old Baroness Mary Vetsera, before shooting himself in the head in Mayerling in AD 1889. The whole affair was covered up by the Habsburg court. Rudolph received a Christian funeral and was deposited in the Habsburg dynastic burial place, the Capuchin Vault in Vienna (Hawlik-van de Water 1993, 301–3).

Murder Victims (g)

Eleven people had been murdered (stabbed, shot and decapitated), and two additional individuals (Medieval) were possibly poisoned. The most famous and best documented murder cases are the shooting of Archduke Franz Ferdinand and his wife Sophie in Sarajevo in AD 1914, the stabbing of Empress Elizabeth in Geneva in AD 1898, the killing of King Albert

I by his nephew John in AD 1308, the murder of Henry of Almain, the son of Richard of Cornwall in AD 1271, the decapitation of Mary of Brabant by her jealous husband in AD 1256, and the murder of Engelbert, Archbishop of Cologne in AD 1225.

The burials of Empress Elizabeth, Archduke Ferdinand and Sophie followed the norm. The corpses were not eviscerated because this was no longer fashionable at that time. Elizabeth was laid to rest in the Capuchin Vault in Vienna. Archduke Franz Ferdinand and his wife Sophie were not buried at the Habsburg vault in Vienna, but rather in the castle of Artstetten because of their morganatic marriage (Hawlik-van de Water 1993).

German-Roman King Albert I was assassinated in AD 1308 by his nephew John at Brugg at the Aaare. He was probably not eviscerated (Meyer 2000, 211) but instead temporarily buried in close proximity to the location of the murder at the monastery of Wettingen. A year later the family sought permission from the new German-Roman King Henry VII to rebury the corpse at Speyer Cathedral. Speyer was the burial place of the Holy Roman emperors from the Salian and Staufen Dynasties as well as the burial place of Rudolph I, Albert's father (Klimm 1953). Albert was reburied in a single ceremony along with the preceding German-Roman King Adolph of Nassau whom he had killed in the battle at Göllheim in AD 1298 and who was exhumed from Rosenthal. Since Rudolph I had already taken the last burial spot in the cathedral, Adolph of Nassau was buried in the sarcophagus of Barbarossa's little daughter and Albert I was interred with Barbarossa's wife (Meyer 2000, 19–52; Weiss-Krejci 2004, 391).

Henry of Almain was murdered in AD 1271 in Viterbo, Italy. He received the same treatment as all the other Crusaders who had died from other causes. He was eviscerated and defleshed and his bones and heart were returned to England (Bradford 1933, 78; Brown 1981, 232).

As with Albert I, the murder of the Archbishop of Cologne, Engelbert, had a direct impact on the fate of his corpse. While Albert I had been exhumed and reburied one year after death, Engelbert of Cologne was excarnated and displayed. In contrast to most other excarnated individuals (see Figure 10.1), he was neither killed during a Crusade nor killed in southern Europe. After he was murdered by Count Frederick of Isenburg in AD 1225 at Gevelsberg near Cologne, his corpse was first brought to the monastery of Altenberg (seven hours away), where it was eviscerated and filled with myrrh and salt. Then it was publicly exhibited at Saint Peter's Church in Cologne. Since it was decided to leave the body of evidence unburied for a while, it was subsequently boiled and defleshed (Schäfer 1920, 485).

'Social Deviants'

Convicted and Executed (h)

Up until the nineteenth century the primary method of execution for members of the aristocracy was decapitation. Seven people had been decapitated (two by the guillotine) – Frederick of Baden and Prince Conradin, the last Staufen, both in AD 1268; Zavis of Falkenstein in AD 1290, Mary, Queen of Scots in AD 1587, Charles I of England, Scotland and Ireland in AD 1649 and Louis XVI and Marie Antoinette, both in AD 1793. The two latest executed individuals – Maximilian of Mexico in AD 1867 and Tsar Nicholas II in 1918 – had been shot. All of these executions were based on charges of treason.

Maximilian of Mexico was executed in Mexico in June 1867. Six months after the execution his body was disinterred and brought to Trieste on the Austrian frigate Novara and buried in the Capuchin Vault in Vienna in January 1868 (Hawlik-van de Water 1993, 264). Tsar Nicholas II and his family were killed in Yekaterinburg during the night of July 16–17, in 1918, and their remains were hidden in the ground. After the breakdown of the Communist regime, their bodies were exhumed in 1991 and reburied exactly 80 years after death in St. Petersburg. The reburial took place on July 17 1998 in a huge public ceremony in the presence of President Boris Yeltsin (Follath 1998).

Exhumation and reburial is also a characteristic of other corpses in this group. Mary, Queen of the Scots was executed at Fotheringhay Castle in AD 1587 and buried at Peterborough Cathedral. Her body was exhumed 25 years after her death in AD 1612 and reinterred within a pompous monument in Westminster Abbey by the order of her son King James I of England (Carr 1999). King Louis XVI of France was guillotined on January 21 1793; his wife Marie Antoinette suffered the same fate on 16 October 1793. Their bodies were buried at the cemetery of the Madeleine but, when the monarchy was restored, they were exhumed and reburied at St. Denis in AD 1815 (Brown 1985, 255).

The reasons for these exhumations are obvious. The original grave location and the funeral rites of the executed individuals were not proper according to their original status. Through exhumation and reburial at some later point in time the mistake of their improper burial was rectified.

Outlaw (i)

John, the posthumous and only son of Rudolph II, was cheated out of his inheritance by his uncle King Albert I and subsequently he decided to kill him in AD 1308 at Brugg at the Aare. The murder, one of the great catastrophes of German history (Honemann 1997, 109), caused the loss of the German-Roman kingship for the House of Habsburg. What made John's crime so special was not the murder – Albert I had also ordered the murder of King Adolph of Nassau – but rather the killing of a patrilineal blood relative. John was soon called *Parricida*, the Parricide, and outlawed in AD 1309 by the newly elected German-Roman King Henry VII. He managed to escape, but died in Italy a few years later (possibly in AD 1313) and was buried at San Niccolo in Pisa (Dienst 1988). John the Parricide is one of the few adult people in the House of Habsburg who was buried in isolation from relatives. No effort was ever made to retrieve his body.

Excommunication (j)

One of the most powerful – and therefore frequently used – political instruments that a pope could direct against a ruler who did not follow his orders was excommunication. Such a ban on a person denied the right for burial in consecrated ground and thus seriously endangered the destiny of the soul. Three people died while excommunicated. These were Emperor Henry IV from the Salian Dynasty († 1106); Ottokar II of Bohemia (Przemyslid), who died in AD 1278 and Louis the Bavarian from the House of Wittelsbach († 1347).

Emperor Henry IV – one of his many crimes against the church was the expulsion of Pope Gregory VII – died excommunicated on 7 August 1106 in Liege. After four weeks his eviscerated corpse was transported to Speyer Cathedral and buried in an unconsecrated side chapel of the cathedral, where he remained for five years. When the ban was lifted, he was reburied on 7 August 1111 beside his father Henry III (Klimm 1957; Ohler 1990, 147).

After the Babenbergs had died out in the male line in AD 1246, Ottokar II the King of Bohemia, ruled over the former Babenberg territory – the duchies of Austria, Styria, Carinthia and Crain – for 26 years. In AD 1273 Rudolph of Habsburg was elected German-Roman king and granted the Babenberg territory by the German electors. Ottokar, who himself had wanted to become the new German-Roman king, rebelled and was excommunicated by the pope. In AD 1278 Ottokar and Rudolph met for a final confrontation in a battle on the Marchfeld near Dürnkrut. Ottokar lost his life and Rudolf became the uncontested ruler of the Austrian lands. After the fight Ottokar's body was eviscerated and his corpse publicly displayed for 30 weeks in Vienna. In AD 1279 Ottokar was buried at Znojmo, but he was exhumed and reburied in St. Vitus Cathedral in Prague in AD 1297, by order of his son (Millauer 1830, 35–8).

Before the fourteenth century excommunication had a direct impact on the fate of the corpse and often caused significant delays between death and final deposition. Dying excommunicated in later times was no longer considered to be as serious. Louis the Bavarian, who died excommunicated in AD 1347, for example, was almost immediately buried in consecrated ground. Many diverging stories exist, however, concerning his burial in Munich (Meyer 2000, 76–87).

Protestant (k)

Several Protestant women married into the Habsburg Dynasty. All but one converted to Roman Catholicism. The one notorious exception is Henrietta of Nassau-Weilburg, wife of Archduke Karl. Although Henrietta was very popular among the Austrian population – she introduced the Christmas tree in Vienna (Hawlik-van de Water 1993, 260) – her confession created a problem when she died in AD 1829. Though her corpse was buried according to the norm, i.e. in the Habsburg vault in Vienna by order of her brother in law, Austrian emperor Francis I (Timmermann 1996, 137), her entrails were not deposited in the proper location. When Henrietta died it was still a custom to bury the hearts at the Augustinian church in Vienna and the intestines at St. Stephen's, Vienna. Henrietta's heart and intestinal urns instead were deposited in the Capuchin Vault beside her coffin (Wolfsgruber 1887, 293).

Small Children

Babenberg

The Medieval records regarding children of the Babenberg Dynasty are incomplete. There were only seven dead children – all belonging to Leopold III – listed in the entire Babenberg genealogy [Table 10.2; Category (q)]. The seven infants were probably all buried at Klosterneuburg in Lower Austria, the foundation and later burial place of their father. Since other Babenbergs probably had lost children too, but these are missing from the record, it is impossible to evaluate child mortality or mortuary behavior concerning children in this dynasty.

Habsburg and Habsburg-Lorraine

In the House of Habsburg child mortality was higher than in the House of Habsburg-Lorraine. Of the 237 blood relatives born into the House of Habsburg 24% died in the first year of life (including premature and stillborn babies), while another 8% perished between the ages of one and four years. In the House of Habsburg-Lorraine only 8% died in their first year, whereas 9% perished between the ages of one and four years.

Children were treated differently than adults. No child was excarnated; only 19 were eviscerated. The earliest evisceration of a child took place in AD 1629 (a two-year old), the last in AD 1855. All eviscerated children had lived for at least a few weeks. While the internal organs of adults at that time were buried in two containers – one for the heart and another for the intestines – and in separate locations in Vienna (hearts at the Augustinian Church, intestines at St. Stephen's), the internal organs of six very small children were each buried within single urns at St. Stephen's. If a child's heart and intestines were enclosed in two urns, they were – with a few exceptions – also buried only at St. Stephen's.

Official mourning ceremonies for children were also much simpler and shorter than for older persons (the borderline was the age of 12 years). Exceptions were made when the child was an important heir to the throne and the only surviving male heir. Leopold Johann, for example, was only seven months old when he died in AD 1716. Since he was the only son of Emperor Charles VI and the last descendent in the male line, a different protocol was followed. As was customary at that time also for children the corpse was eviscerated and laid in state for a few hours. However, a funeral conduct – much larger than usual – which consisted of priests, courtly personnel, and knights from the Order of the Golden Fleece accompanied the body to the Capuchin Vault. Additionally, 23 years later Charles VI commissioned a pompous tin coffin for the corpse of his little son (Hawlik-van de Water 1989, 99–107).

Sources from the seventeenth and eighteenth centuries also show that babies were usually baptised within the first days of life, either by midwives or by a priest. A six-month old live foetus was cut out of the corpse of the deceased Empress Maria Anna in AD 1646. The child was baptised before it died (Wolfsgruber 1887, 94).

In contrast to the House of Habsburg-Lorraine, burial locations for children are very diverse in the House of Habsburg. In the House of Habsburg-Lorraine almost all children were buried in dynastic family crypts and with close patrilineal relatives in Austria, Hungary and Italy (Vienna, Budapest, Florence and Modena). One baby († 1911) was buried in a graveyard in Bad Ischl, the emperor's summer residence. In the House of Habsburg children were buried all over Europe and in all manner of combinations – with adults or with other children; with close patrilineal relatives or with distant relatives. This behaviour is a direct result of the political conditions and geographical extension of the Habsburg territory from the fourteenth to the early eighteenth century. As a result of travels through the vast empire, children often died a long way from their home. Whereas adults were either transported immediately to their burial place or temporarily stored and transported later, deceased infants (as well as adolescents and sometimes even young unmarried adults) were usually interred within the most convenient available crypt. Of 76 children younger than five years in the Habsburg sample 28 (37%) had been buried in the city were they had died and an additional 18 (24%) were transported only between 20 km and 40 km for burial. Only six individuals (8%) were transported more than 40 km for burial. The maximum transport distance for a child younger than five years is 180 km. However, this child was transported with the mother. For the remaining 24 (31%) children of the Habsburg sample the location of death or burial, and thus transport distance, is unknown (see Weiss-Krejci 2004 for House of Habsburg statistics including older children and adolescents).

The transport distance of children's remains is higher in the House of Habsburg-Lorraine. Of 36 children from the House of Habsburg-Lorraine who died younger than five years, eleven (31%) were transported long-distance between 80 km and 380 km. The remaining 25 (69%) individuals were buried at, or close to, the place of death.

In order to avoid the long-distance transport of the remains of a small child, some older Habsburg vaults had to be reopened. The crypt at St. Stephen's Cathedral in Vienna for example, which was used by Habsburg generations four to seven and was out of use since AD 1463, was reopened in AD 1552, 1564 and 1566 to receive the corpses of three infants of Emperor Maximilian II from generation eleven. These children, who had died during visits of the royal family to Vienna, were buried at the entrance of the crypt (Weiss-Krejci 2001, 773). In other instances children were buried alone and away from the dynasty. Five young children from the second marriage of Styrian Duke Ernest († 1424) were buried in the cathedral of the residential city Wiener Neustadt between AD 1421 and 1432. Their father and his first wife († 1407) were buried at the monastery of Rein (Lein 1978), while their mother, Cimburgis of Masovia († 1429), rests at the Babenberg foundation in Lilienfeld (Lein 1978; Jahn 2001).

The monastery of Tulln, a foundation of Rudolph of Habsburg, was also only used for children. No adult from the dynasty was ever buried in this city. A monument in front of the altar steps (Figure 10.4) holds the remains of approximately 16 infants (Lein 1978, 7). These are patrilineal as well as matrilineal grandchildren and great grandchildren of the founder.

If no patrilineal contemporary tomb was available a child or adolescent could also be buried in the dynastic vault of matrilineal relatives. This did not happen with any subadult patrilineal blood relatives of the Habsburg Dynasty, but it explains why several non-dynasty members – i.e. children of Habsburg-born women – were buried in Habsburg tombs. The permission for burial was granted through this connection of blood in the female line (Weiss-Krejci 2004).

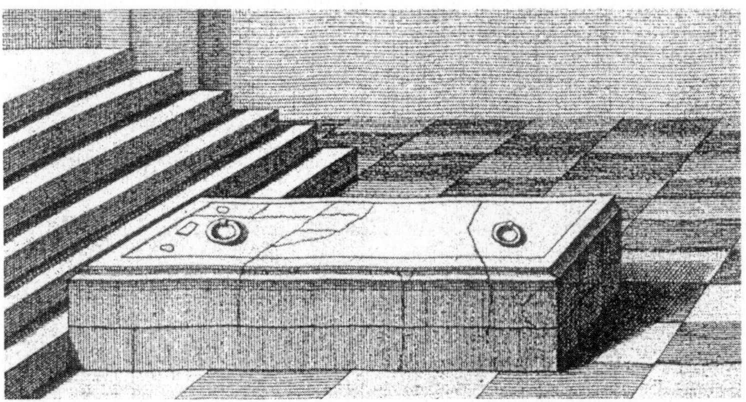

Figure 10.4. Tulln monastery: monument with infant remains in front of the altar steps (late thirteenth/ early fourteenth century). The monument was destroyed in the eighteenth century (Gerbert et al. *1772, 4/2, plate IX, drawn by Franz Rosenstingl, engraved by Nicolai).*

The Deviant Burial of Maximilian I

Differential treatment of the death has also occurred for other reasons, for example penitence (see Holloway, this volume). One example is the burial of Emperor Maximilian I who died in Wels, Austria, in January 1519 (Figure 10.5). He gave very specific instructions for his funerary treatment. He did not want his body to be opened; his hair should be cut off and his teeth knocked out and buried in the graveyard of Wels together with burning coals. His body was to be whipped and covered with lime and ash, wrapped in a bag of coarse linen, covered with bags of fine linen, white silk and damask and publicly displayed to show the perishableness of all earthly glory. The opening of Maximilian's coffin in Wiener Neustadt in both AD 1573 and 1770 confirm the historic accounts of his mortuary treatment. The corpse was covered with lime and all teeth but one were missing. Beside the skeleton several twig whips were encountered (Schmid 1997, 203).

Final Remarks

The investigation had shown that in some instances there exists a relationship between differential life, death and mortuary treatment. High ranking persons who had died during a Crusade were usually defleshed; other warriors were either defleshed or eviscerated in order to be transported home. People who died from plague in the fifteenth century were not eviscerated. The bodies of murdered, executed and excommunicated individuals have been used by survivors for political purposes and therefore were exhumed and reburied in pompous ceremonies. Finally children were buried close to their place of death, and sometimes – at least in pre-industrial times – away from their parents and together with distant relatives or other related children.

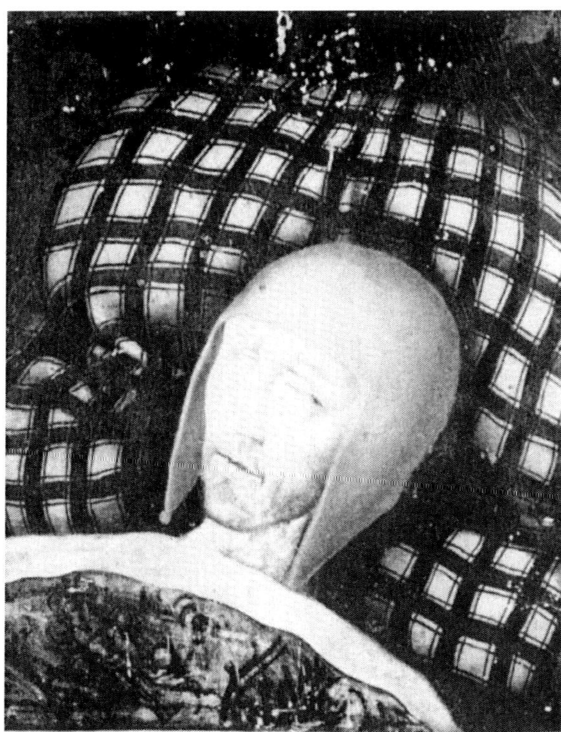

Figure 10.5. Maximilian I one day after his death. Sixteenth century copy from Innsbruck after the original in Wels (Gutkas 1968/1969, fig. 3).

The study also shows that deviant treatment of the corpse can sometimes happen to persons who are the opposite of criminals or misfits. Both the mutilated Don John of Austria and the tortured Maximilian I, for example, were people of tremendous political significance and their deviant treatment is a sign of high and very special status.

Despite a certain relationship between deviant life, death and burial, without historic sources it is quite difficult for an archaeologist to understand why an individual was treated in a certain way. In this sample travellers and pilgrims who died a long way from home were also defleshed in order to be transported home. The remains of some were stored for later exhumation and reburial. Exhumation and reburial were also practiced for many other reasons. In the past investigation of 868 Babenberg and Habsburg burials (Weiss-Krejci 2001) I have shown that at least 40% of the entire sample had been tampered with. Coffins have been opened, bones have been relocated either within buildings, from one building to another, or between towns and even distant countries. The reasons for these frequent manipulations of the dead body are manifold and include territorial shifts, reconstruction of buildings, warfare, etc. They are not necessarily related to the lives or deaths of the deceased.

Every individual in this sample has his/her own story and exceptions from the norm are always possible. This investigation proves that deviant life and deviant death does have an effect on treatment and deposition of the corpse, but in the absence of historic records it is highly recommended that the interpretation of any deviant burial is undertaken in a cautious manner.

Acknowledgements

The original research on which this article is based was funded by the Austrian Science Fund FWF (Project H140-SPR). The article was completed in 2006 under Austrian Science Fund grant P18949-G02. I would like to thank Eileen Murphy for her efforts in organising the EAA session in Cork and for editing this book.

References

Bergdolt, K. 2000. Medizin und Naturwissenschaften zur Zeit Karls V., pp. 99–107 in Seipel, W. (ed.), *Kaiser Karl V. (1500–1558): Macht und Ohnmacht Europas*. Vienna: Kunsthistorisches Museum. (Medical and natural sciences during the time of Charles V in Emperor Charles V (1500–1558): Europe's Power and Powerlessness).

Binford, L. R. 1971. Mortuary practices: their study and their potential, pp. 6–29 in Brown, J. (ed.), *Approaches to the Social Dimensions of Mortuary Practices* (Memoirs of the Society for American Archaeology 25). Washington D.C.: Society for American Archaeology.

Binski, P. 1996. *Medieval Death: Ritual and Representation*. London: British Museum Press.

Bláhová, M. 1997. Die königlichen Begräbniszeremonien im spätmittelalterlichen Böhmen, pp. 89–111 in Kolmer L. (ed.), *Der Tod des Mächtigen*. Paderborn: Schöningh. (Royal burial ceremonies in late medieval Bohemia in Death of the Mighty).

Boase, T. S. R. 1972. *Death in the Middle Ages*. New York: McGraw-Hill Book Company.

Bradford, C. A. 1933. *Heart Burial*. London: George Allen & Unwin Ltd.

Brown, E. A. R. 1981. Death and the human body in the later Middle Ages: the legislation of Boniface VIII on the division of the corpse. *Viator* 12, 221–70.

Brown, E. A. R. 1985. Burying and unburying the kings of France, pp. 241–66 in Trexler, R. (ed.), *Persons in Groups: Social Behavior as Identity Formation in Medieval and Renaissance Europe* (Medieval and Renaissance Texts and Studies 36). Binghamton: Medieval and Renaissance Texts and Studies.

Carr, C. 1995. Mortuary practices: their social, philosophical-religious, circumstantial and physical determinants. *Journal of Archaeological Method and Theory* 2, 105–200.

Carr, W. 1999. *Westminster Abbey*. London: Dean and Chapter of Westminster and Jarrold Publishing.

Dienst, H. 1988. Johann 'Parricida', pp. 174–5 in Hamann, B. (ed.), *Die Habsburger*. Vienna: Ueberreuter. (John 'the Parricide' in The Habsburg Dynasty).

Dodson, A. 1994. The king is dead, pp. 71–95 in Eyre, C., Leahy, A. and Leahy, L. (eds), *The Unbroken Reed*. London: Egypt Exploration Society.

Duncan, W. N. 2005. Understanding veneration and violation in the archaeological record, pp. 207–27 in Rakita, G., Buikstra, J., Beck, L. and Williams, S. (eds), *Interacting with the Dead: Perspectives on Mortuary Archaeology for the New Millennium*. Gainesville: University Press of Florida.

Finucane, R. C. 1981. Sacred corpse, profane carrion: social ideals and death rituals in the later Middle Ages, pp. 40–60 in Whaley, J. (ed.), *Mirrors of Mortality*. London: Europa Publications Limited.

Follath, E. 1998. Verrat, Feigheit, Betrug. *Der Spiegel* 30/1998, 118–9. (Treason, cowardice, fraud).

Forgey, K. and Williams, S. R. 2005. Were Nasca trophy heads war trophies or revered ancestors?: insight from the Kroeber collection, pp. 251–76 in Rakita, G., Buikstra, J., Beck, L. and Williams, S. (eds), *Interacting with the Dead: Perspectives on Mortuary Archaeology for the New Millennium*. Gainesville: University Press of Florida.

Gerbert, M., Herrgott M. and Heer, R. 1772. *Taphographia principum Austriae, Monumenta Augustae domus Austriae 4* (1–2). St Blasien: Monastery St Blasien. (Description of the Burials of the Austrian Lords: Imperial Monuments of the House of Austria).

Giesey, R. E. 1960. *The Royal Funeral Ceremony in Renaissance France*. Geneva: Libraire E. Droz.

Gut, J. 1999. Memorialorte der Habsburger im Südwesten des Alten Reiches: politische Hintergründe und Aspekte, pp. 94–113 in Württembergisches Landesmuseum Stuttgart (ed.), *Vorderösterreich*. Ulm: Süddeutsche Verlagsgesellschaft. (Locations of Habsburg commemoration in the southwest of the Old Empire: political background and aspects in 'Fore' Austria).

Gutkas, K. 1968/1969. Kaiser Maximilian I (1459–1519). *Jahrbuch des Musealvereines Wels* 15, 11–34.

Hamann, B. 1988. Die Herrscherdynastie Habsburg, pp. 11–25 in Hamann, B. (ed.), *Die Habsburger*. Vienna: Ueberreuter. (The ruling Habsburg dynasty in The Habsburg Dynasty).

Hawlik-van de Water, M. 1989. *Der schöne Tod: Zeremonialstrukturen des Wiener Hofes bei Tod und Begräbnis zwischen 1640 und 1740*. Vienna: Herder. (Beautiful Death: Ceremonial Structure at the Viennese Court during Death and Burial between 1640 and 1740).

Hawlik-van de Water, M. 1993. *Die Kapuzinergruft* (second edition). Vienna: Herder. (The Capuchin Vault).

Honemann, V. 1997. A medieval queen and her stepdaughter: Agnes and Elizabeth of Hungary, pp. 109–19 in Duggan, A. (ed.), *Queens and Queenship in Medieval Europe*. Woodbridge: The Boydell Press.

Hutchinson, D. L. and Aragon, L. V. 2002. Collective burials and community memories: interpreting the placement of the dead in the southeastern and mid-Atlantic United States with reference to ethnographic cases from Indonesia, pp. 27–54 in Silverman, H. and Small, D. (eds), *The Space and Place of Death* (Archaeological Papers of the American Anthropological Association 11). Arlington: American Anthropological Association.

Jahn, A. 2001. *Die Grabstätten der Habsburger und der mit ihnen verwandten Häuser in Österreichs Kirchen: Das Haus Habsburg* 2, 2.Vienna: Alois Jahn. (Graves of the Habsburg Dynasty and Related Houses in Austrian Churches: House of Habsburg 2, 2).

Klimm, F. 1953. *Der Kaiserdom zu Speyer*. Speyer: Verlag Jaeger. (The Imperial Cathedral at Speyer).

Lechner, K. 1976. *Die Babenberger*. Vienna: Böhlau. (The Babenberg Dynasty).

Lein, E. 1978. *Begräbnisstätten der Alt-Habsburger in Österreich*. Vienna: Lein-Neubacher. (Burial Places of the Early House of Habsburg in Austria).

Martínez Cuesta, J. 1992. *Guide to the Monastery of San Lorenzo El Real*. Madrid: Editorial Patrimonio Nacional.

Meyer, R. J. 2000. *Königs- und Kaiserbegräbnisse im Spätmittelalter* (Beihefte zu J. F. Böhmer, Regesta Imperii 19). Cologne: Böhlau. (Burials of German-Roman Kings and Emperors in the Late Middle Ages).

Millauer, M. 1830. *Die Grabstätten und Grabmäler der Landesfürsten Böhmens*. (Abhandlungen der königlichen böhmischen Gesellschaft der Wissenschaften, Neue Folge 2). Prague: Gottlieb Haase Söhne. (Graves and Grave Monuments of the Bohemian Lords).

Mraz, G. 1988. Albrecht VI, pp. 42–3 in Hamann, B. (ed.), *Die Habsburger.* Vienna: Ueberreuter. (Albert VI in The Habsburg Dynasty).

Niemetz, P. 1974. *Die Grablege der Babenberger in der Abtei Heiligenkreuz.* Heiligenkreuz: Heiligenkreuzer Verlag. (The Burial Place of the Babenberg Dynasty at Heiligenkreuz Abbey).

Ohler, N. 1990. *Sterben und Tod im Mittelalter.* Munich: Artemis. (Dying and Death in the Middle Ages).

O'Shea, J. 1984. *Mortuary Variability: An Archaeological Investigation.* New York: Academic Press.

Petrie, C. 1967. *Don John of Austria.* New York: W. W. Norton and Company.

Prutz, H. 1879. *Kaiser Friedrich I. Grabstätte: Eine kritische Studie.* Danzig: Ernst Gruihn. (The Burial Place of Emperor Frederick I: A Critical Study).

Schäfer, D. 1920. Mittelalterlicher Brauch bei der Überführung von Leichen. *Sitzungsberichte der preussischen Akademie der Wissenschaften* n.n., 478–98. (Medieval custom at the transport of corpses).

Schmid, P. 1997. Sterben - Tod - Leichenbegängnis Kaiser Maximilians I., pp. 185–215 in Kolmer, L. (ed.), *Der Tod des Mächtigen.* Paderborn: Schöningh. (Dying - death - funeral of Emperor Maximilian I in Death of the Mighty).

Shay, T. 1985. Differentiated treatment of deviancy at death as revealed in anthropological and archaeological material. *Journal of Anthropological Archaeology* 4, 221–41.

Störmer, W. 1980. Die Hausklöster der Wittelsbacher, pp. 139–50 in Glaser, H. (ed.), *Die Zeit der frühen Herzöge: Von Otto I. zu Ludwig dem Bayern.* Munich: Hirmer. (The house monasteries of the Wittelsbach dynasty in Times of the Early Dukes: From Otto I to Louis the Bavarian).

Timmermann, B. 1996. *Die Begräbnisstätten der Habsburger in Wien.* Vienna: Modul Verlag. (The Burial Places of the Habsburg Dynasty in Vienna).

Ucko, P. J. 1969. Ethnography and archaeological interpretation of funerary remains. *World Archaeology* 1, 262–80.

Vocelka, K. and Heller, L. 1997. *Die Lebenswelt der Habsburger.* Graz: Styria. (The Social World of the Habsburg Dynasty).

Waterson, R. 1995. Houses, graves and the limits of kinship groupings among the Sa'dan Toraja'. *Bijdragen tot de Taal-, Land- en Volkenkunde* 151, 194–217.

Weiss-Krejci, E. 2001. Restless corpses: 'secondary burial' in the Babenberg and Habsburg dynasties. *Antiquity* 75, 769–80.

Weiss-Krejci, E. 2004. Mortuary representations of the noble house: a cross-cultural comparison between collective tombs of the ancient Maya and dynastic Europe. *Journal of Social Archaeology* 4, 368–404.

Weiss-Krejci, E. 2005. Excarnation, evisceration, and exhumation in medieval and post-medieval Europe, pp. 155–72 in Rakita, G., Buikstra, J., Beck, L. and Williams, S. (eds), *Interacting with the Dead: Perspectives on Mortuary Archaeology for the New Millennium.* Gainesville: University Press of Florida.

Wolfsgruber, C. 1887. *Die Kaisergruft bei den Kapuzinern in Wien.* Vienna: Alfred Hölder. (The Imperial Capuchin Vault in Vienna).

11. The Origins of *Cillini* in Ireland

Colm J. Donnelly and Eileen M. Murphy

Abstract

Cillini, *or children's burial grounds, were the designated resting places for individuals considered unsuitable for burial within consecrated ground. Traditionally associated with the burial of unbaptised infants, oral lore has also identified the mentally disabled, strangers, the shipwrecked, criminals, famine victims and people who had committed suicide as individuals who could also be buried within a* cillín. *These poignant burial grounds are a recognised class of monument found throughout Ireland but, other than an assumption that they originated at some stage in Ireland's Christian past, there has been a lack of clarity on exactly how and when these cemeteries came into use. The paper attempts to resolve this issue through a review of the dating evidence obtained from 16 excavations that have been undertaken during the period from 1966 to 2004. The result of this survey suggests that the* cillín *is a monument that proliferates in the Post-Medieval period and it is suggested that their development is connected with the reinvigorated Catholicism of the Counter-Reformation in Ireland.*

Introduction

Cillini were the designated resting places for stillborn and unbaptised children and other members of Irish society who were considered unsuitable for burial in consecrated ground. These cemeteries are traditionally associated with the burial of unbaptised infants, although the mentally disabled, strangers, the shipwrecked, criminals, famine victims, and people who had committed suicide could also be buried within *cillini*. Locations for this class of burial ground were diverse and included deserted churches and graveyards; ancient monuments (including megalithic tombs, secular earthworks and castles); natural landmarks and boundary ditches; sea or lake shores and cross-roads. They are not only referred to as *cillini* and they have a variety of different names including *caldragh*, *calluragh*, *cealltrach*, *ceallúnach*, *ceallúrach*, *lisín*, children's burial grounds, cill burial grounds, killeens and kyle burial grounds.

The recognition of these burial sites as a monument class can be gauged by their inclusion in the archaeological surveys and inventories of Ireland and their presence in both the sites and monuments records in Northern Ireland and the Republic of Ireland, while individual examples have been subject to excavation during the course of the last 40 years. Despite this work, however, there remains a lack of clarity over their origins, other than a general assumption that they have their roots at some stage in Ireland's Christian past.

The following paper will attempt to provide some definition to the issue of the origins of *cillíní*, although it can be stated from the outset that this is research in progress; new evidence may alter – or further confirm – the thesis that is set out in this paper. At the core of this work is a review of the available dating evidence for when *cillíní* come into use on the Irish landscape, based on information obtained from historical sources and archaeological excavations. What this exercise will demonstrate is the fact that while *cillíní* may have their origin in the period between AD 500 and AD 1600 there is an apparent lack of evidence in the historical documentation to suggest their existence during this period in Ireland; it is only with the advent of the seventeenth century that we find a first definitive historical reference to their use. This concurs with the archaeological evidence obtained during excavations undertaken since the 1960s, the results of which overwhelmingly date the monuments to the Post-Medieval[1] period.

Historical Evidence and Regional Surveys: An Overview

The first scholars to make reference to *cillíní* in their works were the nineteenth-century antiquarians. During his discussion of the Parish of Ballykinler, Co. Down, in his seminal work on the ecclesiastical antiquities of Down, Connor and Dromore, Rev. William Reeves (1847, 212) made reference to the discovery of a cemetery on the summit of Lisnashimmer, a small hill 'formerly surrounded by a trench':

> Within the enclosed space, a discovery was made, some years ago, of several small graves, about three feet in length, and ten inches in width and depth. The cavities were lined and covered with thin stones, and contained human remains, which, from the charcoal found with them, appeared to have undergone partial incineration. Molar teeth and fragments of full-grown bones, which were interspersed, proved that these graves were not, as might at first appear, intended for unbaptised infants. They may reasonably be supposed to date their formation from a period anterior to the introduction of Christianity into Ireland.

Leaving aside the fact that adults could and were interred within *cillíní*, the significance of Reeves' account lay not in whether we can identify the re-use of an enclosure on the hill-top at Lisnashimmer as the location of a *cillín*, but that Reeves demonstrated that he was well aware of the existence of *cillíní*; this is further emphasised in the sections of his text where he dealt with the Parish of Cary in Co. Antrim, of which he stated: 'This parish is remarkable for the number of its small burying-grounds. These are called by the country people *Keels* (from Cill, 'a church'), and are principally employed for the interment of still-born children' (Reeves 1847, 282). A similar awareness was displayed by William Wakeman (1879–82, 189–90) when he stated that:

> … in many districts of Ireland, in fact all over the face of the country, are ancient cemeteries, usually of small dimensions, which 'time out of mind' have not been used for the purpose of Christian burial. They were, and numbers of them are to this day, the depositories only of the remains of still-born or unbaptised children and suicides. They are looked upon with horror by the modern Celt, who in no case will approach them after dark. These dreary and unhallowed places are generally designated by the name of keel, or Killeen.

In his book *Pagan Ireland* Wood-Martin (1895, 299) briefly noted the existence of 'Keels, Killeens, Caltraghs, and Calluraghs' as 'ancient burial-places originally quite unconnected with Christian remains or associations, and, where still made use of, it is, as a rule, solely for the interment of unbaptised children, suicides, and unknown strangers'. Wood-Martin viewed these burial grounds as pagan cemeteries that had become abandoned after the arrival of Christianity in Ireland, 'though still held in some degree of reverence by the peasantry, and to this feeling must be attributed the preservation of such vast numbers as are even still to be found throughout the kingdom'. He also noted that they were generally unenclosed, with 'no fence around them, such as might be supposed would surround the last resting-place of the dead'.

A more detailed consideration of the monuments was presented by MacNamara (1900, 32–3) towards the end of his account of the old churches in the townland of Kells in Co. Clare. He noted that half-a-mile to the north of Kells Bridge was the *cillín* at Skeaghavan-noe, a site with no known history, but the location of an old stone cross and small building which may have been a church, and he stated that the local populace considered this to be holy ground that should not be interfered with. His discussion then turned to the origins of *cillíní* and, after noting that a significant number of them were situated 'very near forts, or actually in them', he advanced the following theory as to their origins:

> In the very early days of Christianity in Ireland, the secular clergy, as distinguished from those who lived in communities, must have attached themselves in most cases to tribes or families, and not to the territorial divisions afterwards known as parishes. When, however, in the natural evolution of Church government, the ecclesiastical authorities divided the Irish Church into well-defined dioceses and parishes, new places of worship of improved design were erected in great numbers throughout the country to meet the growing needs of the people, and the old sites, nearly always in or close to the residences of the chief men, namely the forts, became, naturally enough, objects of veneration to succeeding generations. In some instances these places may have been contaminated by old, or even contemporary, pagan interments, a debased reverence for them in course of time sprang up, and they eventually became the killeens in which unbaptised children alone were buried.
>
> It is well to remember, however, that the ancient Romans, who, like the Gaedhils, were mainly of Aryan blood, and for centuries dwelt in close geographical contact with the Gauls, had special customs for the burial of children who died before the appearance of their teeth. These were always buried, never burned on a pyre; and the place set apart for their interment is said to have been called a Suggrundarium. There may have been no real connexion between the two customs, but the Irish one of burying unbaptised children altogether by themselves in a killeen, may, perhaps, have a possible origin in far away pagan times, and, like other customs

> of the kind, been so far modified and transformed by the early Irish Church, as not to clash in any way with the tenets of the Christian faith.

The next significant discussion of *cillini*, however, did not occur until 1939 when Seán Ó Súilleabháin published an article on child burial. The text commenced with a review of the evidence from the Classical World, central to which was a study of the information contained in Virgil's tale from the sixth book of the *Aeneid*, and the journey of Aeneas, guided by Sibyl, through the Underworld; they crossed over a river between the outer reaches and the middle of Hades where, among the different people they encountered, were children who had died young. Ó Súilleabháin noted that children who died young were treated as a separate group in pagan times, with a separate place marked out for them in the Afterlife (Ó Súilleabháin 1939, 145), while he also drew attention to the Roman practice that children who had died before their fortieth day would be buried in a *suggrundarium*, a grave located under a wing of the family house. Ó Súilleabháin then suggested that a similar situation may have existed in Ireland, but one that was later Christianised and included separate burial for children who were not baptised (Ó Súilleabháin 1939, 145). He reviewed the evidence from Wakeman, Wood-Martin, and MacNamara and concluded that these three sources were in agreement that *cillini* had their origins in pagan burial grounds dating to before the arrival of Christianity into Ireland (Ó Súilleabháin 1939, 146).

Ó Súilleabháin's work also contained new folklore information that he had extracted from the archives of the Irish Folklore Commission; he provided an overview of the types of location for the sites – in a haggard or garden beside a house, in ancient forts, at crossroads, beside a well, in a sea-cliff or above the high-tide line, in boundary ditches and in the corners of fields, and outside the boundaries of a graveyard (Ó Súilleabháin 1939, 148) – and he discussed their associated folklore and burial customs, before noting that the usage of such sites was coming to an end (Ó Súilleabháin 1939, 151).

Cillini featured in Sean P. Ó Ríordáin's book *The Antiquities of the Irish Countryside*, first published in 1942, in which he discussed the folklore associated with the monuments in Co. Kerry (1991, 57–9). The period from the late 1960s also witnessed renewed interest in the study of the monument type, commencing with Aldridge (1969) who published a short article that elaborated on the location and appearance of the burial grounds in Co. Mayo. In addition, the paper represented the first detailed regional survey to have been undertaken on the monuments in a defined area. By the 1980s *cillini* had become a recognised class of archaeological monument, as demonstrated by their inclusion in the county surveys and inventories published in the Republic of Ireland. A review of the information contained in the introductory chapters to the monuments in 22 volumes indicates, however, that there exists a general vagueness within the archaeological community over the origins of the monuments in Ireland (Table 11.1). In eleven cases no specific information is provided on their date or origins; an Early Christian origin is suggested in three volumes and a Medieval origin suggested in a further four volumes.

In four cases the authors note that the practice was carried out 'from at least the 18th century'. In all four cases the same source for this statement is quoted as 'Cuppage 1986'.

County	Volume type	Year	Comments on dating and origins	Page
Donegal	Survey	1983	'Ó Súilleabháin (1939, 143–51) has pointed out that the custom of setting apart a special burial place and ritual for young children was practiced amongst the ancient Greeks and Romans'.	309
Kerry (Dingle)	Survey	1986	'The custom of setting apart a special place for the burial of very young or unbaptised children appears to have been common practice in Ireland until the 19th century'. 'When the custom began in this country has not yet, however, been established'.	347
Monaghan	Inventory	1986	No statement on dating or origins.	88
Meath	Inventory	1987	No statement on dating or origins.	155
Louth	Survey	1991	'… and neither can they be closely dated to or be associated with a particular period in the Christian era'.	268
Cork 1	Inventory	1992	'The burial of very young unbaptised infants in specially set apart places was a common practice in Ireland from at least the 18th century (Cuppage 1986). It resulted largely from the refusal by church authorities to allow such burials in consecrated graveyards. The practice finally died out in the early decades of the 20th century'.	291
Carlow	Inventory	1993	No statement on dating or origins.	62
Galway 1	Inventory	1993	Following reference to Greek and Roman practice it is stated that: 'In Ireland such burial places are generally thought to be more recent, the majority probably dating to the second millennium AD'.	146
Cork 2	Inventory	1994	'The burial of very young unbaptised infants in specially set apart places was a common practice in Ireland from at least the 18th century (Cuppage 1986). It resulted largely from the refusal by church authorities to allow such burials in consecrated graveyards. The practice finally died out in the early decades of the 20th century'.	179
Cavan	Inventory	1995	'The practice dates back at least as far as Early Medieval times'.	214
Laois	Inventory	1995	'The custom of setting apart a separate burial place for unbaptised children has a long tradition in Ireland'.	98
Kerry (North)	Survey	1995	'The tradition of setting aside a special burial place for children who died at birth or in infancy was a common practice in Ireland right up until the early 20th century'.	213

Table 11.1. Review of comments on dating and origins contained within the county surveys and inventories for the Republic of Ireland published between 1983 and 2005 (continued overleaf).

County	Volume type	Year	Comments on dating and origins	Page
Kerry (Iveragh)	Survey	1996	'The custom of burying infants and young children in a separately designated place appears to have been practiced in Ireland from at least late Medieval times'. 'It is not known when the custom of burying children in *ceallúnaigh* began in Ireland. The practice was certainly widespread throughout the Iveragh Peninsula during the 19th century, and it was common in many areas until the early decades of the 20th'.	323
Wexford	Inventory	1996	No statement on dating or origins.	150
Offaly	Inventory	1997	'… dating from at least the Early Medieval period'.	121
Wicklow	Inventory	1997	'They were in use from at least the Early Medieval period …'.	153
Cork 3	Inventory	1997	'These alternative burial grounds resulted mainly from refusal by church authorities to allow burial of unbaptised infants in consecrated ground'.	334
Galway 2	Inventory	1999	Following reference to Greek and Roman practice it is stated that: 'In Ireland such burial places are generally thought to be more recent, the majority probably dating to the second millennium AD'.	356
Cork 4	Inventory	2000	'These alternative burial grounds resulted mainly from refusal by church authorities to allow burial of unbaptised infants in consecrated ground'.	475
Tipperary 1	Inventory	2002	'Many are known as children's burial grounds as they were used for the burial of unbaptised children who were not permitted by the Roman Catholic church to be buried in consecrated ground … The practice of burying children in a separate designated location has a long tradition, going back to ancient Greek and Roman times (Ó Súilleabháin 1939). In Ireland this practice was certainly carried out from the 18th century (Cuppage 1986) …'.	282
Leitrim	Inventory	2003	The monuments ' … could date at least from the Medieval period and continued in use, in some cases, into the 20th century'.	194
Sligo	Inventory	2005	'Sixteen of these are children's burial grounds, which were used for the burial of unbaptised children who were not permitted by the Roman Catholic church to be buried in consecrated ground. This practice was carried out in Ireland from the 18th century (Cuppage 1986) and continued into the mid 20th century'.	455

Table 11.1 (continued). Review of comments on dating and origins contained within the county surveys and inventories for the Republic of Ireland published between 1983 and 2005.

This source would seem to be the archaeological survey of the Dingle peninsula in Co. Kerry, edited by Judith Cuppage and published in 1986. Upon reading Cuppage's text, however, it does not become apparent where the association with the eighteenth century originates. With reference to origins Cuppage stated that: 'The custom of setting apart a special place for the burial of very young or unbaptised children appears to have been common practice in Ireland until the 19th century' (Cuppage 1986, 347). She goes on to state that:

> The Ordnance Survey recorded many instances of the continued use of children's burial grounds into the 19th century, and an example of the custom was recorded in Co. Mayo as recently as 1964 (Aldridge 1969, 83–7). When the custom began in this country has not, however, been established. The Early Christian settlement at Reask [Co. Kerry] was reused as a calluragh after the abandonment of its oratory and clochauns, and Fanning (1981, 158) suggests that Reask and other similar sites "were only finally abandoned and adopted as ceal-lúnacha in early Medieval times". However, it is possible that the custom is older than this and, without excavation, the antiquity of individual examples remains uncertain.

In his work on the early church in south-west Ireland Hurley (1982, 304) briefly made mention of *cillini*, which he stated 'could date to anywhere from the sixth century to the nineteenth century, though many of them must have had early ecclesiastical associations. Others were simply ring-forts, or even ordinary fields with no associations of sanctity or antiquity, which were utilised as makeshift burial grounds'. Giving Reask as an example, Hurley went on to state that 'a great many definite early church sites, especially in Kerry, were later reused in this manner when they had long ceased to have any official ecclesiastical function, but they still retained the "aura of sanctity"'. Within Northern Ireland Hamlin and Foley (1983) published an important paper on the Woman's Graveyard at Carrickmore, Co. Tyrone, which further highlighted the various categories of individuals who would have been unsuitable for burial within consecrated ground. Also in 1983 Fanning and Sheehan discussed *cillini* in the diocese of Galway in a study that added to our knowledge of the corpus of characteristics that are associated with the sites, including features such as small grave markers and the inclusion of quartz pebbles in graves. They also discussed the significance of the reuse of earlier sites for these burial grounds, particularly early ecclesiastical sites.

In 1988 Crombie published an article on *cillini* in the barony of Dunmore in Co. Galway. This work was then expanded to include the entire county in her M.A. dissertation research, which was completed in 1990. This work was extremely significant since she undertook a comprehensive field survey involving some 458 *cillini* in the county, while also reporting on the archaeological, literary and folklore evidence associated with these sites. She recorded that some 65% of *cillini* in Galway were located on, or within 200 m of, a townland boundary which led her to consider that Irish society had deliberately selected boundary locations because of their supernatural qualities. She then related this finding to the Roman Catholic concept of limbo and the notion of placelessness associated with the unbaptised and other individuals buried within *cillini* (Crombie 1990, 64).

A survey of 12 *cillini* in east Kerry was published by Patricia O'Hare in 1997, the same year in which Emer Dennehy completed her Masters dissertation on the *cillini* of that county. Dennehy's work comprised a field-based study of a similar type to that undertaken by Crombie for Co. Galway. In addition to undertaking a detailed study of some 257 sites, she too looked in considerable depth at the apparent liminal nature of the location of the monuments; the results of this aspect of her research have been summarised in Finlay (2000). Dennehy has continued her studies in this field and has published a survey of the children's burial ground and ogham stone from Gowlane, Farranfore, Co. Kerry (Dennehy 2001) and an overview of the main results obtained during her Masters research (Dennehy 2003). The first regional survey of disused graveyards to have been undertaken in the northern half of the island was completed for the Parish of Ballintoy, Co. Antrim (Donnelly *et al.*, 1999), work which should indicate how important oral tradition and the records of antiquarians are for researchers when trying to identify the locations of these sites on the modern landscape.

From this brief review it is evident that *cillini* are a subject that have received past and ongoing academic attention, yet there remains either a general uncertainty among archaeologists as to their point of origin, or an assumption that all is resolved with regards this matter. The statement by Finlay (2000, 408) that the 'provision of separate burial grounds for unbaptised infants and children was well established in Ireland from the medieval period onwards …' is a particularly fine example of the latter. The preceding review has highlighted, however, that the primary question on this matter still requires an answer: when did these sites come into use?

Excavated Cillini, *1966 to 2004: The Dating Evidence*[2]

It might be expected that Wakeman, Wood-Martin and MacNamara would know that official Roman Catholic doctrine in late nineteenth-century Ireland actively supported the existence and use of *cillini* as the place for the burial of unbaptised children. From what they wrote, however, they did not suggest an origin for the monuments in the Christian period of Ireland's past, but one which dated back to pagan practices. This view was reaffirmed by Ó Súilleabháin who suggested that this class of site had pagan origins but that they were then Christianised and put to use for the burial of the unbaptised. The lack of clarity on the question of their origins was acknowledged by Sean P. Ó Ríordáin (1991, 59) in 1942 when he stated that 'the *cillin* remains … a tantalizing subject of study on which excavation of suitable examples … would be hoped to throw some light'. Ó Ríordáin's hope was realised, although not immediately; it was not until 1966 that the first *cillín* would be excavated by modern archaeologists. The following section of the paper outlines the principal discoveries made through these investigations, and the dating evidence obtained through archaeological fieldwork (Figure 11.1).

In 1966 the first excavation of a possible *cillín* was undertaken by Etienne Rynne after human remains were discovered at the site of a sand quarry known locally as Madden's Hill

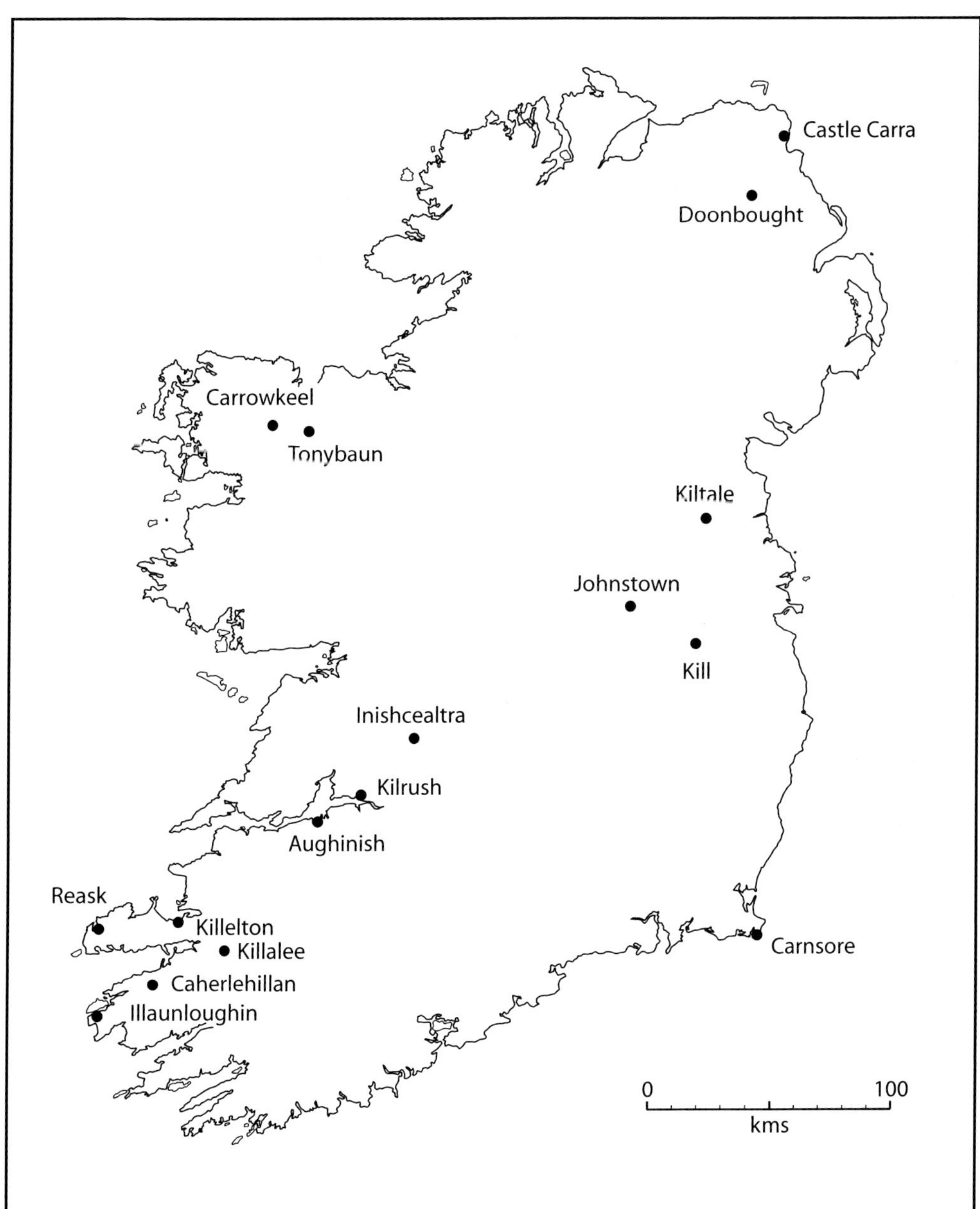

Figure 11.1. Location map of sites mentioned in the text.

at Kiltale, Co. Meath. The monument comprised the site of a ringfort with a souterrain in its interior. Excavation to define the line of the enclosing ditch led to the discovery of human remains, with evidence to suggest that some of the burials had been disturbed when the ringfort ditch had been dug. Further burials were discovered in a natural mound some 35 m to the south-east of the ditch. A concentration of children's burials had been inserted into the mound, while at its centre was observed a setting of stones forming three sides of a rectangle, with each stone set on its end or edge, which was devoid of any traces of human remains. Rynne considered the burials in the ditch and in the mound to represent a single cemetery, with the implication that the human remains were of pre-Christian date since the burials in the ditch predated the construction of the rath. The latest burials were considered to be those located on the mound at the perimeter of the cemetery:

> The reason for the presence of numerous child-burials in this area, a feature not noticed elsewhere on the site, is a matter for speculation but might perhaps be explicable in terms of the recognised practice of burying unbaptised children in ancient pre-Christian burial grounds. If this were so, then it would indicate that the pagan cemetery on "Madden's Hill" was known during Christian times which would, in turn, independently suggest a date in the immediately pre-Christian period for it (Rynne 1974, 273).

In reaching this conclusion Rynne seems to have been influenced by the work of Ó Súilleabháin, whose 1939 article on the subject he referenced in his text (Rynne 1974, 273), and hence he was willing to view the children's burials as pre-Christian and pagan. Given the lack of dating evidence and the fact that natural landscape features could be used as sites for *cillíní*, it can equally be suggested that the two burial groups are chronologically distinct and that the mound was a children's burial ground that developed at this location at a period after the construction of the ringfort. In the absence of scientific dating evidence, however, it is not possible to say with any degree of certainty when this children's burial ground first came into use.

Tom McNeill excavated at the Medieval fort of Doonbought, Co. Antrim, in 1969. The site comprised a sub-circular rock platform with an outer oval earthwork enclosure. Two groups of burials were identified within the fort. Group 1 comprised the remains of nine individuals buried within or at the base of a dump containing thirteenth-century artefacts. Six of the individuals were adults, one was a child and two were infants (Murphy and McNeill 1993, 133). Group 2 consisted of thirteen individuals recovered from the upper levels or the surface of the dump. This group comprised four adults, four juveniles, two children and three infants (Murphy and McNeill 1993, 134). While the range of this age profile would not be exactly typical for a *cillín*, the stratigraphic and artefactual evidence suggested a possibility that the site may represent a Medieval *cillín* or perhaps some form of proto-*cillín*. Recent radiocarbon dates obtained by the current authors from two samples of human bone removed from two of the individuals buried within the thirteenth-century dump, however, would now suggest that the second group of burials belong to the sixteenth to seventeenth century (Table 11.2). It may be the case that the individuals who were buried here represent a group of unfortunates killed by famine or disease and then buried within

Sample 1			
Sample ID:	DB69, Skeleton F12b (6 to 7 year-old juvenile with hydrocephalus) from Group 2		
Lab ID:	UB-6787		
Date:	265±32 BP	68.2% probability	AD 1526–1555 (21.6%) AD 1632–1665 (40.8%) AD 1784–1794 (5.8%)
		95.4% probability	AD 1514–1600 (37.0%) AD 1616–1670 (47.1%) AD 1780–1800 (9.6%) AD 1943–1954 (1.7%)
Sample 2			
Sample ID:	DB69, Skeleton F27 (8 to 9 year old juvenile) from Group 2		
Lab ID:	UB-6788		
Date:	324±33 BP	68.2% probability	AD 1514–1600 (55.4%) AD 1618–1637 (12.8%)
		95.4% probability	AD 1474–1645 (95.4%)

Table 11.2. Radiocarbon dates from Doonbought, Co. Antrim. Dates were calibrated using OxCal v4.0.5 (Bronk Ramsey 1995; 2001) using the IntCal04 calibration curve (Reimer et al. *2004).*

the old fort. Alternatively, it still remains possible that this corpus does represent a *cillín* of post AD 1500 date.

During the period between 1972 and 1975 Tom Fanning undertook excavations at the ecclesiastical complex at Reask, Co. Kerry. As was the case with Madden's Hill and Doonbought Fort, an investigation of a *cillín* was not the primary reason for the excavation and the work principally concentrated on the Early Christian cemetery and settlement at the site. To the north and south of the oratory a number of small graves were discovered directly under the humus, lined with erect slabs and small stones, and in some instances covered with a mantle of quartz and sea pebbles (Fanning 1975, 6). Three of the graves had been inserted within the western end of the oratory with two early cross-slabs re-used as side stones. The preservation of the associated bone was poor, although grave goods appear to have been associated with a number of the burials, most notably with the smallest grave, which was considered to be the earliest in the cemetery. It was found to have contained four pebbles similar to jackstones and locally called *puirthíní,* as well as a small stone anthropogenic figurine (Fanning 1981, 74). The excavator considered it possible that the figurine was a doll and was of the opinion it resembled an infant in swaddling clothes (Fanning 1981, 127–8). He tentatively suggested that this Early Christian ecclesiastical and settlement complex had been adapted for use as a *cillín* in 'early medieval times' (Fanning 1981, 158). He considered the second main phase of ecclesiastical activity at the site to have broadly extended from the seventh/eighth century to the twelfth century, while the site appears to have been used as a *cillín* only after the abandonment of the structures associated with this second phase of activity (Fanning 1981, 158). A reassessment of the site's chronology, however, was undertaken by Emer Dennehy as part of her Master's dissertation on the *cillíní* of County Kerry, and she noted that the presence of seventeenth and eighteenth century pottery within the graves would suggest that the *cillín* was first utilised during this period (Dennehy 1997, 79-80).

Liam De Paor undertook a series of excavations at a monastic site at Inishcealtra, Co. Clare, in the early 1970s. The site remains unpublished, but on the basis of information contained within the annually published excavation summary accounts for the years 1971 to 1976 it would appear that Site 4 'St. Michael's Church', excavated in 1972, had been used as a *cillín.* The site comprised a D-shaped enclosure around the summit of the island, with a roughly square-shaped smaller enclosure located at its centre, marked by a low stony bank prior to excavation. The inner enclosure had been used as a burial ground for children, and finds of coins and other objects suggested that 'the main period of activity here was in the chronological range c. AD1500 to 1800' (de Paor 1973, 31). Further excavation at Site 4 undertaken in 1973 enabled the burials exposed in the previous year to be studied *in situ* by Dr Maire Delaney and it was noted that they were 'mainly of recently born infants. It had been customary to deposit in each infant grave a handful of quartz pebbles and a long stone pebble (sometimes a whetstone, sometimes a shaped stone of phallic appearance)' (de Paor 1974, 5).

In 1974 Ann Lynch (1975, 22) excavated within the bawn of a tower house at Aughinish Island, Co. Limerick, during the course of which she encountered 31 skeletons, 29 of which were located in Cutting 7, to the northern side of the castle; the majority represented the remains of young children and babies. Linda Lynch (1998) undertook the analysis of skeletal remains from the site as part of her Masters dissertation and noted that 64.5% of the sample comprised individuals less than sixteen years of age at the time of death, with the highest number of deaths (22.7%) having occurred between birth and one year of age; infants with age-at-death values of less than six months accounted for 35% of the population (Lynch 1998, 77). The stratigraphy encountered during the excavation was extremely shallow, while there were no artefacts to assist with the dating of the burials. As Lynch (1998, 38) has noted, however, the fact that none of the burials underlay the tower house wall would suggest they post-date the construction of the building. Since the tower house as a building series does not significantly commence until the start of the fifteenth century in the county (Donnelly 1995, i, 66–9), this would suggest that the earliest date for the origin of the cemetery at this site would be after c. AD 1400. Given that the active life of the castle at Aughinish continued through to the mid-seventeenth century, however, it can be suggested it is more probable that the use of a portion of its bawn for a cemetery was a development that commenced following the abandonment of the complex in the Post-Medieval period. Three of the seven juveniles (42.9%) and three of the six adults (50%) with preserved teeth from Aughinish Castle displayed dental caries (Lynch 1998, 78). Despite the small sample size, this would tend to suggest the group had suffered from notably high levels of the lesion. Catryn Power's (1994, 100–2) research on a selection of Munster populations suggested there was a rise in the frequencies of individuals affected by caries from 25.1% (76/303) during Medieval times to 44.9% (22/49) in the Post-Medieval period. As such, the high caries rate from Aughinish Castle would appear to suggest a late date for many of the burials (Lynch 1998, 105).

Excavation at St. Vogue's Church and its associated enclosure at Carnsore, Co. Wexford, in 1975 revealed evidence for the use of the site as a *cillín* in the Early Modern period, although local tradition stated that over the past 200 to 300 years the enclosure and church had been used as the burial place for bodies washed-up on the nearby shore. Seventeen burials were found in the enclosure and a further ten were recovered from the interior of the church. Representing Phase 3 in the chronological use of the site, fragments of military uniforms, buttons and leather boots and shoes were recovered from some of the burials, thereby indicating a Post-Medieval date for the inhumations (Lynch and Cahill 1977, 20).

Six trenches were excavated at Kilrush Church, Co. Limerick, during 1980 by Larry Walsh to establish the extent of archaeological remains on the site prior to the construction of six dwelling houses in its vicinity. The excavation revealed a total of 37 inhumations in Trench 1, while a further two individuals were discovered in Trench 6a. The stratigraphic sequence was extremely poor, and prevented any phasing for the burials to be achieved. There was, however, a very high percentage of infants (40.5%) in the excavated population, a fact that was revealed during Linda Lynch's study of the skeletons as part of her Masters dissertation (Lynch 1998, 110). The presence of the infants, a possible burial of a mother and her infant, and possible stillborn children all hinted that this church site had been in use as a *cillín* (Lynch 1998, 112). Three of the five juveniles (60%) and four of the five adults (80%) with observable teeth displayed dental caries (Lynch 1998, 88–9). Despite the small sample size, these figures would tend to suggest the group had suffered from notably high levels of the lesion. As was the case for Aughinish Castle (see above), Lynch noted that the caries rates for the individuals from Kilrush were most similar to the frequencies for Post-Medieval Munster populations described by Catryn Power (1994, 101). On the basis of these values she suggested the Kilrush population was likely to date to 'at least the Post-Medieval period' (Lynch 1998, 95).

Two seasons of excavation were undertaken by Conleth Manning in 1987 and 1988 at Killelton Oratory in Co. Kerry. The work concentrated on the eastern half and south-west corner of the church and the eastern side of the small irregular enclosure surrounding the building. During the course of the investigation a series of 'child burials' were discovered inside the church, which took the form of small oval pits; the graves did not contain any skeletal remains (considered to be due to the acidic nature of the soil) or grave goods. Outside the building, on the southern side of the enclosure, the remains of two adult burials were discovered which were dated to the eighteenth or nineteenth centuries (Manning 1988, 17). While the date for the origin of the use of this site as a *cillín* was not resolved during the excavation, Dennehy (1997, 80) has noted that the *Ordnance Survey Name Books* attest to the use of the site for the burial of children during the nineteenth century.

Excavation at Illaunloughan – a small island used as the site of a hermitage during the Early Christian period in Co. Kerry – by Claire Walsh and Jenny White-Marshall during the years from 1992 to 1995 focused on a small dry-stone oratory and a dry-stone hut with associated midden. The latter structure was shown to have been pre-dated by two conjoined round huts, while the area of the huts was overlain by infant burials; the site was known to have been used as a children's burial ground until the early decades of the twentieth century, with the last known burial on the island having occurred in 1940. While the chronology of the population was not investigated in detail it was considered to be post seventeenth century in origin (White-Marshall and Walsh 2005, 86), although in her osteoarchaeological study of the assemblage Laureen Buckley (1996, 42) noted that the *cillín* burials were of nineteenth century date or later. The corpus comprised 112 individuals, 91% of whom were non-adults, with over half of this group having died during the first year of life (Buckley 1996, 51). Most of the graves had been marked with simple un-inscribed headstones, while many of the infants had been buried within small wooden coffins manufactured from Scots Pine, imported from the eighteenth century onwards. Additional protection was provided in numerous cases by the placement of the coffins in stone-lined and slab-covered graves (White Marshall and Walsh 2005, 166).

Since 1992 John Sheehan has been directing a multi-seasoned programme of excavation at Caherlehillan, Co. Kerry. The site is an early ecclesiastical enclosure that is known to have been used as a *cillín* from local tradition, with burials continuing until the early twentieth century (O'Sullivan and Sheehan 1996, 264). The principal discoveries from the site during its first five years of investigation (1992 to 1996) were summarised by Dennehy (1997, 86–95). Four stratigraphic layers were encountered during the excavation of Area 1, with the upper layer (Context 10) containing eleven graves, all of which contained the remains of iron nails which would indicate that coffins were used in the latest phase of the site's development (Dennehy 1997, 88). A number of possible shroud pins were also retrieved but these were from the disturbed upper levels of Area 1, and none were associated with a specific burial context (Dennehy 1997, 87). Context 17 underlay the uppermost layer and contained four graves; there was no evidence for the use of coffins during this phase, but two white buttons were discovered with a burial of a neonate, thereby indicating that the infant had been buried clothed (Dennehy 1997, 89). A further six graves were encountered in Context 61, the third burial layer of the *cillín*. In two cases the graves were found to contain iron nails (Dennehy 1997, 90), indicating a use of coffins for at least some of the burials belonging to this stage in the use of the burial ground. The lowest layer of the sequence (Context 82) contained a total of six graves. A ceramic tube and a perforated slate were found associated with one grave, but no nails or wood were retrieved from any of the graves to indicate if the bodies were buried in coffins. Within Area 2 two graves were investigated in Context 2, both of which contained coffins manufactured from Scots Pine (Dennehy 1997, 92), a wood imported into Ireland from the eighteenth century onwards and also used for the manufacture of coffins at Illaunloughan (White Marshall and Walsh 2005, 166).

Excavation continued at the site in 1997 and there was further investigation of the lowest layer of the *cillín* in Area 1 (Sheehan 1998, 82). This work revealed that the graves overlay an oxidized sub-soil, similar to that which had been encountered in Area 3 where it was found to contain Early Christian features. A thin lens of soil, which survived in patches, was identified as the Early Christian ground surface in 1999 (Sheehan 2000b, 112), with a number of adult graves, first encountered in 1997 (Sheehan 1998, 82), and other features cut into this layer, including a drain and a soak-pit (Sheehan 2000b, 112).

In 1997 investigations commenced in Area 8, which centred on the *leacht* or shrine-structure located in the site's north-east quadrant. The morphology of the shrine was investigated, and it was shown to be covered by a deposit of quartz pebbles within which was contained at least one '*ceallúnach*-type burial' (Sheehan 1998, 82). Further infant graves were excavated in the vicinity of the *leacht* in 1999 and these were considered to be Post-Medieval or Early Modern in date (Sheehan 2000b, 112). The summary account of investigations in 2002 describes how excavation under the *leacht* demonstrated that it had been constructed over a stone-lined grave, while a second grave of the same construction type was discovered to the north of the shrine; both of these graves were judged to be similar in form to the Early Christian graves excavated in Area 1 (Sheehan 2004, 212), and further adult graves were investigated in 2003 (Sheehan 2006, 214). A new trench was opened in 2002 to investigate the stratigraphic relationship between the Early Christian burials in Area 1 and those encountered in Area 8. During the course of this work a further 13 graves associated with the *cillín* were excavated (Sheehan 2004, 212). Work continues at Caherlehillan, but from the content of the various summary reports published by the excavator there does not appear to be any suggestion that the *cillín* burials are anything other than Post-Medieval or Early Modern in date. The artefacts that have been retrieved from the three upper levels within Area 1 and the *cillín* graves discovered in the vicinity of the *leacht* in Area 8 would certainly suggest that the main phase of use of the *cillín* was in Post-Medieval or later times.

Excavation under the direction of Declan Hurl took place within the interior of Castle Carra, near Cushendun in Co. Antrim, during 1995 that revealed the re-use of this small abandoned castle as a *cillín* (Hurl and Murphy 1996, 20–3) (Figure 11.2). The removal of a 0.75 m layer of modern deposits within the southern half of the building revealed a layer of sandy soil, some 0.4 m in depth, within which were discovered the remains of a child, approximately two-and-a-half years old, and 15 infants, each of whom had been placed in shallow scoops in the sand. In the summer of 2002 Declan Hurl returned to continue excavations and additional infant burials were discovered within the southern interior of

Figure 11.2. General view of Castle Carra, Co. Antrim (Crown Copyright).

the building (Hurl 2004, 6); the programme of fieldwork ended in 2004 when several infant burials, including nine neonates, were uncovered within the north-west sector of the interior (Hurl 2007, 9–10). The analysis of the Castle Carra infants is ongoing but they are considered by the excavator to be Post-Medieval in date.

Excavation at a ruined Medieval church at Killalee in Co. Kerry during 2000 identified a group of inhumation burials to the south of the old building, with the extent of the burial area delineated by an earth-cut ditch. The site appeared to have been only used for a short period of time in the Medieval period, and there is no evidence that it was used as a burial ground. A total of 23 grave-cuts, however, were recorded following topsoil stripping, with the four graves closest to the church subsequently excavated in full. This revealed that three of the graves were earth-cut, while the fourth was stone-lined. The graves were shallow and the human remains within were poorly preserved but it could be determined that they represented the bodies of two adults (one male and the other possibly female) and two infants. Artefacts recovered with the bodies including shroud pins (associated with the two infants) and a bead and two coins located with the possible female adult, who seems to have been buried fully clothed; the coins were a 1737 halfpenny and a 1738 farthing (Dennehy and Lynch 2001, 20–3).

In 2002 excavations took place at Johnstown, Co. Meath, in advance of the construction of a new motorway. The excavations focused on a series of enclosures, which were found to be Early Medieval in date and appear to have been mainly for settlement and industrial purposes although one did contain a contemporary cemetery. A *cillín* located adjacent to the enclosures on a gravel bank was also excavated and around 60 burials, almost exclusively of premature or newborn babies, were discovered (Fibiger 2005, 102). Shroud pins were associated with the majority of infant burials and it was considered that they dated to the past 100 to 200 years. Nails and traces of wood are evidence that the infants were buried in coffins (Clarke 2002, 13–15). In the same year, preliminary investigations were undertaken at Kill near Monasterevin, Co. Kildare, by John Channing (2004, 259) in advance of the construction of the M7 Heath-Mayfield Motorway Scheme. The site was noted as a children's burial ground in the 1939 edition Ordnance Survey six-inch map sheet, although its existence was not depicted on the first edition map series. As such, the excavator described this as a nineteenth-century burial ground, presumably on the basis that it must have come into use at some stage after the mid-1800s. The site comprised two tree stumps surrounded by an oval concentration of stones, some 9 m in diameter. The discovery of a disarticulated infant during test-trenching led to a full excavation of the site in 2003, when approximately 70 child inhumations were discovered within a disused sandpit, accompanied by shroud pins and coffin nails (Channing 2006, 244).

A children's burial ground was discovered in the interior of a ringfort at Carrowkeel, Co. Mayo, which was excavated in 2002 (Zajac 2004, 390–1). The burials were in two phases, each in a confined area in the northern sector of the site, with a possible earlier phase represented by four infants, each one placed within an oval cut in redeposited boulder clay, and two of whom were accompanied by bronze or copper pins. Beside these graves were further infant burials, with neonatal skeletons present in very shallow cuts at the lowest level of this second phase of burial activity. Shroud pins found with these skeletons suggested that they dated to the nineteenth or twentieth centuries. Of note, however, was the fact that the excavator could report no local tradition of the site having been used as a burial ground. In other cases in recent years sites that do have local tradition of having been used as *cilliní* have been excavated, but no archaeological evidence has been retrieved during the course of fieldwork, as was the case at Lysterfield, Co. Roscommon (Byrne 2006, 424). At Caher Point on Achill Island, Co. Mayo (McDonald 2004, 397–8), and Treanoughteragh, Co. Kerry (Collins 2006, 228), limited fieldwork was undertaken at known *cilliní*. At the former site a foundation trench for a remembrance plaque was excavated but no archaeological evidence was encountered, while at the latter site 25 post-pits were excavated by hand to facilitate the erection of a new perimeter fence around the monument; nothing of archaeological significance was encountered.

An example of a known *cillín* that was excavated in its own right in recent years and that has delivered significant new data was at Tonybaun, Co. Mayo, which was investigated in 2003 under the direction of Joanna Nolan (2006). A total of 248 skeletons from the site were retrieved – 181 children and 67 adults. Of the 181 children there were 147 infants under the age of two years old. The cemetery was excavated in two stratigraphic layers. Samples of bone were selected from nine skeletons from the stratigraphically lowest layer of graves for radiocarbon dating and this produced seven dates ranging from 345±29 BP [OxA-13120;

Figure 11.3. Plan of the upper layer of burials of the cillín *at Tonybaun, Co. Mayo (Mayo County Council).*

two sigma; 1475–1638 cal. AD] to 159±30 BP [OxA-13124; two sigma; 1664–1951 cal. AD] (Nolan 2006, 93; see also O'Sullivan and Stanley 2006, 134–5); as such, the excavator suggested that the cemetery was in continual use from the late fifteenth century through to the mid-twentieth century (Nolan 2006, 89). It should be noted, however, that the majority of the infant skeletons were associated with the upper stratigraphic layer of burials (Nolan 2006, 96), which the excavator described as 'modern' (Nolan 2006, 93) (Figure 11.3). Given this, it is probable that the cemetery was indeed in use from the Late Medieval period, but that it did not take on the function of a *cillín* until the Post-Medieval era. It can also be noted that all of the skeletons were studied as a single population (Murphy 2004). If the lower layer of skeletons – some 30 individuals, all of whom are adults – are taken out of the equation then the age profile of the upper layer becomes more typical of a *cillín*, with 71% infants under the age of two years.

The review of the excavated evidence from sixteen *cillini* (summarised in Table 11.3) should provide the reader with a broad indication as to when each of these burial grounds were in use, based on the evidence obtained during fieldwork; there are only a few cases where the evidence is ambiguous. Manning's excavation at Killelton, Co. Kerry, failed to produce clear dating evidence for when the site came into use as a *cillín*; however, it was certainly being used for this purpose by, and during, the nineteenth century. The thirteen individuals, who comprised the second group of burials from Doonbought Fort, Co. Antrim, were buried in the upper levels and surface of a dump containing thirteenth-century artefacts, but samples from two of these individuals returned radiocarbon dates that indicate they are of sixteenth or seventeenth century date. If this corpus does represent a *cillín* population, then the radiocarbon dates make it possible that it has its origins in the Late Medieval period. In a similar manner, the date-range of AD 1500 to AD 1800 suggested by the excavator for the *cillín* at St. Michael's Church in Inishcealtra, Co. Clare, was based on the discovery of 'coins and other objects' (de Paor 1973, 31). This might also suggest a Late Medieval origin point for these burials. The excavation, however, remains unpublished and, as a consequence, it is not possible to determine which of the artefacts led the excavator to propose an origin for the *cillín* to c. AD 1500.

It should become apparent from the overall exercise, however, that the dating evidence suggests that over half of the corpus of excavated *cillini* – nine out of 16 – had their origins in, and were in use during, the Post-Medieval period or later. It can also be reasonably argued that a further three sites – Reask, Aughinish and Kilrush – were very probably used as *cillini* during the Post-Medieval period and had their origins during this period as well, with the high prevalence of dental caries present among the dead from Aughinish and Kilrush proxy-dating evidence in support of this contention. A further two sites – Doonbought and Inishcealtra – were possibly in use in the Late Medieval or Post-Medieval period. We are hampered by a lack of dating evidence from Killelton that might specifically identify when this site first came into use as *cillín* but we do know, however, that it was being used for this purpose by the nineteenth century. To conclude, the only excavated site that is of significant variance from the norm is the first example of the monument type to have been

Site name	County	Date of excavation	Dating evidence	Date
Madden's Hill, Kiltale	Meath	1966	A natural mound located 35 m south-east of a rath; human remains disturbed during the excavation of the ditch in antiquity. The excavator viewed these remains and those of children inserted into the mound as a single cemetery.	Pre-Christian
Doonbought	Antrim	1969	Artefacts. Radiocarbon dating.	post-13th century (i) 265±32 BP (ii) 324±33 BP
Reask	Kerry	1973–5	Stratigraphy. Reassessment of pottery (Dennehy 1997, 79–80).	post 12th century 17th/18th century
St. Michael's Church, Inishcealtra	Clare	1972–3	Artefacts.	AD 1500–1800
Aughinish Castle	Limerick	1974	Stratigraphy and architecture. Dental caries (Lynch 1998, 105).	Post c. AD 1400 Post-Medieval
St. Vogue's Church, Carnsore	Wexford	1975	Oral tradition and artefacts.	Post-Medieval
Kilrush Church	Limerick	1980	Dental caries (Lynch 1998, 110–11).	Post-Medieval
Killelton Oratory	Kerry	1987–8	Ordnance Survey Name Books (Dennehy 1997, 80). Two adult and one child burial to south of the enclosure dated to 19th century due to associated artefacts.	No dating evidence for origin of use as a *cillín* obtained from within the oratory, but site in use as such during 19th century.
Illaunloughin Island	Kerry	1992–4	Stratigraphy, oral history and artefacts.	Post 17th century; probably 18th century or 19th century.

Table 11.3. Summary of dating evidence obtained from excavated sites.

Site name	County	Date of excavation	Dating evidence	Date
Caherlehillan	Kerry	1992–2003	Area 1: three upper layers indicate Post-Medieval usage of the site. Area 2: Scots Pine coffins indicate 18th century use of the site. Area 8: Graves in vicinity of *leacht* Post-Medieval or Early Modern in date. Local tradition that the site was a *cillín*, with burial terminating in the early 20th century.	Post-Medieval or Early Modern
Castle Carra	Antrim	1995, 2002, 2004	Stratigraphy.	Post-Medieval
Killalee Church	Kerry	2000	Shroud pins and coins (AD 1737 and 1738).	Post-Medieval
Johnstown	Meath	2002	Shroud pins.	18th to 19th century
Kill	Kildare	2002	Oral tradition, map evidence and artifacts.	19th century
Carrowkeel	Mayo	2002	Shroud pins.	19th century or 20th century
Tonybaun	Mayo	2003	Radiocarbon dating (lower layer) Stratigraphy (upper layer)	AD 1475 to 1950 Post-Medieval or 'modern' (Nolan 2006, 93).

Table 11.3 (continued). Summary of dating evidence obtained from excavated sites.

investigated – Madden's Hill, Co. Meath – which was considered by the excavator to have been of pre-Christian date. The dating evidence in support of this conclusion, however, is poor, while the excavator seems to have been heavily influenced by the contents of Ó Súilleabháin's paper from 1939, and hence his willingness to accept a pre-Christian date for the infant burials.

History and Theology

The research presented in the preceding section should indicate that the excavated evidence does not provide explicit evidence for *cillíní* dating to the Early Christian or Medieval periods, although this situation may change in the future, and a *cillín* dating from these periods of Ireland's Christian past may be discovered. Even if this were to happen, however, the majority of the sites listed above have produced dating evidence for their use during the past 400 years and the excavated evidence points to *cillíní* being a monument that proliferates in the Post-Medieval period. What forces, however, were at play within Irish society that might explain how this may have come about?

Within the early Christian church baptism was considered essential to cleanse a person of Original Sin, the sin committed by Adam and Eve in the Garden of Eden and subsequently inherited by humankind ever since, with baptism required to cleanse the soul of the stain of that sin (Walsh 2005, 108). Writing in the fourth century, St. Augustine of Hippo had stated that the souls of unbaptised children were condemned to hell because of their Original Sin. To avoid eternal damnation he recommended that all infants were baptised as soon as possible after birth. This harsh doctrine was later modified by the Medieval church which introduced the concept of limbo, and most theologians followed the beliefs of St. Thomas Aquinas, the thirteenth century theologian, who taught that unbaptised infants would definitely not have any personal suffering after death. Limbo did not appear within the official catechism of the church, but it provided a means to reconcile the problem of what happened to the souls of those who – through no fault of their own – were barred from heaven; 'for this reason, the idea of "limbo" was invented, a kind of in-between state, neither the happiness of heaven nor the torments of hell' (Walsh 2005, 109).

Theologians could engage in debates into what might happen to the souls of unbaptised infants, but it was Canon Law that dictated what would happen to the body of a dead unbaptised child. Canon Law is the formal law of the Catholic Church and is contained in the Code of Canon Law. Up until the start of the twentieth century this law was contained in many different pieces of legislation which had accumulated over the centuries, having been issued piecemeal by various bishops, councils and popes. The Synod of Nîmes in AD 1284, for example, set out that Christian burial was to be refused to the excommunicated, to heretics and suicides, and to men killed in tournaments (Minois 1999, 35). These laws were to be observed by the whole church and were known as the *Corpus Iuris Canonici* (the Body of Canon Law). It was then decided to organise and rationalise this collection of laws into a Code of Canon Law, containing 2,414 different laws, which was first published in 1917 (Walsh 2005, 46–8). It is within this code of laws that we find reference to how the unbaptised were to be dealt with after death, although not within the laws relating to matters concerning baptism, but under those laws relating to burial. In Canon 1239 it is stated that infants of Catholic parents who died without baptism were not to be buried in a blessed cemetery (Woywod 1957, II, 51), while under Canon 1240 other individuals who were to be denied ecclesiastical burial are listed. These included apostates, excommunicates, persons guilty of deliberate suicide, individuals killed in a duel or from wounds received during a duel, 'and other public and manifest sinners' (Woywod 1957, II, 52). Within these two groupings we find a range of individuals that we might find buried within a *cillín*. These laws remained in place until the Second Vatican Council (also known as Vatican II), a council of the Catholic Church held during the years from 1962 to 1965 that led to a major reformulation of the church.

In recent years two synthetic works have been published relating to the subjects of death and burial in historic Ireland – Susan Leigh Fry's *Burial in Medieval Ireland, 900-1500: A Review of the Written Sources* and Clodagh Tait's *Death, Burial and Commemoration in Ireland, 1550–1650*. A section of the former book deals with the burial of 'unfortunates' (Fry 1999, 180–7) and notes that certain types of people could not be buried within consecrated ground: men who had died in battle, women who had died in or shortly after childbirth, strangers, and children who had died before receiving baptism. These would be exactly the people that we might expect to find in a Medieval *cillín*, but – perhaps significantly – Fry could find no reference or information in any of the historic sources relating to their burial: 'In surveying the sources used in this study, no information regarding the burial of unbaptised children, of persons who had taken their own lives or of those who had died while excommunicate has been found' (Fry 1999, 183). In a similar manner, Tait does not provide major comment on *cillíní* in her study other than to state that the evidence obtained from archaeological excavations suggests that 'in certain parts of the country infant children may not have usually been buried in churches or churchyards' (Tait 2002, 69). It would appear, therefore, that the historical record for Ireland is silent on this matter, although there is documentary evidence from Medieval England for the separate burial of the unbaptised in unconsecrated ground.

Nicholas Orme (2001, 124) has noted that by AD 1400 the church in England had forbade the burial of stillborn and unbaptised infants within consecrated ground since they were not considered to be Christians, and this is supported by historical references. A royal licence of AD 1389 permitted Hereford Cathedral to surround its precinct and graveyard with walls and gates which were to be locked at night. One of the reasons for the construction work was stated as being to prevent the secret burials of unbaptised infants (Orme 2001, 126). Likewise, a church court-case in London in AD 1493 relates how a woman from the parish of St. Nicolas in the Shambles had been beaten when pregnant and had then given birth to a stillborn baby. The court was told that the mid-wife who delivered the baby had requested another woman to illegally bury the child within the confines of Pardon graveyard (Orme 2001, 126). Similar restrictions may have been in operation in Medieval

Ireland – particularly in the area around the Pale, which was under English influence – but if so, the documents have not survived. What the English texts do not imply, however, is the existence of a separate class of burial ground for the unbaptised; there is no evidence for a Medieval English equivalent of the *cillín*.

The earliest direct historical reference that the current authors have encountered for the use of *cillíní* in Ireland comes from the north of the island in the decade following the introduction of the English Crown's plantation scheme which saw newcomers from England and Scotland settled on lands in Ulster that had been confiscated from the region's Gaelic lords in the aftermath of the Nine Years' War (1594–1603). In a letter written on 23rd July 1619 by Mr. Goodwyn to the Grocers' Company in London it is stated that the company's representatives in Ulster had decided not to reuse an old church site about half a mile from Muff (later renamed Eglinton) as the location for a new church. The old church was deemed to be too small; in addition, however, it had been used as a burial-place for unbaptised children and suicides – presumably by the local Gaelic Catholic population – and the general opinion was that Muff would be a better site for the new parish church of Faughanvale (Curl 1986, 155).

Catholicism had remained a religious force in Ulster and the church still retained the support of the majority of the Gaelic population. In a deposition by Teag Modder McGlone to the English planter Sir Toby Caulfield, dated 21st October 1613, the former reports on a Franciscan friar, Tirlagh McCroddan, who had preached a seditious sermon in the woods of Loughinsholin in Ulster to a company of 1,000 people including 14 priests. McGlone's deposition is illustrative of this continued adherence to the Catholic faith; the text also demonstrates, however, that McCroddan was more than just the average friar; he was a man on a mission:

> The examinant [McGlone] further says, that the friar has deprived many [priests] of their benefices; – some for keeping women, others for presuming to exercise the function of priest, who had not been properly called [ie: ordained], and for having more benefices than one. Some who had three benefices he deprived of all, but upon submission and acknowledgment he gave them one back again, and such as were not lawfully called, and had married any, he pronounced those marriages unlawful, and made the husbands and wives get married again, whereof this examinant is one. He compels all priests to put away their wives and whores, or else he deprives them of their livings and makes them incapable to say mass or exercise their functions. That day he deprived the priest O'Mott [O'Mollan] and the vicar of Cullan (the one for having two benefices, the other for keeping a woman) (Russell and Prendergast 1877, 430).

The Council of Trent was originally convened in AD 1545 to explore reform within the Catholic Church due to the pressure then being exerted on the church by the new Protestant reformers across Europe. By the time it had concluded in AD 1563 the council had indeed reformed the Catholic Church in areas such as the discipline, education and training of the clergy, but it had also reaffirmed Catholic doctrine and Canon Law. Clearly, by dealing harshly with abuses among the clergy, McCroddan was shepherding them into line with Counter-Reformation teaching; in addition, reform the lifestyle and activities of the clergy and it should follow that you will reform those of their congregation. McCroddan, however, was not alone in his work; like the other Irish seminaries and colleges on the continent, the Franciscans of Louvain College in Belgium, established in AD 1606, were at the heart of the Counter-Reformation's efforts in Ireland (Swords 2007, 45–52).

The first Tridentine catechism in the Irish language was produced in manuscript format by Flaithrí Ó Maolchonaire, a Franciscan friar, translated from a Spanish text in AD 1593 and brought to Ireland in AD 1598 (Ó Cuív 1950). Set out in question-and-answer format between Master and Discipline, the text dealt with issues such as Purgatory and the types of people who would go there after their death (Ó Cuív 1950, 169), the importance of baptism and how it removed Original Sin (Ó Cuív 1950, 184), and Extreme Unction and the final spiritual cleansing of the soul (Ó Cuív 1950, 187). Other catechisms followed, with the first printed catechism in the Irish language published in Antwerp in AD 1611 (O'Connor 1991, 23). The official Roman Catechism, composed by the decree of the Council of Trent, was published in AD 1566 by command of Pius V (Corish 1981, 16). Translated into English in 1829, the contents of this text remained in force until the Second Vatican Council. Within this text the importance of the sacrament of baptism is stressed:

> The faithful are earnestly to be exhorted, to take care that their children be brought to the church, as soon as it can be done with safety, to receive solemn baptism: infants, unless baptized, cannot enter Heaven, and hence we may well conceive how deep the enormity of their guilt, who, through negligence, suffer them to remain without the grace of the sacrament, longer than necessity may require; particularly at an age so tender as to be exposed to numberless dangers of death (O'Donovan 1829, 173).

While the fate of the body of an unbaptised infant is not discussed, the spiritual implication is explicit: a child would not go to heaven if it died unbaptised and it was the responsibility of the parents to ensure that this did not happen. Although designed primarily for the training of the clergy, the new catechisms were to be used for the formal instruction of the laity in the new Tridentine Catholicism. 'The old, easy-fitting "civic religion" belonged to the past. Now to know the faith you had to know why you were a Catholic and not a Protestant' (Corish 1981, 16).

Baptism had always been an important rite within pre-Counter-Reformation Ireland, but not necessarily for its religious significance, for it was seen as a means of incorporating the baptised into the kin group and was an occasion of celebration for this reason. 'The baptismal sacrament, for the populace, provided an opportunity to strengthen the bonds of kinship, through the provision of a number of godparents, who acted as sponsors for the baptized' (Forrestal 1998, 18). Following the closing session of the Council of Trent the church in Ireland first promulgated its new teachings at the Synod of Tuam in AD 1566 (Brady 1946, 193–4); subsequent synods in the early seventeenth century continued the reformation of the Irish church, with baptism receiving particular attention from the bishops. The uniform administration of the sacrament was a central concern at five synods, with the meetings at Dublin and Armagh in AD 1614 devoting whole sections to this matter (Forrestal 1998, 56). There was to be a font, the holy oils were to be replaced annually, and a register of baptisms was to be maintained. The Dublin Synod also discussed the procedures to be followed in cases where the death of an infant was a probable outcome during birth. If the baby was still in the uterus then baptism could not be undertaken, but if the head had been released then baptism could occur, although – once completed – the sacrament could not be administered again following full birth. If, however, a hand or foot was visible then the limb could be baptised, with formal baptism administered after full birth, provided the baby had survived (Forrestal 1998, 56). The Dublin Synod of AD 1614 also stressed that there was to be only one godparent of either sex or, at most, two of both sexes (Forrestal 1998, 67). Prospective godparents needed to be instructed in religion to the satisfaction of the church, since it was the godparents who would be responsible for the spiritual instruction of the newly baptised person. This was in direct contrast to the situation in the past when the function of multiple godparents was to strengthen the kin-group (Corish 1981, 15–16). This change of emphasis, however, was not only restricted to the sacrament of baptism but was reflected in other sacraments as well, such as marriage, which was also removed from the kin-group and now placed within the firm control of the priests and bishops. This helps explain why marriage was such a prominent theme in Friar McCroddan's sermon at Loughinsholin in AD 1613.

Lennon (1986) has explored the impact of the Counter-Reformation among the Old English of the Pale region and Dublin. The descendants of the Anglo-Normans who arrived in this area in the late twelfth century, the population in this area remained loyal to the English Crown throughout the Medieval period and viewed themselves as culturally distinct from their Gaelic neighbours elsewhere on the island. Given this, one might expect that this section of Irish society would be more open to the religious revolution of the Reformation. This was not, however, the case and the majority of the Old English adhered to Catholicism. This rejection of Protestantism, however was not pre-ordained; it was only a very gradual process whereby 'many uncommitted members of the aristocracy and gentry came to view their religious heritage as part of a patrimony to be defended against attack by newcomers' (Lennon 1986, 77). The closure of religious houses in the Pale in the 1540s did not generate significant resistance and the Old English hoped the religious reforms and the declaration of Henry VIII as King of Ireland in AD 1541 might be the forerunners to a whole-scale programme of political and social change throughout the island. The more aggressive nature of the reforms advocated under Edward VI and Elizabeth I were not enthusiastically met by clergy and laity, nor particularly well implemented by the government, but it was only really the threat to their liberties and privileges that developed in the 1570s that turned them back to Rome: 'In this way the fund of religious experience of the community – worship, institutions, devotions, civic piety – became a legacy to be cherished in the face of innovation and change' (Lennon 1986, 82). The result was their support for the efforts of the Counter-Reformation and, in particular, the Jesuits, with the children of landowners and merchants being sent to the continent for their education in colleges where they were taught of the new Tridentine Catholic faith.

Within mid-sixteenth-century Gaelic Ireland there is little evidence that there was any wide-scale desire for a religious reformation. Anticlericalism was not an issue, and local lords were seemingly content with the Medieval *status quo* (Meigs 1997, 16). A study by Jefferies (2000, 163–80) of a visitation report for sixteen parishes within Armagh's *inter Hibernicos* (the rural deaneries of Orior and Tullaghoge) in AD 1546 provides valuable insight into the state of the church in Gaelic Ulster at this time. The report indicated that few of the churches visited were in very good order, with 25% in a poor or ruinous condition, but that the liturgical equipment was satisfactory in the majority of cases. While some of the priests had concubines, the Mass was being celebrated and the clergy were providing pastoral ministry. Jefferies concluded that 'it is becoming increasingly apparent that historians must take greater account of the strengths of the pre-Reformation church and of Irish Catholicism in any consideration of the religious history of Ireland in the Late Medieval and Early Modern periods' (Jefferies 2000, 175). There was, therefore, an existing foundation upon which a Tridentine Catholic Church could build upon in the early seventeenth century, and the strength of this adherence to Catholicism in Gaelic and Old English society was a fundamental reason why the Reformation failed to convert the majority of the Irish away from their old religion to Protestantism.

Although it is estimated that they represented only 30% of the secular clergy in the 1620s (Corish 1981, 26), the direction and leadership that the new priests trained in the continental seminaries brought to the Catholic Church in Ireland was vitally important. A commission of the Londonderry Plantation in AD 1632, for example, indicates that the church in Ulster had re-established itself relatively well in the decades following the crisis caused by the Plantation and the introduction of Protestantism. Within the territory owned by the London Companies there were 24 priests who held 29 parishes, while the annual financial support that both priests and friars received from their parishioners amounted to the equivalent of £1,000, at a time when King Charles' annual revenues from the county amounted to only £855 and 17 shillings. In addition, there had been nine mass-houses erected on the company's properties, one on each of the proportions of the Grocers, Fishmongers, Ironmongers, Vintners and Drapers, and two each on those of the Salters and Skinners (Moody 1939, 263).

The role played by the friars was central to this revival of Catholic fortunes. Popular since their arrival in the thirteenth century, the Medieval friars had preached, undertook religious teaching and administered the sacraments. In return, they had received financial support and patronage from their host communities (Meigs 1997, 46). They also had a close relationship with the learned families, or *aes dána*, of Gaelic society – particularly the hereditary families of poets – and Meigs has contended that this relationship grew more important in the aftermath of the Nine Years' War when Gaelic society lost many of its traditional institutions and the surviving lords and learned families had to adapt to a changed world. 'For the learned elites the dual roles of poet and priest were well established, as was the practice of going abroad for further education, so it is not surprising that as soon as Irish seminaries were established on the Continent in the early seventeenth century, many sons of the old learned orders now flocked to the Continent as clerics-in-training' (Meigs 1997, 81). The result of this process was the development of a new order of 'bard-priests', men such as Flaithrí Ó Maolchonaire, who – as we have seen – produced the first Irish language catechism in AD 1593, and who was a member of an important northern family of poets, or Giolla Brighde Ó hEodhusa who had been a poet with the Maguires before moving to Louvain as a novice in AD 1607. These men put their training as poets and writers to the good use of the Counter-Reformation with the works that they produced at Louvain. Of particular note to our current study, however, is the work of Aodh MacAingil, another member of a hereditary family of poets from the north of Ireland, who composed an Irish religious tract in AD 1618 entitled *Sgáthán Shacramuinte na hAithridhe*, or the 'Mirror of Penance'. The content of the tract has been commented upon by O'Connor (2005, 194–5) in her study of how Tridentine doctrine, tradition and teaching influenced Irish religious folklore. In MacAingil's text there is a section which relates how the spirit of an unrepentant woman, damned to hell for the murder of her illegitimate baby, appears to her son, now in a religious order. MacAingil's tract enjoyed widespread circulation in Ireland through to the nineteenth century, but this particular story does not appear to have been his own creation; it seems to have been cribbed from a corpus of tales then popular among preachers on the Continent. O'Connor (2005, 195) noted that the same story and motifs featured in the Medieval *Gesta Romanorum*, while Gregg (1997, 164) had cited a version as No. 63 in Tubach's *Index Exemplorum*.

O'Connor (2005, 133) has also highlighted clear parallels between one Irish folk tale and a similar tale from France. The story, entitled the 'Intentional Baptism of the Dead Child Spirit', has close parallel to French legend material and, in particular, in Breton traditions. Through her work on folklore the '"Celtic" or Gaelic linkages between Ireland and Brittany have come to the fore, and are especially noticeable in the traditions of the spirits of infants seeking to be baptised by a priest in order to attain eternal rest' (O'Connor 2005, 202). No definitive sources could be identified to demonstrate a direct link between Medieval stories and the folktales concerning sinful women and unbaptised children that were collected in Ireland by the Irish Folklore Commission during the twentieth century. 'Rather … the evidence exists to suggest that "medieval" themes and motifs were re/introduced into Irish folklore during the ensuing centuries, and that these are particularly well represented in the religious stories of Ireland' (O'Connor 2005, 208). In her view the spread of such stories was facilitated by the teaching of Counter-Reformation clergy, trained in the continental seminaries and, in particular, with the introduction of French Catholic teaching methods and materials into Ireland from the eighteenth century through to the twentieth century (O'Connor 2005, 209). These tales then permeated into the religious folklore of the Irish, most notably in the form of the folk concept of a shadowy otherworld – *Dorchadas gan Phain*, or 'Darkness without Pain' – inhabited by unbaptised children and seemingly an Irish folk-version of limbo (O'Connor 2005, 38).

That baptism was viewed as a matter of the importance in seventeenth-century Catholic society can be gauged through Raymond Gillespie's study of the sorry tale of Ellen Ní

Gilwey, burnt at the stake in Knocknagoole, Co. Meath, in AD 1647 as punishment for allegedly murdering her newborn illegitimate baby. The upheaval caused by the war that was then raging in Ireland provided the context for the story, for Ellen was executed by a party of Catholic Confederate soldiers, under the orders of Captain George Cusack. The extreme nature of her execution, however, would suggest that this was not viewed as a straightforward case of murder by Cusack, since the normal punishment for such a crime would be hanging. As Gillespie (1999, 75) has noted: 'Ellen's crime was not simply that she had murdered a child but that she had deprived it of baptism and hence consigned it to limbo'. Ellen seems to have had two other children who disappeared, yet it was the discovery by a dog of the body of her third child in a dung-heap that led to her death. This was viewed as Divine intervention and meant that the crime had to be dealt with in an appropriate God-fearing manner by the soldiers. As such, it can be argued that Cusack was religiously motivated when he ordered Ellen to be burnt at the stake; while the extreme nature of the events at Knocknagoole in AD 1647 may mark it as a one-off incident, it is not hard to envisage how similarly held fundamentalist beliefs at play throughout Ireland during the seventeenth century might have ensured compliance among Irish Catholics to bury their unbaptised infants and other unfortunates within *cillini.*

Conclusion

Antiquarians who commented on *cillini* viewed the monuments as having a pre-Christian origin, and this was a position reaffirmed by Ó Súilleabháin in his paper published in 1939. The dating of the monument series had to await the excavation of a large enough corpus of sites that might enable archaeological insight into this matter, and the current paper has undertaken an assessment of the results obtained from 16 excavations that have taken place across Ireland since 1966. Historical evidence from England would indicate that the separate burial of unbaptised infants was happening in that country during the Medieval period, and this may also have been the case in Medieval Ireland. The archaeological dating evidence, however, suggests a sixteenth century, if not seventeenth century, origin point for the advent in Ireland of the *cillín* as a distinct monument type that then proliferates and continues in use into the twentieth century. It has been suggested in this paper that this proliferation is directly associated with the Counter-Reformation.

Despite being under the rule of a Protestant monarch, and the introduction of a significantly sized Protestant population into the north of Ireland, by the first decades of the seventeenth century the majority of the Irish – both Gaelic and Old English – had retained their allegiance to Catholicism. This was not, however, the Catholicism of Medieval times, but the reinvigorated Catholicism of the Counter-Reformation, spearheaded by Jesuit priests and Franciscan friars trained in the new Continental seminaries and who, armed with their new Tridentine catechisms and religious tracts, returned to Ireland to administer to the people with the zeal of revolutionaries. There was to be strict control of the faithful by the bishops and clergy, and there was to be strict adherence to the doctrines and theology of the Church, with particular emphasis placed on the correct administration of the sacraments, including baptism. The official catechism of the Counter-Reformation church, published in AD 1566, had stressed the importance of baptism, while placing responsibility for the baptism of babies with their parents. The Council of Trent had also re-affirmed Canon Law, with its measures on who could and could not be buried in consecrated ground. As such, if an infant remained unbaptised at the time of its death its soul was bound for limbo; its body, however, was bound for the *cillín*.

Notes

1. Post-Medieval: Within a British context this might be viewed as commencing in the period following AD 1534 but in an Irish context the period after AD 1603 is more appropriate since it was in this year that the English Crown finally completed the conquest of Ireland. This initiated great changes in social and religious organisation and economic activity, with Ireland becoming the first major colony of the fledgling British Empire.
2. The review of excavated evidence ends in 2004 since this is the date of the most recent *Excavations Bulletin* available to the authors at the time of writing.

Acknowledgements

We would like to thank Dr John Ó Neill, School of Archaeology, University College Dublin, for providing us with access to his translation of 'Adhlacadh Leanbhaí', Seán Ó Súilleabháin's seminal paper of 1939 on children's burial grounds in Ireland. We are also indebted to Dr William Roulston, Ulster Historical Foundation, for bringing our attention to Mr Goodwyn's letter of 1619. Our thanks are also due to Libby Mulqueeny, School of Geography, Archaeology and Palaeoecology, Queen's University Belfast, for the production of Figure 11.1 and to Joanna Nolan for permitting us to use the plan of the *cillín* at Tonybaun. We are also grateful to Declan Hurl, RSK (Ireland) Ltd., for providing us with the image of Castle Carra.

References

Albridge, R. B. 1969. Notes on children's burial grounds in Mayo. *Journal of the Royal Society of Antiquaries of Ireland* 99, 83–7.

Brady, J. 1946. Ireland and the Council of Trent. *Irish Ecclesiastical Record* 68, 188–95.

Bronk Ramsey, C. 1995. Radiocarbon calibration and analysis of stratigraphy: the OxCal program. *Radiocarbon* 37, 425-30.

Bronk Ramsey, C. 2001. Development of the radiocarbon calibration program OxCal. *Radiocarbon* 43, 355-63.

Buckley, L. 1996. *Appendix 5: Illaunloughan (92EO87) Skeletal Report.* pdf report available at www.wordwellbooks.com/ftp/Wordwell/Illaunloughan/Appendices/Appendix-5.pdf

Byrne, M. 2006. Lysterfield, Co. Roscommon. *Excavations 2003*, 424.

Channing, J. 2004. Kill, Monasterevin, Co. Kildare. *Excavations 2002*, 259.

Channing, J. 2006. Sites 20 and K, Kill, Co. Kildare. *Excavations 2003*, 244.

Clarke, L. 2002. An Early Medieval enclosure and burials, Johnstown, Co. Meath. *Archaeology Ireland* 16 (4), 13–15.

Collins, T. 2006. Treanoughteragh, Co. Kerry. *Excavations 2003*, 228.

Corish, P. J. 1981. *The Catholic Community in the Seventeenth and Eighteenth Centuries.* Dublin: Helicon History of Ireland, Helicon Limited.

Crombie, D. 1988. Children's burial grounds in the Barony of Dunmore: a preliminary note. *Journal of the Galway Archaeological and Historical Society* 41, 149–51.

Crombie, D. 1990. *Children's Burial Grounds in County Galway.* Unpublished M.A. thesis, Department of Archaeology, National University of Ireland, Galway.

Cuppage, J. 1986. *Corca Dhuibhne. Dingle Peninsula Archaeological Survey.* Ballyferriter: Oidhreacht Chorca Dhuibhne.

Curl, J. S. 1986. *The Londonderry Plantation, 1609–1914.* Sussex: Phillimore and Co. Ltd.

Dennehy, E. A. 1997. *The Ceallúnaigh of County Kerry: An Archaeological Perspective.* Unpublished M.A. thesis, Department of Archaeology, University College Cork.

Dennehy, E. A. 2001. Children's burial ground. *Archaeology Ireland* 15 (1), 20–3.

Dennehy, E. A. 2003. *Dorchadas gan Phian*: The history of *ceallúnaigh* in Co. Kerry. *Journal of the Kerry Archaeological and Historical Society* 2, 5–21.

Dennehy, E. A. and Lynch, L. G. 2001. Unearthed secrets: a clandestine burial-ground. *Archaeology Ireland* 15 (4), 20–3.

De Paor, L. 1973. Inishcaltra, Co. Clare. *Excavations 1972*, 30–1.

De Paor, L. 1974. Inishcaltra, Co. Clare. *Excavations 1973*, 5–6.

Donnelly, C. 1995. *The Tower Houses of County Limerick.* Unpublished Ph.D. thesis, Queen's University Belfast.

Donnelly, S., Donnelly, C. and Murphy, E. 1999. The forgotten dead: the *cillíní* and disused burial grounds of Ballintoy, Co. Antrim. *Ulster Journal of Archaeology* 58, 109–13.

Fanning, T. 1975. Excavations at Reask: preliminary report – seasons 1973–5. *Journal of the Kerry Archaeological and Historical Society* 8, 5–10.

Fanning, T. 1981. Excavation of an Early Christian cemetery and settlement at Reask, County Kerry. *Proceedings of the Royal Irish Academy* 81C, 67–172.

Fanning, T. and Sheehan, J. 1983. Killeens, or children's burial grounds, in the Diocese of Galway. *Galway Diocesan Directory* 18, 97–100.

Fibiger, L. 2005. Minor ailments, furious fights and deadly diseases: investigating life in Johnstown, County Meath, AD 400–1700, pp. 99–110 in O'Sullivan, J. and Stanley, M. (eds), *Recent Archaeological Discoveries on National Road Schemes 2004* (Archaeology and the National Roads Authority Monograph Series No. 2). Dublin: National Roads Authority.

Finlay, N. 2000. Outside of life: traditions of infant burial in Ireland from *cillín* to cist. *World Archaeology* 31, 407–22.

Forrestal, A. 1998. *Catholic Synods in Ireland, 1600–1690.* Dublin: Four Courts Press.

Fry, S. L. 1999. *Burial in Medieval Ireland 900–1500.* Dublin: Four Courts Press.

Gillespie, R. 1999. The burning of Ellen Ní Gilwey: a sidelight on popular belief in Meath. *Ríocht na Midhe: Records of the Meath Archaeological and Historical Society* 10, 71–7.

Gregg, J. Y. 1997. *Devils, Women and Jews: Reflections of the Other in Medieval Sermon Stories.* New York: State University of New York Press.

Hamlin, A. and Foley, C. 1983. A Women's Graveyard at Carrickmore, County Tyrone, and the separate burial of women. *Ulster Journal of Archaeology* 46, 41–6.

Hurl, D. P. 2004. Castle Carra, Co. Antrim. *Excavations 2002*, 6.

Hurl, D. P. 2007. Castle Carra, Co. Antrim. *Excavations 2004*, 9–10.

Hurl, D. P. and Murphy, E. M. 1996. Life and death in a County Antrim tower house. *Archaeology Ireland* 10 (2), 20–3.

Hurley, V. 1982. The early church in the south-west of Ireland: settlement and organization, pp. 297–332 in Pearce, S. (ed.), *The Early Church in Western Britain and Ireland: Studies presented to C. A. Ralegh Radford* (BAR British Series 102). Oxford: Tempvs Reparatvm.

Jefferies, H. A. 2000. The visitation of the parishes of Armagh *Inter Hibernicos* in 1546, pp. 163–80 in Dillon, C. and Jefferies, H. A. (eds), *Tyrone: History and Society*. Dublin: Geography Publications.

Lennon, C. 1986. The Counter-Reformation in Ireland, 1542–1641, pp. 75–92 in Brady, C. and Gillespie, R. (eds), *Natives and Newcomers: Essays on the Making of Irish Colonial Society, 1534–1641*. Dublin: Irish Academic Press.

Lynch, A. 1975: Aughinish Island, Co. Limerick. *Excavations 1974*, 22.

Lynch, A. and Cahill, M. 1977. Carnsore, Co. Wexford. *Excavations 1975–76*, 19–20.

Lynch, L. 1998. *Placeless Souls: Bioarchaeology and Separate Burial in Historic Ireland.* Unpublished M.A. thesis, Department of Archaeology, University College Cork.

MacNamara, G. 1900. The ancient stone crosses of Uí-Fearmaic, County Clare. *Journal of the Royal Society of Antiquaries of Ireland* 10, 32–3.

McDonald, T. 2004. Caher Point, Tonatanvally, Achill Island, Co. Mayo. *Excavations 2002*, 397–8.

Manning, C. 1988. Killelton Oratory, Co. Kerry. *Excavations 1987*, 17.

Meigs, S. A. 1997. *The Reformations in Ireland: Tradition and Confessionalism, 1400 to 1690*. Dublin: Gill and Macmillan Ltd.

Minois, G. 1999. *History of Suicide: Voluntary Death in Western Culture* (translated by L. G. Cochrane). London: John Hopkins University Press.

Moody, T. W. 1939. *The Londonderry Plantation, 1609–41*. Belfast: William Mullan & Son.

Murphy, E. M. 2004. *Osteological and palaeopathological analysis of human remains recovered from Tonybaun, Co. Mayo*. Unpublished report prepared for Joanna Nolan and Mayo County Council.

Murphy, E. M. and McNeill, T. E. 1993 (published 1996). Human remains excavated at Doonbought Fort, Co. Antrim, 1969. *Ulster Journal of Archaeology* 56, 120–38.

Nolan, J. 2006. Excavation of a children's burial ground at Tonybaun, Ballina, County Mayo, pp. 89–101 in O'Sullivan, J. and Stanley, M. (eds), *Settlement, Industry and Ritual* (Archaeology and the National Roads Authority Monograph Series No. 3). Dublin: National Roads Authority.

O'Connor, A. 1991. *Child Murderess and Dead Child Traditions* (FF Communications No. 249). Helsinki: Academia Scientiarum Fennica.

O'Connor, A. 2005. *The Blessed and the Damned: Sinful Women and Unbaptised Children in Irish Folklore*. Bern: Peter Lang AG, European Academic Publishers.

Ó Cuív, B. 1950. Flaithrí Ó Maolchonaire's Catechism of Christian Doctrine. *Celtica* 1, 161–206.

O'Dónovan, J. 1829. *The Catechism of the Council of Trent, Published by Command of Pope Pius V, and Translated into English by the Rev. J. Donovan*. Dublin: Richard Coyne.

O'Hare, P. 1997. A brief note on a number of children's burial grounds in East Kerry. *The Kerry Magazine* 8, 11–17.

Ó Ríordáin, S. P. 1991. *Antiquities of the Irish Countryside* (fifth edition, revised by R. De Valera). London: Routledge.

Orme, N. 2001. *Medieval Children.* London: Yale University Press.

Ó Súilleabháin, S. 1939. Adhlacadh leanbhí. *Journal of the Royal Society of Antiquaries of Ireland* 69, 143–51.

O'Sullivan, A. and Sheehan, J. 1996. *The Iveragh Peninsula: An Archaeological Survey of South Kerry.* Cork: Cork University Press.

O'Sullivan, J. and Stanley, M. 2006. Appendix 1: radiocarbon dates from excavated archaeological sites described in these proceedings, pp. 129–35 in O'Sullivan, J. and Stanley, M. (eds), *Settlement, Industry and Ritual* (Archaeology and the National Roads Authority Monograph Series No. 3). Dublin: National Roads Authority.

Power, C. 1994 (published 1997). A demographic study of human skeletal populations from Historic Munster. *Ulster Journal of Archaeology* 57, 95–118.

Reeves, W. Rev. 1847. *Ecclesiastical Antiquities of Down, Connor, and Dromore.* Dublin: Hodges and Smith.

Reimer, P. J., Baillie, M. G. L., Bard, E., Bayliss, A., Beck, J. W., Bertrand, C. J. H., Blackwell, P. G., Buck, C. E., Burr, G. S., Cutler, K. B., Damon, P. E., Edwards, R. L., Fairbanks, R. G., Friedrich, M., Guilderson, T. P., Hogg, A. G., Hughen, K. A., Kromer, B., McCormac, G., Manning, S., Bronk Ramsey, C., Reimer, R. W., Remmele, S., Southon, J. R., Stuiver, M., Talamo, S., Taylor, F. W., van der Plicht, J. and Weyhenmeyer, C. E. 2004. IntCal04 terrestrial radiocarbon age calibration, 0–26 cal kyr BP. *Radiocarbon* 46, 1029–58.

Russell, C. W. and Prendergast, J. P. (eds) 1877. *Calendar of the State Papers Relating to Ireland of the Reign of James I, 1611–1614.* London: Longman & Co.

Rynne, E. 1974. Excavations at Madden's Hill, Kiltale, Co. Meath. *Proceedings of the Royal Irish Academy* 74C, 267–75.

Sheehan, J. 1998. Caherlehillan, Co. Kerry. *Excavations 1997*, 82.

Sheehan, J. 2000a. Caherlehillan, Co. Kerry. *Excavations 1998*, 89.

Sheehan, J. 2000b. Caherlehillan, Co. Kerry. *Excavations 1999*, 112.

Sheehan, J. 2004. Caherlehillan, Co. Kerry. *Excavations 2002*, 211–12.

Sheehan, J. 2006. Caherlehillan, Co. Kerry. *Excavations 2003*, 214.

Swords, L. 2007. *The Flight of the Earls: A Popular History.* Blackrock: The Columba Press.

Tait, C. 2002. *Death, Burial and Commemoration in Ireland, 1550–1650.* Basingstoke: Palgrave MacMillan.

Wakeman, W. F. 1879–82. Some recent antiquarian discoveries at Toam and Killicarney, near Blacklion, in the County of Cavan. *Journal of the Royal Society of Antiquaries of Ireland* 5, 189–90.

Walsh, M. 2005. *Roman Catholicism: The Basics.* Abingdon: Routledge.

White Marshall, J. and Walsh, C. 2005. *Illaunloughan Island: An Early Medieval Monastery in County Kerry.* Bray: Wordwell Ltd.

Wood-Martin, W. G. 1895. *Pagan Ireland.* London: Longmans, Green & Co.

Woywod, S., Rev. 1957. *A Practical Commentary on the Code of Canon Law* (revised and enlarged edition of combined Volumes I and II, revised by Rev. C. Smith). New York City: Joseph F. Wagner Inc.

Zajac, S. 2004. Carrowkeel, Co. Mayo. *Excavations 2002*, 390–1.

12. Grief, Grievance and Grandeur: An Eighteenth-Century Mausoleum in Mainham, Co. Kildare

Mark Gordon

Abstract

This is the story of a mausoleum in Mainham, Co. Kildare, which dates to AD 1743. The circumstances surrounding its creation were unusual, as is the memorial sculpture it contains. Contrary to the original design of its Catholic patron, Stephen Fitzwilliam Browne, it was built outside the confines of the graveyard of Mainham Church in order to house a funerary monument which had become the focus of a dispute between Browne and the Anglican Minister, John Daniel. Browne consequently placed a prominent plaque over the entrance of the mausoleum, detailing at length what had occurred and the reason he felt he had been 'obliged' to build this structure in that particular location. In light of this and a number of other historical factors, as well as the unusual nature of the sculpture within the mausoleum, it is apparent that there may have been a number of impulses involved in the creation of this building and its interior monument. This paper will focus on one of the less obvious alleged functions of the 'mausoleum' and offer perhaps a more accurate explanation than that volunteered on the plaque, of what may have transpired here over 250 years ago.

Introduction

Nothing is as it seems. In the graveyard of Mainham Church, in the rural townland of Mainham, Co. Kildare, stands an unusual-looking building. The church itself, which once belonged to the Knights Hospitallers and is built on a possible Early Christian site, has been in ruins since the middle of the seventeenth century (Cullen 1997, 33–4). Just a few metres south of it, beyond the lichen-covered headstones and occasional wooden benches nestled in the well-kept grass, sits this curious little building, only about 8 m long, but almost the same again in height, its steep slate roof intact thanks to some recent repair work. A second glance reveals something even more intriguing about the building; it is in fact situated outside the churchyard wall (Figures 12.1 and 12.2).

Figure 12.1. The Wogan-Browne mausoleum from the south, with Mainham church and graveyard in the background (M. Gordon).

Figure 12.2. The mausoleum from the north-east, within the graveyard, which is separated from the structure by the churchyard wall (M. Gordon).

The entrance to the building is in the west-facing elevation. Placed directly above it, written on a stone plaque, is the following inscription:

> The within Monument was prepared
> By ye directio^{ns} of Stephen Browne, Esqr
> ye day it bears date, wch he designd-
> puting up in ye opposite church, or ad-
> -ioyning to it; & s^{d} Browne applyd sever
> :al times to his parishminister ye R^{d} Iohn
> Daniel for his consent wch he refusd
> him unless s^{d} Browne would give him
> Five Guineas for soe doing. A gentlema^{n}
> whose character is remarkably well kno
> wn as well as his behaviour on several-
> occasions to s^{d} Browne, & ye onely-
> Clergyman in ye diocese whose passi-
> -on would prevent their church to-
> be Imbellished or Enlarged, & to de-
> pr^{i}ve themselves and their successors
> From ye burial fees; & he has been
> ye occasion of oblidging s^{d} Bro^{w}ne
> to erect s^{d} monument here on
> his own Estate of Inheritance
> wch S^{d} Browne thinks proper
> to incert here to shew it was
> not by choice he did it
> May ye 1st 1743

Extraordinarily, it outlines how this unusual edifice came to be, and why it was built beyond the perimeter of the churchyard. According to the plaque, a gentleman by the name of Stephen Browne had a monument 'within' this structure commissioned, intending to erect it in the 'opposite church' or 'adjoining to it'. It seems he several times requested permission to do so from his Parish Minister, the Rev. John Daniel, but was refused unless he agreed to pay him five guineas. The inscription further asserts that the 'character' of Rev. Daniel was 'remarkably well known', as was his 'behaviour to' Browne 'on several occasions'. According to the inscription, he was the only clergyman in the diocese whose temperament would not allow his parishioners' church to be 'embellished or enlarged' and it goes on to say that it was this that forced Browne to 'erect said monument here on his own estate of inheritance, which said Browne thinks proper to incert here to shew it was not by choice he did it'. The plaque is inscribed with the date May 1st 1743. The building is cast in an even stranger light. Nothing, indeed, is as it seems.

Stephen Fitzwilliam Browne's residence was in Clongowes Wood (or 'Castle Browne', as it is named on an inscription within the mausoleum), only 1 km south-east of Mainham Church. Even prior to falling into the hands of the Browne family this estate had a long history, first mentioned in the Close Roll of King Henry IV on 24th February 1418 as the dowerlands of Anastasia Wogan, widow of Sir David Wogan of Rathcoffey, and the 'third part of the Silva de Clongowes, in the western part therein, that is to say forty acres' (Devitt 1901, 207). The castle itself was built about AD 1450 by a branch of the Eustaces who later became involved in the rebellion of AD 1641, when James Eustace joined forces with, among others, the head of the Wogan family, Nicholas Wogan of Rathcoffey and Sir Andrew Aylmer of Donadea. The family subsequently lost the estate, failing to regain it even after the Restoration. It was granted by King Charles II to Sir Richard Reynell in AD 1667 and, not long after, sold by Reynell for the sum of £2,100 to a Catholic Dublin barrister, Thomas Browne (Devitt 1901, 213).

This barrister was Stephen Browne's grandfather. An inscription on a central panel of the monument within the mausoleum records that Thomas Browne, who died on the 2nd April 1693, was married to Begnet Stephens (died AD 1665). Their only son was John Browne who married Mary Fitzwilliam and had three children: the eldest was Stephen, Christopher was the second son, and they had a daughter, Anne. All these names bar Stephen's are recorded on a number of inscriptions on the monument and all, according to these inscriptions, are buried here.

That they should be buried within the mausoleum was Stephen Browne's design. The monument's central inscription also records that the remains of Thomas Browne and his wife Begnet, their son John and his wife Mary:

> with several others of said Browne's family were removed from their burial place in St. Audoen's Church, Dublin, by the direction of Stephen Fitzwilliam Browne, Esqr, said John and Mary's eldest son, who with Judith his wife daughter to John Wogan of Rathcoffey … erected this monument Anno. Dom. 1739.

So despite buying the Clongowes Wood estate some time between AD 1667 and his death in AD 1693, Thomas Browne was buried in his Dublin parish church of St. Audoen's, as was the succeeding generation of his family. But his grandson, Stephen Browne, whom we know lived at Clongowes Wood (and may have been responsible for the change of its name to 'Castle Browne') had their remains exhumed and reburied at Mainham, commemorated by a monument which was commissioned for the purpose by Browne and his wife Judith, she a member of the Wogan family, powerful Catholics who were long established in the area (Murphy 1890).

According to the exterior plaque, the erection of this monument was then the centre of a dispute between Stephen Browne and the Minister of Mainham, the Rev. John Daniel. Details of the dispute were inscribed above the entrance to the mausoleum, a building which itself would appear to have been born almost as a direct result of the feud. The dispute was obviously a bitter episode, to judge from both the details inscribed upon the plaque as well as the fact that it was recorded at all, and in stone, prominently displayed in a very public place. This was not a simple matter of angry tempers flaring only to dissipate a day or a week later. Browne built his own separate edifice within which to bury his family, outside church grounds, surmounted with a detailed public explanation as to why this was done and to stress that 'it was not by choice he did it'. This was a very permanent and emphatic gesture.

There is, therefore, far more to this building than may initially meet the eye. As a funerary monument the structure and its contained sculpture serve an explicitly commemorative function as spatial expressions of grief. If the plaque is to be taken at its word, considerable grievance also played a very significant role in its conception. But there is a third, less obvious and somewhat disguised impulse already hinted at in the reinterral of Stephen Browne's family, as well as in the intermarriage of this Dublin man with a prominent local family.

It would seem that Stephen Browne was intent upon making 'Castle Browne' the familial seat, interweaving his own family's history with that of the prominent Catholic families of north Kildare. This may be evident in his marriage to Judith Wogan from nearby Rathcoffey, whose family we have seen was linked with the earlier years of Clongowes Wood and who were very influential at various times in history. In her study of Irish burial and commemoration between AD 1550 and AD 1650 Clodagh Tait (2002, 105) writes that in this period 'tactics employed by those seeking to integrate themselves with a new peer group can include intermarriage with well-established families'. It can also be more strongly inferred when the above union is considered alongside the reinterment of Browne's family at Mainham. This is particularly indicative. As Tait (2002, 86) observes (again in reference to the period AD 1550–1650):

> In Ireland, a country where fortunes and reputations could be made and lost with unusual rapidity and where families on the rise had to be willing to exploit the geography of the opportunity, often leaving deceased family members behind them in their path to wealth and status, disinterment and reburial occasionally proved an important strategic tool.

The intention of this paper is not only to explore the presence of this agenda at Mainham but to do so through an examination of the available archaeological evidence, *viz.* the sculpture and architecture. Tait (2002, 105) refers to funerary monuments as being 'very often the documents of the upwardly mobile'. Not only will this paper present Mainham as a particularly apposite illustration of this assertion, but it will also demonstrate to what extent an exploration of these and other motives in the construction of commemorative monuments can potentially profit from an archaeological reading of these material 'documents'.

The Mausoleum

The Wogan-Browne mausoleum is oriented along an east–west axis, just under 9 m long and 6 m wide on the exterior. The west elevation is 8 m high, measuring to the top of the bell tower. The east elevation, which has no such feature, is 6 m high. There are two windows, one in each of the north and south walls, directly opposite one another. There is no window in the east wall, where one might expect to find one, and since the wall has been rendered with pebbledash it is not possible to say if there are any exterior joints to indicate that an opening had been filled. Neither is there any evidence in the interior for the existence of an east-facing window at any time. The entrance is in the west wall, now closed with a barred iron gate. Framing the door are large slabs of finely cut and dressed limestone and above it is to be found the tale-telling plaque (Figures 12.3 and 12.4).

Inside, the mausoleum is 4 m wide and just under 7 m long from the entrance to the back wall behind the altar. Just inside the entrance, on the left on the west wall, is a small recess and holy water font. On it is carved 'S.B. 1743', referring to the patron and year of the mausoleum's construction. On the floor in front of this is a large slate or shale slab, some 2 m long and 1 m wide, covering the entrance to a burial vault below. The rest of the floor is made of red brick which may not represent the original floor covering. In any case this flooring only makes up a little over half of the surface area; three steps rise to a platform at the east end and it is on this and to one side of it that the mausoleum's sculptural ensemble is arranged (Figure 12.5). In the south wall, directly opposite the Wogan-Browne monument is a large rectangular recess, about 0.5 m wide. Also on this side of the altar, but in the east wall, there is another slightly smaller recess with a hollow in the centre of its basal slab.

Figure 12.3. The west-facing elevation of the mausoleum. The plaque is visible above the entrance (M. Gordon).

The Sculpture

The interior of the building is remarkably plain, conveying a simple austerity that very likely signifies a cognisance of Neo-Classical taste. Despite this restraint, however, there is enough sculptural work within these sepulchral walls to bear a range of motifs that demonstrate widely differing concerns. There are two principal areas; the altar and its associated blank niche framed by Doric pilasters and surmounted by a decorated gable or pediment, and the 'altar-tomb' of the Wogan-Brownes – the building's 'within monument' and *raison d'être*, positioned to the left of the altar.

The stone altar is perhaps the most striking feature. A rectangular stone structure a little under 2 m long, 1 m deep and 1 m high, its front panel bears the kneeling effigies of Stephen and Judith Browne, carved in shallow relief (Figure 12.6). They are depicted on either side of the figure of the crucified Christ, whose body is almost in the round, protruding from the shallowly carved cross. Not unusually, the cross is surmounted by the inscription 'INRI', and at its foot there is a depiction of a human skull. Both Stephen and his wife are shown in contemporary eighteenth-century dress, Stephen wearing a wig

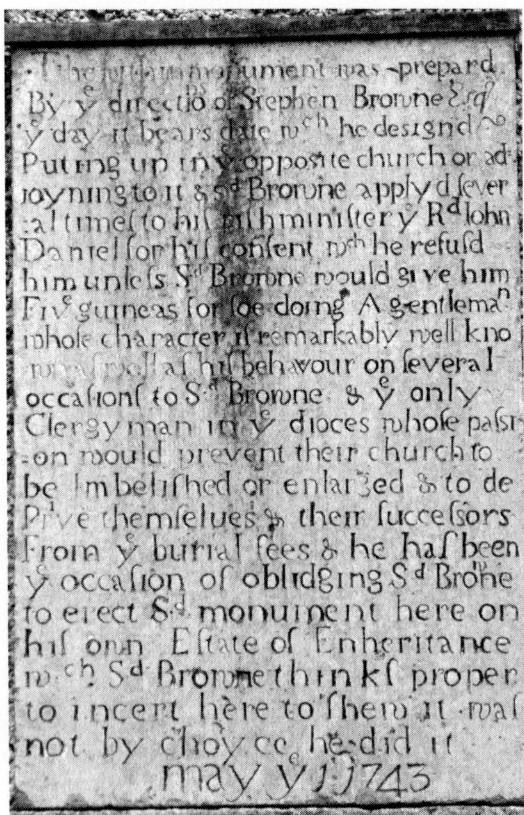

Figure 12.4. The inflammatory plaque (courtesy of Rob Sands).

Figure 12.5. The interior of the mausoleum (courtesy of Rob Sands).

Figure 12.6. The altar frontal showing the kneeling effigies of Stephen Browne and Judith Wogan (courtesy of Rob Sands).

and three-quarter-length coat, his three-corner hat placed respectfully on the ground beside him as he kneels in prayer. He also holds what is presumably a bible in his left hand. Judith is shown wearing a long gown and holding Rosary beads and both figures kneel on tassel-cushioned faldstools. Above their heads are engraved each of their initials; 'S.B' for Stephen and 'I. B. als W.' for Judith, the latter referring to her maiden name, Wogan. The north and east panels are undecorated, but on the altar's flat horizontal surface is a shallow engraving of two cherubs and five crosses.

Above the altar is a large blank niche, some 2 m high, defined by two engaged pilasters of the Doric order rising from either end of the altar, which is backed against the wall. At the centre of this niche, at its foot, there is a small and rather inconspicuous base, the function of which may have been to support an altar cross. However, should one ever have existed it has been gone for some time as an illustration of the interior of the mausoleum after Walter Fitzgerald in a 1901 article on Mainham also shows the niche as empty (1901, 260). At the top of this niche, adjoining the columns is a curved gable. This area could not really be defined as a pediment as such, at least not in the Classical sense, since there is no entablature, and the pilasters are barely even illusorily structural. Within this gabled area is a decorative motif of two cherubs flanking an image of the sun, the anthropomorphic visage of which looks serenely down upon the mausoleum. The decoration at the tops of the pilasters, visible now only on the right pilaster though presumably on both originally, appears to be some sort of floral pattern.

To the left of this group, as one faces the altar, is where the eye would next be drawn. This is our second sculptural group, the Wogan-Browne monument itself; a composite structure, consisting of two principal parts – the tomb-chest on the ground and the mural monument on the wall above (Figure 12.7). The tomb-chest or altar-tomb part of the monument is not dissimilar to the altar described above, just over 1.5 m in length, 1 m deep (to the wall), and reaching to a height of just under 1 m off the ground. It bears the recumbent effigy of Stephen's brother, Christopher Browne (Figure 12.8). Only his shoulders and head are shown, however, the rest of his form hidden by the coffin in which he is depicted. He also appears to be wearing contemporary dress, and his calm expression speaks silently of the peace of his eternal rest. The coffin itself is carved in a deep rectangular recess in the altar-tomb. Imitations of decorative clasps adorn its surface, little putti and hourglasses set within them. These, along with the skull and cross-bones at the foot of the coffin, as well as the coffin itself perhaps, constitute a body of motifs known as mortality symbols which were very common in the period (and had been since Medieval times), particularly on tombstones and other exterior funerary sculpture (McCormick 1983, 281). On the coffin is an inscribed cartouche identifying Christopher Browne as the deceased. The remainder of the upper surface of the altar-tomb presents another inscription, which elaborates on that which is on the coffin.

Above this is the wall-tablet component of the tomb, 2.5 m in height and just over 1 m in width. It is divided into three main parts. The lowest is a single panel, its only decoration a large putto head in high relief. Above this, beneath a coat-of-arms with the Browne,

Figure 12.7. The Wogan-Browne monument (courtesy of Rob Sands).

Fitzwilliam and Wogan crests, is the central panel, bearing a long inscription. The third and uppermost section is above the architrave, on either corner of which sits a skull, crowned with leaves. Between these *memento mori* rests an elaborately decorated flaming urn.

In terms of church monuments, in Ireland especially, memorials in the form of wall tablets or mural monuments were reasonably common among the wealthy classes. By comparison, more elaborately structured monuments built from the ground up are relatively rare from the period, although quite commonplace in Britain (Potterton 1975; Bindman and Baker 1995; Curl 2002, 129–33). In Ireland these elaborate monuments were the preserve of the particularly wealthy Protestant upper class. Among the well known Irish examples of this type of memorial are the monument to Sir Donat O'Brien in Kilnasoolagh, Co. Clare, dating to AD 1717; the monument to Speaker and Mrs Conolly of AD 1736 in Celbridge, Co. Kildare; and in Tashinny, Co. Longford, from AD 1753, the monument to Judge Gore (see Potterton 1972). However, these monuments were particularly lavish, and

Figure 12.8. Detail of the Wogan-Browne monument showing the altar-tomb and the effigy of Christopher Browne (courtesy of Rob Sands).

more common inside churches at this time were the aforementioned mural monuments or tablets, though still the preserve of the moneyed classes. The mural component of the Wogan-Browne monument fits neatly into this latter category, comparable to any one of a large number of contemporary Irish examples of commemorative sculpture (again for examples see Potterton 1972).

Altar-tombs on the other hand are simply not a feature of Irish or British eighteenth-century commemorative sculpture. They do appear later in the nineteenth century, as in the example of the monument to the Marquis of Ormonde from AD 1855 in Kilkenny Cathedral, but this is during the Romantic era when historicism influenced patrons and practitioners of the arts to look back in time for inspiration, in this case, back to the Medieval period, when the use of altar-tombs was at its zenith. In creating the memorial sculptural ensemble at Mainham, and particularly by associating the mural monument with the tomb-chest, Stephen Browne was looking to the past, a past over 100 years before his own time. To explain this we need to look to Mainham's immediate locality, at two monuments in particular, in neighbouring Clane and Donadea (Figure 12.9). When taken together and compared with the whole sculptural ensemble at Mainham, these monuments prove to be rather revealing, particularly given to whom they belonged.

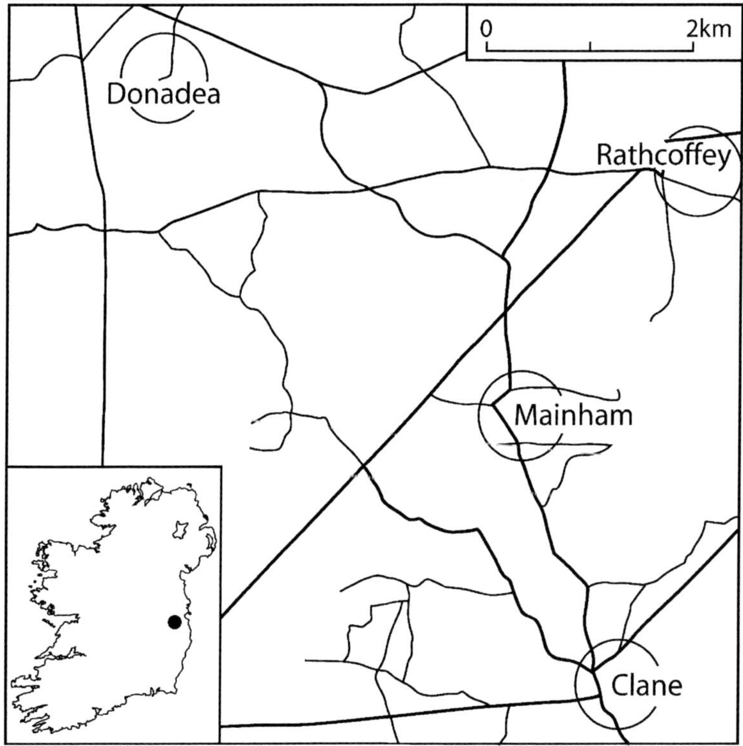

Figure 12.9. Locations of Mainham, Clane, Rathcoffey and Donadea (copyright Ordnance Survey Ireland/Government of Ireland – Copyright Permit No. MP 003206).

Clane

Clane Abbey in the town of Clane, 2.5 km from Mainham, is the location of the first of these two monuments (Figure 12.10). According to its main inscription, this altar-tomb commemorates the death of William Wogan of Rathcoffey in December 1616 (see Cooke-Trench 1899 for details of the inscriptions). The formal resemblance of this monument to the Wogan-Browne monument at Mainham is not exactly overwhelming, but given that it is an immediately local example of the use of an altar-tomb and associated reredos, albeit from the previous century, and moreover one associated with the family into which Browne married, there is an undeniable link. Furthermore, considering the lack of eighteenth-century parallels for the use of altar-tombs and the Classical taste dominant in Browne's day it is not difficult to see the memorial at Mainham as an eighteenth-century adaptation of such Medieval monuments, one which cleverly incorporated the use of the more fashionable wall tablet. It is not unreasonable to suggest that Browne was making a deliberate reference to this monument and those like it in his Mainham ensemble.

Figure 12.10. The Wogan monument in the grounds of Clane Abbey (courtesy of Rob Sands).

Donadea

This second and more elaborate example of the sculptural context for Mainham is housed in St. Peter's Church in Donadea, some 4 km from the Wogan-Browne mausoleum (Figure 12.11). This monument is far more elaborate than those at either Mainham or Clane, though it follows the same structural pattern of both in its altar-tomb and reredos. According to its inscriptions, it was built in AD 1626, commissioned by Sir Gerald Aylmer to commemorate his wife, Dame Julia Nugent who died in AD 1617. Aylmer himself died in AD 1634 and is also commemorated on the monument. In appearance it is absolutely typical of a more elaborate funerary monument type of the late sixteenth and early seventeenth centuries of which there are many examples in Ireland and particularly Britain (Potterton 1975; Curl 2002). Although there is none in this case, these monuments quite often incorporate a recumbent effigy where there is an altar-tomb. Just as common is the use of a reredos without any altar-tomb at all, such as the monument to Francis Agard and Lady Cecilia Harrington

Figure 12.11. The Aylmer memorial in the chancel of St. Peter's Church, Donadea (courtesy of Rob Sands).

demonstrates at Christ Church Cathedral, Dublin, or the O'Connor Don monument in Sligo Abbey (see Potterton 1975, 17–19). Particularly significant on the Aylmer memorial is its use of kneeling effigies; Sir Gerald Aylmer, Dame Julia Nugent and their children are depicted kneeling in separate aedicules on the reredos (Figure 12.12). This kneeling posture is one in which sculptors of the period typically depicted their patrons and/or the deceased, and it is exactly how we find the effigies of Stephen Browne and his wife Judith on the altar front at Mainham. The latter even kneel on tassel-cushioned faldstools, just as praying Medieval figures usually do. Predictably, however, this is very unusual in an eighteenth-century context. At present, no other Irish parallels are known to the author. Conversely, they are an extremely common feature of the Medieval period, continuing up to the beginning of the seventeenth century on monuments like the Aylmer memorial. Once again, this is a strange anomaly in the sculptural ensemble at Mainham for which a local comparison can be found in the memorial monuments of prominent Catholic families from over a century before.

Figure 12.12. Detail of the Aylmer memorial showing the kneeling effigies of Sir Gerald Aylmer, his wife Dame Julia Nugent and their children (courtesy of Rob Sands).

There is another very important facet to the situation at Donadea. One of the inscriptions on the Aylmer memorial, clearly a later insertion, reads: 'This Monument was removed from the old Church Novber 1812 by Sir Fenton Aylmer, Bart'. The 'old Church' is referred to on another inscription on the monument:

> The inscripte pray for the sovle of Sr Gerald Aylmer Knight & Barronett whoe bvylt this chappell tombe & monument & with all the chvrch & chancll adioyning ther vnto ANNO DO 1626 diceased the 19th of Avgst AO DOMINI 1634.

Outside, in the grounds of St. Peter's on the south side of the present church, are the heavily overgrown ruins of a building which may well be the chapel referred to in this inscription. It is not clear from either the seventeenth- or nineteenth-century inscription whether the Aylmer memorial was housed in the chapel or the old church. What is important, however, is that it was located in one of these buildings, both of which had been built by Gerald Aylmer, and it is in this architectural context that Stephen Browne and his contemporaries would have been familiar with the elaborate Jacobean memorial.

What is a Mausoleum?

Stephen Browne's unusual edifice at Mainham is referred to as a mausoleum in all previous literature which discusses or mentions the building (Devitt 1894, 317; Fitzgerald 1901, 261; Craig 1975, 416; Craig and Craig 1999, 21), as well on the six inch and 25 inch Ordnance Survey maps, on which it is marked. But what do we mean when we use the term 'mausoleum'? A definition on English Heritage's website carefully describes a mausoleum as 'a building designed solely for the purpose of human internment' (2003). Craig (1975, 410; 1999, 4) defines such a building as a 'funerary structure having the character of a roofed building, and large enough to stand up in'. The *Oxford English Reference Dictionary*, on the other hand, refers to a mausoleum as 'a large and stately tomb or place of burial' (Pearsall and Trumble 1996, 893). The last two definitions are rather more broad than the first, but given that English Heritage is so particular in its categorisation, what definition should we assume an author is using when referring, for example, to the distribution of mausolea in a particular area? This discussion may seem somewhat pedantic, but the phrases we use not only express our perceptions but feed back into our preconceptions; the use of the word 'mausoleum', particularly with reference to a structure that is next to a church as in the case at Mainham, may lead one to assume that the building's purpose was solely one of interment. There is certainly no reference to any other function it may have served in the literature outlined above.

Yet an initial examination of the structure at an early stage in this investigation revealed the niches at the east end of the interior, previously unmentioned in any of the literature. According to the description of similar features by Leask (1966, 155–7) it is very likely that the niches here were designed to function as a piscina and aumbry. Piscinae were used to wash the sacred vessels. They often had a hollow in their base and a drain through the wall and were usually located in the south wall. At Mainham, the recess with the hollow in its base is in the east wall, though on the south end. There is no drain leading to the exterior, at least that is visible now, though Leask (1966, 140) has pointed out that there was not always one present, and that in such cases the bowl (lavabo) would have been emptied elsewhere. Aumbries are mostly very simple features, usually consisting of a rectangular recess and were used for storing the sacred vessels (Leask 1966, 139; Fleming *et al.* 1999, 29). The presence of two niches such as these as well as the use of a stone altar adorned with strongly Catholic iconography, and the creation of a chancel-like area with steps on which the altar and Wogan-Browne monument is placed, suggests very strongly that this building was designed to facilitate the celebration of mass, adding a whole new dimension to the issue of the dispute that took place here over the erection of the 'within monument'.

What exactly was it that Browne 'applyd several times to his parishminister' to erect? The wording on the plaque is more revealing than may at first have seemed. Browne intended to erect the monument 'in' the church or 'adjoining to it'. Erecting it 'in' the building would presumably have meant placing it against an interior wall, perhaps in the nave or chancel, as was often the case with eighteenth-century mural monuments and indeed, late sixteenth/early seventeenth-century memorials. 'Adjoining' it to the church would almost assuredly mean building an extension on to the main building, forming a chapel in which to house the monument, also not an uncommon context for monuments of the early sixteenth century.

Significantly, however, both of these possibilities also have echoes of other earlier practices, perhaps unsurprisingly given the reference to the past we have seen in the altar-tomb at Mainham. Eighteenth-century mural monuments were also erected in the context of a church or private chapel interior, but we have seen that the Wogan-Browne monument is not a typical eighteenth-century monument. Its composition harks back to an earlier period, and a monument of that type, erected in the same fashion as normal eighteenth-century church memorials, but by a Catholic and during the Penal era, has entirely different connotations. Whether erected 'in' or 'adjoining to' the church, the use of a reredos with an altar-tomb element strongly recalls the pre-Reformation concept of chantry.

Chapels, Chantries and 'Chancers'

Colvin (1991, 154) defines a chantry as 'essentially an endowment for the performance of masses and other works of charity for the benefit of the souls of specified persons'. Chantries could be established for eternity or for a certain term, and could consist of anything from a single priest saying masses at an existing altar in a parish church to a collegiate foundation with a church built specially for the purpose, as well as residential quarters for the clergy (Colvin 1991, 154). The practice was rejected by the Protestant Churches of the Reformation across Europe. In England, the government went so far as to confiscate all chantry revenues by Act of Parliament in AD 1574 (Colvin 1991, 255). What is of concern here, however, is their physical manifestation. Minimally, a chantry required an altar and usually an associated place of burial. A number of altars could be found ranged along the nave walls of a church interior for example, each shared perhaps by a number of families, and at which a priest would serve mass for intercession on behalf of their souls (Colvin 1991, 155). Had the eighteenth-century Wogan-Browne monument been placed against a wall in this manner within Daniel's church, it would have resembled strongly the appearance of such chantries of pre-Reformation Europe. Although an altar-*tomb*, and not an actual altar, these monuments have an altar's shape, and are made of stone, as opposed to the wood of Protestant Communion Tables. Members of the Established Church had used such monuments, but they had not been in fashion for a century and even at that time they had also been widely used by Catholic recusants (Colvin 1991, 257). How would one expect an eighteenth-century Anglican minister to react if a Catholic applied to erect such a monument in his church?

What if the monument had been erected 'adjoining to' the church? The use of this phrase in the inscription would appear to imply the building of an architectural extension to the parish church to house the Wogan-Browne monument. The building of such chapels, pre- and post-Reformation, was not an uncommon practice. Their pre-Reformation use could have been to facilitate chantry or serve simply as private family chapels with which the wealthy and powerful could further distinguish themselves from the rest of the congregation. We have already seen that Sir Gerald Aylmer built his own church and private chapel in Donadea, housing his family monument in the latter. It would appear then that there is an architectural as well as a sculptural parallel between Mainham and Donadea. Had Stephen Browne brazenly intended to build a chantry at a time when Catholic practices were illegal? Whatever the case, he built a private family chapel in which to erect the disputed memorial, and in so doing created a strong material association with the previous monumental activities of two local prominent Catholic families, the Aylmers and the Wogans, whose history was not only long entwined with that of the area, but also marked by the power and influence to resist Protestant authority, whether Crown or government (Murphy 1890, 122–7; Aylmer 1896, 301–2).

Perhaps Stephen Browne's original intention for the Wogan-Browne monument was not all that deliberately rebellious or antagonistic. He may on the one hand have deliberately avoided ruffling the feathers of the Established Church by commissioning a monument which bore no Catholic iconography and which employed the use of form and symbols deemed acceptable under Protestant convention, while at the same time subtly associating his family with the established Catholic dynasties of the area by including as part of that monument an altar tomb component which echoed the form of locally known Aylmer and Wogan memorials.

Two Angry Men

However, something had clearly irked the Anglican Reverend John Daniel. Could it have been that this blow-in from Dublin wanted to erect a memorial to his family 'in the opposite church or adjoining to it' using a monument which, while partly conventional, also had this highly unusual altar-tomb element which had not been in fashion for over a century and smacked rather strongly of Catholicism and the outlawed practice of chantry? Could it have been that although Browne had no ancestry in the area, and was not aristocracy, he intended building his family this grand tomb to be placed in the local church for all to see as well as reburying his parents and grandparents here as though they had lived in the locality for generations? Perhaps Minister Daniel thought Browne possessed ideas well above his station? Or perhaps he had objections to the Catholic Wogan family into whom Browne had married? We do not know. What we do know, however, is that the plaque makes explicit reference to Daniel's 'well known' character and 'his behaviour on several occasions' to Browne. It claims there was a history between these two gentlemen, whatever the cause, and that the Reverend's request for burial fees was the straw that broke the camel's back.

Conceivably it was at this point that Stephen took matters a step further, building a fully fledged private family chapel adjoining the churchyard 'on his own estate of inheritance', a chapel in which he placed not only his disputed Wogan-Browne monument, but also a stone altar suffused with Catholic imagery and 'idolatrous' effigies of himself and his wife Judith kneeling before Christ. Mass may never have been celebrated here, but it could have been, and after suffering the affront of refusal at the hands of John Daniel in front of his new, powerful north Kildare peer group, this may have been the point Browne wanted to make. He had married into a family whose influence was such that they had been able, in AD 1710, to have built a Catholic church in nearby Rathcoffey during the reign of Queen Anne and at the height of the Penal period. He had made reference in his Wogan-Browne monument to the tombs of these powerful Catholic families – both of whom had joined in the AD 1641 rebellion (Murphy 1890, 122; Aylmer 1896, 297) – and now Browne responded to this (possibly calculated) affront by erecting his very own monument of defiance. Having reburied his ancestors within an openly Catholic chapel on the grounds of Castle Browne, the new familial seat of the Wogan-Brownes, he had effectively demonstrated that this newly established lineage, like those of his influential peers, was one to be reckoned with.

Conclusion

In the eighteenth century there was often a cynicism among social commentators regarding the erection of grandiose monuments, particularly by those who had made their fortune through business. This led to a fear among those wishing to commemorate themselves and their families that their commissions might be read as vain testimonies to wealth and status rather than spiritual monuments to the mortality of man. Consequently, many placed on their memorials written denials of any motive so base (Bindman and Baker 1995, 3; Tait 2002, 107). An earlier example cited by Clodagh Tait (2002, 107) reads: 'Be my witness, O Christ, that this stone does not lie here to ornament the body, but to have the soul remembered'. This sentiment is rather reminiscent of the last line on Stephen Browne's disapproving plaque, saying of John Daniel that 'he has been the occasion of oblidging sd Browne to erect sd monument here on his own Estate of Inheritance wch sd Browne thinks proper to incert here to shew it was not by choice he did it'. The tone is almost apologetic. Given the criticism in some circles of grandiose funerary monuments at that time, that they were 'yet another expression of the decadence of the age' (Bindman and Baker 1995, 4), it is possible that Browne was concerned about how this chapel and its sculpture would be received by his contemporaries; the erection of such a recusant monument, not only outside of holy ground but on Browne's own land, may have been perceived as particularly brazen, especially since they were the actions not of a local gentleman, but a Dublin man, an outsider.

Perhaps it is to this end that the plaque claims that Browne's hand was forced, that he was obliged to construct it here. Browne was not forced, however, and certainly not to commission the sculpture that made up the final ensemble. Honour and prestige may have prevented him from simply paying the Reverend his five guineas, or not paying him at all and desisting with his project, but the claim that he had no choice may in truth have been a means of deflecting attention away from the fact that he had erected such a large and elaborate monument to himself and his family. Tait (2002, 134) writes:

> What may still be lacking is antiquity, a long-established claim to high standing. In this scenario, the endlessly manipulable nature of funeral monuments could become invaluable. By choosing an identity from the most socially acceptable elements of one's past, present and future, and rendering this in stone, a medium by which its very nature could convey added veracity, solidity and permanency, reality could be controlled by the patron. Moreover, once reality is constructed in this manner, monuments allow for no doubt or argument.

The dispute at Mainham was in fact the 'occasion' of providing Stephen Browne with an opportunity rather than a burdensome obligation. An opportunity to create a monument which would forever portray the Wogan Brownes' ancestors and descendants as people of influence, status, and nobility, worthy of their place among the powerful Catholic gentry of Kildare.

Acknowledgements

Special thanks are due to: Dorothy Kelly, Tadhg O'Keefe, Rob Sands, Ed Lyne, Denis Dunne and the Mainham Graveyard Committee, Heather King, Michael McCarthy, Finbar McCormick, Joshua Rose, Brendan Cullen, Conor McDermott, Carol Holohan, Brian Dolan, and Aimée Little. Particular thanks are due to Séamus Cullen, who so freely and generously shared his time and expert knowledge whenever and wherever it was needed.

References

Aylmer, H. H. 1896. The Aylmer family. *Journal of the County Kildare Archaeological Society* 1, 295–307.

Bindman, D. and Baker, M. 1995. *Roubilliac and the Eighteenth-Century Monument: Sculpture as Theatre.* London: Yale University Press.

Colvin, H. 1991. *Architecture and the After-Life.* London: Yale University Press.

Cooke-Trench, T. 1899. The Wogan monument. *Journal of the County Kildare Archaeological Society* 3, 98–100.

Craig, M. 1975. Mausoleums in Ireland. *Studies* winter, 410–23.

Craig, M. and Craig, M. 1999. *Mausolea Hibernica.* Dublin: Lilliput.

Cullen, S. 1997. *Manor of Mainham 1170s – 1642.* Unpublished Diploma thesis, St. Patrick's College, National University of Ireland Maynooth.

Curl, J. S. 2002. *Death and Architecture.* Stroud: Sutton.

Devitt, Rev. M. 1894. The grave of Buan, near Clane. *Journal of the County Kildare Archaeological Society* 1, 310–17.

Devitt, Rev. M. 1901. Clongowes Wood. *Journal of the County Kildare Archaeological Society* 3, 206–15.

English Heritage 2003. *Mausolea (Post Medieval)*. http://www.eng-h.gov.uk/mpp/mcd/sub/maus1.htm (accessed 17/01/2003).

Fitzgerald, W. 1901. The Browne Mausoleum at Mainham. *Journal of the County Kildare Archaeological Society* 3, 260–4.

Fleming, J., Nikolaus, P. and Hugh, H. 1999. *The Penguin Dictionary of Architecture and Landscape Architecture* (fifth edition). West Drayton, Middlesex: Penguin Books Ltd.

Leask, H. G. 1966. *Irish Churches and Monastic Buildings: Gothic Architecture to A.D. 1400*. Vol. 2. Dundalk: Dundalgan.

McCormick, F. 1983. The symbols of death and the tomb of John Forster in Tydavnet, Co. Monaghan. *Clogher Record* 6, 273–86.

Murphy, Rev. D. 1890. The Wogans of Rathcoffey. *Journal of the Royal Society of Antiquaries of Ireland* 21, 119–30.

Pearsall, J. and Trumble, B. (eds) 1996. *The Oxford English Reference Dictionary*. Oxford: Oxford University Press.

Potterton, H. 1972. William Kidwell, sculptor, c. 1664 – 1736 and some contemporary mason-sculptors in Ireland. *Irish Georgian Society* 14–15, 80–124.

Potterton, H. 1975. *Irish Church Monuments 1570–1880*. Belfast: Ulster Architectural Heritage Society.

Tait, C. 2002. *Death, Burial and Commemoration in Ireland, 1550–1650*. Hampshire: Palgrave Macmillan.